THE WORKS OF JOHN MILTON

Gul. Faithorne ad Vivum   Delin. et sculpsit.

Ioannis Miltoni Effigies Ætat: 62.
1670.

JOHN MILTON ÆT. LXII

THE WORKS OF JOHN MILTON

VOLUME X

NEW YORK
Columbia University Press
1932

PRINTED IN THE UNITED STATES OF AMERICA
BY THE PRINTING HOUSE OF WILLIAM EDWIN RUDGE, INC.
MOUNT VERNON, NEW YORK

CONTENTS

	PAGE
The History of Britain	1
EDITED BY GEORGE PHILIP KRAPP	
A Brief History of Moscovia	327
EDITED BY GEORGE PHILIP KRAPP	
Notes	383

ILLUSTRATIONS

PAGE

Frontispiece to the History of Britain, 1670 . *Frontispiece*

Title-page to the History of Britain, 1670 . . I

ix

HISTORY OF BRITAIN

THE
HISTORY
OF
BRITAIN,

That part especially now call'd

ENGLAND.

From the first Traditional Beginning, continu'd to the
NORMAN CONQVEST.

Collected out of the antientest and best Authours
thereof by

JOHN MILTON.

LONDON,

Printed by *J. M.* for *James Allestry*, at the *Rose*
and *Crown* in St. *Paul's Church-Yard,*
MDCLXX.

THE HISTORY OF
BRITAIN,

That Part especially now call'd *England*;
Continu'd to the *Norman Conquest*.

THE FIRST BOOK

THE beginning of Nations, those excepted of whom
sacred Books have spok'n, is to this day unknown.
Nor only the beginning, but the deeds also of many
succeeding Ages, yea periods of Ages, either wholly unknown,
5 or obscur'd and blemisht with Fables. Whether it were that
the use of Letters came in long after, or were it the violence of
barbarous inundations, or they themselves at certain revolu-
tions of time, fatally decaying, and degenerating into Sloth
and Ignorance; wherby the monuments of more ancient
10 civility have bin som destroy'd, som lost. Perhaps dis-esteem
and contempt of the public affairs then present, as not worth
recording, might partly be in cause. Certainly oft-times we
see that wise men, and of best abilitie have forborn to write the
Acts of thir own daies, while they beheld with a just loathing
15 and disdain, not only how unworthy, how pervers, how corrupt, but often how ignoble, how petty, how below all His-

tory the persons and thir actions were; who either by fortune, or som rude election had attain'd as a sore judgment, and ignominie upon the Land, to have cheif sway in managing the Commonwealth. But that any law, or superstition of our old
5 Philosophers the *Druids* forbad the *Britans* to write thir memorable deeds, I know not why any out of *Cæsar* should allege: he indeed saith, that thir doctrine they thought not *Cæs.* l. 6. lawful to commit to Letters; but in most matters else, both privat, and public, among which well may History be reck'nd,
10 they us'd the Greek Tongue: and that the *British Druids* who taught those in *Gaule* would be ignorant of any Language known and us'd by thir Disciples, or so frequently writing other things, and so inquisitive into highest, would for want of recording be ever Children in the Knowledge of Times
15 and Ages, is not likely. What ever might be the reason, this we find, that of *British affairs,* from the first peopling of the Iland to the coming of *Julius Cæsar,* nothing certain, either by Tradition, History, or Ancient Fame hath hitherto bin left us. That which we have of oldest seeming, hath by the greater
20 part of judicious Antiquaries bin long rejected for a modern Fable.

Nevertheless there being others besides the first suppos'd Author, men not unread, nor unlerned in Antiquitie, who admitt that for approved story, which the former explode for
25 fiction, and seeing that oft-times relations heertofore accounted fabulous have bin after found to contain in them many footsteps, and reliques of somthing true, as what we read in Poets of the Flood, and Giants little beleev'd, till un-

doubted witnesses taught us, that all was not fain'd; I have therfore determin'd to bestow the telling over ev'n of these reputed Tales; be it for nothing else but in favour of our English Poets, and Rhetoricians, who by thir Art will know,
5 how to use them judiciously.

I might also produce example, as *Diodorus* among the *Greeks, Livie* and others of the *Latines, Polydore* and *Virunnius* accounted among our own Writers. But I intend not with controversies and quotations to delay or interrupt the
10 smooth course of History; much less to argue and debate long who were the first Inhabitants, with what probabilities, what authorities each opinion hath bin upheld, but shall endevor that which hitherto hath bin needed most, with plain, and lightsom brevity, to relate well and orderly things worth the
15 noting, so as may best instruct and benefit them that read. Which, imploring divine assistance, that it may redound to his glory, and the good of the *British* Nation, *I now begin.*

That the whole Earth was inhabited before the Flood, and to the utmost point of habitable ground, from those effectual
20 words of *God* in the Creation, may be more then conjectur'd. Hence that this Iland also had her dwellers, her affairs, and perhaps her stories, eev'n in that old World those many hunderd years, with much reason we may inferr. After the Flood, and the dispersing of Nations, as they journey'd leasurely
25 from the East, *Gomer* the eldest Son of *Japhet,* and his offspring, as by Authorities, Arguments, and Affinitie of divers names is generally beleev'd, were the first that peopl'd all these West and Northren Climes. But they of our own Writers,

who thought they had don nothing, unless with all circumstance they tell us when, and who first set foot upon this Iland,
presume to name out of fabulous and counterfet Authors a
certain *Samothes* or *Dis,* a fowrth or sixt Son of *Japhet,* whom
5 they make about 200 years after the Flood, to have planted
with Colonies; first the Continent of *Celtica,* or *Gaule,* and
next *this Iland;* Thence to have nam'd it *Samothea,* to have
reign'd heer, and after him lineally fowr Kings, *Magus,*
Saron, Druis, and *Bardus.* But the forg'd *Berosus,* whom
10 only they have to cite, no where mentions that either hee, or
any of those whom they bring, did ever pass into *Britain,* or
send thir people hither. So that this outlandish figment may
easily excuse our not allowing it the room heer so much as of
a *British* Fable.

15   That which follows, perhaps as wide from truth, though
seeming less impertinent, is, that these *Samotheans* under the
Reign of *Bardus* were subdu'd by *Albion* a Giant, Son of
Neptune: who call'd the Iland after his own name, and rul'd
it 44 years. Till at length passing over into *Gaul,* in aid of his
20 Brother *Lestrygon,* against whom *Hercules* was hasting out
of *Spain* into *Italy,* he was there slain in fight, and *Bergion*
also his Brother.

    Sure anough we are, that *Britain* hath bin anciently term'd
Albion, both by the *Greeks* and *Romans.* And *Mela* the Geog-
25 rapher makes mention of a stonie shoar in *Languedoc,* where
by report such a Battel was fought. The rest, as his giving name
to the Ile, or ever landing heer, depends altogether upon late
surmises. But too absurd, and too unconscionably gross is

that fond invention that wafted hither the fifty daughters of a strange *Dioclesian King of Syria;* brought in doubtles by som illiterat pretender to somthing mistak'n in the Common Poetical Story of *Danaus King of Argos,* while his vanity, not 5 pleas'd with the obscure beginning which truest Antiquity affords the Nation, labour'd to contrive us a Pedigree, as he thought, more noble. These Daughters by appointment of *Danaus* on the mariage-night having murder'd all thir Husbands, except *Linceus,* whom his Wives loialty sav'd, were by 10 him at the suit of his Wife thir Sister, not put to death, but turn'd out to Sea in a Ship unmann'd; of which whole Sex they had incurr'd the hate: and as the Tale goes, were driv'n on *this Iland.* Where the Inhabitants, none but Devils, as som write, or as others, a lawless crew left heer by *Albion* without 15 Head or Governour, both entertain'd them, and had issue by them a second breed of Giants, who tyranniz'd *the Ile,* till *Brutus* came.

The Eldest of these Dames in thir Legend they call *Albina;* and from thence, for which cause the whole scene was fram'd, 20 will have the name *Albion* deriv'd. Incredible it may seem so sluggish a conceit should prove so ancient, as to be authoriz'd by the Elder *Ninnius,* reputed to have liv'd above a thousand years agoe. This I find not in him; but that *Histion* sprung of Holinshed. *Japhet,* had four Sons; *Francus, Romanus, Alemannus,* and 25 *Britto,* of whom the *Britans;* as true, I beleeve, as that those other Nations whose names are resembl'd, came of the other three; if these Dreams give not just occasion to call in doubt the Book it self, which bears that title.

Hitherto the things themselves have giv'n us a warrantable dispatch to run them soon over. But now of *Brutus* and his Line, with the whole Progeny of Kings, to the entrance of *Julius Cæsar,* we cannot so easily be discharg'd; Descents of
5 Ancestry, long continu'd, laws and exploits not plainly seeming to be borrow'd, or devis'd, which on the common beleif have wrought no small impression: defended by many, deny'd utterly by few. For what though *Brutus,* and the whole *Trojan* pretence were yeelded up, seeing they who first devis'd
10 to bring us from som noble Ancestor were content at first with *Brutus* the Consul; till better invention, although not willing to forgoe the name, taught them to remove it higher into a more fabulous Age, and by the same remove lighting on the *Trojan* Tales in affectation to make the *Britan* of one Origi-
15 nal with the *Roman,* pitch'd there, yet those old and inborn names of successive Kings, never any to have bin real persons, or don in thir lives at least som part of what so long hath bin remember'd, cannot be thought without too strict an incredulity.
20   For these, and those causes above mention'd, that which hath receav'd approbation from so many, I have chos'n not to omitt. Certain or uncertain, be that upon the credit of those whom I must follow; so far as keeps alooff from impossible and absurd, attested by ancient Writers from Books more
25 ancient I refuse not, as the due and proper subject of Story. The principal Author is well know'n to be *Geoffrey of Monmouth;* what he was, and whence his authority, who in his age or before him have deliver'd the same matter, and such

like general discourses, will better stand in a Treatise by themselvs. All of them agree in this, that *Brutus* was the Son of
Silvius; he of *Ascanius;* whose Father was *Æneas a Trojan
Prince,* who at the burning of that City, with his Son *Asca-*
5 *nius,* and a collected number that escap'd, after long wandring on the Sea, arriv'd in *Italy.* Where at length by the
assistance of *Latinus King of Latium,* who had giv'n him *his
Daughter Lavinia,* he obtain'd to succeed in that Kingdom,
and left it to *Ascanius,* whose Son *Silvius* (though *Roman*
10 Histories deny *Silvius* to be Son of *Ascanius*) had maried
secretly a Neece of *Lavinia.*

    She being with Child, the matter became known to *Asca-
nius.* Who commanding his *Magicians to enquire by Art,
what sex the Maid had conceiv'd,* had answer, *that it was one
15 who should be the death of both his Parents; and banish'd for
the fact, should after all in a farr Country attain to highest
honour.* The prediction fail'd not, for in travel the Mother
di'd. And *Brutus* (the Child was so call'd) at fifteen years of
Age, attending his Father to the Chace, with an arrow un-
20 fortunately kill'd him.

    Banish'd therefore by his kindred he retires into *Greece.*
Where meeting with the race of *Helenus King Priams Son,*
held there in servile condition by *Pandrasus then King,* with
them he abides. For *Pirrhus* in revenge of his Father slain at
25 *Troy* had brought thither with him *Helenus,* and many others
into servitude. There *Brutus* among his own stock so thrives
in vertue and in Arms, as renders him belov'd to Kings, and
great Captains above all the Youth of that Land. Wherby the

*Henry of
Huntingdon.
Matthew of
Westminster.*

Trojans not only beginn to hope, but secretly to move him, that he would lead them the way to liberty. They allege their numbers, and the promis'd help of *Assaracus* a Noble Greekish Youth, by the Mothers side a *Trojan;* whom for that cause
5 his Brother went about to dispossess of certain Castles bequeath'd him by his Father. *Brutus* considering both the Forces offer'd him, and the strength of those Holds, not unwillingly consents.

First therfore having fortifi'd those Castles, he with *Assa-*
10 *racus* and the whole multitude betake them to the Woods and Hills; as the safest place from whence to expostulate; and in the name of all sends to *Pandrasus* this Message; *That the* Trojans *holding it unworthy thir Ancestors to serv in a Foren Kingdom, had retreated to the Woods; choosing rather a*
15 *Savage life then a slavish; If that displeas'd him, that then with his leave they might depart to some other soil.*

As this may pass with good allowance, that the *Trojans* might be many in these parts, for *Helenus* was by *Pirrhus* made King of the *Chaonians,* and the Sons of *Pirrhus* by *An-*
20 *dromache Hectors Wife* could not but be powerful through all *Epirus,* so much the more it may be doubted, how these *Trojans* could be thus in bondage, where they had Freinds and Country-men so Potent. But to examin these things with diligence, were but to confute the Fables of *Britan* with the
25 Fables of *Greece* or *Italy;* for of this Age, what we have to say, as well concerning most other Countries, as this Iland, is equally under Question. Be how it will, *Pandrasus* not expecting so bold a message from the Sons of Captives, gathers

an Army. And marching toward the Woods, *Brutus* who had notice of his approach nigh to a Town call'd *Sparatinum*, (I know not what Towne, but certaine of no Greek name) over night planting himself there with good part of his men, sud-
5 denly sets upon him, and with slaughter of the *Greeks* pursues him to the passage of a River, which mine Author names *Akalon*, meaning perhaps *Achelous*, or *Acheron:* where at the Ford he overlaies them afresh. This victory obtain'd, and a sufficient strength left in *Sparatinum*, *Brutus* with *Antig-*
10 *onus*, the Kings Brother and his Freind *Anacletus*, whom he had tak'n in the fight, returns to the residue of his freinds in the thick Woods. While *Pandrasus* with all speed recollecting, beseiges the Town. *Brutus* to releive his men beseig'd, who earnestly call'd him, distrusting the sufficiency of his force,
15 bethinks himself of this Policy. Calls to him *Anacletus,* and threatning instant death else, both to him and his freind *An-tigonus,* enjoyns him, that he should goe at the second howr of night to the Greekish Leagre, and tell the Guards he had brought *Antigonus* by stealth out of Prison to a certain woody
20 Vale; unable through the waight of his Fetters to move furder: entreating them to come speedily and fetch him in. *Ana-cletus* to save both himself and his freind *Antigonus,* swears this; and at fit howr setts on alone toward the Camp: is mett, examin'd, and at last unquestionably known. To whom, great
25 profession of fidelity first made, he frames his Tale, as had bin taught him: and they now fully assur'd, with a credulous rashness leaving thir Stations, far'd accordingly by the ambush that there awaited them. Forthwith *Brutus* dividing his men

into three parts, leads on in silence to the Camp; commanding first each part at a several place to enter, and forbear Execution, till he with his Squadron possess'd of the Kings Tent, gave Signal to them by Trumpet. The sound whereof no
5 sooner heard, but huge havock begins upon the sleeping, and unguarded Enemy; whom the beseiged also now sallying forth, on the other side assaile. *Brutus* the while had special care to seise and secure the *Kings Person;* whose life still within his Custody, he knew was the surest pledge to obtain
10 what he should demand. Day appearing, he enters the Town, there distributes the *Kings Treasury,* and leaving the place better fortify'd, returns with the King his Prisner to the Woods. Strait the ancient and grave men he summons to Counsell, what they should now demand of the *King.*

15 After long debate *Mempricius,* one of the gravest, utterly dissuading them from thought of longer stay in *Greece,* unlesse they meant to be deluded with a suttle peace, and the awaited revenge of those whose freinds they had slain, advises them to demand first the *Kings Eldest Daughter Innogen*
20 in mariage to thir Leader *Brutus,* with a rich dowry, next shipping, mony, and fitt provision for them all to depart the Land.

This resolution pleasing best, the King now brought in, and plac'd in a high Seat, is breifly told, that on these condi-
25 tions granted, he might be free, not granted, he must prepare to die.

Prest with fear of death the *King* readily yeelds: especially to bestow his Daughter on whom he confess'd so Noble and so

Valiant: offers them also the third part of his Kingdom, if they like to stay; if not, to be thir Hostage himself, till he had made good his word.

The Mariage therfore solemniz'd, and shipping from all
5 parts got together, the *Trojans* in a Fleet, no less writt'n then three hunderd fowr and twenty Sail, betake them to the wide Sea; where with a prosperous course two daies and a night bring them on a certain Iland long before dispeopl'd and left wast by Sea-Roavers; the name wherof was then *Leogecia,*
10 now unknow'n. They who were sent out to discover, came at length to a ruin'd City; where was a Temple and Image of *Diana* that gave Oracles: but not meeting first or last save wild Beasts, they return with this notice to thir Ships: Wishing thir General would enquire of that Oracle what voiage to
15 pursue.

Consultation had, *Brutus* taking with him *Gerion* his Diviner, and twelv of the ancientest, with wonted Ceremonies before the inward shrine of the Goddess, in Verse, as it seems the manner was, utters his request, *Diva potens nemo-*
20 *rum,* &c.

> *Goddess of Shades, and Huntress, who at will*
> *Walk'st on the rowling Sphear, and through the deep,*
> *On thy third Reigne the Earth look now, and tell*
> *What Land, what Seat of rest thou bidst me seek,*
> 25 *What certain Seat, where I may worship thee*
> *For aye, with Temples vow'd, and Virgin quires.*

To whom sleeping before the Altar, *Diana* in a Vision that
night thus answer'd, *Brute sub occasum Solis,* &c.

    Brutus *far to the West, in th' Ocean wide*
    Beyond the Realm of Gaul, *a Land there lies,*
5   *Sea-girt it lies, where Giants dwelt of old,*
    Now void, it fitts thy people; thether bend
    Thy course, there shalt thou find a lasting seat,
    There to thy Sons another Troy *shall rise,*
    And Kings *be born of thee, whose dredded might*
10 *Shall aw the World, and Conquer Nations bold.*

These Verses Originally Greek, were put in Latin, saith
Virunnius, by *Gildas* a British Poet, and him to have liv'd
under *Claudius.* Which granted true, adds much to the Antiquitie of this Fable; and indeed the Latin Verses are much
15 better, then for the Age of *Geoffrey* ap-*Arthur,* unless perhaps
Joseph of Exeter, the only smooth Poet of those times, befreinded him; in this *Diana* overshot her Oracle thus ending,
Ipsis totius terræ subditus orbis erit, That to the race of *Brute*
Kings of this Iland, the whole Earth shall be subject.
20 But *Brutus* guided now, as he thought, by divine conduct,
speeds him towards the West; and after som encounters on
the *Afric* side, arrives at a place on the *Tyrrhen* Sea; where he
happ'ns to find the Race of those *Trojans* who with *Antenor*
came into *Italy;* and *Corineus* a man much fam'd, was thir
25 Cheif: though by surer Authors it be reported, that those *Tro-*
jans with *Antenor,* were seated on the other side of *Italie,* on
the *Adriatic,* not the *Tyrrhen* shoar. But these joyning Com-

pany, and past the *Herculean Pillars,* at the mouth of *Ligeris in Aquitania* cast Anchor, Where after som discovery made of the place, *Corineus* Hunting nigh the shoar with his Men, is by Messengers of the King *Goffarius Pictus* mett, and ques-
5 tion'd about his Errand there. Who not answering to thir mind, *Imbertus,* one of them, lets fly an Arrow at *Corineus,* which he avoiding, slaies him: and the *Pictavian* himself heerupon levying his whole Force, is overthrown by *Brutus,* and *Corineus;* who with the Battell Ax which he was wont to
10 manage against the *Tyrrhen Giants* is said to have done mar-vells. But *Goffarius* having draw'n to his aid the whole Coun-try of *Gaul,* at that time govern'd by *twelv Kings,* puts his Fortune to a second Trial, Wherin the *Trojans* over-born by multitude, are driv'n back, and beseigd in thir own Camp,
15 which by good foresight was strongly situate. Whence *Brutus* unexpectedly issuing out, and *Corineus* in the mean while, whose device it was, assaulting them behind from a Wood, where he had convayd his men the night before: The *Trojans* are again Victors, but with the loss of *Turon* a Valiant Nefew
20 of *Brutus;* whose Ashes left in that place, gave name to the City of *Tours,* built there by the *Trojans. Brutus* finding now his powers much lessn'd, and this yet not the place foretold him, leaves *Aquitain,* and with an easie course, arriving at *Totness* in *Dev'nshire,* quickly perceivs heer to be the prom-
25 is'd end of his labours.

The Iland not yet *Britain* but *Albion,* was in a manner desert and inhospitable; kept only by a remnant of *Giants;* whose excessive Force and Tyranie had consum'd the rest.

Them *Brutus* destroies, and to his people divides the Land, which with som reference to his own name he thenceforth calls *Britain*. To *Corineus, Cornwal,* as now we call it, fell by Lot; the rather by him lik't, for that the hugest Giants, in
5 Rocks and Caves were said to lurk still there; which kind of Monsters to deal with was his old exercise.

And heer, with leave bespok'n to recite a grand Fable, though dignify'd by our best Poets; while *Brutus* on a certain Festival day solemnly kept on that shoar, where he first landed,
10 was with the people in great jollity and mirth, a crew of these Savages breaking in upon them, began on the suddain another sort of Game then at such a meeting was expected. But at length by many hands overcome, *Goëmagog* the hugest, in higth twelv Cubits, is reserv'd alive; that with him
15 *Corineus,* who desir'd nothing more, might try his strength; Whom in a Wrestle the Giant catching aloft, with a terrible hugg broke three of his Ribs: nevertheless *Corineus* enrag'd, heaving him up by main force, and on his Shoulders bearing him to the next high Rock, threw him headlong all shatter'd
20 into the Sea, and left his name on the Cliff, call'd ever since *Langoëmagog,* which is to say, the Giants leap.

After this, *Brutus* in a chosen place builds *Troia nova,* chang'd in time to *Trinovantum,* now *London:* and began to enact Laws; *Heli* beeing then high Preist in *Judæa:* and hav-
25 ing govern'd the whole Ile 24 Years, dy'd, and was buried in his new *Troy.* His three Sons *Locrine, Albanact,* and *Camber* divide the Land by consent. *Locrine* had the middle part *Loëgria; Camber* possess'd *Cambria* or *Wales; Albanact Al-*

bania, now *Scotland.* But he in the end by *Humber* King of the *Hunns,* who with a Fleet invaded that Land, was slain in fight, and his people driv'n back into *Loëgria. Locrine* and his Brother goe out against *Humber;* who now marching on-

5 ward, was by them defeated, and in a River drown'd, which to this day retains his name. Among the spoils of his Camp and Navy, were found certain young Maids, and *Estrildis,* above the rest, passing fair; the Daughter of a *King in Germany;* from whence *Humber,* as he went wasting the Sea-

10 Coast, had led her Captive: whom *Locrine,* though before contracted to the Daughter of *Corineus,* resolvs to marry. But beeing forc'd and threatn'd by *Corineus,* whose Autority, and power he fear'd, *Guendolen* the Daughter he yeelds to marry, but in secret loves the other: and oft-times retiring as

15 to som privat Sacrifice, through Vaults and passages made under ground; and seven years thus enjoying her, had by her a Daughter equally fair, whose name was *Sabra.* But when once his fear was off by the Death of *Corineus,* not content with secret enjoyment, divorcing *Guendolen,* he makes *Es-*

20 *trildis* now his Queen. *Guendolen* all in rage departs into *Cornwall;* where *Madan,* the Son she had by *Locrine,* was hitherto brought up by *Corineus* his Grandfather. And gathering an Army of her Fathers Freinds and Subjects, gives Battail to her Husband by the River *Sture;* wherin *Locrine*

25 shot with an Arrow ends his life. But not so ends the fury of *Guendolen;* for *Estrildis* and her Daughter *Sabra,* she throws into a River: and to leave a Monument of revenge, proclaims, that the stream be thenceforth call'd after the

Damsels name; which by length of time is chang'd now to *Sabrina*, or *Severn*.

Fifteen Years she governs in behalf of her Son; then resigning to him at Age, retires to her Fathers Dominion. This saith my Author, was in the daies of *Samuel*. *Madan* hath the praise to have well and peacefully rul'd the space of 40 years; leaving behind him two Sons, *Mempricius*, and *Malim*. *Mempricius* had first to doe with the ambition of his Brother, aspiring to share with him in the Kingdom; whom therfore at a meeting to compose matters, with a treachery which his cause needed not, he slew.

Nor was he better in the sole possession, wherof so ill he could endure a Partner, killing his Nobles, and those especially next to succeed him; till lastly giv'n over to unnaturall lust, in the twentith of his Reigne, hunting in a Forest, he was devowr'd by Wolves.

His Son *Ebranc* a man of mighty strength and stature, Reign'd 40 Years. He first after *Brutus* wasted *Gaul;* and returning rich and prosperous, builded *Caerebranc,* now *York;* in *Albania Alclud, Mount Agned, or the Castle of Maydens, now Edinburgh.* He had 20 Sons and 30 Daughters by 20 Wives. His Daughters he sent to *Silvius Alba* into *Italy,* who bestow'd them on his Peers of the *Trojan* Line. His Sons under the leading of *Assaracus* thir Brother, won them Lands and Signories in *Germany;* thence call'd, from these Brethren *Germania:* a derivation too hastily suppos'd, perhaps before the word *Germanus* or the Latin Tongue was in use. Som who have describ'd *Henault,* as *Jacobus Bergomas,* and *Les-*

sabeus, are cited to affirm that *Ebranc* in his Warre there, was by *Brunchildis Lord of Henault* put to the worse.

Brutus therfore surnamed *Greenshield* succeeding, to repair his Fathers losses, as the same *Lessabeus* reports, fought a
5 second Battail in *Henault* with *Brunchild* at the mouth of *Scaldis,* and Encamp'd on the River *Hania.* Of which *our Spencer* also thus Sings.

> *Let* Scaldis *tell, and let tell* Hania,
> *And let the Marsh of* Esthambruges *tell*
10 *What colour were thir Waters that same day,*
> *And all the Moar twixt* Elversham *and* Dell,
> *With blood of* Henalois *which therin fell;*
> *How oft that day did sad* Brunchildis *see*
> *The* Greenshield *dy'd in dolorous Vermeil,* &c.

15 But *Henault,* and *Brunchild,* and *Greenesheild,* seeme newer names then for a Story pretended thus Antient.

Him succeeded *Leil,* a maintainer of Peace and Equity; but slackn'd in his latter end, whence arose som civil discord. He built in the North *Cairleil;* and in the daies of *Solomon.*
20 *Rudhuddibras,* or *Hudibras* appeasing the commotions which his Father could not, fownded *Caerkeynt* or *Canterbury, Caerguent,* or *Winchester,* and *Mount Paladur,* now *Septonia* or *Shaftsbury:* but this by others is contradicted.

Bladud his Son built *Caerbadus* or *Bathe,* and those med-
25 cinable Waters he dedicated to *Minerva,* in whose Temple there he kept fire continually burning. He was a man of great invention, and taught Necromancie: till having made him

Wings to fly, he fell down upon the Temple of *Apollo* in *Trinovant,* and so dy'd after twenty years Reigne.

Hitherto from Father to Son the direct Line hath run on: but *Leir* who next Reign'd, had only three Daughters, and no

5 Male Issue: govern'd laudably, and built *Caer-Leir,* now *Leicestre,* on the Bank of *Sora.* But at last, failing through Age, he determines to bestow his Daughters, and so among them to divide his Kingdom. Yet first to try which of them lov'd him best (a Trial that might have made him, had he

10 known as wisely how to try, as he seem'd to know how much the trying behoov'd him) *he resolves a simple resolution, to ask them solemnly in order; and which of them should profess largest, her to beleev. Gonorill* th' Eldest apprehending too well her Fathers weakness, makes answer invoking Heav'n,

15 *That she lov'd him above her Soul. Therfore,* quoth the old man overjoy'd, *since thou so honourst my declin'd Age, to thee and the Husband whom thou shalt choose, I give the third part of my Realm.* So fair a speeding for a few words soon utter'd, was to *Regan* the second, ample instruction what

20 to say. She on the same demand spares no protesting, and the Gods must witness, that otherwise to express her thoughts she knew not, but that *she lov'd him above all Creatures;* and so receavs an equal reward with her Sister. But *Cordelia* the youngest, though hitherto best belov'd, and now before

25 her Eyes the rich and present hire of a little easie soothing, the danger also, and the loss likely to betide plain dealing, yet moves not from the solid purpose of a sincere and vertuous answer. *Father,* saith she, *my love towards you, is as my duty*

*bids; what should a Father seek, what can a Child promise
more? they who pretend beyond this, flatter.* When the old
man, sorry to hear this, and wishing her to recall those words,
persisted asking, with a loiall sadness at her Fathers infirmity,
5 but somthing on the sudden, harsh, and glancing rather at her
Sisters, then speaking her own mind, *Two waies only,* saith
she, *I have to answer what you require mee; the former, Your
command is, I should recant; accept then this other which is
left mee; look how much you have, so much is your value, and
10 so much I love you. Then hear thou,* quoth *Leir* now all in
passion, *what thy ingratitude hath gain'd thee; because thou
hast not reverenc'd thy aged Father equall to thy Sisters, part in
my Kingdom, or what else is mine reck'n to have none.* And
without delay gives in mariage his other Daughters, *Gonorill*
15 to *Maglaunus* Duke of *Albania, Regan* to *Henninus* Duke
of *Cornwall;* with them in present half his Kingdom; the
rest to follow at his Death. In the mean while Fame was
not sparing to divulge the wisdom, and other Graces of *Cordeilla,* insomuch that *Aganippus a great King in Gaul* (how-
20 ever he came by his Greek name) seeks her to Wife, and
nothing alter'd at the loss of her Dowry, receavs her gladly
in such manner as she was sent him. After this *King Leir,*
more and more drooping with Years, became an easy prey to
his Daughters and thir Husbands; who now by dayly en-
25 croachment had seis'd the whole Kingdom into thir hands:
and the old King is put to sojorn with his Eldest Daughter,
attended only by threescore Knights. But they in a short while
grudg'd at, as too numerous and disorderly for continuall

Guests, are reduc'd to thirty. Not brooking that affront, the
old King betakes him to his second Daughter: but there also
discord soon arising between the Servants of differing Masters in one Family, five only are suffer'd to attend him. Then
5 back again he returns to the other; hoping that she his Eldest
could not but have more pity on his Gray Hairs: but she now
refuses to admitt him, unless he be content with one only of
his followers. At last the remembrance of his youngest *Cordeilla* comes to his thoughts; and now acknowledging how
10 true her words had bin, though with little hope from whom
he had so injur'd, be it but to pay her the last recompence she
can have from him, his confession of her wise forewarning,
that so perhaps his misery, the prooff and experiment of her
Wisdom, might somthing soft'n her, he takes his Journey into
15 *France*. Now might be seen a difference between the silent,
or down-right spok'n affection of som Children to thir Parents, and the talkative obsequiousness of others; while the
hope of Inheritance over-acts them, and on the Tongues
end enlarges thir duty. *Cordeilla* out of meer love, without
20 the suspicion of expected reward, at the message only of her
Father in distress, powrs forth true filial tears. And not enduring either that her own, or any other Eye should see him
in such forlorn condition as his Messenger declar'd, discreetly
appoints one of her trusted Servants, first to convay him pri-
25 vately toward som good Sea Town, there to array him, bathe
him, cherish him, furnish him with such Attendance and
State, as beseemd his Dignity. That then, as from his first
Landing, he might send word of his Arrival to her Husband

Aganippus. Which don with all mature, and requisite contrivance, *Cordelia* with the King her Husband, and all the
Barony of his Realm, who then first had news of his passing
the Sea, goe out to meet him; and after all honourable and
5 joyfull entertainment, *Aganippus,* as to his Wives Father, and
his Royall Guest, surrenders him, during his abode there, the
power, and disposal of his whole Dominion: permitting his
Wife *Cordeilla* to go with an Army, and set her Father upon
his Throne. Wherin her piety so prosper'd, as that she van-
10 quish'd her impious Sisters with those Dukes, and *Leir* again,
as saith the story, three years obtain'd the Crown. To whom
dying, *Cordeilla* with all regal Solemnities gave Burial in the
Town of *Leicestre.* And then as right Heir succeeding, and
her Husband dead, rul'd the Land five years in Peace. Untill
15 *Marganus* and *Cunedagius* her two Sisters Sons, not bearing
that a Kingdom should be govern'd by a Woman, in the un-
seasonablest time to raise that quarrel against a Woman so
worthy, make War against her, depose her, and imprison her;
of which impatient, and now long unexercis'd to suffer, she
20 there, as is related, killd her self. The Victors between them
part the Land: but *Marganus* the Eldest Sisters Son, who held
by agreement from the North-side of *Humber* to *Cathness,*
incited by those about him, to invade all as his own right,
warres on *Cunedagius;* who soon met him, overcame, and
25 overtook him in a Town of *Wales,* where he left his life, and
ever since his name to the place.

    Cunedagius was now sole King, and govern'd with much
praise many years; about the time when *Rome* was built.

Him succeeded *Rivallo* his Son, wise also and fortunat; save what they tell us of three daies raining blood, and swarmes of stinging Flies, whereof men dy'd. In order then *Gurgustius, Jago* or *Lago,* his Nefew; *Sisillius, Kinmarcus.* 5 Then *Gorbogudo,* whom others name *Gorbodego,* and *Gorbodion,* who had two Sons, *Ferrex,* and *Porrex.* They in the old Age of thir Father falling to contend who should succeed, *Porrex* attempting by treachery his Brothers life, drives him into *France;* and in his return, though aided with the 10 force of that Country, defeats and slaies him. But by his Mother *Videna* who less lov'd him, is himself, with the assistance of her Women, soon after slain in his Bed: With whom ended, as is thought, the Line of *Brutus.* Whereupon, the whole Land with civil broils was rent into five Kingdoms, 15 long time waging Warr each on other; and som say 50 Years. At length *Dunwallo Molmutius* the Son of *Cloten King of Cornwall,* one of the foresaid five, excelling in valour, and goodliness of person, after his Fathers decease found means to reduce again the whole Iland into a Monarchy: subduing 20 the rest at opportunities. First *Ymner King of Loegria* whom he slew; then *Rudaucus of Cambria, Staterius of Albania,* confederat together. In which fight *Dunwallo is reported,* while the Victory hung doubtfull, to have us'd this Art. He takes with him 600 Stout men, bids them put on the Armour 25 of thir slain Enemies; and so unexpectedly approaching the Squadron, where those two Kings had plac'd themselvs in fight, from that part which they thought securest, assaults, and dispatches them. Then displaying his own Ensignes

which before he had conceal'd, and sending notice to the other part of his Army what was don, adds to them new courage, and gains a final Victory. This *Dunwallo was the first in Britain that wore a Crown of Gold; and therfore by som re-*
5 *puted the first King.* He established the *Molmutine* Laws, famous among the English to this day; writt'n long after in Latine by *Gildas,* and in Saxon by King *Alfred:* so saith *Geofrey,* but *Gildas* denies to have known aught of the *Britans* before *Cæsar;* much less knew *Alfred.* These Laws, whoever
10 made them, bestow'd on Temples the privilege of Sanctuary; to Cities also, and the waies thether leading, yea to Plows granted a kind of like refuge: and made such riddance of Theeves and Robbers, that all passages were safe. Forty Years he Govern'd alone, and was buried nigh to *the Temple of*
15 *Concord;* which he, to the memory of peace restor'd, had built in *Trinovant.*

His two Sons *Belinus* and *Brennus* contending about the Crown, by decision of Freinds came at length to an accord; *Brennus* to have the North of *Humber, Belinus* the Sovran-
20 tie of all. But the younger not long so contented, that he, as they whisper'd to him, whose valour had so oft repell'd the invasions of *Ceulphus the Morine Duke,* should now be subject to his Brother, upon new Designe sails into *Norway;* enters League and Affinitie with *Elsing* that King; which
25 *Belinus* perceaving, in his absence disposseses him of all the North. *Brennus* with a Fleet of *Norwegians* makes toward *Britain;* but encounter'd by *Guithlac* the *Danish King,* who laying claim to his Bride, pursu'd him on the Sea, his hast was

retarded, and he bereft of his Spouse: who from the fight by a sudden Tempest, was by the *Danish King* driv'n on *Northumberland,* and brought to *Belinus. Brennus* nevertheless recollecting his Navy, lands in *Albania,* and gives Battell to 5 his Brother in the Wood *Calaterium;* but loosing the day, escapes with one single Ship into *Gaul.* Mean while the *Dane* upon his own offer to become tributary, sent home with his new prise, *Belinus* returns his thoughts to the administring of Justice, and the perfeting of his Fathers Laws; and to explain 10 what High-waies might enjoy the foresaid privileges, he caus'd to be drawn out and pav'd fowr main Roades to the utmost length and bredth of the Iland; and two others athwart; which are since attributed to the *Romans. Brennus* on the other side solliciting to his aid the Kings of *Gaul,* happ'ns at 15 last on *Seginus Duke of the Allobroges;* where his worth, and comliness of person wan him the Dukes Daughter and Heir. In whose right he shortly succeeding, and by obtain'd leave passing with a great Host through the length of *Gaul,* gets footing once again in *Britain.* Nor was *Belinus* unprepar'd, 20 and now the Battell ready to joyn, *Conuvenna* the Mother of them both all in a fright, throws her self between; and calling earnestly to *Brennus* her Son, whose absence had so long depriv'd her of his sight, after imbracements and teares, assails him with such a motherly power, and the mention of things 25 so dear and reverend, as irresistibly wrung from him all his enmity against *Belinus.*

Then are hands joyn'd, reconciliation made firm, and Counsel held to turn thir united preparations on Foren parts.

Thence that by these two all *Gallia* was overrun, the story tells; and what they did in *Italy,* and at *Rome,* if these be they, and not *Gauls,* who took that City, the Roman Authors can best relate. So far from home I undertake not for the
5 *Monmouth Chronicle;* which heer against the stream of History carries up and down these Brethren, now into *Germany,* then again to *Rome,* pursuing *Gabius* and *Porsena,* two unheard of Consuls. Thus much is more generally beleev'd, that both this *Brennus,* and another famous Captain, *Britomarus,*
10 whom the Epitomist *Florus* and others mention, were not *Gauls* but *Britans;* the name of the first in that Tongue signifying a King, and of the other a Great *Britan.* However *Belinus* after a while returning home, the rest of his daies rul'd in Peace, Wealth, and Honour above all his Predeces-
15 sors; building som Cities, of which one was *Caerose* upon *Osca,* since *Caerlegion;* beautifying others, as *Trinovant* with a Gate, a Hav'n, and a Towr, on the Thames, retaining yet his name; on the top wherof his Ashes are said to have bin laid up in a Golden Urne.
20 After him *Gurguntius Barbirus* was King, mild and just, but yet inheriting his Fathers Courage, he subdu'd the *Dacian,* or *Dane,* who refus'd to pay the Tribute Covnanted to *Belinus* for his enlargement. In his return finding about the *Orkneies* 30 Ships of *Spain,* or *Biscay,* fraught with Men and
25 Women for a Plantation, whose Captain also *Bartholinus* wrongfully banish't, as he pleaded, besaught him that som part of his Territory might be assign'd them to dwell in, he sent with them certain of his own men to *Ireland,* which then

lay unpeopl'd; and gave them that Iland to hold of him as in
Homage. He was buried in *Caerlegion,* a City which he had
wall'd about.

Guitheline his Son, is also remember'd, as a just and good
5 Prince, and his Wife *Martia* to have excell'd so much in wisdom, as to venture upon a new Institution of Laws. Which
King Alfred translating call'd *Marchen Leage,* but more truly
therby is meant, the Mercian Law; not translated by *Alfred,*
but digested or incorporated with the West-Saxon. In the
10 minority of her Son she had the rule, and then, as may be
suppos'd, brought forth these Laws, not her self, for Laws
are Masculin Births, but by the advice of her sagest Counse-
lors; and therin she might doe vertuously, since it befell her
to supply the nonage of her Son: else nothing more awry from
15 the Law of God and Nature, then that a Woman should give
Laws to Men.

Hir Son *Sisilius* comming to Yeares receav'd the Rule; then
in order *Kimarus,* then *Danius* or *Elanius* his Brother. Then
Morindus, his Son by *Tanguestela* a Concubine, who is re-
20 corded a man of excessive Strength, Valiant, Liberal, and fair
of Aspect, but immanely Cruell; not sparing in his Anger,
Enemy, or Freind, if any Weapon were in his hand. A certain
King of the Morines, or *Picards* invaded *Northumberland;*
whose Army this King, though not wanting sufficient num-
25 bers, cheifly by his own prowess overcame: But dishonour'd
his Victory by the cruel usage of his Prisners, whom his own
hands, or others in his presence put all to several Deaths: well
fitted to such a bestiall Cruelty was his end; for hearing of a

huge Monster that from the Irish Sea infested the Coast, and in the Pride of his Strength foolishly attempting to set manly valour against a Brute vastness, when his Weapons were all in vain, by that horrible mouth he was catch't up and de-
5 vour'd.

Gorbonian the Eldest of his five Sons, then whom a Juster man liv'd not in his Age, was a great builder of Temples, and gave to all what was thir due; to his Gods devout Worship, to men of desert honour and preferment, to the Commons
10 encouragement in thir Labours, and Trades, defence and protection from injuries and oppressions, so that the Land florish'd above her Neighbours, Violence and Wrong seldom was heard of: his Death was a general loss: he was buried in *Trinovant*.

15 *Archigallo* the second Brother follow'd not his Example; but depress'd the ancient Nobility, and by peeling the wealthier sort, stuff'd his Treasury, and took the right way to be depos'd.

Elidure the next Brother, surnam'd the Pious, was set up
20 in his place; a mind so noble, and so moderat, as almost is incredible to have bin ever found. For having held the Scepter five Years, hunting one day in the Forest of *Calater,* he chanc'd to meet his deposed Brother, wandring in mean condition: who had bin long in vain beyond the Seas, importun-
25 ing Foren aides to his Restorement: and was now in a poor Habit, with only ten followers, privatly return'd to find subsistence among his secret freinds. At the unexpected sight of him, *Elidure* himself also then but thinly accompanied, runns

to him with open Arms; and after many dear and sincere wel-
comings, convaies him to the Citty *Alclud;* there hides him in
his own Bed-Chamber. Afterwards faining himself sick, summons all his Peers as about greatest affairs; where admitting
5 them one by one, as if his weakness endur'd not the disturbance of more at once, causes them willing, or unwilling, once
more to swear Allegiance to *Archigallo.* Whom after reconciliation made on all sides, he leads to *York;* and from his own
Head, places the Crown on the Head of his Brother. Who
10 thenceforth, Vice it self dissolving in him, and forgetting her
firmest hold with the admiration of a deed so Heroic, became
a true converted man; rul'd worthily 10 Years; dy'd, and was
Buried in *Caerleir.* Thus was a Brother sav'd by a Brother, to
whom love of a Crown, the thing that so often dazles, and
15 vitiats mortal men, for which, thousands of neerest blood have
destroy'd each other, was in respect of Brotherly dearness, a
contemptible thing.

Elidure now in his own behalf re-assumes the Government,
and did as was worthy such a man to doe. When providence,
20 that so great vertue might want no sort of trial to make it
more illustrious, stirs up *Vigenius,* and *Peredure* his youngest
Brethren, against him who had deserv'd so nobly of that relation, as lest of all by a Brother to be injur'd. Yet him they
defeat, him they Imprison in the Towr of *Trinovant,* and
25 divide his Kingdom; the North to *Peredure,* the South to
Vigenius. After whose Death *Peredure* obtaining all, so
much the better us'd his power, by how much the worse
he got it. So that *Elidure* now is hardly miss't. But yet in all

right owing to his Elder the due place wherof he had depriv'd
him, Fate would that he should die first: and *Elidure* after
many years Imprisonment, is now the third time seated on
the Throne; which at last he enjoy'd long in Peace; finishing
5 the interrupted course of his mild, and just Reign, as full of
vertuous deeds, as daies to his end.

After these five Sons of *Morindus,* succeeded also thir Sons   * *Matthew*
in Order. **Regin of Gorbonian, Marganus of Archigallo,*   *Westmin.*
both good Kings. But *Enniaunus* his Brother taking other
10 courses, was after six years depos'd. Then *Idwallo* taught by
a neer Example, Govern'd soberly. Then *Runno,* then *Ge-
runtius,* He of *Peredure,* this last the Son of *Elidure.* From
whose Loyns (for that likely is the durable, and surviving
Race that springs of just Progenitors) issu'd a long descent of
15 Kings, whose names only for many successions without other
memory stand thus register'd, *Catellus, Coillus, Porrex, Che-
rin,* and his three Sons, *Fulgenius, Eldadus,* and *Andragius,*
his Son *Urianus; Eliud, Eledaucus, Clotenus, Gurguntius,
Merianus, Bleduno, Capis, Oënus, Sisillius,* twentie Kings in
20 a continu'd row, that either did nothing, or liv'd in Ages that
wrote nothing, at least a foul pretermission in the Author of
this, whether Story or Fable; himself wearie, as seems, of his
own tedious Tale.

But to make amends for this Silence, *Blegabredus* next suc-
25 ceeding, is recorded to have excell'd all before him in the Art
of Music; opportunely, had he but left us one Song of his 20
Predecessors doings.

Yet after him nine more succeeded in name; His Brother

Archimailus, Eldol, Redion, Rederchius, Samulius, Penissel, Pir, Capoirus, but *Cliguellius,* with the addition of Modest, Wise and Just.

His Son *Heli* Reign'd 40 Years, and had three Sons, *Lud,* 5 *Cassibelaun,* and *Nennius.* This *Heli* seems to be the same whom *Ninnius* in his fragment calls *Minocan;* for him he writes to be the Father of *Cassibelan. Lud* was he that en-larg'd, and wall'd about *Trinovant,* there kept his Court, made it the prime City, and call'd it from his own name *Caer-* 10 *lud,* or *Luds Town,* now *London.* Which, as is alledg'd out of *Gildas,* became matter of great dissention betwixt him, and his Brother *Nennius;* who took it hainously that the name of *Troy* thir ancient Country should be abolish'd for any new one. *Lud* was hardy, and bold in Warr, in Peace a jolly 15 Feaster. He conquer'd many Ilands of the Sea, saith *Hunt-* ingdon, and was buried by the Gate which from thence wee call *Ludgate.* His two Sons *Androgeus,* and *Tenuantius,* were left to the tuition of *Cassibelan;* whose bounty, and high demeanor so wraught with the common people, as got him 20 easily the Kingdom transferr'd upon himself. He neverthe-less continuing to favour and support his Nefews, conferrs freely upon *Androgeus, London* with *Kent,* upon *Tenuan-tius, Cornwall:* reserving a superiority both over them, and all the other Princes to himself; till the *Romans* for a while 25 circumscrib'd his power. Thus farr, though leaning only on the credit of *Geffrey Monmouth,* and his assertors, I yet for the specify'd causes have thought it not beneath my purpose, to relate what I found. Wherto I neither oblige the beleif of

Hunting L. 1.

other person, nor over-hastily subscribe mine own. Nor have
I stood with others computing, or collating years and Chro-
nologies, lest I should be vainly curious about the time and
circumstance of things wherof the substance is so much in
5 doubt. By this time, like one who had set out on his way by
night, and travail'd through a Region of smooth or idle
Dreams, our History now arrivs on the Confines, where day-
light and truth meet us with a cleer dawn, representing to our
view, though at a farr distance, true colours and shapes. For
10 albeit, *Cæsar,* whose Autority we are now first to follow,
wanted not who tax'd him of mis-reporting in his Commen-
taries, yea in his Civil Warrs against *Pompey,* much more,
may wee think, in the *British affairs,* of whose little skill in
writing he did not easily hope to be contradicted, yet now in
15 such variety of good Authors, we hardly can miss from one
hand or other to be sufficiently inform'd as of things past so
long agoe. But this will better be referr'd to a second discourse.

The End of the First Book.

THE HISTORY OF
BRITAIN.

THE SECOND BOOK

I AM now to write of what befell the *Britans* from *fifty
and three years before the Birth of our Saviour,* when
first the *Romans* came in, till the decay and ceasing of
that Empire; a story of much truth, and for the first hunderd
5 years and somwhat more, collected without much labour. So
many and so prudent were the Writers, which those two, the
civilest, and the wisest of *European Nations,* both *Italy* and
Greece, afforded to the actions of that Puissant Citty. For
worthy deeds are not often destitute of worthy relaters: as by
10 a certain Fate great Acts and great Eloquence have most commonly gon hand in hand, equalling and honouring each other
in the same Ages. 'Tis true that in obscurest times, by shallow
and unskilfull Writers, the indistinct noise of many Battels,
and devastations, of many Kingdoms over-run and lost, hath
15 come to our Eares. For what wonder, if in all Ages, Ambition and the love of rapine hath stirr'd up greedy and violent
men to bold attempts in wasting and ruining Warrs, which to
posterity have left the work of Wild Beasts and Destroyers,
rather then the Deeds and Monuments of men and Conquer-
20 ours. But he whose just and true valour uses the necessity of
Warr and Dominion, not to destroy but to prevent destruction, to bring in liberty against Tyrants, Law and Civility
among barbarous Nations, knowing that when he Conquers
all things else, he cannot Conquer *Time,* or *Detraction,* wisely

conscious of this his want as well as of his worth not to be forgott'n or conceal'd, honours and hath recourse to the aid of Eloquence, his freindliest and best supply; by whose immortal Record his noble deeds, which else were transitory,

5 becoming fixt and durable against the force of Yeares and Generations, he fails not to continue through all Posterity, over *Envy, Death,* and *Time,* also victorious. Therfore when the esteem of Science, and liberal study waxes low in the Common-wealth, wee may presume that also there all civil

10 Vertue, and worthy action is grown as low to a decline: and then Eloquence, as it were consorted in the same destiny, with the decrease and fall of vertue corrupts also and fades; at least resignes her office of relating to illiterat and frivolous Historians; such as the persons themselvs both deserv, and are best

15 pleas'd with; whilst they want either the understanding to choose better, or the innocence to dare invite the examining, and searching stile of an intelligent, and faithfull Writer to the survay of thir unsound exploits, better befreinded by obscurity then Fame. As for these, the only Authors wee have of

20 *Brittish* matters, while the power of *Rome* reach'd hither, (for *Gildas* affirms that of the *Roman* times noe *Brittish* Writer was in his daies extant, or if any ever were, either burnt by Enemies, or transported with such as fled the *Pictish* and *Saxon* invasions) these therfore only *Roman* Authors there

25 bee who in the English Tongue have laid together, as much, and perhaps more then was requisite to a History of *Britain.* So that were it not for leaving an unsightly gap so neer to the beginning, I should have judg'd this labour, wherin so little

seems to be requir'd above transcription, almost superfluous. Notwithstanding since I must through it, if ought by diligence may bee added, or omitted, or by other disposing may be more explain'd, or more express'd, I shall assay.

5 *Julius Cæsar* (of whom, and of the *Roman* Free State, more then what appertains, is not here to be discours'd) having subdu'd most part of *Gallia,* which by a potent faction, he had obtain'd of the Senat as his Province for many years, stirr'd up with a desire of adding still more glory to his name, 10 and the whole *Roman* Empire to his ambition, som say, with a farr meaner and ignobler, the desire of *Brittish* Pearls, whose bigness he delighted to ballance in his hand, determins, and that upon no unjust pretended occasion, to trie his Force in the Conquest also of *Britain.* For he understood that the 15 *Britans* in most of his *Gallian* Warrs had sent supplies against him, had receiv'd fugitives of the *Bellovaci* his Enemies, and were call'd over to aid the Citties of *Armorica,* which had the year before conspir'd all in a new Rebellion. Therfore *Cæsar,* though now the Summer well nigh ending, and the season 20 unagreeable to transport a Warr, yet judg'd it would be great advantage, only to get entrance into the *Ile,* knowledge of the men, the places, the ports, the accesses; which then, it seems, were eev'n to the *Gauls* thir Neighbours almost unknown. For except Merchants and Traders, it is not oft, saith he, that 25 any use to Travel thether; and to those that doe, besides the Sea Coast, and the Ports next to *Gallia,* nothing else is known. But heer I must require, as *Pollio* did, the diligence, at least the memory of *Cæsar:* for if it were true, as they of *Rhemes*

Suetoniu
vit. Cæs.

Year befo
Christ, 5

Suetoniu
Cæsar C
L. 1.

told him, that *Divitiacus,* not long before, a Puissant King of
the *Soissons,* had *Britain* also under his Command, besides
the *Belgian Colonies* which he affirms to have nam'd and
peopl'd many Provinces there, if also the *Britans* had so fre-
5 quently giv'n them aid in all thir Warrs, if lastly the *Druid*
learning honour'd so much among them, were at first taught
them out of *Britain,* and they who soonest would attain that
Discipline, sent hether to learn; it appears not how *Britain* at
that time should be so utterly unknow'n in *Gallia,* or only
10 know'n to Merchants, yea to them so little, that beeing call'd
together from all parts, none could be found to inform *Cæsar*
of what bigness the Ile, what Nations, how great, what use of
Warr they had, what Laws, or so much as what commodious
Havens for bigger Vessels. Of all which things as it were then
15 first to make discovery, he sends *Caius Volusenus,* in a long
Galley, with command to return assoon as this could be effected. Hee in the mean time with his whole power draws
nigh to the *Morine* Coast, whence the shortest passage was
into *Britain.* Hether his Navy which he us'd against the
20 *Armoricans,* and what else of Shipping can be provided, he
draws together. This known in *Britain,* Embassadors are sent
from many of the States there, who promise Hostages, and
Obedience to the *Roman Empire.* Them, after Audience
giv'n, *Cæsar* as largely promising, and exhorting to continue
25 in that mind, sends home, and with them *Comius of Arras,*
whom he had made King of that Country, and now secretly
employ'd to gain a *Roman* party among the *Britans,* in as
many Citties as he found inclinable, and to tell them, that he

*Cæsar Com.
L. 4.*

himself was speeding thether. *Volusenus* with what discovery of the *Iland* he could make from aboard his Ship, not daring to venture on the shoar, within five daies returns to *Cæsar*. Who soon after, with two Legions, ordnarily amounting, of
5 *Romans* and thir Allies, to about 25000 *Foot, and* 4500 *Horse,* the Foot in 80 Ships of burden, the Horse in 18, besides what Gallies were appointed for his chief Commanders, setts off about the third watch of night with a good Gale to Sea; leaving behind him *Sulpitius Rufus* to make good the
10 Port with a sufficient strength. But the Horse whose appointed Shipping lay Wind-bound 8 mile upward in another Hav'n, had much trouble to Imbark. *Cæsar* now within sight of *Britain* beholds on every Hill multitudes of armed men, ready to forbid his landing; and *Cicero* writes to his friend *Cic. Att.*
15 *Atticus,* that the accesses of the Iland were wondrously forti- *4. Ep. 17* fy'd with strong workes or moles. Heer from the fowrth to the ninth hour of day he awaits at Anchor the coming up of his whole Fleet. Mean while with his Legatts and Tribuns consulting, and giving order to fitt all things for what might
20 happ'n in such a various, and floating water-fight as was to be expected. This place, which was a narrow Bay, close inviron'd with Hills, appearing no way commodious, he removes to a plain and open shoar 8 Mile distant; commonly suppos'd about *Deal in Kent.* Which when the *Britans* per- *Camden*
25 ceav'd, thir Horse and Chariots, as then they us'd in fight, scowring before, thir main powr speeding after, som thick upon the shoar, others not tarrying to be asail'd, ride in among the Waves to encounter, and assault the *Romans* eev'n under

thir Ships; with such a bold, and free hardihood, that *Cæsar*
himself between confessing and excusing that his Souldiers
were to come down from thir Ships, to stand in water heavy
arm'd, and to fight at once, denies not but that the terrour of
5 such new and resolute opposition made them forget thir
wonted valour. To succour which, he commands his Gallies,
a sight unusual to the *Britans,* and more apt for motion, drawn
from the bigger Vessels, to row against the op'n side of the
Enemy, and thence with Slings, Engines, and Darts, to beat
10 them back. But neither yet, though amaz'd at the strangeness
of those new Sea Castles, bearing up so neer, and so swiftly as
almost to overwhelm them, the hurtling of Oares, the battring
of feirce Engines against thir bodies barely expos'd, did the
Britans give much ground, or the *Romans* gain; till *he who*
15 *bore the Eagle of the Tenth Legion,* yet in the Gallies, first
beseeching his gods, said thus alowd, *leap down Souldiers,*
unless ye mean to betray your Ensigne; I for my part will per-
form what I ow to the Commonwealth and my General. This
utter'd, over-board he leaps, and with his Eagle feircly ad-
20 vanc'd runs upon the Enemy; the rest hartning one another
not to admit the dishonour of so nigh loosing thir cheif Standard, follow him resolutely. Now was fought eagerly on both
sides. Ours who well knew thir own advantages, and expertly
us'd them, now in the shallows, now on the Sand, still as the
25 *Romans* went trooping to their Ensignes, receav'd them, dispatch'd them, and with the help of thir Horse, put them every
where to great disorder. But *Cæsar* causing all his Boats and
Shallops to be fill'd with Souldiers, commanded to ply up and

down continually with releif where they saw need; Whereby
at length all the Foot now dis-imbark't, and got together in
som order on firm ground, with a more steddy charge put the
Britans to flight: but wanting all thir Horse, whom the winds
5 yet withheld from Sailing, they were not able to make poursuit. In this confused fight *Scæva a Roman Souldier,* having
press'd too farr among the *Britans,* and besett round, after incredible valour shewn, single against a multitude, swom back
safe to his General; and in the place that rung with his praises,
10 earnestly besought pardon for his rash adventure against Discipline: which modest confessing after no bad event, for such
a deed wherin valour, and ingenuity so much out-weigh'd
transgression, easily made amends and preferr'd him to be a
Centurion. *Cæsar* also is brought in by *Julian,* attributing to
15 himself the honour (if it were at all an honour to that person
which he sustain'd) of being the first that left his Ship, and
took Land: but this were to make *Cæsar* less understand what
became him then *Scæva.* The *Britans* finding themselvs maister'd in fight, forthwith send Embassadors to treat of peace;
20 promising to give Hostages, and to be at command. With
them *Comius of Arras* also return'd; whom hitherto since his
first coming from *Cæsar,* they had detain'd in Prison as a spy:
the blame wherof they lay on the common people; for whose
violence, and thir own imprudence they crave pardon. *Cæsar*
25 complaining they had first sought peace, and then without
cause had begun Warr, yet content to pardon them, commands Hostages: wherof part they bring in strait, others farr
up in the Country to be sent for, they promise in a few daies.

Valer. M.
Plutarch.

In Cæsari

Mean while the people disbanded and sent home, many
Princes, and cheif men from all parts of the Ile submit themselves and thir Citties to the dispose of *Cæsar,* who lay then
encamp'd, as is thought, on *Baram down.* Thus had the *Brit-*
5 *ans* made thir peace; when suddenly an accident unlook'd for
put new counsels into thir minds. Fowr daies after the coming
of *Cæsar,* those 18 Ships of burden, which from the upper
hav'n had tak'n in all the *Roman Horse,* born with a soft wind
to the very Coast, in sight of the *Roman Camp,* were by a
10 sudden tempest scatter'd, and driv'n back, some to the Port
from whence they loos'd, others down into the West Country;
who finding there no safety either to land, or to cast Anchor,
chose rather to commit themselvs again to the troubl'd Sea;
and as *Orosius* reports, were most of them cast away. The
15 same night, it being full Moon, the Gallies left upon dry
Land, were unaware to the Romans, cover'd with a Spring-
tide, and the greater Ships that lay off at Anchor, torn and
beat'n with Waves, to the great perplexity of *Cæsar,* and his
whole Army; who now had neither Shipping left to convay
20 them back, nor any provision made to stay heer, intending to
have winter'd in *Gallia.* All this the *Britans* well perceaving,
and by the compass of his Camp, which without baggage appear'd the smaller, guessing at his numbers, consult together,
and one by one slily withdrawing from the Camp, where they
25 were waiting the conclusion of a peace, resolve to stop all provisions, and to draw out the business till Winter. *Cæsar*
though ignorant of what they intended, yet from the condition wherin he was, and thir other hostages not sent, suspect-

ing what was likely, begins to provide apace, all that might be,
against what might happ'n: laies in Corn, and with materials
fetch'd from the Continent, and what was left of those Ships
which were past help, he repairs the rest. So that now by the
5 incessant labour of his Souldiers, all but twelve were again
made serviceable. While these things are doing, one of the
Legions being sent out to forrage, as was accustom'd, and no
suspicion of Warr, while som of the *Britans* were remaining
in the Country about, others also going and coming freely to
10 the *Roman Quarters,* they who were in station at the Camp
Gates sent speedy word to *Cæsar,* that from that part of the
Country, to which the Legion went, a greater dust then usual
was seen to rise. *Cæsar* guessing the matter, commands the
Cohorts of Guard to follow him thether, two others to suc-
15 ceed in thir stead, the rest all to arm and follow. They had not
march'd long, when *Cæsar* discerns his Legion sore over-
charg'd: for the *Britans* not doubting but that thir Enemies
on the morrow, would be in that place which only they had
left unreap'd of all thir Harvest, had plac'd an Ambush; and
20 while they were disperst and busiest at thir labour, set upon
them, kill'd som, and routed the rest. The manner of thir
fight was from a kind of Chariots; wherin riding about, and
throwing Darts, with the clutter of thir Horse, and of thir
Wheels, they oft-times broke the rank of thir Enemies; then
25 retreating among the Horse, and quitting thir Chariots, they
fought on Foot. The Charioters in the mean while somwhat
aside from the Battell, set themselvs in such order, that thir
Maisters at any time oppress'd with odds, might retire safely

thether, having perform'd with one person both the nimble
service of a Horse-man, and the stedfast duty of a Foot Souldier. So much they could with thir Chariots by use, and
exercise, as riding on the speed down a steep Hill, to stop
5 suddenly, and with a short rein turn swiftly, now runing on
the beam, now on the Yoke, then in the Seat. With this sort
of new skirmishing, the *Romans* now overmatch'd, and terrify'd, *Cæsar* with opportune aid appears; for then the *Britans*
make a stand: but he considering that now was not fitt time to
10 offer Battell, while his men were scarce recover'd of so late a
fear, only keeps his ground, and soon after leads back his
Legions to the Camp. Furder action for many days following was hinder'd on both sides by foul weather; in which time
the *Britans* dispatching Messengers round about, to how few
15 the *Romans* were reduc'd, what hope of prise and booty, and
now if ever of freeing themselvs from the fear of like invasions
heerafter by making these an example, if they could but now
uncamp thir Enemies, at this intimation multitudes of Horse
and Foot coming down from all parts make towards the Ro-
20 mans. *Cæsar* foreseeing that the *Britans* though beat'n and
put to flight would easily evade his Foot, yet with no more
then 30 Horse, which *Comius* had brought over, draws out
his men to Battell, puts again the *Britans* to flight, poursues
with slaughter, and returning burns and laies waste all about.
25 Whereupon Embassadors the same day being sent from the
Britans to desire peace, *Cæsar,* as his affairs at present stood,
for so great a breach of Faith, only imposes on them double
the former hostages, to be sent after him into *Gallia:* And

because *September* was nigh half spent, a season not fit to
tempt the Sea with his weather-beat'n Fleet, the same night
with a fair wind he departs towards *Belgia;* whether two only
of the *Britan* Citties sent Hostages, as they promis'd, the rest
5 neglected. But at *Rome* when the news came of *Cæsars* acts
here, whether it were esteem'd a Conquest, or a fair Escape,
supplication of 20 days is decreed by the Senate, as either for
an exploit done, or a discovery made, wherin both *Cæsar* and
the *Romans* gloried not a little, though it brought no benefit
10 either to him, or the Commonwealth.

The Winter following, *Cæsar,* as his custom was, going   *Dion.*
into *Italy,* when as he saw that most of the *Britans* regarded *Cæsar*
not to send thir Hostages, appoints his Legats whom he left   *Com. 5.*
in *Belgia,* to provide what possible Shipping they could either
15 build, or repair. Low built they were to bee, as therby easier
both to fraught, and to hale ashoar; nor needed to be higher,
because the Tyde so often changing, was observ'd to make the
Billows less in our Sea then those in the Mediterranean:
broader likewise they were made, for the better transporting
20 of Horses, and all other fraughtage, being intended cheifly to
that end. These all about 600. in a readiness, with 28 Ships of
burden, and what with adventurers, and other hulks above
200, *Cotta* one of the Legates wrote them, as *Athæneus* affirms, in all 1000, *Cæsar* from Port *Iccius,* a passage of som
25 30 mile over, leaving behind him *Labienus* to guard the hav'n,
and for other supply at need, with five Legions, though but
2000 Horse, about sun sett hoysing saile with a slack South-
West, at midnight was becalm'd. And finding when it was

light, that the whole Navy lying on the current, had fal'n of
from the Ile, which now they could descry on thir left hand,
by the unwearied labour of his Souldiers, who refus'd not to
tugg the Oare, and kept course with Ships under sayl, he bore
5 up as neer as might bee, to the same place where he had landed
the yeer before; where about noon arriving, no Enemy could
be seen. For the *Britans,* which in great number, as was after
know'n, had bin there, at sight of so huge a Fleet durst not
abide. *Cæsar* forthwith landing his Army, and encamping to
10 his best advantage, som notice being giv'n him by those he
took, where to find the Enemy, with his whole power, save
only ten cohorts, and 300 Horse, left to *Quintus Atrius* for
the guard of his Ships, about the third watch of the same night
marches up twelv mile into the Country. And at length by a
15 River commonly thought the *Stowre* in *Kent,* espies embat-
tail'd *the British Forces.* They with thir Horses and Chariots
advancing to the higher Banks, oppose the *Romans* in thir
March, and begin the fight; but repuls't by the *Roman Cavalrie* give back into the Woods to a place notably made strong
20 both by Art and Nature; which, it seems, had bin a Fort, or
Hold of strength rays'd heertofore in time of Warrs among
themselvs. For entrance, and access on all sides, by the felling
of huge Trees overthwart one another, was quite barr'd up;
and within these the *Britans* did thir utmost to keep out the
25 Enemy. But the Souldiers of the seventh Legion locking all
thir Sheilds together like a rooff close over head, and others
raysing a Mount, without much loss of blood took the place,
and drove them all to forsake the Woods. Pursuit they made

Before the
Birth of
Christ, 52.

not long, as beeing through ways unknow'n; and now ev'ning
came on, which they more wisely spent, in choosing out where
to pitch and fortify thir Camp that night. The next Morning
Cæsar had but newly sent out his men in three bodies to pour-
5 sue, and the last no furder gon then yet in sight, when Horse-
men all in Poste from *Quintus Artrius* bring word to *Cæsar,*
that almost all his Ships in a Tempest that night had suffer'd
wrack, and lay brok'n upon the shoar. *Cæsar* at this news
recalls his Legions, himself in all hast riding back to the Sea-
10 side, beheld with his own Eyes the ruinous prospect. About
forty Vessels were sunk and lost, the residue so torn, and
shak'n as not to be new rigg'd without much labour. Strait he
assembles what number of Ship-wrights either in his own Legions or from beyond Sea, could be summon'd; appoints *La-*
15 *bienus* on the *Belgian* side to build more; and with a dreadful
industry of ten days, not respiting his Souldiers day or night,
drew up all his Ships, and entrench'd them round within the
circuit of his Camp. This don, and leaving to thir defence the
same strength as before, he returns with his whole Forces to
20 the same Wood, where he had defeated the *Britans:* who pre-
venting him with greater powers then before, had now re-
possess'd themselvs of that place, under *Cassibelan* thir cheif
Leader. Whose Territory from the States bordering on the Sea
was divided by the *River Thames* about 80 mile inward.
25 With him formerly other Citties had continual Warr; but
now in the common danger had all made choise of him to be
thir Generall. Heer the *British* Horse and Charioters meeting
with the *Roman* Cavalrie fought stoutly; and at first, som-

thing overmatch'd they retreat to the neer advantage of thir
Woods and Hills, but still follow'd by the *Romans,* make
head again, cut of the forwardest among them, and after some
pause, while *Cæsar,* who thought the days work had bin don,
5 was busied about the entrenching of his Camp, march out
again, give feirce assault to the very Stations of his Guards
and Senteries, and while the main cohorts of two Legions that
were sent to the Alarme, stood within a small distance of each
other terrify'd at the newness and the boldness of thir fight,
10 charg'd back again through the midst, without loss of a man.
Of the Romans that day was slain *Quintus Laberius Durus* a
Tribune: the *Britans* having fought thir fill at the very entrance of *Cæsars* Camp, and sustain'd the resistance of his
whole Army entrench'd, gave over the assault. *Cæsar* heer
15 acknowledges that the *Roman* way both of arming, and of
fighting, was not so well fitted against this kind of Enemy;
for that the Foot in heavy Armour could not follow thir cunning flight, and durst not by ancient Discipline stirr from thir
Ensigne; and the Horse alone, disjoyn'd from the Legions,
20 against a foe that turn'd suddenly upon them with a mixt encounter both of Horse and Foot, were in equall danger both
following and retiring. Besides thir fashion was, not in great
bodies, and close order, but in small divisions, and open distances to make thir onset; appointing others at certain spaces,
25 now to releev and bring of the weary, now to succeed and
renew the conflict; which argu'd no small experience, and
use of Armes. Next day the *Britans* afarr off upon the Hills
begin to shew themselves heer and there, and though less

boldly then before, to skirmish with the *Roman* Horse. But
at Noon *Cæsar* having sent out 3 Legions, and all his Horse
with *Trebonius* the Legat, to seek fodder, suddenly on all sides
they set upon the Forragers, and charge up after them to the
5 very Legions, and thir Standards. The *Romans* with great
courage beat them back, and in the chace, beeing well seconded by the Legions, not giving them time either to rally, to
stand, or to descend from thir Chariots as they were wont,
slew many. From this overthrow, the *Britans,* that dwelt
10 farder off, betook them home; and came no more after that
time with so great a power against *Cæsar.* Whereof advertis'd
he marches onward to the Frontiers of *Cassibelan,* which on
this side were bounded by the *Thames,* not passable except in   *Camden.*
one place and that difficult, about *Coway stakes neer Oat-*
15 *lands,* as is conjectur'd. Hither coming he descries on the
other side great Forces of the Enemy, plac'd in good Array;
the bank sett all with sharp stakes, others in the bottom, cover'd with water; whereof the marks in *Beda*'s time, were to
be seene, as he relates. This having learnt by such as were
20 tak'n, or had run to him, he first commands his Horse to pass
over; then his Foot, who wadeing up to the neck went on so
resolutely, and so fast, that they on the furder side not enduring the violence, retreated and fled. *Cassibelan* noe more now
in hope to contend for Victorie, dismissing all but 4000. of
25 those Charioters, through Woods, and intricate waies attends
thir motion; where the *Romans* are to pass, drives all before
him; and with continuall sallies upon the Horse, where they
least expected, cutting off some and terrifying others, com-

pells them soe close together, as gave them no leave to fetch in
prey or bootie without ill success. Whereupon *Cæsar* strictly
commanding all not to part from the Legions, had nothing
left him in his way but empty Fields and Houses, which he
5 spoil'd and burnt. Meane while the *Trinobantes* a State, or
Kingdome, and perhaps the greatest then among the *Britans,*
less favouring *Cassibelan* send Embassadors, and yeild to *Cæsar*
upon this reason. *Immanuentius* had bin thir King: him *Cassibelan* had slaine, and purpos'd the like to *Mandubratius* his
10 Son, whom *Orosius* calls *Androgorius, Beda Androgius;* but
the youth escaping by flight into *Gallia,* put himself under
the protection of *Cæsar.* These entreat that *Mandubratius* may
be still defended; and sent home to succeed in his Fathers
right. *Cæsar* sends him, demands 40 Hostages and provision
15 for his Armie, which they immediately bring in, and have thir
Confines protected from the Souldier. By their example the
Cenimagni, Segontiaci, Ancalites, Bibroci, Cassi (so I write
them for the modern names are but guess'd) on like terms
make thir peace. By them he learns that the Town of *Cassi-
20 belan,* suppos'd to be *Verulam,* was not farr distant; fenc't
about with Woods and Marshes, well stuff't with men and
much Cattel. For Towns then in *Britain* were only Wooddy
places Ditch't round and with a Mud Wall encompass'd
against the inrodes of Enemies. Thether goes *Cæsar* with his
25 Legions, and though a place of great strength both by art and
nature, assaults it in two places. The *Britans* after some defence fled out all at another end of the Town; in the flight
many were taken, many slain, and great store of Cattel found

there. *Cassibelan* for all these losses yet deserts not himself;
nor was yet his authoritie so much impair'd, but that in *Kent,*
though in a manner possest by the Enemie, his Messengers
and commands finde obedience anough to raise all the people.
5 By his direction *Cingetorix, Carvilius, Taximagulus* and
Segonax, fowr Kings Reigning in those Countries which ly
upon the Sea, lead them on to assault that Camp wherein the
Romans had entrench'd thir Shipping: but they whom *Cæsar*
left there, issuing out slew many, and took Prisners *Cingetorix*
10 a noted Leader, without loss of thir own. *Cassibelan* after so
many defeats, mov'd especially by revolt of the Citties from
him, thir inconstancie and falshood one to another, uses mediation by *Comius of Arras* to send Embassadors about treatie of
yeilding. *Cæsar* who had determin'd to Winter in the Con-
15 tinent, by reason that *Gallia* was unsettl'd and not much of
the Summer now behind, commands him only Hostages, and
what yearly Tribute the Iland should pay to *Rome,* forbidds
him to molest the *Trinobants,* or *Mandubratius;* and with his
Hostages, and great number of Captives he puts to Sea, have-
20 ing at twise embark't his whole Armie. *At his return to*   Pliny.
Rome, as from a glorious enterprise, he offers to Venus *the*
Patroness of his Family, a Corslet of British Pearles.

Howbeit other antient writers have spok'n more doubtfully of *Cæsars* Victories heer; and that in plaine termes he
25 fled from hence; for which the common verse in *Lucan* with
divers passages heer and there in *Tacitus* is alleg'd. *Paulus*   Oros. Lib
Orosius, who took what he wrote from a Historie of *Sueto-*   c. 7. & 9.
nius now lost, writes that *Cæsar* in his first journey entertain'd

with a sharp fight lost no small number of his Foot, and by tempest nigh all his Horse. *Dion* affirms that once in the second expedition all his Foot were routed, *Orosius* that another time all his Horse. The *British* Author, whom I use only then

5 when others are all silent, hath many trivial discourses of *Cæsars* beeing heer, which are best omitted. Nor have wee more of *Cassibelan,* then what the same storie tells, how he warr'd soon after with *Androgeus,* about his Nefew slain by *Evelinus* Nefew to the other; which business at length com-

10 pos'd, *Cassibelan* dies and was buried in *Yorke, if the Monmouth Booke Fable not.* But at *Cæsars* coming hither, such likeliest were the *Britans,* as the Writers of those times, and thir own actions represent them; in courage and warlike readiness to take advantage by ambush or sudden onset, not in-

15 feriour to the *Romans,* nor *Cassibelan* to *Cæsar,* in Weapons, *Dion.*
Armes, and the skill of Encamping, Embattailing, Fortify- *Mela.*
Cæsar.
ing, overmatch't; thir Weapons were a short Speare and light
Target, a Sword also by thir side, thir fight sometimes in
Chariots phang'd at the Axle with Iron Sithes, thir bodies

20 most part naked, only painted with woad in sundrie figures *Herodian.*
to seeme terrible as they thought, but poursu'd by Enemies,
not nice of thir painting to run into Bogs, worse then *wild*
Irish up to the Neck, and there to stay many daies holding a
certain morsel in thir mouths no bigger then a bean, to suffice *Dion.*

25 hunger; but that receit, and the temperance it taught, is long
since unknown among us: thir Towns and strong holds were
spaces of ground fenc't about with a Ditch and great Trees *Cæsar.*
Strabo.
fell'd overthwart each other, thir buildings within were

thatch't Houses for themselves and thir Cattell: in peace the
Upland Inhabitants besides hunting tended thir flocks and *Dion.*
heards, but with little skill of Countrie affaires; the makeing
of Cheese they commonly knew not, Woole or Flax they spun *Strabo.*
5 not, gard'ning and planting many of them knew not; cloth-
ing they had none, but what the skins of Beasts afforded them, *Herodia*
and that not alwaies; yet gallantrie they had, painting thir
own skins with severall Portratures of Beast, Bird, or Flower, *Solimus*
a Vanitie which hath not yet left us, remov'd only from the
10 *skin to the skirt behung now with as many colour'd Ribands*
and gewgawes; towards the Sea side they till'd the ground and *Cæsar.*
liv'd much after the manner of *Gaules* thir Neighbours, or
first Planters: thir money was brazen pieces or Iron Rings, *Tacitus,*
thir best Merchandise Tin, the rest trifles of Glass, Ivorie and *dor. Str*
15 such like; yet Gemms and Pearles they had, saith *Mela,* in
some Rivers: thir Ships of light timber wickerd with Oysier *Lucan.*
betweene, and coverd over with Leather, serv'd not therefore
to tranceport them farr, and thir commodities were fetch't
away by Foren Merchants: thir dealing, *saith Diodorus,*
20 plaine and simple without fraude; thir civil Government
under many Princes and States, not confederate or consulting *Tacitus*
in common, but mistrustfull, and oft-times warring one with *Mela.*
the other, which gave them up one by one an easie Conquest
to the *Romans:* thir Religion was governd by a sort of Priests
25 or Magicians call'd *Druides* from the Greek name of an *Oke,*
which Tree they had in greate reverence, and the *Missleto* especially growing theron; *Plinie* writes them skill'd in Magic
no less then those of *Persia:* by thir abstaining from a Hen, a *Dion.*

Hare, and a Goose, from Fish also, *saith Dion,* and thir opinion of the Soules passing after Death into other Bodies, they Caesar.
may be thought to have studied *Pythagoras;* yet Philosophers
I cannot call them, reported men factious and ambitious,
5 contending somtimes about the archpriesthood not without Caesar.
civil Warr and slaughter; nor restrein'd they the people under them from a lew'd adulterous and incestuous life, ten or
twelve men absurdly against nature, possessing one woman
as thir common Wife, though of neerest Kin, Mother, Daugh-
10 ter, or Sister; Progenitors not to be glori'd in. But the Gospel,
not long after preach't heer, abolish'd such impurities, and of
the *Romans* we have cause not to say much worse, then that
they beate us into some civilitie; likely else to have continu'd
longer in a barbarous and savage manner of life. After *Julius*
15 (for *Julius* before his Death tyrannously had made himself
Emperor of the *Roman* Common-wealth, and was slaine in
the Senate for so doeing) he who next obtain'd the Empire,
Octavianus Caesar Augustus, either contemning the *Iland,* as Strabo L. 2.
Strabo would have us think, whose neither benefit was worth
20 the having, nor enmitie worth the fearing; or out of a whol-
some state maxim, as some say, to moderate and bound the
Empire from growing vast and unweildie, made no attempt
against the *Britans.* But the truer cause was partly civil Warr Year before
among the *Romans,* partly other affairs more urging. For the Birth of Christ, 32.
25 about 20 Years after, all which time the *Britans* had liv'd at *Dion. L.* 49.
thir own dispose, *Augustus* in imitation of his Uncle *Julius,* Year before the Birth of Christ, 25.
either intending or seeming to intend an expedition hither, *Dion. L.* 53.
was com into *Gallia,* when the news of a revolt in *Pannonia* 24.

diverted him: about 7 year after in the same resolution, what
with the unsettl'dness of *Gallia,* and what with Embassadors
from *Britain* which met him there, he proceeded not. The
next year, difference arrising about Covnants, he was again
5 prevented by other new commotions in *Spaine.* Nevertheless
som of the *British Potentates* omitted not to seek his friendship by guifts offerd in the Capitol, and other obsequious
addresses. Insomuch that the whole *Iland* became eev'n in   *Strabo L*
those daies well known to the *Romans;* too well perhaps for
10 them, who from the knowledge of us were so like to prove
Enemies. But as for Tribute, the *Britans* paid none to *Augus-*
tus, except what easie customes were levied on the slight commodities wherewith they traded into *Gallia.*

After *Cassibelan, Tenantius* the younger Son of *Lud,* accord-
15 ing to the *Monmouth* Storie was made King. For *Androgeus*
the Elder, conceaving himself generally hated, for sideing
with the *Romans,* forsook his claime heer, and follow'd *Cæsars*
Fortune. *This King is recorded Just and Warlike.*

His Son *Kymbeline* or *Cunobeline* succeeding, was brought
20 up, as is said, in the Court of *Augustus,* and with him held
friendly correspondences to the end; was a warlike Prince;
his chief seat *Camalodunum,* or *Maldon,* as by certain of his
coines, yet to be seen, appears. *Tiberius* the next Emperor,
adhering alwaies to the advice of *Augustus,* and of himself
25 less careing to extend the bounds of his Empire, sought not
the *Britans;* and they as little to incite him, sent home cour-
teously the Souldiers of *Germanicus,* that by Shipwrack had
bin cast on the *Britan shoar.* But *Caligula* his Successor, a

wild and dissolute Tyrant, haveing past *the Alpes* with intent
to rob and spoile those Provinces, and stirr'd up by *Adminius*
the Son of *Cunobeline;* who by his Father banish'd, with a
small number fled thether to him, made semblance of march-
5 ing toward *Britain;* but beeing come to the Ocean, and there
behaveing himself madly, and ridiculously, went back the
same way: yet sent before him boasting letters to the Senate,
as if all *Britain* had bin yeilded him. *Cunobeline* now dead,
Adminius the Eldest by his Father banish'd from his Country,
10 and by his own practice against it, from the Crown, though
by an old coine seeming to have also reign'd; *Togodumnus,*
and *Caractacus* the two younger, uncertaine whether equal or
subordinat in power, were advanc'd into his place. But
through civil discord, *Bericus* (what he was furder, is not
15 known) with others of his party flying to *Rome,* persuaded
Claudius the Emperor to an invasion. *Claudius* now Consul
the third time, and desirous to do something, whence he
might gain the honour of a Triumph, at the persuasion of
these fugitives, whom the *Britans* demanding, he had deny'd
20 to render, and they for that cause had deny'd furder amity
with *Rome,* makes choise of *this Iland* for his Province: and
sends before him *Aulus Plautius the Prætor,* with this command, if the business grew difficult to give him notice. *Plautius* with much ado persuaded the Legions to move out of
25 *Gallia,* murmuring that now they must be put to make Warr
beyond the Worlds End; for so they counted *Britain;* and
what welcom *Julius* the Dictator found there, doubtless they
had heard. At last prevail'd with, and hoyssing saile from

Tacit. an.
L. 2.
Year after
the Birth of
Christ, 16.
Dion. Sue-
ton. Cal.
An. Dom.
40.

Dion.

43.
Sueton.

three several Ports, lest thir landing should in any one place
be resisted, meeting cross winds, they were cast back and dis-
heartn'd: till in the night a meteor shooting flames from the
East, and, as they fansi'd, directing thir course, they took
5 heart againe to try the Sea, and without opposition landed.
For the *Britans* haveing heard of thir unwillingness to come,
had bin negligent to provide against them; and retireing to
the Woods and Moares, intended to frustrate, and wear them
out with delaies, as they had serv'd *Cæsar* before. *Plautius*
10 after much trouble to find them out, encountring first with
Caractacus, then with *Togodumnus,* overthrew them; and
receaving into conditions part of the *Boduni,* who then were
subject to the *Catuellani,* and leaving there a Garrison, went
on toward a River; where the *Britans* not imagining that
15 *Plautius* without a bridge could pass, lay on the furder side
careless and secure. But he sending first the *Germans,* whose
custome was, arm'd as they were, to swim with ease the
strongest current, commands them to strike especially at the
Horses, whereby the Chariots, wherein consisted thir chief
20 art of fight, became unserviceable. To second them he sent
Vespatian, who in his later daies obtain'd the Empire, and
Sabinus his Brother; who unexpectedly assailing those who
were least aware, did much execution. Yet not for this were
the *Britans* dismaid; but reuniteing the next day fought with
25 such a courage, as made it hard to decide which way hung the
Victorie: till *Caius Sidius Geta,* at point to have bin tak'n,
recover'd himself so valiantly, as brought the day on his side;
for which at *Rome* he receav'd high honours. After this the

Britans drew back toward the mouth of *Thames,* and acquainted with those places, cross'd over; where the *Romans* following them through bogs and dangerous flats, hazarded the loss of all. Yet the *Germans* getting over, and others by a
5 bridge at some place above, fell on them again with sundry Alarmes and great slaughter; but in the heat of pursuit running themselves again into Bogs and Mires, lost as many of thir own. Upon which ill success, and seeing the *Britans* more enrag'd at the Death of *Togodumnus,* who in one of these
10 Battels had bin slain, *Plautius* fearing the worst, and glad that he could hold what he held, as was enjoyn'd him, sends to *Claudius.* He who waited ready with a huge preparation, as if not safe anough amidst the flowr of all his *Romans,* like a great Eastern King, with armed Elephants marches through
15 *Gallia.* So full of perill was this enterprise esteem'd, as not without all this Equipage, and stranger terrors then *Roman* Armies to meet the native and the naked *British valour* defending their Country. Joyn'd with *Plautius* who encamping on the Bank of *Thames* attended him, he passes the River.
20 The *Britans,* who had the courage, but not the wise conduct of old *Cassibelan,* laying all Stratagem aside, in down right manhood scrupl'd not to affront in op'n field almost the whole power of the *Roman Empire.* But overcome and vanquish'd, part by force, others by treatie com in and yeild. *Claudius*
25 therfore who took *Camalodunum,* the Royal Seat of *Cunobeline,* was oft'n by his Armie saluted *Imperator;* a Militarie Title which usually they gave thir Generall after any notable exploit; but to others not above once in the same Warr; as if

Claudius by these acts had deservd more then the Laws of
Rome had provided honour to reward. Haveing therefore
disarm'd the *Britans,* but remitted the confiscation of thir   *Dion. L.*
goods, for which they worship'd him with Sacrifice and
5 Temple as a God, leaving *Plautius* to subdue what remain'd;   *Tacit. a*
he returnes to *Rome,* from whence he had bin absent only six   44.
moneths, and in *Britain* but 16 daies; sending the news before
him of his Victories, though in a small part of the *Iland*. To
whom the Senate, as for atchievments of highest merit, de-
10 cree'd excessive honours; *Arches, Triumphs, annual Solem-*
nities, and the Sirname of Britannicus both to him and his
Son.

    Suetonius writes that *Claudius* found heer no resistance,
and that all was done without stroke: but this seems not prob-
15 able. *The Monmouth Writer* names these two Sones of *Cu-*
nobeline, Guiderius, and *Arviragus; that Guiderius* beeing
slaine in fight, *Arviragus* to conceale it, put on his Brothers
Habillements, and in his person held up the Battel to a Victorie; the rest, as of *Hamo* the *Roman Captaine, Genuissa* the
20 Emperors Daughter, and such like stuff, is too palpably un-
true to be worth rehersing in the midst of Truth. *Plautius*
after this, employing his fresh Forces to Conquer on, and
quiet the rebelling Countries, found worke anough to deserve
at his returne a kind of Tryumphant riding into *the Capitol*   *Sueton.*
25 side by side with the Emperour. *Vespatian* also under *Plautius*   *Claud.*
had thirtie conflicts with the Enemie; in one of which en-
compass'd and in great danger, he was valiantly and piously   *Sueton.*
rescu'd by his Son *Titus:* two powerfull Nations he subdu'd   *Dio. L.*
                                                                    47.

heer, above 20 Townes and *the Ile of Wight;* for which he ·
receav'd at *Rome* Tryumphal Ornaments, and other great
dignities. *For that Cittie in reward of vertue was ever mag-*
nificent: and long after when true merit was ceas't among
5 *them, lest any thing resembling vertue should want honour,*
the same rewards were yet allow'd to the very shadow and
ostentation of merit. Ostorius in the room of *Plautius* Vice- 50.
prætor, met with turbulent affaires; the *Britans* not ceasing to *Tacit. an.* 12.
vex with inrodes all those Countries that were yeilded to the
10 *Romans;* and now the more eagerly, supposing that the new
Generall unacquainted with his Armie, and on the edge of
Winter, would not hastily oppose them. But he waighing that
first events were most available to breed fear or contempt,
with such cohorts as were next at hand sets out against them:
15 whome having routed, so close he followes, as one who meant
not to be everie day molested with the cavils of a slight peace,
or an emboldn'd Enemie. Lest they should make head againe,
he disarmes whom he suspects; and to surround them, places
many Garrisons upon the Rivers of *Antona* and *Sabrina.* But
20 the *Icenians,* a stout people untouch'd yet by these Warrs, as
haveing before sought alliance with the *Romans,* were the
first that brook'd not this. By their example others rise; and
in a chosen place, fenc't with high Banks of Earth, and narrow
Lanes to prevent the Horse, warily Encampe. *Ostorius,*
25 though yet not strengthn'd with his Legions, causes the
auxiliar Bands, his Troops also allighting, to assault the ram-
part. They within though pester'd with thir own number,
stood to it like men resolv'd, and in a narrow compass did re-

markable deeds. But overpowerd at last, and others by thir
success quieted, who till then waverd, *Ostorius* next bends
his Force upon the *Cangians,* wasting all eeven to the Sea of
Ireland, without foe in his way, or them, who durst, ill
5 handl'd; when the *Brigantes* attempting new matters, drew
him back to settle first what was unsecure behind him. They,
of whome the chief were punish'd, the rest forgiv'n, soon gave
over, but the *Silures* no way tractable were not to be repress'd
without a set Warr. To furder this, *Camalodunum* was
10 planted with a Colony of *Veteran Souldiers;* to be a firme and
readie aid against revolts, and a means to teach the Natives
Roman Law and Civilitie. *Cogidunus* also a *British King,*
thir fast friend, had to the same intent certain Citties giv'n *Tacit. v*
him: a haughtie craft, which the *Romans* us'd, to make Kings *Agric.*
15 also the servile agents of enslaving others. But the *Silures*
hardie of themselves, rely'd more on the valour of *Caractacus;*
whome many doubtfull, many prosperous successes had made
eminent above all that rul'd in *Britain.* He adding to his
courage Policie, and knowing himself to be of strength infe-
20 rior, in other advantages the better; makes the Seat of his
Warr among the *Ordovices;* a Country wherein all the odds
were to his own partie, all the difficulties to his Enemie. The
Hills and every access he fortifi'd with heapes of Stones, and
guards of men; to com at whom a River of unsafe passage
25 must be first waded. The place, *as Camden conjectures,* had
thence the name of *Caer-Caradoc on the West edge of Shrop-*
shire. He himself continually went up and down, animating
his Officers and Leaders, *that this was the day, this the field*

either to defend thir Libertie, or to die free; calling to mind
the names of his glorious Ancestors, who drove *Cæsar* the
Dictator out of *Britain,* whose valour hitherto had preserv'd
them from bondage, thir Wives and Children from dishonour.
5 Inflam'd with these words, they all vow thir utmost, with
such undaunted resolution as amaz'd the *Roman Generall;*
but the Souldier less waighing, because less knowing, clam-
ourd to be led on against any danger. *Ostorius* after wary
circumspection bidds them pass the River: the *Britans* no
10 sooner had them within reach of thir Arrowes, Darts, and
Stones, but slew and wounded largly of the *Romans.* They
on the other side closeing thir ranks, and over head closeing
thir Targetts, threw down the loose rampires of the *Britans,*
and persue them up the Hills both light arm'd and Legions;
15 till what with gauling Darts and heavie strokes, the *Britans*
who wore neither Helmet nor Cuirass to defend them, were
at last overcome. This the *Romans* thought a famous Victorie;
wherein the Wife and Daughter of *Caractacus* were tak'n, his
Brothers also reduc'd to obedience; himself escapeing to *Cartis-*
20 *mandua Queene of the Brigantes,* against faith giv'n was to the
Victors deliverd bound: having held out against the *Romans*
nine year, saith Tacitus, but by truer computation, *Seaven.*
Whereby his name was up through all the adjoyning Provinces, eev'n to *Italy and Rome:* many desiring to see who he
25 was, that could withstand so many years the *Roman* Puissance: and *Cæsar* to extoll his own Victorie, extoll'd the man
whom he had vanquish'd. Beeing brought to *Rome,* the
people as to a Solemn spectacle were call'd together, the Em-

perors Guard stood in Armes. In order came first the Kings
Servants, bearing his Trophies won in other Warrs, next, his
Brothers, Wife, and Daughter, last himself. The behaviour
of others through fear was low and degenerate: he only nei-
5 ther in countenance, word, or action, submissive standing at
the Tribunal of *Claudius,* briefly spake to this purpose. *If
my mind, Cæsar, had bin as moderate in the highth of Fortune, as my Birth and Dignitie was eminent, I might have
come a friend rather then a Captive into this Cittie. Nor
10 couldst thou have dislik'd him for a confederate, so noble of
descent, and ruling so many Nations. My present estate to me
disgracefull, to thee is glorious. I had Riches, Horses, Armes,
and men; no wonder then if I contended, not to loose them.
But if by Fate, yours only must be Empire, then of necessitie
15 ours among the rest must be subjection. If I sooner had bin
brought to yeild, my misfortune had bin less notorious, your
Conquest had bin less renown'd; and in your severest determining of me, both will be soon forgott'n. But if you grant that
I shall live, by me will live to you for ever that praise which is
20 so neer divine, the clemency of a Conquerour. Cæsar* mov'd at
such a spectacle of Fortune, but especially at the nobleness of
his bearing it, gave him pardon, and to all the rest. They all
unbound, submissely thank him, and did like reverence to
Agrippina the Emperors Wife, who sat by in State: a new and
25 disdained sight to the manly Eyes of *Romans,* a Woeman
sitting public in her Female pride among Ensignes and
Armed Cohorts. To *Ostorius* Tryumph is decreed; and his
acts esteem'd equall to theirs, that brought in Bonds to *Rome*

famousest Kings. But the same prosperitie attended not his later actions heer. For the *Silures,* whether to reveng thir loss of *Caractacus,* or that they saw *Ostorius,* as if now all were done, less earnest to restrain them, besett the Prefect of his
5 Camp, left there with Legionarie Bands to appoint Garrisons: and had not speedie aid com in from the neighbouring Holds and Castles, had cutt them all off; notwithstanding which, the *Præfect with 8 Centurions,* and many thir stoubtest men were slaine: and upon the neck of this, meeting first with
10 *Roman* Forragers, then with other Troops hasting to thir relief, utterly foyl'd and broke them also. *Ostorius* sending more after, could hardly stay thir flight; till the waighty Legions coming on, at first poys'd the Battel, at length turn'd the Scale: to the *Britans* without much loss; for by that time
15 it grew night. Then was the Warr shiverd as it were into small frayes and bickerings; not unlike sometimes to so many robberies, in Woods, at Waters, as chance or valour, advice or rashness led them on, commanded or without command. That which most exasperated the *Silures,* was a report of
20 certaine words cast out by the *Emperor, that he would root them out to the verie name.* Therefore two Cohorts more of Auxiliars, by the avarice of thir Leaders too securely pillageing, they quite intercepted: and bestowing liberally the Spoils and Captives, whereof they took plentie; drew other Countries to joyne with them. These losses falling so thick upon the
25 tries to joyne with them. These losses falling so thick upon the *Romans, Ostorius* with the thought, and anguish thereof ended his daies: the *Britans* rejoycing, although no Battel, that yet adverse Warr had worne out so great a Souldier.

Cæsar in his place ordaines *Aulus Didius:* but ere his coming, though much hastn'd, that the Province might not want a Governour; the *Silures* had giv'n an overthrow to *Manlius Valens* with his Legion, rumor'd on both sides greater then
5 was true, by *the Silures* to amate the new Generall; by him in a double respect, of the more praise if he queld them, or the more excuse if he fail'd. Meane time the *Silures* forgett not to infest the *Roman* pale with wide excursions; till *Didius* marching out, kept them somwhat more within bounds. Nor
10 were they long to seek, who after *Caractacus* should lead them; for next to him in worth and skill of Warr, *Venutius a Prince of the Brigantes* merited to be thir chief. He at first faithfull to the *Romans,* and by them protected, was the Husband of *Cartismandua Q. of the Brigantes,* himself perhaps
15 reigning elsewhere. She who had betray'd *Caractacus* and her Countrie to adorne the Tryumph of *Claudius,* thereby grown powerfull and gratious with the *Romans,* presuming on the hire of her treason, deserted her Husband; and marrying *Vellocatus* one of his Squires, conferrs on him the Kingdome
20 also. This deed so odious and full of infamie, disturb'd the whole State: *Venutius* with other Forces, and the help of her own Subjects, who detested the example of so foule a fact, and with all the uncomeliness of thir Subjection to the Monarchie of a Woeman, a peece of manhood not every day to be
25 found among *Britans,* though shee had got by suttle train his Brother with many of his kindred into her hands, brought her soon below the confidence of beeing able to resist longer. When imploring the *Roman* aid, with much adoe, and after

many a hard encounter she escap'd the punishment which was readie to have seis'd her. *Venutius* thus debar'd the autority of ruling his own Houshold, justly turnes his anger against the *Romans* themselves; whose magnanimitie not
5 wont to undertake dishonorable causes, had arrogantly intermeddl'd in his domestic affaires, to uphold the Rebelion of an adultress against her Husband. And the Kingdome he retain'd against thir utmost opposition; and of Warr gave them thir fill: first in a sharpe conflict of uncertaine event,
10 then against the Legion of *Cæsius Nasica*. Insomuch that *Didius* growing old and mannageing the Warr by Deputies, had worke anough to stand on his defence, with the gaining now and then of a small Castle. And *Nero* (for in that part of the *Ile* things continu'd in the same plight to the
15 Reigne of *Vespatian*) was minded but for shame to have withdrawn the *Roman* Forces out of *Britain:* In other parts whereof, about the same time, other things befell. *Verannius,* whom *Nero* sent hither to succeed *Didius,* dying in his first Year, save a few inrodes upon the *Silures,* left only a
20 great boast behind him, *that in two years, had he liv'd, he would have Conquerd all.* But *Suetonius Paulinus,* who next was sent hither, esteem'd a Souldier equall to the best in that age, for two years together went on prosperously; both confirming what was got, and subdueing onward. At last over-
25 confident of his present actions, and æmulating others, of whose deeds he heard from abroad, marches up as farr as *Mona, the Ile of Anglesey,* a populous place. For they it seemes had both entertain'd fugitives, and giv'n good assist-

*Tacit. vit.
Agric.
Tacit. Hist.
3. Sueton.*

tance to the rest that withstood him. He makes him Boates with flat bottoms, fitted to the Shallows which he expected in that narrow frith: his Foot so pass'd over, his Horse waded or swom. Thick upon the shoar stood several gross bands of

5 men well weapn'd, many women like furies running to and fro in dismal habit with hair loose about thir shoulders, held Torches in thir hands. The *Druids,* those were thir Priests, of whome more in another place, with hands lift up to Heav'n uttering direfull praiers, astonish'd the *Romans;* who at so

10 strange a sight stood in a-maze though wounded: at length awak'd and encourag'd by thir Generall, not to feare a barbarous and lunatic rout, fall on, and beat them down scorch't and rouling in thir own fire. Then were they yoak'd with Garrisons, and the places consecrate to thir bloodie supersti-

15 tions destroi'd. For whom they took in Warr they held it lawfull to Sacrifice; and by the entrails of men us'd divination. While thus *Paulinus* had his thought still fix'd before, to goe on winning, his back lay broad op'n to occasion of loosing more behind. For the *Britans* urg'd and oppress'd with many

20 unsufferable injuries, had all banded themselves to a generall revolt. The particular causes are not all writt'n by one Author; *Tacitus* who liv'd next those times of any to us extant, writes that *Prasutagus King of the Icenians* abounding in wealth had left *Cæsar* Coheir with his two Daughters; thereby hope-

25 ing to have secur'd from all wrong both his Kingdom and his House; which fell out farr otherwise. For under colour to oversee and take possession of the Emperors new Inheritance, his Kingdome became a prey to Centurions, his House to

rav'ning Officers, his Wife *Boadicea* violated with stripes, his Daughters with Rape, the wealthiest of his Subjects, as it were by the will and testament of thir King thrown out of thir Estates, his kindred made little better then slaves. The new
5 Colony also at *Camalodunum* took House or Land from whome they pleas'd; terming them Slaves and Vassals; the Souldiers complying with the Colony, out of hope hereafter to use the same licence themselves. Moreover the Temple erected to *Claudius* as a badge of thir eternal slaverie, stood a
10 great Eye sore; the Priests whereof under pretext of what was due to the religious service, wasted and imbezl'd each mans substance upon themselves. And *Catus Decianus* the Procu- *Dion.* rator endeavour'd to bring all thir goods within the compass of a new confiscation, by disavowing the remittment of *Clau-*
15 *dius*. Lastly, *Seneca* in his Books a Philosopher, having drawn the *Britans* unwillingly to borrow of him vast summs upon faire promises of easy loan, and for repayment to take thir own time, on a sudden compells them to pay in all at once with great extortion. Thus provock't by heaviest sufferings,
20 and thus invited by opportunities in the absence of *Paulinus,* the *Icenians,* and by their Example the *Trinobantes,* and as many else as hated servitude, rise up in Armes. Of these ensueing troubles many foregoing signes appear'd: the image of Victorie at *Camalodunum* fell down of it self with her face
25 turn'd as it were to the *Britans;* certaine women in a kind of ecstasie foretold of calamities to come; in the Counsel-House were heard by night barbarous noises, in the Theater hideous howlings, in the Creek horrid sights betok'ning the destruc-

tion of that Colony; heerto the Ocean seeming of a bloody hew, and human shapes at a low ebb, left imprinted on the sand, wrought in the *Britans* new courage, in the *Romans* unwonted feares. *Camalodunum,* where the *Romans* had 5 seated themselves to dwell pleasantly, rather then defensively, was not fortifi'd: against that therefore the *Britans* make first assault. The Souldiers within were not very many. *Decianus* the Procurator could send them but 200, those ill arm'd: and through the treachery of some among them, who secretly 10 favour'd the insurrection, they had deferr'd both to entrench, and to send out such as bore not Armes; such as did, flying to the Temple, which on the second day was forcibly tak'n, were put all to the Sword, the Temple made a heap, the rest rifl'd and burnt. *Petilius Cerealis* coming to his succour, is in his 15 way met, and overthrown, his whole Legion cut to peeces; he with his Horse hardly escaping to the *Roman Camp.* *Decianus,* whose rapine was the cause of all this, fled into *Gallia.* But *Suetonius* at these tideings not dismay'd, through the midst of his Enemies Countrie marches to *London* (though 20 not term'd a Colony, yet full of *Roman* Inhabitants, and for the frequency of trade and other commodities, a Town eev'n then of principal note) with purpose to have made there the seat of Warr. But considering the smallness of his numbers, and the late rashness of *Petilius,* he chooses rather with the loss 25 of one Town to save the rest. Nor was he flexible to any prayers or weeping of them that besought him to tarry there; but taking with him such as were willing, gave signal to depart; they who through weakness of Sex or Age, or love of the

place went not along, perish'd by the Enemie; so did *Verulam a Roman free Town.* For the *Britans* omitting Forts and Castles, flew thether first where richest bootie, and the hope of pillageing toald them on. In this massacre, about 70 thou-
5 sand *Romans* and thir associats in the places above-mention'd, of a certaine, lost thir lives. None might be spar'd, none ransom'd, but tasted all either a present or a lingring Death; no crueltie that either outrage or the insolence of success putt into thir heads, was left unacted. The *Roman* Wives and Virgins   *Dion. L.* 62.
10 hang'd up all naked, had thir Breasts cut off, and sow'd to thir mouthes; that in the grimness of Death they might seem to eat thir own flesh; while the *Britans* fell to feasting and carousing in the Temple of *Andate* thir Goddess of Victorie. *Suetonius* adding to his Legion other old Officers, and Soul-
15 diers thereabout, which gatherd to him, were neer upon ten thousand; and purposing with those not to deferr Battel, had chos'n a place narrow, and not to be overwing'd, on his rear a Wood; being well inform'd that his Enemies were all in Front on a plain unapt for ambush: the Legionaries stood thic in
20 order, impal'd with light armed; the Horse on either Wing. The *Britans* in Companies and Squadrons were every where shouting and swarming, such a multitude as at other time never; no less reckon'd then 200 and 30 thousand, so feirce and confident of Victorie, that thir Wives also came in Wag-
25 gons to sit and behold the sport, as they made full account, of killing *Romans*: a folly doubtless for the serious *Romans* to smile at, as a sure tok'n of prospering that day: a Woeman also was thir Commander in Chief. For *Boadicea* and her

Daughters ride about in a Chariot, telling the tall Champions
as a great encouragement, that with the *Britans* it was usual
for Woemen to be thir Leaders. A deal of other fondness they
put into her mouth, not worth recital; how she was lash'd,
5 how her Daughters were handl'd, things worthier silence, re-
tirment, and a Vail, then for a Woeman to repeat, as don to
hir own person, or to hear repeated before an host of men.
The Greek Historian setts her in the field on a high heap of   *Dion.*
Turves, in a loose-bodied Gown declaming, a Spear in her
10 hand, a Hare in her bosome, which after a long circumlocu-
tion she was to let slip among them for lucks sake, then praying to *Andate the British Goddess,* to talk again as fondly as
before. And this they do out of a vanity, hoping to embellish
and set out thir Historie with the strangness of our manners,
15 not careing in the mean while to brand us with the rankest
note of Barbarism, as if in *Britain* Woemen were Men, and
Men Woemen. I affect not set speeches in a Historie, unless
known for certain to have bin so spok'n in effect as they are
writ'n, nor then, unless worth rehearsal; and to invent such,
20 though eloquently, as some Historians have done, is an abuse
of posteritie, raising, in them that read, other conceptions of
those times and persons then were true. Much less therefore
do I purpose heer or elsewhere to Copie out tedious Orations
without decorum, though in thir Authors compos'd ready to
25 my hand. Hitherto what we have heard of *Cassibelan, Toga-
dumnus, Venusius,* and *Caractacus* hath bin full of magnanimitie, soberness, and martial skill: but the truth is, that in
this Battel, and whole business, the *Britans* never more plainly

manifested themselves to be right *Barbarians;* no rule, no
foresight, no forecast, experience or estimation, either of
themselves or of thir Enemies; such confusion, such impotence, as seem'd likest not to a Warr, but to the wild hurrey of
5 a distracted Woeman, with as mad a Crew at her heeles.
Therefore *Suetonius* contemning thir unruly noises, and fierce
looks, heart'ns his men but to stand close a while, and strike
manfully this headless rabble that stood neerest, the rest would
be a purchase, rather then a toil. And so it fell out; for the
10 Legion, when they saw thir time, bursting out like a violent
wedge, quickly broke and dissipated what oppos'd them; all
else held only out thir necks to the slayer, for thir own Carts
and Waggons were so plac'd by themselves, as left them but
little room to escape between. The *Roman* slew all; men,
15 women, and the very drawing Horses lay heap'd along the
Field in a gory mixture of slaughter. About fowrscore thousand *Britans* are said to have bin slain on the place; of the
Enemy scarse 400 and not many more wounded. *Boadicea*
poysond her self, or, as others say, sick'n'd and dy'd. She was *Dion.*
20 of Stature big and tall, of visage grim and stern, harsh of
voice, her hair of bright colour flowing down to her hipps;
she wore a plighted Garment of divers colours, with a great
gold'n Chain; button'd over all a thick robe. *Gildas* calls her
the craftie lioness, and leaves an ill fame upon her doeings.
25 *Dion* sets down otherwise the order of this fight, and that the
field was not won without much difficultie, nor without intention of the *Britans* to give another Battel, had not the Death
of *Boadicea* come betweene. Howbeit *Suetonius* to preserve

Discipline, and to dispatch the reliques of Warr, lodg'd with all his Armie in the op'n field; which was supply'd out of *Germany* with 1000 Horse, and 10000 Foot; thence dispers'd to Winter, and with incursions to wast those Countries that
5 stood out. But to the *Britans* famin was a worse affliction; having left off dureing this uproar, to till the ground, and made reck'ning to serve themselves on the provisions of thir Enemie. Nevertheless those Nations that were yet untaimd, hearing of some discord ris'n betweene *Suetonius,* and the new
10 Procurator *Classicianus,* were brought but slowly to terms of peace; and the rigor us'd by *Suetonius* on them that yeilded, taught them the better course to stand on thir defence. For it *Tacit. vi.* is certaine, that *Suetonius,* though else a worthie man, over- *Agric.* proud of his Victorie, gave too much way to his anger against
15 the *Britans. Classician* therefore sending such word to *Rome,* that these severe proceedings would beget an endless Warr, *Polycletus,* no *Roman* but a Courtier, was sent by *Nero* to examin how things went. He admonishing *Suetonius* to use more mildness, aw'd the Armie, and to the *Britans* gave mat-
20 ter of Laughter. Who so much eeven till then were nurs'd up in thir native libertie, as to wonder that so great a Generall with his whole Armie should be at the rebuke and ordering of a Court Servitor. But *Suetonius* a while after having lost a few Gallies on the shoar, was bid resigne his command to *Petro-*
25 *nius Turpilianus,* who not provoking the *Britans,* nor by them provok'd, was thought to have pretended the love of peace to what indeed was his love of ease and sloth. *Trebellius Maximus* follow'd his steps, usurping the name of gentle Gover-

ment to any remisness or neglect of Discipline; which brought
in first licence, next disobedience into his Camp; incens'd
against him partly for his covetousness, partly by the incitement of *Roscius Cælius* Legat of a Legion; with whom for-
5 merly disagreeing, now that civil Warr began in the Empire,
he fell to op'n discord; charging him with disorder, and
sedition, and him *Cælius* with peeling and defrauding the
Legions of thir pay; insomuch that *Trebellius* hated, and deserted of the Souldiers, was content a while to govern by base
10 entreaty, and forc'd at length to flie the Land. Which notwithstanding remain'd in good quiet, govern'd by *Cælius* and
the other Legate of a Legion, both faithfull to *Vitellius* then
Emperour; who sent hither *Vectius Bolanus;* under whose
lenity, though not tainted with other fault, against the *Britans*
15 nothing was done, nor in thir own Discipline reform'd. *Petilius Cerealis* by appointment of *Vespasian* succeeding, had to
doe with the populous *Brigantes* in many Battails, and som of
those, not unbloodie. For as we heard before, it was *Venusius*
who eeven to these times held them tack, both himself re-
20 maining to the end unvanquish'd, and some part of his Countrie not so much as reach't. It appeares also by several passages
in the Histories of *Tacitus,* that no small number of *British
Forces* were commanded over Sea the year before to serve in
those bloodie Warrs betweene *Otho* and *Vitellius, Vitellius*
25 and *Vespasian* contending for the Empire. To *Cerealis* succeeded *Julius Frontinus* in the Government of *Britain,* who by
tameing the *Silures,* a people warlike and strongly inhabiting, augmented much his reputation. But *Julius Agricola,*

Tacit. Hist.
8. 1. & vit.
Agric.

69.
Tacit. Hist.
2. & vit.
Agric.
70.

74.
Calvis.
Tacit. Hist.
3. & vit.
Agric.

79.

whom *Vespatian* in his last year sent hither, train'd up from his youth in the *British* Warrs, extended with victories the *Roman* Limit beyond all his Predecessors. His coming was in the midst of Summer; and the *Ordovices* to welcome the
5 new General, had hew'n in peeces a whole Squadron of Horse, which lay upon thir bounds, few escapeing. *Agricola,* who perceav'd that the noise of this defeat had also in the Province desirous of novelty, stirr'd up new expectations, resolves to be before-hand with the danger: and drawing together the
10 choice of his Legions with a competent number of Auxiliars, not beeing met by the *Ordovices,* who kept the Hills, himself in the head of his men hunts them up and down through difficult places, almost to the final extirpating of that whole Nation. With the same current of success, what *Paulinus* had
15 left unfinish'd he Conquers in the *Ile of Mona:* for the Ilanders altogether fearless of his approach, whom they knew to have no Shipping, when they saw themselves invaded on a sudden by the Auxiliars, whose Countrie use had taught them to swimm over with Horse and Armes, were compel'd to
20 yeild. This gain'd *Agricola* much opinion; who at his verie entrance, a time which others bestow'd of course in hearing complements and gratulations, had made such early progress into laborious and hardest enterprises. But by farr not so famous was *Agricola* in bringing Warr to a speedie end, as in
25 cutting off the causes from whence Warr arises. For he knowing that the end of Warr was not to make way for injuries in peace, began reformation from his own house; permitted not his attendants and followers to sway, or have to doe at all in

public affairs: laies on with equallitie the proportions of corn
and tribute that were impos'd; takes off exactions, and the
Fees of encroaching Officers, heavier then the tribute it self.
For the Countries had bin compell'd before, to sitt and wait
5 the op'ning of public Granaries, and both to sell and to buy thir
Corn at what rate the Publicans thought fitt; the Pourveyers
also commanding when they pleas'd to bring it in, not to the
neerest, but still to the remotest places, either by the com-
pounding of such as would be excus'd, or by causing a Dearth,
10 where none was, made a particular gain. These greevances
and the like, he in the time of peace removing, brought peace
into some credit; which before, since the *Romans* coming,
had as ill a name as Warr. The Summer following, *Titus then
Emperor,* he so continually with inroads disquieted the Ene-
15 mie over all the Ile, and after terror so allur'd them with his
gentle demeanour, that many Citties which till that time
would not bend, gave Hostages, admitted Garrisons, and came
in voluntarily. The Winter he spent all in worthie actions;
teaching and promoting like a public Father the institutes
20 and customes of civil life. The Inhabitants rude and scatter'd,
and by that the proner to Warr, he so perswaded as to build
Houses, Temples, and Seats of Justice; and by praysing the
forward, quick'ning the slow, assisting all, turn'd the name
of necessitie into an emulation. He caus'd moreover the
25 Noblemens Sons to be bred up in liberal Arts; and by pre-
ferring the Witts of *Britain,* before the Studies of *Gallia,*
brought them to affect the Latine Eloquence, who before
hated the Language. Then were the *Roman* fashions imitated,

80.

and the Gown; after a while the incitements also and materials of Vice, and voluptuous life, proud Buildings, Baths, and
the elegance of Banqueting; which the foolisher sort call'd
civilitie, but was indeed a secret Art to prepare them for bond-
5 age. Spring appearing, he took the Field, and with a pros-   81.
perous expedition wasted as farr Northward as the Frith of
Taus all that obey'd not; with such a terror, as he went, that
the *Roman* Army, though much hinderd by tempestuous
weather, had the leasure to build Forts and Castles where they
10 pleas'd, none dareing to oppose them. Besides, *Agricola* had
this excellence in him, so providently to choose his places
where to fortifie, as not another General then alive. No sconce,
or fortress of his raising was ever known either to have bin
forc't, or yeilded up, or quitted. Out of these impregnable
15 by seige, or in that case duely releev'd, with continual irrup-
tions he so prevail'd, that the Enemie, whose manner was in
Winter to regain, what in Summer he had lost, was now alike
in both seasons kept short, and streit'n'd. For these exploits
then esteem'd so great, and honourable, *Titus* in whose Reign *Dion. L*
20 they were atcheev'd, was the fifteenth time saluted Imperator;
and of him *Agricola* receaved triumphal honours. The fourth   82.
Summer, *Domitian* then ruleing the Empire, he spent in set-
tling and confirming what the year before he had travail'd
over with a running Conquest. And had the valour of his
25 Souldiers bin answerable, he had reach'd that year, as was
thought, the utmost bounds of *Britain*. For *Glota,* and *Bo-*
dotria, now *Dunbritton,* and the Frith of *Edinburrow;* two
opposite Armes of the Sea, divided only by a neck of Land,

and all the Creeks and Inlets on this side, were held by the *Romans,* and the Enemie driv'n as it were into another Iland. In his fift year he pass'd over into the *Orcades,* as we may probably guess, and other Scotch Iles; discovering and sub-
5 dueing Nations till then unknown. He gain'd also with his Forces that part of *Britain* which faces *Ireland,* as aiming also to conquer that Iland; where one of the Irish Kings driv'n out by civil Warrs, comming to him, he both gladly receav'd, and retain'd him as against a fitt time. The Summer ensueing,
10 on mistrust that the Nations beyond *Bodotria* would generally rise, and forelay the passages by land, he caus'd his Fleet, makeing a great shew, to bear along the Coast, and up the Friths and Harbours; joyning most commonly at night on the same shoar both Land and Sea Forces, with mutual shouts and
15 loud greetings. At sight whereof the *Britans,* not wont to see thir Sea so ridd'n, were much daunted. Howbeit the *Caledonians* with great preparation, and by rumor, as of things unknown much greater, taking Armes, and of thir own accord begining Warr by the assault of sundry Castles, sent
20 back some of thir fear to the *Romans* themselves: and there were of the Commanders, who cloaking thir fear under shew of sage advice, counsel'd the General to retreat back on this side *Bodotria.* He in the mean while having intelligence, that the Enemie would fall on in many Bodies, devided also his
25 Armie into three parts. Which advantage the *Britans* quickly spying, and on a sudden uniting what before they had disjoyn'd, assaile by night with all thir Forces that part of the Roman Armie, which they knew to be the weakest; and

83.

84.

breaking in upon the Camp surpris'd between sleep and fear, had begun some Execution. When *Agricola,* who had learnt what way the Enemies took, and follow'd them with all speed, sending before him the lightest of his Horse and Foot to
5 charge them behind, the rest as they came on to affright them with clamour, so ply'd them without respite, that by approach of day the *Roman* Ensigns glittering all about, had encompass'd the *Britans:* who now after a sharp fight in the very Ports of the Camp, betook them to thir wonted refuge, the
10 Woods and Fens, poursu'd a while by the Romans, that day else in all appearance had ended the Warr. The Legions reincourag'd by this event, they also now boasting, who but lately trembl'd, cry all to be led on as farr as there was *British* ground. The *Britans* also not acknowledging the loss of that
15 day to *Roman* valour, but to the policy of their Captaine, abated nothing of their stoutness; but arming thir youth, conveying thir Wives and Children to places of safty, in frequent assemblies, and by solemn covnants bound themselves to mutual assistance against the common Enemy. About the same
20 time a Cohort of *Germans* having slain thir Centurion with other *Roman* Officers in a mutiny, and for fear of punishment fled a Shipboard, launch'd forth in three light Gallies without *Dion. L.* Pilot: and by tide or weather carried round about the Coast, using Piracy where they landed, while their Ships held out,
25 and as thir skill serv'd them, with various fortune, were the first discoverers to the *Romans* that *Britain* was an Iland. The following Summer, *Agricola* having before sent his Navie to   85. hover on the Coast, and with sundrie and uncertaine landings

to divert and disunite the *Britans,* himself with a power best
appointed for expedition, wherein also were many *Britans,*
whom he had long try'd both valiant and faithful, marches
onward to the Mountaine *Grampius,* where the *British,* above
30 thousand, were now lodg'd, and still encreasing: for neither would thir old men, so many as were yet vigorous and
lusty, be left at home, long practis'd in Warr, and every one
adorn'd with some badge, or cognisance of his warlike deeds
long agoe. Of whom *Galgacus,* both by birth and merit the
prime Leader, to thir courage, though of it self hot and violent, is by his rough Oratory, in detestation of servitude and
the *Roman* yoke, said to have added much more eagerness of
fight; testifi'd by thir shouts and barbarous applauses. As
much did on the others side *Agricola* exhort his Souldiers to
Victorie and Glorie; as much the Souldiers by his firm and
well grounded Exhortations were all on a fire to the onset.
But first he orders them in this sort. Of 8000 Auxiliar Foot
he makes his middle ward, on the wings 3000 Horse, the
Legions as a reserve, stood in array before the Camp; either to
seise the Victorie won without their own hazard, or to keep
up the Battaile if it should need. The *British* powers on the
Hill side, as might best serve for shew and terrour, stood in
thir Battalions; the first on eeven ground, the next rising behind, as the Hill ascended. The field between rung with the
noise of Horsemen and Chariots ranging up and down. *Ag-*
ricola doubting to be over wing'd, stretches out his front,
though somwhat with the thinest, insomuch that many advis'd to bring up the Legions: yet he not altering, alights from

his Horse, and stands on foot before the Ensignes. The fight began aloof, and the *Britans* had a certain skill with their broad swashing Swords and short Bucklers either to strike aside, or to bear off the Darts of thir Enemies; and withall to

5 send back showers of thir own. Until *Agricola* discerning that those little Targets and unweildie Glaves ill pointed, would soon become ridiculous against the thrust and close, commanded three *Batavian* Cohorts, and two of the *Tungrians* exercis'd and arm'd for close fight, to draw up, and come to

10 handy-strokes. The *Batavians*, as they were commanded, running in upon them, now with their long Tucks thrusting at the face, now with their piked Targets bearing them down, had made good riddance of them that stood below; and for hast omitting furder Execution, began apace to advance up

15 Hill, seconded now by all the other Cohorts. Mean while the Horse-men fly, the Charioters mixe themselves to fight among the Foot; where many of thir Horse also fall'n in disorderly, were now more a mischief to thir own, then before a terrour to thir Enemies. The Battaile was a confus'd heap; the ground

20 unequal; men, horses, Chariots crowded pelmel; sometimes in little roome, by and by in large, fighting, rushing, felling, over-bearing, over-turning. They on the Hill, which were not yet come to blows, perceaving the fewness of thir Enemies, came down amain; and had enclos'd the *Romans* unawares

25 behind, but that *Agricola* with a strong Body of Horse, which he reserv'd for such a purpose, repell'd them back as fast: and others drawn off the front, were commanded to wheel about and charge them on the backs. Then were the *Romans* clearly

Maisters; they follow, they wound, they take, and to take
more, kill whom they take: the *Britans* in whole Troops with
weapons in thir hands, one while flying the pursuer, anon
without weapons desperately running upon the slayer. But
5 all of them, when once they got the Woods to thir shelter, with
fresh boldness made head again, and the forwardest on a sudden they turn'd and slew, the rest so hamper'd, as had not
Agricola, who was every where at hand, sent out his readiest
Cohorts, with part of his Horse to alight and scowr the Woods,
10 they had receiv'd a foyle in the midst of Victorie; but following with a close and orderly poursuit, the *Britans* fled again,
and were totally scatter'd; till night and weariness ended the
chase. And of them that day 10 thousand fell; of the *Romans*
340, among whom *Aulus Atticus* the Leader of a Cohort;
15 carried with heat of youth and the firceness of his Horse too
far on. The *Romans* jocond of this Victorie, and the spoile
they got, spent the night; the vanquished wandring about the
field, both men and women, some lamenting, some calling
thir lost friends, or carrying off their wounded; others for-
20 saking, some burning thir own Houses; and it was certain
enough, that there were who with a stern compassion laid
violent hands on thir Wives and Children to prevent the more
violent hands of hostile injurie. Next day appearing manifested more plainly the greatness of thir loss receav'd; every
25 where silence, desolation, houses burning afar off, not a man
seen, all fled, and doubtful whether: such word the scouts
bringing in from all parts, and the Summer now spent, no fit
season to disperse a Warr, the *Roman* General leads his Armie

among the *Horestians;* by whom Hostages being giv'n, he
commands his Admiral with a sufficient Navie to saile round
the Coast of *Britain:* himself with slow marches, that his delay
in passing might serve to awe those new conquer'd Nations,
5 bestowes his Armie in their Winter-quarters. The Fleet also
having fetch't a prosperous and speedy compass about the Ile,
put in at the Haven *Trutulensis,* now *Richborrow* neer *Sand-*   *Camden*
wich, from whence it first set out: and now likeliest, if not   *Juvenal,*
two years before, as was mention'd, the *Romans* might dis-   *sat.* 2.
10 cover and subdue the Iles of *Orkney;* which others with less
reason following *Eusebius* and *Orosius,* attribute to the deeds   *Eutrop.*
of *Claudius.* These perpetual exploits abroad won him wide
fame; with *Domitian,* under whom great virtue was as pun-
ishable as op'n crime, won him hatred. For he maligning the   *Dion. L.*
15 renown of these his acts, in shew decreed him honours, in
secret devis'd his ruin. *Agricola* therefore commanded home   86.
for doeing too much, of what he was sent to doe, left the Province to his Successor quiet and secure. Whether he, as is conjectured, were *Salustius Lucullus,* or before him some other,
20 for *Suetonius* only names him Legat of *Britain* under *Domi-*
tian; but furder of him, or ought else done here until the time
of *Hadrian,* is no where plainly to be found. Some gather by
a Preface in *Tacitus* to the Book of his Histories, that what
Agricola won here, was soon after by *Domitian* either through
25 want of valour lost, or through envy neglected. And *Juvenal*
the Poet speaks of *Arviragus* in these days, and not before,
King of *Britain:* who stood so well in his resistance, as not
only to be talk'd of at *Rome,* but to be held matter of a glori-

ous Triumph, if *Domitian* could take him Captive, or overcome him. Then also *Claudia Rufina* the Daughter of a *Britain,* and Wife of *Pudence* a *Roman* Senator, liv'd at *Rome;*
famous by the Verse of *Martial* for beauty, wit, and learning.
5 The next we hear of *Britain,* is that when *Trajan* was Emperor, it revolted, and was subdued. Under *Adrian, Julius*   *Spartianus*
Severus, saith *Dion,* govern'd the Iland, a prime Souldier of   *in vit.*
Hadrian.
that Age, but he being call'd away to suppress the Jews then
in tumult, left things at such pass, as caus'd the Emperor in   122.
Spartianus
10 person to take a journey hither; where many things he re-   *ibid.*
form'd, and, as *Augustus,* and *Tiberius* counsel'd to gird the
Empire within moderate bounds; he rais'd a Wall with great
stakes driv'n in deep, and fastn'd together, in manner of a
strong mound, fourscore mile in length, to devide what was
15 *Roman* from *Barbarian:* no antient Author names the place,
but old inscriptions, and ruin it self yet testifies where it went
along between *Solway* Frith by *Carlile,* and the mouth of
Tine. Hadrian having quieted the Iland, took it for honour   *Camden.*
to be titl'd on his Coine, the Restorer of *Britain.* In his time
20 also *Priscus Licinius,* as appears by an old inscription, was
Lieutenant heer. *Antoninus Pius* reigning, the *Brigantes* ever   *Pausan.*
least patient of Foren servitude, breaking in upon *Genounia*   *archad.*
(which *Camden* guesses to be *Guinethia* or *North-Wales*)
part of the *Roman* Province, were with the loss of much ter-
25 ritory driv'n back by *Lollius Urbicus,* who drew another   *Capitolin.*
Wall of Turves; in likelihood much beyond the former, and   *vit. Anton.*
144.
as *Camden* proves, between the Frith of *Dunbritton,* and of   *Capitolin.*
Marc. Ant.
Edinborrow; to hedge out incursions from the North. And   *Philos.*
162.
Digest. L. 36.

Seius Saturninus, as is collected from the digests, had charge heer of the *Roman* Navie. With like success did *Marcus Aurelius* next Emperor by his Legate *Calphurnius Agricola* finish heer a new Warr: *Commodus* after him obteining the Empire. In his time, as among so many different accounts may seem most probable, *Lucius* a suppos'd King in some part of *Beda.* *Britain,* the first of any King in *Europe,* that we read of, receav'd the Christian Faith, and this Nation the first by publick Authority profess'd it: a high and singular grace from above, if sinceritie and perseverance went along, otherwise an empty boast, and to be fear'd the verifying of that true sentence, *the first shall be last.* And indeed the praise of this action is more proper to King *Lucius* than common to the *Nation;* whose first professing by publick Authority was no real commendation of their true faith; which had appear'd more sincere and praise-worthy, whether in this or other Nation, first profess'd without publick Authority or against it, might else have bin but outward conformity. *Lucius* in our *Monmouth* Storie is made the second by descent from *Marius, Marius* the Son of *Arviragus* is there said to have overthrown the *Picts* then first coming out of *Scythia,* slain *Roderic* their King; and in sign of Victorie to have set up a monument of Stone in the Country since call'd *Westmaria;* but these things have no foundation. *Coilus* the Son of *Marius,* all his reign, which was just and peaceable, holding great amity with the *Romans,* left it hereditary to *Lucius.* He (if *Beda* err not, living neer 500 years after, yet our antientest Author of this report) sent to *Eleutherius* then Bishop of *Rome,* an improbable

Letter, as some of the Contents discover, desiring that by his appointment he and his people might receave Christianitie. From whome two religious Doctors, nam'd in our Chronicles *Faganus* and *Deruvianus,* forthwith sent, are said to have converted and baptiz'd well nigh the whole Nation: thence *Lucius* to have had the sirname of *Levermaur,* that is to say, great light. Nor yet then first was the Christian Faith heer known, but eev'n from the later daies of *Tiberius,* as *Gildas* confidently affirms, taught and propagated, and that as some say by *Simon Zelotes,* as others by *Joseph* of *Arimathæa, Barnabas, Paul, Peter,* and thir prime Disciples. But of these matters, variously written and believ'd, Ecclesiastic Historians can best determin: as the best of them do, with little credit giv'n to the particulars of such uncertain relations. As for *Lucius,* they write, that after a long reigne he was buried at *Gloster;* but dying without issue left the Kingdom in great commotion. By truer testimony we find that the greatest Warr which in those days busy'd *Commodus,* was in this Iland. For the Nations Northward, notwithstanding the Wall rais'd to keep them out, breaking in upon the *Roman* Province, wasted wide; and both the Army and the Leader that came against them wholly routed, and destroy'd; which put the Emperor in such a fear, as to dispatch hither one of his best Commanders, *Ulpius Marcellus.* He a man endu'd with all nobleness of mind, frugal, temperate, mild, and magnanimous, in Warr bold and watchful, invincible against lucre, and the assault of bribes, what with his valour, and these his other virtues, quickly ended this Warr that look'd

Marginal notes: 181. Nennius. Geff. Mon. Dion. L. 72. 183.

so dangerous, and had himself like to have been ended by the
peace which he brought home, for presuming to be so worthy
and so good under the envy of so worthless and so bad an
Emperor. After whose departure the *Roman* Legions fell to
5 sedition among themselves; 15 hundred of them went to
Rome in name of the rest, and were so terrible to *Commodus*
himself, as that to please them he put to death *Perennis* the
Captain of his Guard. Notwithstanding which compliance
they endeavour'd heer to set up another Emperor against him;
10 and *Helvius Pertinax* who succeeded Governour, found it a
work so difficult to appease them, that once in a mutiny he
was left for dead among many slain; and was fain at length to
seek a dismission from his charge. After him *Clodius Albinus*
took the Government; but he, for having to the Souldiers
15 made an Oration against Monarchie, by the appointment of
Commodus was bid resign to *Junius Severus*. But *Albinus* in
those troublesome times ensuing under the short reign of *Per-*
tinax and *Didius Julianus,* found means to keep in his hands
the Government of *Britain;* although *Septimius Severus* who
20 next held the Empire, sent hither *Heraclitus* to displace him;
but in vain, for *Albinus* with all the *British* powers and those
of *Gallia* met *Severus* about *Lyons* in *France,* and fought a
bloody Battail with him for the Empire, though at last vanquish'd and slain. The Government of *Britain, Severus* di-
25 vided between two Deputies; till then one Legat was thought
sufficient; the North he committed to *Virius Lupus.* Where
the *Meatæ* rising in Arms, and the *Caledonians,* though they
had promis'd the contrary to *Lupus,* preparing to defend

Lampria
in comm
186.

Capitoli
in Pert.

Capitoli
in Alb.

193.
Dion.
Did. Jul.
Spartian
in Sever
Herod.

Herod.
Digest.
tit. 6.

them, so hard beset, he was compell'd to buy his peace, and a *Dion.*
few of Pris'ners with great Sums of money. But hearing that
Severus had now brought to an end his other Warrs, he writes *Herod. L. 3.*
him plainly the state of things heer, that the *Britans* of the
5 North made Warr upon him, broke into the Province, and
harrass'd all the Countries nigh them, that there needed suddenly either more aid, or himself in person. *Severus* though
now much weak'nd with Age and the Gout, yet desirous to
leav som memorial of his warlike acheevements heer, as he
10 had don in other places, and besides to withdraw by this
means his two Sons from the pleasures of *Rome,* and his
Souldiers from idleness, with a mighty power far sooner than
could be expected, arrives in *Britain.* The Northern people 208.
much daunted with the report of so great Forces brought over
15 with him, and yet more preparing, send Embassadors to
treat of peace, and to excuse thir former doings. The Emperor
now loath to returne home without some memorable thing
don, whereby he might assume to his other titles the addition
of *Britannicus,* delays his answer and quick'ns his prepara-
20 tions; till in the end, when all things were in readiness to follow them, they are dismiss't without effect. His principal
care was to have many Bridges laid over Bogs and rott'n
Moars, that his Souldiers might have to fight on sure footing.
For it seems through lack of tillage, the Northern parts were
25 then, as *Ireland* is at this day; and the inhabitants in like manner wonted to retire, and defend themselves in such watrie
places half naked. He also being past *Adrians* wall, cut down 209.
Woods, made way through Hills, fast'nd and fill'd up un-

sound and plashy Fens. Notwithstanding all this industrie
us'd, the Enemie kept himself so cunningly within his best
advantages, and seldom appearing, so opportunely found his
times to make irruption upon the *Romans,* when they were
5 most in straits and difficulties, sometimes training them on
with a few Cattel turn'd out, and drawn within ambush cruelly handling them, that many a time enclos'd in the midst
of sloughs and quagmires, they chose rather themselves to *Dion.*
kill such as were faint and could not shift away, than leave
10 them there a prey to the *Caledonians.* Thus lost *Severus,* and
by sickness in those noisome places, no less than 50 thousand
men: and yet desisted not, though for weakness carried in a
Litter, till he had march't through with his Armie to the
utmost Northern verge of the Ile: and the *Britans* offring
15 peace were compell'd to lose much of thir Country not before
subject to the *Romans. Severus* on the Frontiers of what he
had firmly conquer'd builds a Wall cross the Iland from Sea   210.
                                                              Spartia
to Sea; which one Author judges the most magnificent of all   *in Sever*
his other deeds; and that he thence receav'd the stile of *Bri-*
20 *tannicus;* in length 132 Miles. *Orosius* adds it fortify'd with *Eutropi*
                                                              an. Oro
a deep Trench, and between certain spaces many Towers, or   *Cassido*
Battlements. The place whereof som will have to be in *Scot-* *chro.*
                                                              Buchan
land, the same which *Lollius Urbicus* had wall'd before.
Others affirm it only *Hadrians* work re-edifi'd; both plead
25 Authorities and the ancient tract yet visible: but this I leave
among the studious of these Antiquities to be discuss't more
at large. While Peace held, the Empress *Julia* meeting on a
time certain *British* Ladies, and discoursing with the Wife of

Argentocoxus a *Caledonian,* cast out a scoff against the loose-
ness of our Iland Women; whose manner then was to use
promiscuously the company of divers men. Whom straight
the *British* Woman boldly thus answer'd: *Much better do we*
5 Britans *fulfill the work of Nature than you* Romans; *we with*
the best men accustom op'nly; you with the basest commit
private adulteries. Whether she thought this answer might
serve to justifie the practice of her Countrie, as when vices are
compar'd, the greater seems to justifie the less, or whether the
10 law and custom wherein she was bred, had wip't out of her
conscience the better dictate of Nature, and not convinc't her
of the shame; certain it is that whereas other Nations us'd a
liberty not unnatural for one man to have many Wives, the
Britans altogether as licentious, but more absurd and prepos-   *Cæsar.*
15 terous in thir licence, had one or many Wives in common
among ten or twelve Husbands; and those for the most part
incestuously. But no sooner was *Severus* return'd into the
Province, then the *Britans* take Arms again. Against whom
Severus worn out with labours and infirmity, sends *Anto-*
20 *ninus* his eldest Son; expressly commanding him to spare
neither Sex nor Age. But *Antoninus* who had his wicked
thoughts tak'n up with the contriving of his Fathers death, a
safer Enemie then a Son, did the *Britans* not much detriment.
Whereat *Severus* more overcom with grief than any other
25 maladie, ended his life at *York.* After whose decease *Anto-*   211.
ninus Caracalla his impious Son concluding peace with the   *Spartianus*
Britans, took Hostages and departed to *Rome.* The Con-   *in Sever.*
ductor of all this Northern Warr *Scottish* Writers name *Do-*

naldus, he of *Monmouth Fulgenius,* in the rest of his relation
nothing worth. From hence the *Roman* Empire declining
apace, good Historians growing scarce, or lost, have left us
little else but fragments for many years ensuing. Under
5 *Gordian* the Emperour we find by the Inscription of an Altar
stone, that *Nonius Philippus* govern'd heer. Under *Galienus*
we read there was a strong and general revolt from the *Roman*
Legat. Of the 30 Tyrants which not long after took upon
them the style of Emperor, by many Coins found among us,
10 *Lollianus, Victorinus, Posthumus,* the *Tetrici* and *Marius* are
conjectured to have ris'n or born great sway in this Iland.
Whence *Porphyrius* a Philosopher then living, said that *Brit-*
ain was a soil fruitful of Tyrants; and is noted to be the first
Author that makes mention of the *Scottish* Nation. While
15 *Probus* was Emperor, *Bonosus* the Son of a Rhetorician, bred
up a *Spanyard,* though by descent a *Britan,* and a matchless
drinker, nor much to be blamed, if, as they write, he were still
wisest in his cups, having attained in warfare to high honours,
and lastly in his charge over the *German* shipping, willingly,
20 as was thought, miscarried, trusting on his power with the
Western Armies, and join'd with *Proculus,* bore himself
a while for Emperor; but after a long and bloodie fight at
Cullen, vanquish't by *Probus* he hang'd himself, and gave
occasion of a ready jest made on him for his much drinking;
25 *Heer hangs a Tankard, not a man.* After this, *Probus* with
much wisdom prevented a new rising heer in *Britain* by the
severe loyaltie of *Victorinus* a *Moor,* at whose entreatie he
had plac't heer that Governour which rebell'd. For the Em-

242.
Camd.
Cumber

259.
Eumen.
neg. Co
267.
Camder

Gildas.
Hieron;

282.
Vapisc.
Bonos.

Zozim.

peror upbraiding him with the disloyaltie of whom he had
commended, *Victorinus* undertaking to set all right again,
hastes hither, and finding indeed the Governour to intend
sedition, by som contrivance not mention'd in the storie, slew
5 him, whose name som imagin to be *Cornelius Lelianus*. They   *Camd.*
write also that *Probus* gave leave to the *Spanyards, Gauls,* and
Britans to plant Vines, and to make Wine; and having subdu'd the *Vandals,* and *Burgundians* in a great Battail, sent *Zozimus.*
over many of them hither to inhabit, where they did good
10 service to the *Romans* when any insurrection happen'd in the
Ile. After whom *Carus* Emperor going against the *Persians,*
left *Carinus* one of his Sons to govern among other Western   283.
Provinces this Iland with imperial authority; but him *Dio-* *Vopisc. in*
clesian saluted Emperor by the Eastern Armies overcame and *Carin.*
15 slew. About which time *Carausius* a man of low parentage,   284.
born in *Menapia,* about the parts of *Cleves* and *Juliers,* who *Aurel. victor.*
through all militarie degrees was made at length Admiral of *de Cæsar.*
the *Belgic* and *Armoric* Seas, then much infested by the
Franks and *Saxons,* what he took from the Pyrats, neither re-   285.
20 storing to the owners, nor accounting to the Publick, but en- *Eutrop. Oros.*
riching himself, and yet not scowring the Seas, but conniving
rather at those Sea Robbers, was grown at length too great a
Delinquent to be less than an Emperor: for fear and guiltiness
in those days made Emperors ofter than merit: And under-
25 standing that *Maximianus Herculius, Dioclesians* adopted
Son, was com against him into *Gallia,* pass'd over with the *Eumen.*
Navie which he had made his own, into *Britain,* and possess'd *Paneg. 2.*
the Iland. Where he built a new Fleet after the *Roman* fash-   286.

ion, got into his power the Legion that was left heer in Garrison, other outlandish Cohorts detain'd, listed the very Merchants and Factors of *Gallia,* and with the allurement of
spoile invited great numbers of other barbarous Nations to his
5 part, and train'd them to Sea service, wherein the *Romans* at
that time were grown so out of skill, that *Carausius* with his
Navie did at Sea what he listed, robbing on every Coast;
whereby *Maximian,* able to come no neerer than the shoar of
Boloigne, was forc't to conclude a Peace with *Carausius,* and   *Victor.*
10 yeild him *Britain;* as one fittest to guard the Province there   *Eutrop.*
against inroads from the North. But not long after having as-   *291.*
sum'd *Constantius Chlorus* to the dignity of *Cæsar,* sent him
against *Carausius;* who in the mean while had made himself
strong both within the Land and without. *Galfred* of *Mon-*   *Buchana*
15 *mouth* writes that he made the *Picts* his confederates; to
whom lately com out of *Scythia* he gave *Albany* to dwell in:
and it is observ'd that before his time the *Picts* are not known
to have bin any where mentioned, and then first by *Eumenius*
a Rhetorician. He repair'd and fortifi'd the Wall of *Severus*   *Paneg.* 2
20 with 7 Castles, and a round House of smooth stone on the
Bank of *Carron,* which River, faith *Ninnius,* was of his Name
so call'd; he built also a Triumphal Arch in remembrance of
some Victory there obtain'd. In *France* he held *Gessoriacum,*
or *Boloigne;* and all the *Franks* which had by his permission
25 seated themselves in *Belgia,* were at his devotion. But *Con-*   *Paneg.*
stantius hasting into *Gallia,* besieges *Boloigne,* and with   *Sigonius*
Stones and Timber obstructing the Port, keeps out all relief
that could be sent in by *Carausius.* Who ere *Constantius* with

the great Fleet which he had prepar'd, could arrive hither,
was slain treacherously by *Alectus* one of his Friends, who   292.
long'd to step into his place; when he 7 years, and worthily,
as som say, as others, tyrannically, had rul'd the Iland. So
5 much the more did *Constantius* prosecute that opportunity,   *Camd. ex*
before *Alectus* could well strengthen his Affairs: and though   *Nin. Eumen.*
in ill weather, putting to Sea with all urgency from several   *Pan.* 3.
Hav'ns to spread the terror of his landing, and the doubt
where to expect him, in a Mist passing the *British* Fleet un-
10 seen, that lay scouting neer the Ile of *Wight,* no sooner got a
shoar, but fires his own Ships, to leave no hope of refuge but
in Victory. *Alectus* also, though now much dismaid, trans-
fers his fortune to a Battel on the shoar; but encountred by
Asclepiodotus Captain of the *Prætorian* Bands, and desper-
15 ately rushing on, unmindful both of ordering his men, or
bringing them all to fight, save the accessories of his Treason,
and his outlandish hirelings, is overthrown, and slain with
little or no loss to the *Romans,* but great execution on the
Franks. His Body was found almost naked in the field, for
20 his Purple Robe he had thrown aside, lest it should descry
him, unwilling to be found. The rest taking flight to *London,*
and purposing with the pillage of that City to escape by Sea,
are met by another part of the *Roman* Armie, whom the Mist
at Sea disjoining had by chance brought thither, and with a
25 new slaughter chas'd through all the Streets. The *Britans,*
thir Wives also and Children, with great joy go out to meet
Constantius, as one whom they acknowledge their deliverer
from bondage and insolence. All this seems by *Eumenius,*

who then liv'd, and was of *Constantius* houshold, to have bin
don in the course of one continu'd action; so also thinks
Sigonius a learned Writer: though all others allow three years   *Eumen.*
to the tyranny of *Alectus*. In these days were great store of
5 Workmen, and excellent Builders in this Iland, whom after
the alteration of things heer, the *Æduans* in *Burgundie* entertain'd to build thir Temples and publick Edifices. *Dioclesian*
having hitherto successfully us'd his valour against the Enemies of his Empire, uses now his rage in a bloodie persecu-
10 tion against his obedient and harmless Christian Subjects:
from the feeling whereof neither was this Iland, though most   *Gildas.*
remote, far anough remov'd. Among them heer who suffer'd
gloriously, *Aron,* and *Julius* of *Caer leon* upon *Usk,* but chiefly
Alban of *Verulam,* were most renown'd: The story of whose
15 Martyrdom soil'd, and worse martyr'd with the fabling zeal
of some idle fancies, more fond of Miracles, than apprehen-
sive of Truth, deserves not longer digression. *Constantius*
after *Dioclesian,* dividing the Empire with *Galerius,* had
Britain among his other Provinces; where either preparing
20 or returning with victorie from an expedition against the   *Author ig*
Caledonians, he di'd at *York.* His Son *Constantine,* who   *post Mar*
  lin. vales
happily came Post from *Rome* to *Boloigne* just about the time,   306.
saith *Eumenius,* that his Father was setting sail his last time   *Eutrop. I*
  men. ide
hither, and not long before his death, was by him on his death-   *Auth. igi*
25 bed nam'd, and after his Funeral, by the whole Army saluted
Emperor. There goes a fame, and that seconded by most of
our own Historians, though not those the ancientest, that
Constantine was born in this Iland, his Mother *Helena* the

Daughter of *Coilus* a *British* Prince, not sure the Father of King *Lucius,* whose Sister she must then be, for that would detect her too old by an hunderd years to be the Mother of *Constantine.* But to salve this incoherence, another *Coilus* is
5 feign'd to be then Earl of *Colchester.* To this therefore the *Roman* Authors give no testimony, except a passage or two in the *Panegyrics,* about the sense whereof much is argu'd: others neerest to those times clear the doubt, and write him *Idem vit.* certainly born of *Helena,* a mean Woman at *Naisus* in *Dar-* *Auth. ignot.* *Euseb.*
10 *dania.* Howbeit, ere his departure hence he seems to have *Const.* had some bickerings in the North, which by reason of more urgent affairs compos'd, he passes into *Gallia;* and after 4 *307.* years returns either to settle or to alter the state of things heer; *Sigon.* *311.* until a new Warr against *Maxentius* call'd him back, leaving *Camd.*
15 *Pacatianus* his Vicegerent. He deceasing, *Constantine* his eldest Son enjoy'd for his part of the Empire, with all the Provinces that lay on this side the *Alpes,* this Iland also. But fall- *Ammian.* ing to Civil Warr with *Constans* his Brother, was by him slain; *L. 20. & in* *eum* who with his third Brother *Constantius* coming into *Britain,* *Valesius.*
20 seis'd it as Victor. Against him rose *Magnentius,* one of his *340.* *Libanius* chief Commanders, by som affirm'd the Son of a *Britan,* he *in Basilico.* having gain'd on his side great Forces, contested with *Con-* *343.* *Camd. ex* *stantius* in many Battels for the sole Empire; but vanquish't, *Firmico.* in the end slew himself. Somwhat before this time *Gratianus* *350.* *Camden.*
25 *Funarius,* the Father of *Valentinian,* afterwards Emperor, *353.* had chief command of those Armies which the *Romans* kept heer. And the *Arrian* Doctrine which then divided Christen- *Ammian.* dom, wrought also in this Iland no small disturbance: a Land,

saith *Gildas,* greedy of every thing new, stedfast in nothing.
At last *Constantius* appointed a *Synod* of more than 400 Bish-   359.
ops to assemble at *Ariminum* on the Emperors charges, which
the rest all refusing, three only of the *British,* poverty con-
5 streining them, accepted; though the other Bishops among
them offer'd to have born thir charges: esteeming it more
honourable to live on the publick, than to be obnoxious to any
private Purse. Doubtless an ingenuous mind, and far above
the Presbyters of our Age; who like well to sit in Assembly
10 on the publick stipend, but lik'd not the poverty that caus'd
these to do so. After this *Martinus* was Deputy of the Province; who being offended with the cruelty which *Paulus,* an
inquisitor sent from *Constantius,* exercis'd in his enquiry
after those Military Officers who had conspir'd with *Mag-*
15 *nentius,* was himself laid hold on as an accessory; at which
enrag'd he runs at *Paulus* with his drawn Sword; but failing
to kill him, turns it on himself. Next to whom, as may be
guess'd, *Alipius* was made Deputy. In the mean time *Julian,*
whom *Constantius* had made *Cæsar,* having recover'd much
20 Territory about *Rhine,* where the *German* inrodes before had
long insulted, to releeve those Countries almost ruin'd, causes *Liban. O*
800 Pinaces to be built; and with them by frequent Voyages,   10. *Zozir*
plenty of Corn to be fetch'd in from *Britain;* which eev'n   *L. 3.*
then was the usual bounty of this Soil to those parts, as oft as   *Amm. l.*
25 *French* and *Saxon* Pirats hinderd not the transportation.
While *Constantius* yet reign'd, the *Scots* and *Picts* breaking   360.
in upon the Northern confines, *Julian,* being at *Paris,* sends
over *Lupicinus,* a well try'd Souldier, but a proud and cove-   *Amm. L*

tous man; who with a power of light arm'd *Herulians, Batavians,* and *Mæsians,* in the midst of Winter sailing from *Boloigne,* arrives at *Rutupiæ* seated on the opposite shoar, and comes to *London,* to consult there about the Warr; but soon

5 after was recall'd by *Julian* then chosen Emperor. Under whom we read not of ought happning heer; only that *Palladius* one of his great Officers was hither banish'd. This year *Valentinian* being Emperor, the *Attacots, Picts,* and *Scots* roaving up and down, and last the *Saxons* with perpetual

10 landings and invasions harryed the South Coast of *Britain;* slew *Nectaridius* who govern'd the Sea Borders, and *Bulchobaudes* with his Forces by an ambush. With which news *Valentinian* not a little perplext, sends first *Severus* high Steward of his House, and soon recalls him, then *Jovinus,*

15 who intimating the necessity of greater supplies, he sends at length *Theodosius,* a man of try'd valour, and experience, father to the first Emperor of that Name. He with selected numbers out of the Legions, and Cohorts, crosses the Sea from *Boloigne* to *Rutupiæ;* from whence with the *Batavians,*

20 *Herulians,* and other Legions that arriv'd soon after, he marches to *London;* and dividing his Forces into several Bodies, sets upon the dispers'd and plundring Enemie, lad'n with spoile; from whom recovering the booty which they led away, and were forc'd to leave there with thir lives, he restores

25 all to the right owners, save a small portion to his wearied Souldiers, and enters *London* victoriously; which before in many straits and difficulties, was now reviv'd as with a great deliverance. The numerous Enemy with whom he had to

364.
Amm.
L. 26. 27.

367.

deal, was of different Nations, and the Warr scatter'd: which *Theodosius,* getting daily som intelligence from fugitives and prisoners, resolves to carry on by sudden parties and surprisals rather than set Battels; nor omits he to proclaim indemnity to

5 such as would lay down Arms, and accept of peace, which brought in many. Yet all this not ending the work, he requires that *Civilis,* a man of much uprightness, might be sent him, to be as Deputy of the Iland, and *Dulcitius* a famous Captain. Thus was *Theodosius* busy'd, besetting with am-

10 bushes the roaving Enemy, repressing his Rodes, restoring Cities and Castles to thir former safety and defence, laying every where the firm foundation of a long peace, when *Valen-* *tinus* a *Pannonian* for some great offence banish'd into *Britain,* conspiring with certain Exiles and Souldiers against *Theo-*

15 *dosius,* whose worth he dreaded as the only obstacle to his greater design of gaining the Ile into his power, is discover'd, and with his chief accomplices deliver'd over to condign punishment; against the rest, *Theodosius* with a wise lenity suffer'd not inquisition to proceed too rigorously, lest the fear

20 thereof appertaining to so many, occasion might arise of new trouble in a time so unsettl'd. This don, he applies himself to reform things out of order, raises on the confines many strong holds; and in them appoints due and diligent watches; and so reduc'd all things out of danger, that the Province which

25 but lately was under command of the Enemy, became now wholly *Roman,* new nam'd *Valentia* of *Valentinian,* and the City of *London Augusta.* Thus *Theodosius* nobly acquitting himself in all Affairs, with general applause of the whole

368.
Amm. L
Zozim.

Province, accompanied to the Sea-side, returns to *Valentin-ian*. Who about 5 years after sent hither *Fraomarius*, a King of the *Almans*, with authority of a Tribune over his own Country Forces, which then both for number and good service were in high esteem. Against *Gratian* who succeeded in the Western Empire, *Maximus* a *Spanyard*, and one who had serv'd in the *British* Warrs with younger *Theodosius* (for hee also, either with his Father, or not long after him, seems to have done somthing in this Iland) and now General of the *Roman* Armies heer, either discontented that *Theodosius* was preferr'd before him to the Empire, or constrain'd by the Souldiers who hated *Gratian*, assumes the imperial Purple, and having attain'd Victorie against the *Scots* and *Picts*, with the flowr and strength of *Britain*, passes into *France;* there slays *Gratian*, and without much difficultie, the space of 5 years, obtains his part of the Empire, overthrown at length and slain by *Theodosius*. With whom perishing most of his followers, or not returning out of *Armorica*, which *Maximus* had giv'n them to possess, the South of *Britain* by this means exhausted of her youth, and what there was of *Roman* Souldiers on the Confines drawn off, became a prey to savage Invasions; of *Scots* from the *Irish* Seas, of *Saxons* from the *German*, of *Picts* from the North. Against them, first *Chrysanthus* the Son of *Marcian* a Bishop, made Deputy of *Britain* by *Theodosius*, demean'd himself worthily: then *Stilicho* a man of great power, whom *Theodosius*, dying, left Protector of his Son *Honorius*, either came in person, or sending over sufficient aid, repress'd them, and as it seems new fortifi'd the

373.
Amm. L. 29.

Zozim. L. 4.
Sigon.

Prosper.
Aquitanic.
chron.
383.

Gildas.
388.
Beda.
Ninn.

389.
Socrat. L. 7.

Claudian. de
laud. stil. l. 2.
& de. bello
Get.

Wall against them. But that Legion being call'd away, when
the *Roman* Armies from all parts hasted to releive *Honorius*   402.
then besieg'd in *Asta* of *Piemont,* by *Alaric* the *Goth, Britain*
was left expos'd as before, to those Barbarous Robbers. Lest
5 any wonder how the *Scots* came to infest *Britain* from the
Irish Sea, it must be understood, that the *Scots* not many years
before had been driv'n all out of *Britain* by *Maximus;* and
thir King *Eugenius* slain in fight; as thir own Annals report:
whereby, it seems, wandring up and down, without certain
10 seat, they liv'd by scumming those Seas and shoars as Pyrats.
But more authentic Writers confirm us, that the *Scots,* who-   *Ethelwe*
ever they be originally, came first into *Ireland,* and dwelt   *Sax. an.*
there, and nam'd it *Scotia* long before the North of *Britain*   *Bede Ep*
                                                                     the year
took that name. About this time, though troublesom, *Pelagius*   *and Bed*
                                                                     L. 2. c. 4
15 a *Britan* found the leasure to bring new and dangerous Opin-   405.
ions into the Church, and is largely writ against by St. *Austin.*
But the *Roman* powers which were call'd into *Italy,* when
once the fear of *Alaric* was over, made return into several
Provinces: and perhaps *Victorinus* of *Tolosa,* whom *Rutilius*
20 the Poet much commends, might be then Prefect of the Iland:
if it were not he whom *Stilicho* sent hither. *Buchanan* writes,
that endeavouring to reduce the *Picts* into a Province, he gave
the occasion of thir calling back *Fergusius* and the *Scots,*
whom *Maximus* with thir help had quite driv'n out of the
25 Iland: and indeed the Verses of that Poet speak him to have
bin active in those parts. But the time which is assign'd him
later by *Buchanan* after *Gratianus Municeps,* by *Camden,*
after *Constantine* the Tyrant, accords not with that which

follows in the plain course of Historie. For the *Vandals* hav- 407.
Zozim. L. 6.
ing broke in and wasted all *Belgia,* eev'n to those places from
whence easiest passage is into *Britain,* the *Roman* Forces heer,
doubting to be suddenly invaded, were all in uproar, and in
5 tumultuous manner set up *Marcus,* who it may seem was then
Deputy. But him not found agreeable to thir heady courses, *Sozom. L.* 9.
they as hastily kill: for the giddy favour of a mutining rout is
as dangerous as thir furie. The like they do by *Gratian* a *Brit-*
ish Roman, in four Months advanc't, ador'd, and destroy'd. *Oros. L.* 7.
10 There was among them a common Souldier whose name was
Constantine, with him on a sudden so taken they are, upon
the conceit put in them of a luckiness in his name, as without
other visible merit to create him Emperor. It fortun'd that the
man had not his name for nought; so well he knew to lay
15 hold, and make good use of an unexpected offer. He therefore with a wak'n'd spirit, to the extent of his Fortune dilating
his mind, which in his mean condition before lay contracted
and shrunk up, orders with good advice his military affairs:
and with the whole force of the Province, and what of *British*
20 was able to bear Arms, he passes into *France,* aspiring at
least to an equal share with *Honorius* in the Empire. Where
by the valour of *Edobecus* a *Frank,* and *Gerontius* a *Britan,*
and partly by perswasion gaining all in his way, he comes to
Arles. With like felicity by his Son *Constans,* whom of a 408.
25 Monk he had made a *Cæsar,* and by the conduct of *Gerontius*
he reduces all *Spain* to his obedience. But *Constans* after this
displacing *Gerontius,* the affairs of *Constantine* soon went to
wrack: for he by this means alienated, set up *Maximus* one 409.

of his friends against him in *Spain;* and passing into *France,*
took *Vienna* by assault, and having slain *Constans* in that
City, calls on the *Vandals* against *Constantine;* who by him
incited, as by him before they had bin repress't, breaking for-
5 ward, over-run most part of *France.* But when *Constantius*
Comes, the Emperors General, with a strong power came out
of *Italy, Gerontius* deserted by his own Forces, retires into   *Sozom.*
Spain; where also growing into contempt with the Souldiers,
after his flight out of *France,* by whom his House in the night   *Olympi*
10 was beset, having first with a few of his Servants defended   *apud*
Photium
himself valiantly, and slain above 300, though when his Darts
and other Weapons were spent, he might have scap'd at a private dore, as all his Servants did, not enduring to leave his
Wife *Nonnichia,* whom he lov'd, to the violence of an en-
15 raged crew, he first cuts off the head of his friend *Alanus,* as
was agreed; next his Wife, though loth and delaying, yet by
her entreated and importun'd, refusing to outlive her Husband, he dispatches: for which her resolution *Sozomenus* an
Ecclesiastic Writer gives her high praise, both as a Wife, and
20 as a Christian. Last of all against himself he turns his Sword;
but missing the mortal place, with his poinard finishes the
work. Thus farr is poursu'd the story of a famous *Britan,* related negligently by our other Historians. As for *Constantine,*
his ending was not answerable to his setting out: for he with
25 his other Son *Julian* beseig'd by *Constantius* in *Arles,* and
mistrusting the change of his wonted success, to save his head,
poorly turns Priest; but that not availing him, is carried into
Italy, and there put to death; having 4 years acted the Em-

peror. While these things were doing, the *Britans* at home
destitute of *Roman* aid, and the cheif strength of their own *Gildas.*
youth, that went first with *Maximus,* then with *Constantine,* *Beda.*
not returning home, vext, and harras'd by thir wonted Ene-
5 mies, had sent messages to *Honorius;* but he at that time not *Zozim. L. 6.*
being able to defend *Rome* it self, which the same year was
taken by *Alaric,* advises them by his Letter to consult how best
they might for their own safety, and acquits them of the *Ro-*
man jurisdiction. They therefore thus relinquish't, and by all *Procopius*
10 right the Government relapsing into thir own hands, thence- *vandalic.*
forth betook themselves to live after thir own Laws, defending thir bounds as well as they were able, and the *Armoricans,*
who not long after were call'd the *Britans* of *France,* follow'd
thir Example. Thus expir'd this great Empire of the *Romans;*
15 first in *Britain,* soon after in *Italy* it self: having born chief
sway in this Iland, though never throughly subdu'd, or all at
once in subjection, if we reck'n from the coming in of *Julius*
to the taking of *Rome* by *Alaric,* in which year *Honorius*
wrote those Letters of discharge into *Britain,* the space of 462 *Calvis.*
20 years. And with the Empire fell also what before in this *Sigon.*
Western World was cheifly *Roman;* Learning, Valour, Eloquence, History, Civility, and eev'n Language it self, all these
together, as it were, with equal pace diminishing, and decaying. Henceforth we are to stear by another sort of Authors;
25 neer anough to the things they write, as in thir own Countrie,
if that would serve; in time not much belated, some of equal
age; in expression barbarous; and to say how judicious, I sus-
pend a while: this we must expect; in civil matters to find

them dubious Relaters, and still to the best advantage of what they term holy Church, meaning indeed themselves: in most other matters of Religion, blind, astonish'd, and strook with superstition as with a Planet; in one word, Monks. Yet these
5 Guides, where can be had no better, must be follow'd; in gross, it may be true anough; in circumstance each man as his judgment gives him, may reserve his Faith, or bestow it. But so different a state of things requires a several relation.

THE HISTORY OF BRITAIN.

THE THIRD BOOK

THIS third Book having to tell of accidents as various and exemplary, as the intermission or change of Government hath any where brought forth, may deserve attention more than common, and repay it with like benefit
5 to them who can judiciously read: considering especially that the late civil broils had cast us into a condition not much unlike to what the *Britans* then were in, when the imperial jurisdiction departing hence left them to the sway of thir own Councils; which times by comparing seriously with these
10 later, and that confused Anarchy with this intereign, we may be able from two such remarkable turns of State, producing like events among us, to raise a knowledg of our selves both great and weighty, by judging hence what kind of men the *Britans* generally are in matters of so high enterprise, how by
15 nature, industry, or custom fitted to attempt or undergoe matters of so main consequence: for if it be a high point of wisdom in every private man, much more is it in a Nation to know it self; rather than puft up with vulgar flatteries, and encomiums, for want of self knowledge, to enterprise rashly
20 and come off miserably in great undertakings. The *Britans* thus as we heard being left without protection from the Empire, and the Land in a manner emptied of all her youth, consumed in Warrs abroad, or not caring to return home,   *Gild. Bede.* themselves through long subjection, servile in mind, sloathful   *Malins.*

of body, and with the use of Arms unacquainted, sustain'd but ill for many years the violence of those barbarous Invaders, who now daily grew upon them. For although at first greedy *Zozim* of change, and to be thought the leading Nation to freedom

5 from the Empire, they seem'd a while to bestirr them with a shew of diligence in thir new affairs, som secretly aspiring to rule, others adoring the name of liberty, yet so soon as they felt by proof the weight of what it was to govern well themselves, and what was wanting within them, not stomach or

10 the love of licence, but the wisdom, the virtue, the labour, to use and maintain true libertie, they soon remitted thir heat, and shrunk more wretchedly under the burden of thir own libertie, than before under a foren yoke. Insomuch that the residue of those *Romans* which had planted themselves heer,

15 despairing of thir ill deportment at home, and weak resistance in the field by those few who had the courage, or the strength to bear Arms, nine years after the sacking of *Rome* remov'd 418. out of *Britain* into *France,* hiding for haste great part of thir *Ethelw annal.* treasure, which was never after found. And now again the

20 *Britans,* no longer able to support themselves against the prevailing Enemy, sollicit *Honorius* to thir aid, with mournful Letters, Embassages and vows of perpetual subjection to *Rome Gildas* if the *Northern* Foe were but repuls't. He at thir request 422. *Diacor* spares them one Legion, which with great slaughter of the *L. 14.*

25 *Scots* and *Picts* drove them beyond the Borders, rescu'd the *Britans,* and advis'd them to build a Wall cross the Iland, between Sea and Sea, from the place where *Edinburg* now *Bede.* stands to the Frith of *Dunbritton,* by the City *Alcluith.* But *L. 1. c.*

the material being only Turf, and by the rude multitude unar-
tificially built up without better direction, avail'd them little.
For no sooner was the Legion departed, but the greedy   *Gildas.*
spoilers returning, land in great numbers from thir Boats and
5 Pinaces, wasting, slaying, and treading down all before them.
Then are messengers again posted to *Rome* in lamentable sort,
beseeching that they would not suffer a whole Province to be
destroy'd, and the *Roman* name, so honourable yet among
them, to become the subject of barbarian scorn and insolence.
10 The Emperor, at thir sad complaint, with what speed was   423.
possible sends to thir succour. Who coming suddenly on those
ravenous multitudes that minded only spoil, surprise them
with a terrible slaughter. They who escap'd, fled back to those
Seas, from whence yearly they were wont to arrive, and return
15 lad'n with booties. But the *Romans* who came not now to
rule, but charitably to aid, declaring that it stood not longer
with the ease of thir Affairs to make such laborious voyages in
pursuit of so base and vagabond robbers, of whom neither
glory was to be got, nor gain, exhorted them to manage thir
20 own warfare; and to defend like men thir Country, thir
Wives, thir Children, and what was to be dearer than life,
thir liberty, against an Enemy not stronger than themselves,
if thir own sloth and cowardise had not made them so; if they
would but only find hands to grasp defensive Arms, rather
25 than basely stretch them out to receave bonds. They gave them   *Bede ibid.*
also thir help to build a new Wall, not of earth as the former,   *Gildas.*
but of stone (both at the public cost, and by particular contri-
butions) traversing the Ile in direct line from East to West

between certain Cities plac'd there as Frontiers to bear off the
Enemy, where *Severus* had wall'd once before. They rais'd
it 12 Foot high, 8 broad. Along the South shoar, because from
thence also like hostility was fear'd, they place Towers by the
5 Sea side at certain distances, for safety of the Coast. Withall
they instruct them in the art of Warr, leaving Patterns of thir
Arms and Weapons behind them; and with animating words,
and many lessons of valour to a faint-hearted audience, bid
them finally farewell, without purpose to return. And these
10 two friendly Expeditions, the last of any hither by the *Romans,* were perform'd, as may be gather'd out of *Beda,* and
Diaconus, the two last years of *Honorius.* Thir Leader, as
som modernly write, was *Gallio* of *Ravenna; Buchanan,* who   *Blond.*
departs not much from the Fables of his Predecessor *Boethius,*   *Sabellic.*
15 names him *Maximianus,* and brings against him to this Battel *Fergus* first King of *Scots* after thir second suppos'd coming into *Scotland, Durstus* King of *Picts,* both there slain, and
Dioneth an imaginary King of *Britain,* or Duke of *Cornwall,*
who improbablie sided with them against his own Countrie,
20 hardlie escaping. With no less exactness of particular circum-   *Buch. L.*
stances, he takes upon him to relate all those tumultuarie inrodes of the *Scots* and *Picts* into *Britain,* as if they had but
yesterday happen'd, thir order of Battel, manner of fight,
number of slain, Articles of Peace, things whereof *Gildas* and
25 *Beda* are utterly silent, Authors to whom the *Scotch* Writers
have none to cite comparable in Antiquity; no more therefore
to be believ'd for bare assertions, however quaintlie drest, than
our *Geofry* of *Monmouth* when he varies most from authen-

tick storie. But either the inbred vanity of some, in that respect unworthily call'd Historians, or the fond zeal of prais-
ing thir Nations above truth hath so far transported them,
that where they find nothing faithfully to relate, they fall con-
5 fidently to invent what they think may either best set off thir
Historie, or magnifie thir Countrie.

The *Scots* and *Picts* in manners differing somwhat from
each other, but still unanimous to rob and spoile, hearing that
the *Romans* intended not to return, from thir Gorroghs, or
10 Leathern Frigats pour out themselves in swarms upon the *Gildas. Bede.*
Land, more confident than ever: and from the North end of
the Ile to the very wall side, then first took possession as inhabitants; while the *Britans* with idle Weapons in thir hands
stand trembling on the Battlements, till the half-naked Bar-
15 barians with thir long and formidable Iron hooks pull them
down headlong. The rest not only quitting the Wall but
Towns and Cities, leave them to the bloodie pursuer, who
follows killing, wasting, and destroying all in his way. From
these confusions arose a Famin, and from thence discord and
20 civil commotion among the *Britans:* each man living by
what he rob'd or took violently from his Neighbour. When
all stores were consum'd and spent where men inhabited, they
betook them to the Woods, and liv'd by hunting, which was
thir only sustainment. To the heaps of these evils from with- *Bede.*
25 out, were added new divisions within the Church. For *Agric-* *Constantius.*
ola the Son of *Severianus* a *Pelagian* Bishop had spread his
Doctrine wide among the *Britans* not uninfected before. The
sounder part neither willing to embrace his opinion to the

overthrow of divine grace, nor able to refute him, crave assistance from the Churches of *France:* who send them *Germanus*
Bishop of *Auxerre,* and *Lupus* of *Troyes.* They by continual
preaching in Churches, in Streets, in Fields, and not without
5 miracles, as is writt'n, confirm'd som, regain'd others, and at
Verulam in a public disputation put to silence thir chief ad-
versaries. This reformation in the Church was beleev'd to be
the cause of thir success a while after in the field. For the
Saxons and *Picts* with joint force, which was no new thing
10 before the *Saxons* at least had any dwelling in this Iland, during the abode of *Germanus* heer, had made a strong impression from the North. The *Britans* marching out against them,
and mistrusting thir own power, send to *Germanus* and his
Collegue, reposing more in the spiritual strength of those two
15 men, than in thir own thousands arm'd. They came, and thir
presence in the Camp was not less than if a whole Army had
com to second them. It was then the time of *Lent,* and the
people instructed by the daily Sermons of these two Pastors,
came flocking to receave Baptism. There was a place in the
20 Camp set apart as a Church, and trick'd up with boughs upon
Easter-day. The Enemy understanding this, and that the *Britans* were tak'n up with Religions more than with feats of
Arms, advances, after the Paschal Feast, as to a certain Victorie. *German* who also had intelligence of thir approach,
25 undertakes to be Captain that day; and riding out with selected Troops to discover what advantages the place might
offer, lights on a Valley compass't about with Hills, by which
the Enemy was to pass. And placing there his ambush, warns

429.
Prosp. A

Math. W
ad ann. 4

430.

Constan
German

them that what word they heard him pronounce aloud, the same they should repeat with universal shout. The Enemy passes on securely, and *German* thrice aloud cries *Halleluia;* which answered by the Souldiers with a sudd'n burst of
5 clamour, is from the Hills and Valleys redoubled. The *Saxons* and *Picts* on a sudden supposing it the noise of a huge Hoast, throw themselves into flight, casting down thir Arms, and great numbers of them are drown'd in the River which they had newly pass'd. This Victory, thus won without
10 hands, left to the *Britans* plenty of spoile, and to the person and the preaching of *German* greater authority and reverence than before. And the exploit might pass for current, if *Constantius,* the Writer of his life in the next age, had resolv'd us how the *British* Army came to want baptizing; for
15 of any Paganism at that time, or long before, in the Land we read not, or that *Pelagianism* was re-baptiz'd. The place of this Victory, as is reported, was in *Flintshire* by a Town *Usser. Primord p. 333.* call'd *Guid-cruc,* and the River *Allen,* where a field retains the name of *Maes German* to this day. But so soon as *German*
20 was return'd home, the *Scots* and *Picts,* though now so many *431. Prosp. Aquit.* of them Christians, that *Palladius* a Deacon was ordain'd and sent by *Celestine* the Pope to be a Bishop over them, were not so well reclaim'd, or not so many of them as to cease from *Ethelwerd.* doing mischief to thir Neighbours, where they found no im- *Florent. Gild. Bede.*
25 peachment to fall in yearly as they were wont. They therefore of the *Britans* who perhaps were not yet wholly ruin'd, in the strongest and South-west parts of the Ile, send Letters to *Ætius,* then third time Consul of *Rome,* with this superscrip-

tion; *To Ætius thrice Consul, the groanes of the* Britans. And   *Malmsb*
L. 1.c.1.
446.
after a few words thus: *The barbarians drive us to the Sea, the*
Sea drives us back to the barbarians; thus bandied up and
down between two deaths we perish, either by the Sword or
5 *by the Sea.* But the Empire at that time overspread with
Hunns and *Vandals,* was not in condition to lend them aid.
Thus rejected and wearied out with continual flying from
place to place, but more afflicted with Famine, which then
grew outrageous among them, many for hunger yielded to
10 the Enemy, others either more resolute, or less expos'd to
wants, keeping within Woods, and Mountainous places, not
only defended themselves, but sallying out at length gave a
stop to the insulting Foe with many seasonable defeats; led by
some eminent person, as may be thought, who exhorted them
15 not to trust in thir own strength, but in Divine assistance.
And perhaps no other heer is meant than the foresaid deliverance by *German,* if computation would permit, which
Gildas either not much regarded, or might mistake; but that
he tarried so long heer, the Writers of his life assent not. Find-   *Gildas.*
20 ing therefore such opposition, the *Scots* or *Irish* Robbers, for
so they are indifferently term'd, without delay get them home.
The *Picts,* as before was mentioned, then first began to settle
in the utmost parts of the Iland, using now and then to make
inrodes upon the *Britans.* But they in the mean while thus
25 ridd of thir Enemies, begin afresh to till the ground; which
after cessation yields her fruit in such abundance, as had not
formerly bin known for many Ages. But wantonness and
luxury, the wonted companions of plenty, grow up as fast,

and with them, if *Gildas* deserve belief, all other vices incident to human corruption. That which he notes especially to
be the chief perverting of all good in the Land, and so continued in his days, was the hatred of truth, and all such as
5 durst appear to vindicate and maintain it. Against them, as
against the only disturbers, all the malice of the Land was
bent. Lies and falsities, and such as could best invent them,
were only in request. Evil was embrac'd for good, wickedness
honour'd and esteem'd as virtue. And this quality thir valour
10 had, against a foren Enemy to be ever backward and heart-
less; to civil broils eager and prompt. In matters of Government, and the search of truth, weak and shallow, in falshood
and wicked deeds pregnant and industrious. Pleasing to God,
or not pleasing, with them weighed alike; and the worse most
15 an end was the weightier. All things were done contrary to
public welfare and safety; nor only by secular men, for the
Clergy also, whose Example should have guided others, were
as vitious and corrupt. Many of them besotted with continual
drunkenness; or swoln with pride and willfulness, full of
20 contention, full of envy, indiscreet, incompetent Judges to
determine what in the practice of life is good or evil, what
lawful or unlawful. Thus furnish'd with judgment, and for
manners thus qualifi'd both Priest and Lay, they agree to
chuse them several Kings of thir own; as neer as might be,
25 likest themselves; and the words of my Author import as
much. Kings were anointed, saith he, not of Gods anointing,
but such as were cruellest, and soon after as inconsiderately,
without examining the truth, put to death by thir anointers,

to set up others more fierce and proud. As for the election of
thir Kings (and that they had not all one Monarch, appears
both in Ages past and by the sequel) it began, as nigh as may
be guess'd, either this Year or the following, when they saw   *447.*
5 the *Romans* had quite deserted thir claim. About which time   *Constant*
                                                                     Bede.
also *Pelagianism* again prevailing by means of some few, the
British Clergie too weak, it seems, at dispute, entreat the
second time *German* to thir assistance. Who coming with
Severus a Disciple of *Lupus* that was his former associate,
10 stands not now to argue, for the people generally continu'd
right; but enquiring those Authors of new disturbance,
adjudges them to banishment. They therefore by consent of all   *448.*
were deliver'd to *German;* who carrying them over with him,   *Sigon.*
                                                                    Gildas.
dispos'd of them in such place where neither they could infect
15 others, and were themselves under cure of better instruction.
But *Germanus* the same year dy'd in *Italy;* and the *Britans*
not long after found themselves again in much perplexity,
with no slight rumour that thir old troublers the *Scots* and
Picts had prepar'd a strong invasion, purposing to kill all and
20 dwell themselves in the Land from end to end. But ere thir
coming in, as if the instruments of Divine justice had bin at
strife, which of them first should destroy a wicked Nation,
the Pestilence forestalling the Sword left scarce alive whom to
bury the dead; and for that time, as one extremity keeps off
25 another, preserv'd the Land from a worse incumbrance of
those barbarous dispossessors, whom the Contagion gave not
leave now to enter farr. And yet the *Britans* nothing better'd   *Malms. I*
by these heavy judgments, the one threatn'd, the other felt,

instead of acknowledging the hand of Heaven, run to the
Palace of thir King *Vortigern* with complaints and cries of
what they suddenly fear'd, from the *Pictish* invasion. *Vortigern,* who at that time was chief rather than sole King, un-
5 less the rest had perhaps left thir Dominions to the common
Enemy, is said by him of *Monmouth* to have procur'd the
death first of *Constantine,* then of *Constance* his Son, who of
a Monk was made King, and by that means to have usurp'd
the Crown. But they who can remember how *Constantine*
10 with his Son *Constance* the Monk, the one made Emperor,
the other *Cæsar,* perish'd in *France,* may discern the simple
fraud of this Fable. But *Vortigern* however coming to reign,
is decipher'd by truer stories a proud unfortunate Tyrant, and
yet of the people much belov'd, because his vices sorted so well
15 with theirs. For neither was he skill'd in Warr, nor wise in
Counsel, but covetous, lustful, luxurious, and prone to all
vice; wasting the public Treasure in gluttony and riot, careless
of the common danger, and through a haughty ignorance,
unapprehensive of his own. Nevertheless importun'd and
20 awak'd at length by unusual clamours of the people, he summons a general Council, to provide some better means than
heertofore had been us'd against these continual annoyances
from the North. Wherein by advice of all it was determin'd,
that the *Saxons* be invited into *Britan* against the *Scots* and
25 *Picts;* whose breaking in they either shortly expected, or already found they had not strength anough to oppose. The
Saxons were a barbarous and heathen Nation, famous for
nothing else but robberies and cruelties done to all thir Neigh-

bours both by Sea and Land; in particular to this Iland, witness that military force which the *Roman* Emperors maintain'd heer purposely against them, under a special Commander, whose title, as is found, on good record, was Count   *Notitiæ*
5 of the *Saxon* shoar in *Britain;* and the many mischiefs done by   *imperii.*
thir landing heer, both alone and with the *Picts,* as above hath
bin related, witness as much. They were a people thought by
good Writers, to be descended of the *Sacæ,* a kind of *Scy-*   *Florent.*
thian in the North of *Asia,* thence call'd *Sacasons,* or Sons   *Wigorn.*
10 of *Sacæ,* who with a Flood of other Northern Nations came   *ad an.* 370
into *Europe,* toward the declining of the *Roman* Empire;
and using Pyracy from *Denmark* all along these Seas, pos-   *Ethelwerd*
sess'd at length by intrusion all that Coast of *Germany* and
the *Nether-lands,* which took thence the name of old *Sax-*
15 *ony,* lying between the *Rhene* and *Elve,* and from thence
North as far as *Eidora,* the River bounding *Holsatia,* though
not so firmly, or so largely, but that thir multitude wan-
der'd yet uncertain of habitation. Such guests as these the
Britans resolve now to send for, and entreat into thir houses
20 and possessions, at whose very name heertofore they trembl'd
afar off. So much do men through impatience count ever that
the heaviest which they bear at present, and to remove the evil
which they suffer, care not to pull on a greater: as if variety
and change in evil also were acceptable. Or whether it be that
25 men in the despair of better, imagine fondly a kind of refuge
from one misery to another.

    The *Britans* therefore, with *Vortigern,* who was then ac-   *Ethelwe*
counted King over them all, resolve in full Council to send   *Malmsb.*
  Witichir
  gest. Sax
  L. 1. *p.* 3

Embassadors of thir choicest men with great gifts, and saith a *Saxon* Writer in these words, desiring thir aid. *Worthy* Saxons, *hearing the fame of your prowess, the distressed* Britans *wearied out, and overprest by a continual invading Enemy,*
5 *have sent us to beseech your aid. They have a Land fertile and spatious, which to your commands they bid us surrender. Heertofore we have liv'd with freedom, under the obedience and protection of the* Roman *Empire. Next to them we know none worthier than your selves; and therefore become sup-*
10 *pliants to your valour. Leave us not below our present Enemies, and to ought by you impos'd, willingly we shall submit.* Yet *Ethelwerd* writes not that they promis'd subjection, but only amity and league. They therefore who had chief rule *Malms.* among them, hearing themselves entreated by the *Britans,* to
15 that which gladly they would have wish't to obtain of them by entreating, to the *British* Embassy return this answer. Be *Witichind.* assur'd henceforth of the *Saxons,* as of faithful friends to the *Britans,* no less ready to stand by them in thir need, than in thir best of fortune. The Embassadors return joyful, and with
20 news as welcome to thir Countrie, whose sinister fate had now blinded them for destruction. The *Saxons,* consulting first *Gildas.* thir Gods (for they had answer, that the Land whereto they went, they should hold 300 years, half that time conquering, and half quietly possessing) furnish out three long Gallies, *Bede.*
25 or Kyules, with a chos'n company of warlike youth, under the conduct of two Brothers, *Hengist* and *Horsa,* descended in the fourth degree from *Woden;* of whom, deify'd for the fame of his acts, most Kings of those Nations derive thir pedigree.

These, and either mixt with these, or soon after by themselves, two other Tribes, or neighbouring people, *Jutes* and *Angles,* the one from *Jutland,* the other from *Anglen* by the City of *Sleswich,* both Provinces of *Denmark,* arrive in the first year

5 of *Martian* the *Greek* Emperor, from the birth of Christ 450, receav'd with much good will of the people first, then of the King, who after some assurances giv'n and tak'n, bestows on them the Ile of *Tanet,* where they first landed, hoping they might be made heerby more eager against the *Picts,* when they

10 fought as for thir own Countrie, and more loyal to the *Britans,* from whom they had receav'd a place to dwell in, which before they wanted. The *British Nennius* writes that these Brethren were driv'n into exile out of *Germany,* and to *Vortigern* who reigned in much fear, one while of the *Picts,* then

15 of the *Romans,* and *Ambrosius,* came opportunely into the Hav'n. For it was the custom in old *Saxony,* when thir numerous off-spring overflow'd the narrowness of thir bounds, to send them out by lot into new dwellings, wherever they found room, either vacant or to be forc't. But whether sought,

20 or unsought, they dwelt not heer long without employment. For the *Scots* and *Picts* were now come down, som say, as far as *Stamford* in *Lincoln-shire,* whom, perhaps not imagining to meet new opposition, the *Saxons,* though not till after a sharp encounter, put to flight; and that more than once: slay-

25 ing in fight, as some *Scotch* Writers affirm, thir King *Eugenius* the Son of *Fergus. Hengist* percaeving the Iland to be rich and fruitful, but her Princes and other inhabitants giv'n to vicious ease, sends word home, inviting others to a share of

450.
Nennius
Malms.

Malmsb

*Henry
Huntin
Ethelwe*

Bed. N

Nenn.

his good success. Who returning with 17 Ships, were grown
up now to a sufficient Army, and entertain'd without suspicion on these terms, that they should bear the brunt of War
against the *Picts,* receaving stipend and some place to inhabit.

5 With these was brought over the Daughter of *Hengist;* a
Virgin wondrous fair, as is reported, *Rowen* the *British* call
her: she by commandment of her Father, who had invited the
King to a Banquet, coming in presence with a Bowle of Wine
to welcome him, and to attend on his Cup till the Feast ended,

10 won so much upon his fancy, though already wiv'd, as to demand her in mariage upon any conditions. *Hengist* at first,
though it fell out perhaps according to his drift, held off, ex-
cusiing his meanness; then obscurely intimating a desire and
almost a necessity, by reason of his augmented numbers, to

15 have his narrow bounds of *Tanet* enlarg'd to the Circuit of
Kent, had it streit by donation: though *Guorangonus* till then
was King of that place: and so, as it were overcome by the
great munificence of *Vortiger,* gave his Daughter. And still
encroaching on the Kings favour, got furder leave to call over

20 *Octa* and *Ebissa,* his own and his Brothers Son; pretending
that they, if the North were giv'n them, would sit there as a
continual defence against the *Scots,* while himself guarded the
East. They therfore sayling with forty Ships eev'n to the *Orcades,* and every way curbing the *Scots* and *Picts,* possess'd

25 that part of the Ile which is now *Northumberland.* Notwithstanding this they complain that thir monthly pay was grown
much into arrear; which when the *Britans* found means to
satisfie, though alleging withall that they to whom promise

Gildas. Bod.
Ninn.

was made of wages, were nothing so many in number, quieted
with this a while, but still seeking occasion to fall off, they
find fault next, that thir pay is too small for the danger they
undergo, threatning op'n Warr unless it be augmented. *Guor-*
5 *timer* the Kings Son perceaving his Father and the Kingdom
thus betray'd, from that time bends his utmost endeavour to
drive them out. They on the other side making League with
the *Picts* and *Scots,* and issuing out of *Kent,* wasted without
resistance almost the whole Land eev'n to the Western Sea,
10 with such a horrid devastation, that Towns and Colonies over-
turn'd, Preists and people slain, Temples, and Palaces, what
with fire and Sword lay alltogether heap'd in one mixt ruin.
Of all which multitude, so great was the sinfullness that
brought this upon them, *Gildas* adds that few or none were
15 likely to be other then lew'd and wicked persons. The residue
of these, part overtak'n in the Mountains were slain; others
subdu'd with hunger preferr'd slavery before instant death;
som getting to Rocks, Hills, and Woods inaccessible, preferr'd the fear and danger of any Death before the shame of a
20 secure slavery; many fled over Sea into other Countries; some
into *Holland,* where yet remain the ruins of *Brittenburgh,* an
old Castle on the Sea, to be seen at low water not far from
Leiden; either built, as Writers of thir own affirm, or seis'd on
by those *Britans* in thir escape from *Hengist:* Others into
25 *Armorica,* peopl'd, as som think, with *Britans* long before;
either by guift of *Constantine* the *Great,* or else of *Maximus*
to those *British* Forces which had serv'd them in Forein Wars;
to whom those also that miscarried not with the latter *Con-*

Primore
pag. 41?

Malms.
L. 1. *c.* 1
Huntin
L. 1.

stantine at *Arles;* and lastly, these exiles driv'n out by *Saxons,*
fled for refuge. But the antient Chronicles of those Provinces
attest thir coming thether to be then first when they fled the
Saxons, and indeed the name of *Britain* in *France* is not read
5 till after that time. Yet how a sort of fugitives who had quitted
without stroke thir own Country, should so soon win another,
appears not; unless joyn'd to som party of thir own settl'd
there before. *Vortiger* nothing better'd by these calamities, *Ninn.*
grew at last so obdurat as to commit incest with his daughter, *Malmsb.*
10 tempted or tempting him out of an ambition to the Crown.
For which beeing censur'd and condemn'd in a great Synod
of *Clercs,* and *Laics,* and partly for fear of the *Saxons,* according to the Counsel of his Peers he retir'd into *Wales,* and built
him there a strong Castle in *Radnorshire* by the advice of *Ninn.*
15 *Ambrosius* a young prophet, whom others call *Merlin.* Nevertheless *Faustus,* who was the Son thus incestuously begott'n
under the instructions of *German,* or some of his Disciples,
for *German* was dead before, prov'd a religious man, and
liv'd in devotion by the River *Remnis* in *Clamorganshire.*
20 But the *Saxons,* though finding it so easy to subdue the Ile, *Gildas.*
with most of thir Forces, uncertain for what cause, return'd
home: when as the easiness of thir Conquest might seem
rather likely to have call'd in more. Which makes more probable that which the *British* write of *Guortemir.* For he com- *Ninn.*
25 ing to Reigne, instead of his Father depos'd for incest, is said
to have thrice driv'n and beseig'd the *Saxons* in the Ile of
Taneth; and when they issu'd with powerful supplies sent
form *Saxony,* to have fought with them fowr other Batells,

wherof three are nam'd; the first on the River *Darwent,* the
second at *Episford,* wherin *Horsa* the Brother of *Hengist* fell,
and on the *British* part *Catigern* the other Son of *Vortiger.*
The third in a Feild by *Stonar* then call'd *Lapis tituli* in *Tanet,*
5 where he beat them into thir Ships that bore them home, glad
to have so scap'd and not venturing to land again for 5 years
after. In the space wherof *Guortemir* dying, commanded they
should bury him in the Port of *Stonar;* perswaded that his
bones lying there would be terror enough to keep the *Saxons*
10 from ever landing in that place: they, saith *Ninnius,* neglecting his command, buried him in *Lincoln.* But concerning
these times, antientest annals of the *Saxons* relate in this manner. In the year 455. *Hengist* and *Horsa* fought against *Vor-*
tigern, in a place called *Eglesthrip,* now *Ailsford* in *Kent;*
15 where *Horsa* lost his life, of whom *Horsted,* the place of his
burial, took name.

After this first Battel and the Death of his Brother, *Hengist*
with his Son *Esca* took on him Kingly Title, and peopl'd *Kent*
with *Jutes;* who also then or not long after possess'd the Ile of
20 *Wight,* and part of *Hamshire* lying opposite. Two years after
in a fight at *Creganford,* or *Craford, Hengist* and his Son slew
of the *Britans* four Cheif Commanders, and as many thousand
men: the rest in great disorder flying to *London,* with the
total loss of *Kent.* And 8 years passing between, he made new
25 Warr on the *Britans;* of whom in a Battel at *Wippeds-fleot,*
12 Princes were slain, and *Wipped* the *Saxon* Earl, who left
his name to that place, though not sufficient to direct us where
it now stands. His last encounter was at a place not mention'd,

455.
Bede.
Ethelwe
Florent.
Annal. .

The Kii
dome of
Kent.

457.

465.

473.

where he gave them such an overthrow, that flying in great
fear they left the spoil of all to thir Enemies. And these perhaps are the 4 Battells, according to *Nennius,* fought by *Guortemir,* though by these writers far differently related; and
5 happ'ning besides many other bickerings, in the space of 20
years, as *Malmsbury* reck'ns. Nevertheless it plainly appears
that the *Saxons,* by whomsoever, were put to hard shifts, being all this while fought withall in *Kent,* thir own allotted
dwelling, and somtimes on the very edge of the Sea, which the
10 word *Whippeds-fleot* seems to intimat. But *Guortemir* now *Nennius.*
dead, and none of courage left to defend the Land, *Vortigern*
either by the power of his faction, or by consent of all, reas-
sumes the Government: and *Hengist* thus rid of his grand
opposer, hearing gladly the restorement of his old favourer,
15 returns again with great Forces; but to *Vortigern* whom he
well knew how to handle without warring, as to his Son in
Law, now that the only Author of dissention between them
was remov'd by Death, offers nothing but all terms of new
league and amity. The King both for his Wives sake and his
20 own sottishness, consulting also with his Peers not unlike
himself, readily yeilds; and the place of parly is agree'd on; to
which either side was to repair without Weapons. *Hengist,*
whose meaning was not peace, but treachery, appointed his
men to be secretly arm'd, and acquainted them to what in-
25 tent. The watch-word was *Nemet eour Saxes,* that is, *Draw* *Malms.*
your Daggers; which they observing, when the *Britans* were
throughly heated with Wine (for the Treaty it seems was not
without Cups) and provok'd, as was plotted, by som affront,

dispatch'd with those Poniards every one his next man, to the
number of 300. the cheif of those that could do ought against
him either in Counsel or in Field. *Vortigern* they only bound
and kept in Custody, untill he granted them for his ransome
5 three Provinces, which were called afterward *Essex, Sussex,*
and *Middlesex.* Who thus dismist, retiring again to his solitary abode in the Country of *Guorthigirniaun,* so call'd by his
name, from thence to the Castle of his own building in *North-
Wales,* by the River *Tiebi;* and living there obscurely among
10 his Wives, was at length burnt in his Towre by fire from
Heav'n at the Praier, as some say, of *German,* but that co- *Nin. ex*
heres not; as others, by *Ambrosius Aurelian;* of whom as we *end St. C* *Galfrid.*
have heard at first, he stood in great fear, and partly for that *Monmo*
cause invited in the *Saxons.* Who whether by constraint or of
15 thir own accord after much mischeif don, most of them returning back into thir own Country, left a fair opportunity to
the *Britans* of avenging themselves the easier on those that
staid behinde. Repenting therefore, and with earnest supplication imploring divine help to prevent thir final rooting out,
20 they gather from all parts, and under the leading of *Ambrosius Aurelianus,* a vertuous and modest man, the last heer of
Roman stock, advancing now onward against the late Victors, defeat them in a memorable Battell. Common opinion,
but grounded cheifly on the *British* Fables, makes this *Ambro-
25 sius* to be a younger Son of that *Constantine,* whose eldest, as
we heard, was *Constance* the Monk: who both lost thir lives
abroad usurping the Empire. But the express words both of
Gildas and *Bede,* assures us that the Parents of this *Ambro-*

sius having heer born regal dignity, were slain in these *Pictish* Wars and commotions in the Iland. And if the fear of *Ambrose* induc'd *Vortigern* to call in the *Saxons,* it seems *Vortigern* usurp'd his right. I perceave not that *Nennius* makes

5 any difference between him and *Merlin:* for that Child without Father that propheci'd to *Vortigern,* he names not *Merlin* but *Ambrose,* makes him the Son of a Roman Consul; but conceal'd by his mother, as fearing that the King therfore sought his life; yet the youth no sooner had confess'd his par-

10 entage, but *Vortigern* either in reward of his predictions, or as his right, bestow'd upon him all the West of *Britain;* himself retiring to a solitary life. Whose ever Son he was, he was *Gildas. Bed.* the first, according to surest Authors, that led against the *Saxons,* and overthrew them; but whether before this time or

15 after, none have writt'n. This is certain, that in a time when most of the *Saxon* Forces were departed home, the *Britans* gather'd strength; and either against those who were left remaining, or against thir whole powers, the second time returning obtain'd this Victory. Thus *Ambrose* as cheif

20 Monarch of the Ile succeeded *Vortigern;* to whose third Son *Pascentius* he permitted the rule of two Regions in *Wales, Buelth,* and *Guorthigirniaun.* In his daies, saith *Nennius, Ninn.* the *Saxons* prevail'd not much: against whom *Arthur,* as beeing then Cheif General for the *British* Kings, made great

25 War; but more renown'd in Songs and Romances, then in true stories. And the sequel it self declares as much. For in *477.* the year 477. *Ella* the *Saxon,* with his three Sons, *Cymen, Ethelw.* *Pleting,* and *Cissa,* at a place in *Sussex* call'd *Cymenshore, Florent.*

arrive in three Ships, kill many of the *Britans,* chasing them
that remain'd into the Wood *Andreds* Leage. Another Battell
was fought at *Mercreds-Burnamsted,* wherin *Ella* had by far
the Victory; but *Huntingdon* makes it so doubtful, that the
5 *Saxons* were constrain'd to send home for supplies. Four year
after dy'd *Hengist* the first *Saxon* King of *Kent;* noted to have
attain'd that dignity by craft, as much as valour, and giving
scope to his own cruel nature, rather then proceeding by mildness or civility. His Son *Oeric* surnam'd *Oisc,* of whom the
10 Kentish Kings were call'd *Oiscings,* succeeded him, and sate
content with his Fathers winnings; more desirous to settle
and defend, then to enlarge his bounds: he reign'd 24 years.
By this time *Ella* and his Son *Cissa,* beseiging *Andredchester,*
suppos'd now to be *Newenden* in *Kent,* take it by force, and
15 all within it put to the Sword.

   Thus *Ella* 3 years after the death of *Hengist,* began his
Kingdome of the South-Saxons; peopling it with new inhabitants, from the Country which was then old *Saxony,* at this
day *Holstein* in *Denmark,* and had besides at his command
20 all those Provinces which the *Saxons* had won on this side
Humber. Animated with these good successes, as if *Britain*
were become now the field of Fortune, *Kerdic* another *Saxon*
Prince, the tenth by Linage from *Woden* an old and practis'd
Souldier, who in many prosperous conflicts against the En-
25 emy in those parts, had nurs'd up a Spirit too big to live at
home with equals, coming to a certain place which from
thence took the name of *Kerdic-shoar,* with 5 Ships, and
Kenric his Son, the very same day overthrew the *Britans* that

[marginal notes:]
485.
Florent.
Hunting

489.

Malms.

Bed.
L. 2. c. 5

492.
Camden

The Kin
dome of
South-S
Bed. L.
c. 15. &
L. 2. c. 5

Sax. an.
omn.
495.

oppos'd him; and so effectually, that smaller skirmishes after
that day were sufficient to drive them still furder off, leaving
him a large territory. After him *Porta* another *Saxon* with his
two Sons *Bida* and *Megla*, in two Ships arrive at *Portsmouth*
5 thence call'd, and at thir landing slew a young *British* Nobleman, with many others who unadvisedly set upon them. The
Britans to recover what they had lost, draw together all thir
Forces led by *Natanleod*, or *Nazaleod*, a certain King in
Britain, and the greatest saith one; but him with 5000 of his
10 men *Kerdic* puts to rout and slaies. From whence the place in
Hantshire, as far as *Kerdicsford*, now *Chardford*, was call'd
of old *Nazaleod*. Who this King should be, hath bred much
question; som think it to be the *British* name of *Ambrose;*
others to be the right name of his Brother, who for the terror
15 of his eagerness in fight, became more known by the Sirname
of *Uther*, which in the Welch Tongue signifies Dreadful. And
if ever such a King in *Britain* there were as *Uther Pendragon*,
for so also the *Monmouth* Book surnames him, this in all
likelyhood must be he. *Kerdic* by so great a blow giv'n to the
20 *Britans* had made large room about him; not only for the men
he brought with him, but for such also of his friends, as he
desir'd to make great; for which cause, and withall the more
to strengthen himself, his two Nefews *Stuf*, and *Withgar*, in
3 Vessels bring him new levies to *Kerdic* shoar. Who that they
25 might not come sluggishly to possess what others had won
for them, either by thir own seeking or by appointment, are
set in place where they could not but at thir first coming give
a proof of themselves upon the Enemy: and so well they did

501.
Sax. an. omn.
Huntingd.

508.
Annal. omn.
Huntingd.
Camden.

Camd. Uss.
primord.

514.
An. omn.

it, that the *Britans* after a hard encounter left them Maisters
of the field. And about the same time, *Ella* the first *South-*
Saxon King dy'd; whom *Cissa* his youngest succeeded; the
other two failing before him.

5   Nor can it be much more or less then about this time, for
it was before the *West-Saxon* Kingdome, that *Uffa* the 8th.
from *Woden* made himself King of the *East-Angles;* who by
thir name testifie the Country above mention'd from whence
they came in such multitudes, that thir native soil is said to
10 have remain'd in the daies of *Beda* uninhabited. *Huntingdon*
deferrs the time of thir coming in, to the ninth year of *Kerdic*'s
Reigne: for saith he, at first many of them strove for princi-
pality, seising every one his Province, and for som while so
continu'd making petty Warrs among themselves; till in the
15 end *Uffa,* of whom those Kings were call'd *Uffings,* over-
top'd them all in the year 571, then *Titilus* his Son, the Father
of *Redwald,* who became potent.

And not much after the *East-Angles,* began also the *East-*
Saxons to erect a Kingdom under *Sleda* the tenth from
20 *Woden.* But *Huntingdon,* as before, will have it later by 11
years, and *Erchenwin* to be the first King.

Kerdic the same in power, though not so fond of title, for-
bore the name 24 Years after his arrival; but then founded so
firmly the Kingdome of *West-Saxons,* that it subjected all the
25 rest at length, and became the sole Monarchie of *England.*
The same year he had a Victory against the *Britans* at *Ker-*
dics-Ford, by the River *Aven:* and after 8 years, another great
fight at *Kerdics* Leage, but which won the day is not by any

Hunting

The Kin
dom of
East-Ang

Malms.
L. 1. c. 5.
Bed.
L. 1. c. 1
Hunting
L. 2. p. 3
315.
Bede
L. 2. c. 1
Malms.
L. 1. c. 6.

The Kin
dom of
East-Sax

519.
The Kin
dom of
West-Sa

Sax. an.
527.

set down. Hitherto hath bin collected what there is of certainty with circumstance of time and place to be found register'd, and no more then barely register'd in annals of best
note; without describing after *Huntingdon* the manner of
5 those Battels and Encounters, which they who compare, and
can judge of Books, may be confident he never found in any
current Author whom he had to follow. But this disease hath
bin incident to many more Historians: and the age wherof
we now write, hath had the ill hap, more then any since the
10 first fabulous times, to be surcharg'd with all the idle fancies
of posterity. Yet that we may not rely altogether on *Saxon*
relaters, *Gildas,* in Antiquity far before these, and every way
more credible, speaks of these Wars in such a manner, though
nothing conceited of the *British* valour, as declares the *Saxons*
15 in his time and before to have bin foyl'd not seldomer then the
Britans. For besides that first Victory of *Ambrose,* and the
interchangeable success long after, he tells that the last overthrow which they receav'd at *Badon* Hill, was not the least;
which they in thir oldest annals mention not at all. And be-
20 cause the time of this Battell, by any who could do more then
guess, is not set down, or any foundation giv'n from whence
to draw a solid compute, it cannot be much wide to insert it in
this place. For such Authors as we have to follow, give the
conduct and praise of this exploit to *Arthur;* and that this was
25 the last of 12 great Battells which he fought victoriously
against the *Saxons.* The several places writt'n by *Nennius* in *Ninn.*
thir Welch names, were many hunder'd years ago unknown,
and so heer omitted. But who *Arthur* was, and whether ever

any such reign'd in *Britain,* hath bin doubted heertofore, and
may again with good reason. For the Monk of *Malmsbury,*
and others whose credit hath sway'd most with the learneder
sort, we may well perceave to have known no more of this
5 *Arthur* 500 years past, nor of his doeings, then we now living;
And what they had to say, transcrib'd out of *Nennius,* a very
trivial writer yet extant, which hath already bin related. Or
out of a *British* Book, the same which he of *Monmouth* set
forth, utterly unknown to the World, till more then 600 years
10 after the dayes of *Arthur,* of whom (as *Sigebert* in his Chronicle confesses) all other Histories were silent, both Foren and
Domestic, except only that fabulous Book. Others of later
time have sought to assert him by old legends and Cathedrall
regests. But he who can accept of Legends for good story, may
15 quickly swell a volume with trash, and had need be furnish'd
with two only necessaries, leasure, and beleif, whether it be
the writer, or he that shall read. As to *Artur,* no less is in doubt
who was his Father; for if it be true as *Nennius* or his notist
avers, that *Artur* was call'd *Mab-Uther,* that is to say, a cruel
20 Son, for the fierseness that men saw in him of a Child, and
the intent of his name *Arturus* imports as much, it might well
be that som in after ages who sought to turn him into a Fable,
wrested the word *Uther* into a proper name, and so fain'd him
the Son of *Uther;* since we read not in any certain story, that
25 ever such person liv'd, till *Geffry* of *Monmouth* set him off
with the sirname of *Pendragon.* And as we doubted of his
parentage, so may we also of his puissance; for whether that
Victory at *Badon* Hill were his or no, is uncertain; *Gildas* not

naming him, as he did *Ambrose* in the former. Next, if it be
true as *Caradoc* relates, that *Melvas* King of that Country *Caradoc.*
which is now *Summerset,* kept from him *Gueniver* his Wife a *Llancarvon.*
vit. Gild.
whole year in the Town of *Glaston,* and restor'd her at the
5 entreaty of *Gildas,* rather then for any enforcement, that
Artur with all his Chivalry could make against a small Town
defended only by a moory situation; had either his knowledge in War, or the force he had to make, bin answerable to
the fame they bear, that petty King had neither dar'd such an
10 affront, nor he bin so long, and at last without effect, in revenging it. Considering lastly how the *Saxons* gain'd upon
him every where all the time of his suppos'd reign, which began, as som write, in the tenth year of *Kerdic,* who wrung *Malms.*
from him by long Warr the Countries of *Summerset,* and *Antiquit.*
Glaston.
15 *Hamshire;* there will remain neither place nor circumstance 529.
in story, which may administer any likelyhood of those great *Primord.*
p. 468.
Acts that are ascrib'd him. This only is alleg'd by *Nennius* in *Polychronic.*
Arturs behalf, that the *Saxons,* though vanquish't never so oft, *L.* 5. *c.* 6.
grew still more numerous upon him by continual supplies out
20 of *Germany.* And the truth is that valour may be overtoil'd,
and overcom at last with endless overcomming. But as for
this Battell of Mount *Badon* where the *Saxons* were hemm'd
in, or beseig'd, whether by *Artur* won, or whensoever, it
seems indeed to have giv'n a most undoubted and impor-
25 tant blow to the *Saxons,* and to have stop'd thir proceedings
for a good while after. *Gildas* himself witnessing that the
Britans having thus compel'd them to sit down with peace,
fell thereupon to civil discord among themselves. Which

words may seem to let in som light toward the searching out
when this Battell was fought. And we shall find no time since
the first *Saxon* War, from whence a longer peace ensu'd, then
from the fight at *Kerdics* Leage in the year 527. which all the
5 Chronicles mention, without Victory to *Kerdic;* and give us
argument from the custome they have of magnifying thir own
deeds upon all occasions, to presume heer his ill speeding.
And if we look still onward, eev'n to the 44*th* year after,
wherin *Gildas* wrote, if his obscure utterance be understood,
10 we shall meet with very little War between the *Britans* and
Saxons. This only remains difficult, that the Victory first won   *Gildas.*
by *Ambrose,* was not so long before this at *Badon* Seige, but
that the same men living might be eye-witnesses of both; and
by this rate hardly can the latter be thought won by *Artur,*
15 unless we reck'n him a grown youth at least in the daies of
Ambrose, and much more then a youth, if *Malmsbury* be
heard, who affirms all the exploits of *Ambrose,* to have bin
don cheifly by *Artur* as his General, which will add much
unbeleif to the common assertion of his reigning after *Am-*
20 *brose* and *Uther,* especially the fight at *Badon,* being the last
of his twelve Battels. But to prove by that which follows, that
the fight at *Kerdics* Leage, though it differ in name from that
of *Badon,* may be thought the same by all effects; *Kerdic* 3   530.
years after, not proceeding onward, as his manner was, on the   *Sax. an.*
25 continent, turns back his Forces on the Ile of *Wight;* which
with the slaying of a few only in *Withgarburgh,* he soon
maisters; and not long surviving, left it to his Nefews by the
Mothers side, *Stuff* and *Withgar;* the rest of what he had sub-

du'd, *Kenric* his Son held; and reign'd 26 years, in whose
tenth year *Withgar* was buried in the Town of that Iland
which bore his name. Notwithstanding all these unlikely-
hoods of *Artur*'s Reign and great acheivments, in a narration
5 crept in I know not how among the Laws of *Edward* the
Confessor, Artur the famous King of *Britans,* is said not only
to have expell'd hence the *Saracens,* who were not then known
in *Europe,* but to have conquer'd *Freesland,* and all the North
East Iles as far as *Russia,* to have made *Lapland* the Eastern
10 bound of his Empire, and *Norway* the Chamber of *Britain.*
When should this be done? from the *Saxons,* till after twelve
Battells, he had no rest at home; after those, the *Britans* contented with the quiet they had from thir Saxon Enemies, were
so far from seeking Conquests abroad, that, by report of
15 *Gildas* above cited, they fell to civil Wars at home. Surely
Artur much better had made War in old *Saxony,* to repress
thir flowing hither, then to have won Kingdoms as far as
Russia, scarce able heer to defend his own. *Buchanan* our
Neighbour Historian reprehends him of *Monmouth* and
20 others for fabling in the deeds of *Artur,* yet what he writes
thereof himself, as of better credit, shews not whence he had
but from those Fables; which he seems content to believe in
part, on condition that the *Scots* and *Picts* may be thought to
have assisted *Arthur* in all his Wars, and atchievments;
25 wherof appears as little grownd by any credible story, as of
that which he most counts Fabulous. But not furder to contest about such uncertainties.

In the year 547. *Ida* the *Saxon,* sprung also from *Woden*

534.
544.

in the tenth degree, began the Kingdome of *Bernicia* in *North-umberland;* built the Town *Bebbanburg,* which was after wall'd; and had 12 Sons, half by Wives, and half by Concubines. *Hengist* by leave of *Vortigern,* we may remember, had sent *Octa* and *Ebissa* to seek them seats in the North, and there by warring on the *Picts,* to secure the Southern parts. Which they so prudently effected, that what by force and fair proceeding, they well quieted those Countries; and though so far distant from *Kent,* nor without power in thir hands, yet kept themselves nigh 180 years within moderation; and as inferiour Governors, they and their off-spring gave obedience to the Kings of *Kent,* as to the elder Family. Till at length following the example of that Age; when no less then Kingdoms were the prize of every fortunat Commander, they thought it but reason, as well as others of thir Nation, to assume Royalty. Of whom *Ida* was the first, a man in the prime of his years, and of Parentage as we heard; but how he came to wear the Crown, aspiring or by free choise, is not said. Certain enough it is, that his vertues, made him not less noble then his birth, in War undaunted, and unfoil'd; in peace tempring the aw of Magistracy, with a naturall mildness he raign'd about 12 years. In the mean while *Kenric* in a fight at *Searesbirig,* now *Salsbury,* kil'd and put to flight many of the *Britans;* and the fourth year after at *Beranvirig,* now *Banbury,* as some think, with *Keaulin* his son put them again to flight. *Keaulin* shortly after succeeded his father in the *West-Saxons.* And *Alla* descended also of *Woden,* but by another line, set up a second Kingdom in *Deira* the South part of *Northumberland,* and

547.
The Kir
dome of
*Northun
berland.*
*Annal or
Bed. Epi
Malmsb.*

Malmsb.

552.
Annal o
556.
Camden

560.
*Annal.
Florent.*

held it 30 years; while *Adda* the son of *Ida,* and five more
after him reign'd without other memory in *Bernicia:* and in
Kent, Ethelbert the next year began. For *Esca* the son of   561.
Hengist had left *Otha,* and he *Emeric* to rule after him; both
5 which without adding to their bounds, kept what they had in
peace 53 years. But *Ethelbert* in length of reign equal'd both
his progenitors, and as *Beda* counts, 3 years exceeded. Young   *Malms.*
at his first entrance, and unexperienc'd, he was the first raiser
of civill War among the *Saxons;* claiming from the priority of
10 time wherin *Hengist* took possession here, a kind of right
over the later Kingdomes; and thereupon was troublesome to
thir Confines: but by them twise defeated, he who but now
thought to seem dreadfull, became almost contemptible. For   *Ann. omn.*
Keaulin and *Cutha* his Son, persuing him into his own Terri-   568.
15 tory, slew there in Battel, at *Wibbandun* 2 of his Earls, *Oslac,*
and *Cnebban.* By this means the *Britans,* but cheifly by this
Victory at *Badon,* for the space of 44 years ending in 571,
receav'd no great annoyance from the *Saxons:* but the peace
they enjoy'd, by ill using it, prov'd more destructive to them
20 then War. For being rais'd on a sudden by two such eminent
successes, from the lowest condition of thraldome, they whose
Eyes had beheld both those deliverances, that by *Ambrose,*
and this at *Badon,* were taught by the experience of either
Fortune, both Kings, Magistrates, Preists, and privat men, to
25 live orderly. But when the next Age, unacquainted with past   *Gildas.*
Evils, and only sensible of thir present ease and quiet, succeeded, strait follow'd the apparent subversion of all truth,
and justice, in the minds of most men: scarce the lest footstep,

or impression of goodness left remaining through all ranks
and degrees in the Land; except in some so very few, as to be
hardly visible in a general corruption: which grew in short
space not only manifest, but odious to all the Neighbour Nations. And first thir Kings, among whom also, the Sons or
Grand-Children of *Ambrose,* were fouly degenerated to all
Tyranny and vitious life. Wherof to hear som particulars out
of *Gildas* will not be impertinent. They avenge, saith he, and
they protect; not the innocent, but the guilty: they swear oft,
but perjure; they wage War, but civil and unjust War. They
punish rigorously them that rob by the high way; but those
grand Robbers that sit with them at Table, they honour and
reward. They give alms largly, but in the face of thir Alms-
deeds, pile up wickedness to a far higher heap. They sit in the
seat of Judgment, but goe seldome by the rule of right; neglecting and proudly overlooking the modest and harmless;
but countenancing the audacious, though guilty of abomina-
blest crimes; they stuff thir Prisons, but with men committed
rather by circumvention, then any just cause. Nothing better
were the Clergy, but at the same pass or rather worse, then
when the *Saxons* came first in; Unlerned, Unapprehensive,
yet impudent; suttle Prowlers, Pastors in Name, but indeed
Wolves; intent upon all occasions, not to feed the Flock, but
to pamper and well line themselves: not call'd, but seising on
the Ministry as a Trade, not as a Spiritual Charge: teaching
the people, not by sound Doctrin, but by evil Example: usurping the Chair of *Peter,* but through the blindness of thir own
worldly lusts, they stumble upon the Seat of *Judas:* deadly

haters of truth, broachers of lies: looking on the poor Christian with Eyes of Pride and Contempt; but fawning on the wickedest rich men without shame: great promoters of other mens Alms with thir set exhortations; but themselves con-

5 tributing ever least; slightly touching the many vices of the Age, but preaching without end thir own greivances, as don to Christ; seeking after preferments and degrees in the Church more then after Heav'n; and so gain'd, make it thir whole study how to keep them by any Tyranny. Yet lest they should

10 be thought things of no use in thir eminent places, they have thir niceties and trivial points to keep in aw the superstitious multitude; but in true saving knowledge leave them still as gross and stupid as themselves; bunglers at the Scripture, nay forbidding and silencing them that know; but in worldly

15 matters, practis'd and cunning Shifters; in that only art and symony, great Clercs and Maisters, bearing thir heads high, but thir thoughts abject and low. He taxes them also as gluttonous, incontinent, and daily Drunkards. And what shouldst thou expect from these, poor Laity, so he goes on, these beasts,

20 all belly? shall these amend thee, who are themselves laborious in evil doings? shalt thou see with their Eyes, who see right forward nothing but gain? Leave them rather, as bids our Saviour, lest ye fall both blind-fold into the same perdition. Are all thus? Perhaps not all, or not so grosly. But what

25 avail'd it *Eli* to be himself blameless, while he conniv'd at others that were abominable? who of them hath bin envi'd for his better life? who of them hath hated to consort with these, or withstood thir entring the Ministry, or endeavour'd

zealously thir casting out? Yet som of these perhaps by others
are legended for great Saints. This was the state of Goverment, this of Religion among the *Britans,* in that long calm
of peace, which the fight at *Badon* Hill had brought forth.
5 Wherby it came to pass, that so fair a Victory came to nothing.
Towns and Citties were not reinhabited, but lay ruin'd and
wast; nor was it long ere domestic War breaking out, wasted
them more. For *Britain,* as at other times, had then also several Kings. Five of whom *Gildas* living then in *Armorica,* at *Primora*
10 a safe distance, boldly reproves by name; First *Constantine* *p. 444.*
(fabl'd the Son of *Cador,* Duke of *Cornwall, Arturs* half
Brother by the Mothers side) who then reign'd in *Cornwall*
and *Devon,* a Tyrannical and bloody King, polluted also with
many Adulteries: he got into his power, two young Princes of
15 the Blood Royal, uncertain whether before him in right, or
otherwise suspected: and after solemn Oath giv'n of thir safety
the year that *Gildas* wrote, slew them with thir two Governours in the Church, and in thir Mothers Arms, through the
Abbots Coap, which he had thrown over them, thinking by
20 the reverence of his vesture to have withheld the murderer.
These are commonly suppos'd to be the Sons of *Mordred,*
Arturs Nefew, said to have revolted from his Uncle, giv'n him
in a Battel his Deaths wound, and by him after to have bin
slain. Which things were they true, would much diminish
25 the blame of cruelty in *Constantine,* revenging *Artur* on the
Sons of so false a *Mordred.* In another part, but not express'd
where, *Aurelius Conanus* was King: him he charges also with
Adulteries, and Parricide; cruelties worse then the former; to

be a hater of his Countries Peace, thirsting after civil War and
Prey. His condition it seems was not very prosperous; for
Gildas wishes him, being now left alone, like a Tree wither-
ing in the midst of a barren field, to remember the vanity,
5 and arrogance of his Father, and elder Brethren, who came
all to untimely Death in thir youth. The third reigning in
Demetia, or *South Wales,* was *Vortipor,* the Son of a good
Father; he was when *Gildas* wrote, grown old, not in years
only, but in Adulteries, and in governing full of falshood, and
10 cruel Actions. In his latter daies, putting away his Wife, who
dy'd in divorce, he became, if we mistake not *Gildas,* incestuous with his Daughter. The fourth was *Cuneglas,* imbru'd in
civil War; he also had divorc'd his Wife, and tak'n her Sister,
who had vow'd Widdowhood: he was a great Enemy to the
15 Clergy, high-minded, and trusting to his wealth. The last,
but greatest of all in power, was *Maglocune,* and greatest also
in wickedness; he had driv'n out or slain many other Kings,
or Tyrants; and was called the *Island Dragon,* perhaps having
his seat in *Anglesey;* a profuse giver, a great Warrior, and of
20 a goodly stature. While he was yet young, he overthrew his
Uncle, though in the head of a compleat Army, and took from
him the Kingdom: then touch't with remorse of his doings,
not without deliberation took upon him the profession of a
Monk; but soon forsook his vow, and his wife also, which for
25 that vow he had left, making love to the wife of his Brothers
Son then living. Who not refusing the offer, if she were not
rather the first that entic'd, found means both to dispatch her
own Husband, and the former wife of *Maglocune,* to make

her marriage with him the more unquestionable. Neither did
he this for want of better instructions, having had the learned-
est and wisest man reputed of all *Britain,* the instituter of his
youth. Thus much, the utmost that can be learnt by truer
5 story, of what past among the *Britans* from the time of their
useless Victory at *Badon,* to the time that *Gildas* wrote, that
is to say, as may be guess't, from 527 to 571, is here set down
altogether; not to be reduc't under any certainty of years. But
now the *Saxons,* who for the most part all this while had bin
10 still, unless among themselves, began afresh to assault them,
and ere long to drive them out of all which they yet maintain'd on this side *Wales.* For *Cuthulf* the Brother of *Keau-*   571.
lin, by a Victory obtain'd at *Bedanford,* now *Bedford,* took   *Camden*
from them 4 good Towns, *Liganburgh, Eglesburh, Besing-*   *Annal o*
15 *ton,* now *Benson* in *Oxfordshire,* and *Igncsham;* but outliv'd
not many months his good success. And after 6 years more,   577.
Keaulin, and *Cuthwin* his Son, gave them a great overthrow
at *Deorrham* in *Glostershire,* slew three of thir Kings, *Comail,*
Condidan, and *Farinmaile,* and took three of thir Cheif Cit-
20 ties; *Glocester, Cirencester,* and *Badencester.* The *Britans* not-   584.
withstanding, after some space of time, judging to have out-
grown thir losses, gather to a head, and encounter *Keaulin*
with *Cutha* his Son, at *Fethanleage;* whom valiantly fighting,
they slew among the thickest, and as is said, forc'd the *Saxons*
25 to retire. But *Keaulin* reinforcing the fight, put them to a   *Huntin*
main rout, and following his advantage, took many Towns,
and return'd lad'n with rich booty.

The last of those *Saxons* who rais'd thir own acheivments

to a Monarchy, was *Crida,* much about this time, first founder The Kingdome of
Mercia.
of the *Mercian* Kingdom, drawing also his Pedigree from
Woden. Of whom all to write the several Genealogies, though Huntingd.
Mat. Westm.
it might be done without long search, were, in my opinion, to
5 encumber the story with a sort of barbarous names, to little
purpose. This may suffice, that of *Wodens* 3 Sons, from the
Eldest issu'd *Hengist,* and his succession; from the second, Malmsb.
L. 1. c. 3.
the Kings of *Mercia;* from the third, all that reign'd in *West-*
Saxon, and most of the *Northumbers,* of whom *Alla* was one,
10 the first King of *Deira;* which, after his death, the race of *Ida*
seis'd, and made it one Kingdom, with *Bernicia,* usurping on Florent.
ad ann.
559.
the Childhood of *Edwin, Alla*'s Son. Whom *Ethelric* the Son
of *Ida* expel'd. Notwithstanding others write of him; that
from a poor life, and beyond hope in his old Age, coming to
15 the Crown, he could hardly by the access of a Kingdom, have
overcome his former obscurity, had not the fame of his Son
preserv'd him. Once more the *Britans,* ere they quitted all on 588.
this side the Mountains, forgot not to shew some manhood; Annal. omn.
592.
for meeting *Keaulin* at *Wodens* Beorth, that is to say, *Wodens* Florent.
20 Mount in *Wiltshire,* whether it were by thir own Forces, or
assisted by the *Angles,* whose hatred *Keaulin* had incurr'd, Bed. l. 2. c. 3.
Malms.
Florent.
they ruin'd his whole Army, and chas'd him out of his Kingdom, from whence flying, he dy'd the next year in poverty; Sax. an.
Who a little before, was the most potent and indeed sole King
25 of all the *Saxons* on this side *Humber.* But who was cheif
among the *Britans* in this exploit, had bin worth remembring,
whether it were *Maglocune,* of whose prowess hath bin spok'n,
or *Teudric* King of *Glamorgan,* whom the regest of *Landaff*

recounts to have bin alwaies victorious in fight; to have reign'd about this time, and at length to have exchang'd his Crown for a Hermitage; till in the aid of his Son *Mouric,* whom the *Saxons* had reduc'd to extremes, taking armes again, he de-
5 feated them at *Tinterne* by the River *Wye;* but himself re-ceav'd a mortal wound. The same year with *Keaulin,* whom *Keola* the Son of *Cuthulf, Keaulins* Brother succeeded, *Crida*   593. also the *Mercian* King deceas'd, in whose room *Wibba* suc-ceeded; and in *Northumberland, Ethelfrid,* in the room of
10 *Ethelric;* reigning 24 years. Thus omitting Fables, we have the view of what with reason can be rely'd on for truth, don in *Britain,* since the *Romans* forsook it. Wherin we have heard the many miseries and desolations, brought by divine hand on a perverse Nation; driv'n when nothing else would reform
15 them, out of a fair Country, into a Mountanous and Barren Corner, by Strangers and Pagans. So much more tolerable in the Eye of Heav'n is Infidelity profess't, then Christian Faith and Religion dishonoured by unchristian works. Yet they also at length renounc'd thir Heathenism; which how it came to
20 pass, will be the matter next related.

The End of the Third Book.

THE HISTORY OF BRITAIN.

THE FOURTH BOOK

THE *Saxons* grown up now to 7 absolute Kingdoms, and the latest of them establish'd by succession, finding thir power arrive well nigh at the utmost of what was to be gain'd upon the *Britans,* and as little fearing to be
5 displanted by them, had time now to survey at leasure one anothers greatness. Which quickly bred among them, either envy, or mutual jealousies; till the West Kingdom at length grown over powerful, put an end to all the rest. Mean while, *Bed. Malms.* above others, *Ethelbert* of *Kent,* who by this time had well
10 rip'nd his young ambition, with more ability of years and experience in War, what before he attempted to his loss, now successfully attains; and by degrees brought all the other Monarchies between *Kent* and *Humber,* to be at his devotion. To which design the Kingdom of *West-Saxons,* being
15 the firmest of them all, at that time sore shak'n by thir overthrow at *Wodens-beorth,* and the Death of *Keaulin,* gave him no doubt a main advantage; the rest yeilded not subjection, but as he earn'd it by continual Victories. And to win him the *Bed. l. i. c. 25.* more regard abroad, he marries *Bertha* the French Kings
20 Daughter, though a Christian, and with this condition, to have the free exercise of her Faith, under the care and instruction of *Letardus* a Bishop, sent by her Parents along with her; the King notwithstanding and his people retaining thir own Religion. *Beda* out of *Gildas* laies it sadly to the *Bed. l. i. c. 22.*

Britans charge, that they never would voutsafe thir *Saxon* Neighbours the means of conversion: but how far to blame they were, and what hope there was of converting in the *Bed.l.* 2. midst of so much hostility, at least falshood from thir first
5 arrival, is not now easie to determin. Howbeit not long after, they had the Christian Faith preach't to them by a Nation *Malms.* more remote, and (as a report went, accounted old in *Bedas* *l. 1. c. 3.* time) upon this occasion.

The *Northumbrians* had a custom at that time, and many
10 hunder'd yeares after not abolish't, to sell thir Children for a small value into any Foren Land. Of which number, two comly youths were brought to *Rome,* whose fair and honest countnances invited *Gregory* Arch-Deacon of that Citty, among others that beheld them, pittying thir condition, to
15 demand whence they were; it was answer'd by som who stood by, that they were *Angli* of the Province *Deira,* subjects to *Alla* King of *Northumberland,* and by Religion Pagans. Which last *Gregory* deploring, fram'd on a sudden this allusion to the three names he heard; that the *Angli* so like
20 to Angels should be snatch't *de ira,* that is, from the wrath of God, to sing *Hallelujah:* and forthwith obtaining licence of *Benedict* the Pope, had come and preach't heer among them, had not the *Roman* people, whose love endur'd not the absence of so vigilant a Pastor over them, recall'd him then on
25 his journey, though but deferr'd his pious intention. For a   596. while after, succeeding in the Papal Seat, and now in his fourth year, admonisht, saith *Beda,* by divine instinct, he sent *Augustine* whom he had design'd for Bishop of the

English Nation, and other zealous Monks with him, to preach to them the Gospel. Who being now on thir way, discouraged by some reports, or thir own carnal fear, sent back *Austin,* in the name of all, to beseech *Gregory* they
5 might return home, and not be sent a journey so full of hazard, to a fierce and infidel Nation, whose tongue they understood not. *Gregory* with pious and Apostolic perswasions exhorts them not to shrink back from so good a work, but cheerfully to go on in the strength of divine assistance. The
10 Letter it self yet extant among our Writers of Ecclesiastic story, I omit heer, as not professing to relate of those matters more then what mixes aptly with civil affairs. The Abbot *Austin,* for so he was ordain'd over the rest, reincourag'd by the exhortations of *Gregory,* and his fellows by the Letter
15 which he brought them, came safe to the Ile of *Tanet,* in   597.
number about 40, besides some of the French Nation whom they took along as Interpreters. *Ethelbert* the King, to whom *Austin* at his landing had sent a new and wondrous message, that he came from *Rome* to proffer Heav'n and eternal hap-
20 piness in the knowledge of another God then the *Saxons* knew, appoints them to remain where they landed, and necessaries to be provided them, consulting in the mean time what was to be done. And after certain days coming into the Iland, chose a place to meet them under the open Sky, possest
25 with an old perswasion, that all Spells, if they should use any to deceive him, so it were not within doors, would be unavailable. They on the other side call'd to his presence, advancing for thir Standard, a silver cross, and the painted

image of our Saviour, came slowly forward singing thir solemn Litanies: which wrought in *Ethelbert* more suspition perhaps that they us'd enchantments; till sitting down as the King will'd them, they there preach'd to him, and all in that

5 assembly, the tidings of Salvation. Whom having heard attentively, the King thus answer'd. Fair indeed and ample are the promises which ye bring, and such things as have the appearance in them of much good; yet such as being new and uncertain, I cannot hastily assent to, quitting the Religion

10 which from my Ancestors, with all the *English* Nation, so many years I have retain'd. Nevertheless because ye are strangers, and have endur'd so long a journey, to impart us the knowledge of things, which I perswade me you believe to be the truest and the best, ye may be sure we shall not

15 recompence you with any molestation, but shall provide rather how we may friendliest entertain ye; nor do we forbid whom ye can by preaching gain to your belief. And accordingly thir residence he allotted them in *Doroverne* or *Canturbury* his chief Citty, and made provision for thir mainte-

20 nance, with free leave to preach their doctrine where they pleased. By which, and by the example of thir holy life, spent in prayer, fasting, and continual labour in the conversion of Souls, they won many; on whose bounty and the Kings, receiving only what was necessary, they subsisted. There stood

25 without the Citty, on the East-side, an ancient Church built in honour of St. *Martin,* while yet the *Romans* remain'd heer: in which *Bertha* the Queen went out usually to pray: Heer they also began first to preach, baptize, and openly to exercise   598.

divine worship. But when the King himself convinc't by thir good life & miracles, became Christian, and was baptiz'd, which came to pass in the very first year of thir arrival, then multitudes daily, conforming to thir Prince, thought it honour to be reckon'd among those of his faith. To whom *Ethelbert* indeed principally shewed his favour, but compell'd none. For so he had bin taught by them who were both the Instructors and the Authors of his faith, that Christian Religion ought to be voluntary, not compell'd. About this time *Kelwulf* the Son of *Cutha Keaulins* Brother reign'd over the *West-Saxons,* after his Brother *Keola* or *Kelric,* and had continual War either with *English, Welch, Picts,* or *Scots.* But *Austin,* whom with his fellows, *Ethelbert* now had endow'd with a better place for thir abode in the Citty, and other possessions necessary to livelihood, crossing into *France,* was by the Archbishop of *Arles,* at the appointment of Pope *Gregory,* ordain'd Archbishop of the *English:* and returning, sent to *Rome Laurence* and *Peter,* two of his associates, to acquaint the Pope of his good success in *England,* and to be resolv'd of certain Theological, or rather Levitical questions: with answers to which, not proper in this place, *Gregory* sends also to the great work of converting, that went on so happily, a supply of labourers, *Mellitus, Justus, Paulinus, Rufinian,* and many others; who what they were, may be guess't by the stuff which they brought with them, vessels and vestments for the Altar, Coaps, reliques, and for the Archbishop *Austin* a Pall to say Mass in: to such a rank superstition that Age was grown, though some of them yet

Bed. l. 2. c. 5.

Sax. an.
Malms.
601.
Bed. l. 1. c. 27.

retaining an emulation of Apostolic zeal: lastly, to *Ethelbert*
they brought a letter with many presents. *Austin* thus exalted
to Archiepiscopal authority, recover'd from the ruins and
other profane uses, a Christian Church in *Canturbury* built
5 of old by the *Romans;* which he dedicated by the name of
Christs Church, and joyning to it built a seat for himself and
his successors; a Monastery also neer the Citty Eastward,
where *Ethelbert* at his motion built St. *Peters,* and enrich't it
with great endowments, to be a place of burial for the Arch-
10 bishops and Kings of *Kent:* so quickly they step't up into
fellowship of pomp with Kings. While thus *Ethelbert* and   *Bed. l. 2.*
his people had thir minds intent, *Ethelfrid* the *Northum-*
brian King, was not less busied in far different affairs: for
being altogether warlike, and covetous of fame, he more
15 wasted the *Britans* then any *Saxon* King before him; winning
from them large Territories, which either he made tributary,
or planted with his own Subjects. Whence *Edan* King of   603.
those *Scots* that dwelt in *Britain,* jealous of his successes,
came against him with a mighty Army, to a place call'd
20 *Degsastan;* but in the fight loosing most of his men, himself
with a few escap'd: only *Theobald* the Kings brother, and
the whole wing which he commanded, unfortunately cut
off, made the Victory to *Ethelfrid* less intire. Yet from that
time no King of *Scots* in hostile manner durst pass into *Brit-*
25 *ain* for a hunderd and more years after: and what some years
before, *Kelwulf* the *West-Saxon* is annal'd to have done
against the *Scots* and *Picts,* passing through the Land of
Ethelfrid a King so potent, unless in his aid and alliance, is

not likely. *Buchanan* writes as if *Ethelfrid,* assisted by *Keau-lin* whom he mistitles King of *East-Saxons,* had before this time a battel with *Aidan,* wherein *Cutha Keaulins* son was slain. But *Cutha,* as is above written from better authority,

5 was slain in fight against the *Welch* 20 years before. The number of Christians began now to increase so fast, that *Augustine* ordaining Bishops under him, two of his assistants *Mellitus* and *Justus,* sent them out both to the work of thir ministry. And *Mellitus* by preaching converted the *East-*

10 *Saxons,* over whom *Sebert* the son of *Sleda,* by permission of *Ethelbert,* being born of his sister *Ricula,* then reign'd. Whose conversion *Ethelbert* to gratulate, built them the great Church of St. *Paul* in *London* to be their Bishops Cathedral; as *Justus* also had his built at *Rochester,* and both gifted by

15 the same King with fair possessions. Hitherto *Austin* laboured well among Infidels, but not with like commendation soon after among Christians. For by means of *Ethelbert* summoning the *Britan* Bishops to a place on the edge of *Worcestershire,* call'd from that time *Augustines* Oke, he requires

20 them to conform with him in the same day of celebrating *Easter,* and many other points wherein they differ'd from the rites of *Rome:* which when they refus'd to do, not prevailing by dispute, he appeals to a miracle, restoring to sight a blind man whom the *Britans* could not cure. At this something

25 mov'd, though not minded to recede from thir own opinions without furder consultation, they request a second meeting: to which came seven *Britan* Bishops, with many other lerned men, especially from the famous Monastery of *Bangor,* in

604.
Bed. *l.* 2. *c.* 3.

which were said to be so many Monks, living all by thir own
labour, that being divided under seven Rectors, none had
fewer then 300. One man there was who staid behind, a
Hermit by the life he led, who by his wisdom effected more
5 then all the rest who went: being demanded, for they held
him as an Oracle, how they might know *Austin* to be a man
from God, that they might follow him, he answer'd, that if
they found him meek and humble, they should be taught by
him, for it was likeliest to be the yoke of Christ, both what
10 he bore himself, and would have them bear; but if he bore
himself proudly, that they should not regard him, for he was
then certainly not of God. They took his advice, and hasted
to the place of meeting. Whom *Austin* being already there
before them, neither arose to meet, nor receiv'd in any broth-
15 erly sort, but sat all the while pontifically in his Chair.
Whereat the *Britans,* as they were counsel'd by the holy man,
neglected him, and neither hark'n'd to his proposals of conformity, nor would acknowledge him for an Archbishop:
And in name of the rest, *Dinothus* then Abbot of *Bangor,* is *Spelman*
concil.
20 said, thus sagely to have answer'd him. As to the subjection *pag.* 108
which you require, be thus perswaded of us, that in the bond
of love and charity we are all Subjects and Servants to the
Church of God, yea to the Pope of *Rome,* and every good
Christian to help them forward, both by word and deed, to
25 be the Childern of God: other obedience then this we know
not to be due to him whom you term the Pope; and this obedience we are ready to give both to him and to every Christian continually. Besides, we are govern'd under God by the

Bishop of *Caerleon,* who is to oversee us in spiritual matters. To which *Austin* thus presaging, some say menacing, replies, since ye refuse to accept of peace with your brethren, ye shall have War from your enemies; and since ye will not with us preach the word of life, to whom ye ought, from their hands ye shall receive death. This, though Writers agree not whether *Austin* spake it as his prophecy, or as his plot against the *Britans,* fell out accordingly. For many years were not past, when *Ethelfrid,* whether of his own accord, or at the request of *Ethelbert* incens't by *Austin,* with a powerful host came to *Westchester,* then *Caer-legion.* Where being met by the *British* Forces, and both sides in readiness to give the onset, he discernes a company of men, not habited for War, standing together in a place of some safety; and by them a Squadron arm'd. Whom having lernt upon some enquiry to be Priests and Monks, assembl'd thither after three days fasting, to pray for the good success of thir Forces against him, therefore they first, saith he, shall feel our Swords; for they who pray against us, fight heaviest against us by thir prayers, and are our dangerousest enemies. And with that turns his first charge upon the Monks: *Brocmail* the Captain set to guard them, quickly turns his back, and leaves above 1200 Monks to a sudden massacher, whereof scarse fifty scap'd, but not so easie work found *Ethelfrid* against another part of *Britans* that stood in arms, whom though at last he overthrew, yet with slaughter nigh as great to his own souldiers. To excuse *Austin* of this bloodshed, lest some might think it his revengeful policy, *Beda* writes that he was dead long be-

*Sax. an.
Huntingd.
607.*

fore, although if the time of his sitting Archbishop be right
computed sixteen years, he must survive this action. Other
just ground of charging him with this imputation appears not,
save what evidently we have from *Geffry Monmouth,* whose
5 weight we know. The same year *Kelwulf* made War on the
South-Saxons, bloody, saith *Huntingdon,* to both sides, but
most to them of the *South:* and four years after dying left
the Government of *West-Saxons* to *Kinegils* and *Cuichelm*
the sons of his brother *Keola.* Others, as *Florent* of *Worster*
10 and *Mathew* of *Westminster,* will have *Cuichelm* son of
Kinegils, but admitted to reign with his father, in whose
third year they are recorded with joynt Forces or conduct to
have fought against the *Britans* in *Beandune,* now *Bindon* in
Dorsetshire, and to have slain of them above two thousand.
15 More memorable was the second year following, by the death
of *Ethelbert* the first Christian King of *Saxons,* and no less a
favourer of all civility in that rude age. He gave Laws and
Statutes after the example of *Roman* Emperors, written with
the advice of his sagest Counsellors, but in the *English*
20 tongue, and observ'd long after. Wherein his special care was
to punish those who had stoln ought from Church or Church-
man, thereby shewing how gratefully he receiv'd at thir
hands the Christian Faith. Which, he no sooner dead, but
his son *Eadbald* took the course as fast to extinguish; not
25 only falling back to Heathenism, but that which Heathenism
was wont to abhor, marrying his fathers second wife. Then
soon was perceiv'd what multitudes for fear or countenance
of the King had profess't Christianity, returning now as

Malms.
pont. l. 1

Sax. an.

611.
Sax. an.
Malms.

614.

Camd.
616.
Sax. an.

eagerly to thir old Religion. Nor staid the Apostacy within
one Province, but quickly spread over to the *East-Saxons;*
occasion'd there likewise, or set forward by the death of thir
Christian King *Sebert:* whose three sons, of whom two are
5 nam'd *Sexted* and *Seward,* neither in his life time would be *Malms.*
brought to baptism, and after his decease re-establish'd the
free exercise of Idolatry; nor so content, they set themselves
in despight to do some op'n profanation against the other
Sacrament. Coming therfore into the Church, where *Melli-*
10 *tus* the Bishop was ministring, they requir'd him in abuse
and scorn to deliver to them unbaptiz'd the consecrated
bread; and him refuseing, drove disgracefully out of their
dominion. Who cross'd forthwith into *Kent,* where things
were in the same plight, and thence into *France,* with *Justus*
15 Bishop of *Rochester.* But Divine vengeance deferr'd not long
the punishment of men so impious; for *Eadbald,* vext with
an evil Spirit, fell oft'n into foul fits of distraction; and the
Sons of *Sebert,* in a fight against the *West-Saxons* perish'd,
with their whole Army. But *Eadbald,* within the year, by
20 an extraordinary means became penitent. For when *Lau-*
rence the Archbishop and successor of *Austin* was preparing
to ship for *France,* after *Justus* and *Mellitus,* the story goes,
if it be worth beleeving, that St. *Peter,* in whose Church he
spent the night before in watching and praying, appear'd to
25 him, and to make the Vision more sensible, gave him many
stripes for offering to desert his flock; at sight whereof the
King (to whom next morning he shew'd the marks of what
he had suffer'd, by whom and for what cause) relenting and

in great fear dissolv'd his incestuous marriage, and appli'd himself to the Christian Faith more sincerely then before, with all his people. But the *Londoners* addicted still to Paganism, would not be perswaded to receave again *Mellitus* thir Bishop, and to compell them was not in his power. Thus much through all the South was troubl'd in Religion, as much were the North parts disquieted through Ambition. For *Ethelfrid* of *Bernicia*, as was touch't before, having thrown *Edwin* out of *Deira,* and join'd that Kingdome to his own, not content to have bereav'd him of his right, whose known vertues and high parts gave cause of suspition to his Enemies, sends Messengers to demand him of *Redwald* King of *East-Angles;* under whose protection, after many years wandring obscurely through all the Iland, he had plac'd his safety. *Redwald,* though having promis'd all defence to *Edwin* as to his suppliant, yet tempted with continual and large offers of gold, and not contemning the puissance of *Ethelfrid,* yeilded at length, either to dispatch him, or to give him into thir hands: but earnestly exhorted by his Wife, not to betray the Faith and inviolable Law of Hospitality and refuge giv'n, preferrs his first promise as the more Religious, nor only refuses to deliver him; but since War was thereupon denounc't, determins to be beforehand with the danger; and with a sudden Army rais'd, surprises *Ethelfrid,* little dreaming an invasion, and in a fight near to the East-side of the River *Idle,* on the *Mercian* border, now *Nottinghamshire,* slaies him, dissipating easily those few Forces which he had got to march out over-hastily with him; who yet as a testi-

617.

Malmsb.
L. 1. c. 3.

Camden

mony of his Fortune, not his Valour to be blam'd, slew first with his own hands, *Reiner* the Kings Son. His two Sons *Oswald,* and *Oswi,* by *Acca, Edwins* Sister, escap'd into *Scotland.* By this Victory, *Redwald* became so far superior to the
5 other *Saxon* Kings, that *Beda* reck'ns him the next after *Ella* and *Ethelbert;* who besides this Conquest of the North, had likewise all on the hitherside *Humber* at his obedience. He had formerly in *Kent* receav'd Baptism, but coming home and perswaded by his Wife, who still it seems, was his Chief
10 Counseller to good or bad alike, relaps'd into his old Religion; yet not willing to forgoe his new, thought it not the worst way, lest perhaps he might err in either, for more assurance to keep them both; and in the same Temple erected one Altar to Christ, another to his Idols. But *Edwin,* as with
15 more deliberation he undertook, and with more sincerity retain'd the Christian profession, so also in power and extent of dominion far exceeded all before him; subdueing all, saith *Beda,* English or British, eev'n to the Iles, then call'd *Mevanian, Anglesey,* and *Man;* setl'd in his Kingdome by *Red-*
20 *wald,* he sought in mariage *Edelburga,* whom others call *Tate,* the Daughter of *Ethelbert.* To whose Embassadors, *Eadbald* her Brother made answer, that to wed thir Daughter to a Pagan, was not the Christian Law. *Edwin* repli'd, that to her Religion he would be no hindrance, which with
25 her whole Houshold she might freely exercise. And moreover, that if examin'd it were found the better, he would imbrace it. These ingenuous offers, op'ning so fair a way to the advancement of truth, are accepted, and *Paulinus* as a spirit-

Bed.
L. 2. c. 15.

625.

ual Guardian sent along with the Virgin. He being to that
purpose made Bishop by *Justus,* omitted no occasion to plant   626.
the Gospel in those parts, but with small success, till the next
year, *Cuichelm,* at that time one of the two *West-Saxon*
5 Kings, envious of the greatness which he saw *Edwin* growing up to, sent privily *Eumerus* a hir'd Sword-man to assassin
him; who under pretence of doing a message from his Master, with a poison'd Weapon, stabs at *Edwin,* conferring with
him in his House, by the River *Derwent* in *Yorkeshire,* on an
10 Easter-day; which *Lilla* one of the Kings Attendants, at the
instant perceaving, with a loyalty that stood not then to de-
liberate, abandon'd his whole body to the blow; which notwithstanding made passage through to the Kings Person,
with a wound not to be slighted. The murderer encompass'd
15 now with Swords, and desperate, fore-revenges his own fall
with the Death of another, whom his Poinard reach'd home.
Paulinus omitting no opportunity to win the King from misbeleef, obtain'd at length this promise from him; that if
Christ, whom he so magnifi'd, would give him to recover of
20 his wound, and victory of his Enemies who had thus assaulted him, he would then become Christian, in pledge
whereof he gave his young Daughter *Eanfled* to be bred up
in Religion; who with 12 others of his Family, on the day of
Pentecost was baptiz'd. And by that time well recover'd of
25 his wound; to punish the Authors of so foul a fact, he went
with an Army against the *West-Saxons:* whom having
quell'd by War, and of such as had conspir'd against him,
put some to Death, others pardon'd, he return'd home vic-

torious, and from that time worship'd no more his Idols, yet
ventur'd not rashly into Baptism, but first took care to be instructed rightly, what he learnt, examining and still considering with himself and others, whom he held wisest; though
5 *Boniface* the Pope, by large Letters of exhortation, both to
him and his Queen, was not wanting to quicken his beleef.
But while he still deferr'd, and his deferring might seem now
to have past the maturity of wisedome to a faulty lingring,
Paulinus by Revelation, as was beleev'd, coming to the
10 knowledge of a secret, which befell him strangly in the time
of his troubles, on a certain day went in boldly to him, and
laying his right hand on the head of the King, ask'd him if
he rememberd what that sign meant; the King trembling,
and in a maze riseing up, strait fell at his Feet. Behold, saith
15 *Paulinus,* raising him from the ground; God hath deliver'd
you from your Enemies, and giv'n you the Kingdome, as
you desir'd: perform now what long since you promis'd him,
to receave his Doctrine which I now bring you, and the Faith,
which if you accept, shall to your temporal felicity, add Eter-
20 nal. The promise claim'd of him by *Paulinus,* how and
wherefore made, though savouring much of Legend, is thus
related. *Redwald,* as we heard before, dazl'd with the gold of
Ethelfrid, or by his threatning over-aw'd, having promis'd
to yeild up *Edwin,* one of his faithfull Companions, of which
25 he had some few with him in the Court of *Redwald,* that
never shrunk from his adversity, about the first howr of
night comes in hast to his Chamber, and calling him forth
for better secrecy, reveles to him his danger, offers him his

aid to make escape; but that course not approv'd, as seeming
dishonourable without more manifest cause to begin distrust
towards one who had so long bin his only refuge, the friend
departs. *Edwin* left alone without the Palace Gate, full of
5 sadness and perplext thoughts, discerns about the dead of
night, a man neither by countnance nor by habit to him
known, approaching towards him. Who after salutation,
ask'd him why at this howr, when all others were at rest, he
alone so sadly sat waking on a cold Stone? *Edwin* not a little
10 misdoubting who he might be, ask'd him again, what his
sitting within dores, or without, concern'd him to know? To
whom he again, think not that who thou art, or why sitting
heer, or what danger hangs over thee, is to me unknown:
But what would you promise to that man, who ever would
15 befriend you out of all these troubles, and perswade *Redwald*
to the like? All that I am able, answer'd *Edwin*. And he,
what if the same man should promise to make you greater
then any English King hath bin before you? I should not
doubt, quoth *Edwin,* to be answerably gratefull. And what
20 if to all this he would inform you, said the other, in a way to
happiness, beyond what any of your Ancestors hath known?
would you hark'n to his Counsel? *Edwin* without stopping
promis'd he would. And the other laying his right hand on
Edwins head, when this sign, saith he, shall next befall thee,
25 remember this time of night, and this discourse, to perform
what thou hast promis'd, and with these words disappeering,
left *Edwin* much reviv'd, but not less fill'd with wonder, who
this unknown should be. When suddenly the friend who had

bin gon all this while to list'n furder what was like to be decree'd of *Edwin,* comes back and joyfully bids him rise to his repose, for that the Kings mind, though for a while drawn aside, was now fully resolv'd not only not to betray him,

5 but to defend him against all Enemies, as he had promis'd. This was said to be the cause why *Edwin* admonish't by the Bishop of a sign which had befaln him so strangely, and as he thought so secretly, arose to him with that reverence and amazement, as to one sent from Heav'n, to claim that prom-

10 ise of him which he perceav'd well was due to a Divine pow-er, that had assisted him in his troubles. To *Paulinus* there-fore he makes answer, that the Christian Beleef he himself ought by promise, and intended to receave; but would con-ferr first with his Cheif Peers and Counsellers, that if they

15 likewise could be won, all at once might be baptiz'd. They therfore being ask'd in Counsel what thir opinion was con-cerning this new Doctrine, and well perceaving which way the King enclin'd, every one thereafter shap'd his reply. The Cheif-Preist speaking first, discover'd an old grudge he had

20 against his Gods, for advancing others in the Kings Favour above him thir Cheif Preist: another hiding his Court-com-pliance with a grave sentence, commended the choise of cer-tain before uncertain, upon due examination; to like purpose answer'd all the rest of his Sages, none op'nly dissenting

25 from what was likely to be the Kings Creed: wheras the preaching of *Paulinus* could work no such effect upon them, toiling till that time without success. Whereupon *Edwin* re-nouncing Heathenism, became Christian: and the Pagan

Preist, offring himself freely to demolish the Altars of his
former Gods, made some amends for his teaching to adore
them. With *Edwin,* his two Sons *Osfrid* and *Eanfrid,* born   627.
to him by *Quenburga,* Daughter, as saith *Beda,* of *Kearle*
5 King of *Mercia,* in the time of his banishment, and with
them most of the people, both Nobles and Commons, easily
converted, were baptiz'd; he with his whole Family at *York,*
in a Church hastily built up of Wood, the multitude most
part in Rivers. *Northumberland* thus christ'nd, *Paulinus*
10 crossing *Humber,* converted also the Province of *Lindsey,*
and *Blecca* the Governour of *Lincoln,* with his Houshold and
most of that City; wherin he built a Church of Stone, curiously wrought, but of small continuance; for the Roof in
Bedas time, uncertain whether by neglect or Enemies, was
15 down; the Walls only standing. Mean while in *Mercia,*
Kearle a Kinsman of *Wibba,* saith *Huntingdon,* not a Son,
having long withheld the Kingdome from *Penda Wibba*'s
Son, left it now at length to the fiftieth year of his Age: with
whom *Kinegils* and *Cuichelm,* the *West-Saxon* Kings, two   629.
20 year after, having by that time it seems recover'd strength,   *Sax. ann*
since the Inrode made upon them by *Edwin,* fought at *Ciren-*
cester, then made Truce. But *Edwin* seeking every way to
propagate the Faith, which with so much deliberation he had
receav'd, persuaded *Eorpwald* the Son of *Redwald,* King of
25 *East-Angles,* to imbrace the same beleef; willingly or in aw,   632.
is not known, retaining under *Edwin* the name only of a   *Sax. an.*
King. But *Eorpwald* not long surviv'd his conversion, slain   *Florent.*
in fight by *Ricbert* a Pagan: wherby the people having lightly   *Genealc*

follow'd the Religion of thir King, as lightly fell back to thir
old superstitions for above 3 years after: *Edwin* in the mean
while, to his Faith adding vertue, by the due administration
of justice wrought such peace over all his Territories, that
5 from Sea to Sea, man or woman might have travail'd in
safety. His care also was of Fountains by the way side, to
make them fittest for the use of Travellers. And not unmindful of regal State, whether in War or Peace, he had a Royal
Banner carried before him. But having reign'd with much
10 honour 17 years, he was at length by *Kedwalla,* or *Cadwal-*
lon, King of the *Britans,* who with aid of the *Mercian Penda,*
had rebell'd against him, slain in Battel with his Son *Osfrid,*
at a place call'd *Hethfeild,* and his whole Army overthrown
or disperst in the year 633. and the 47*th* of his Age, in the   633.
15 Eye of man worthy a more peacefull end. His Head brought
to *York,* was there buried in the Church by him begun. Sad
was this overthrow, both to Church and State of the *North-*
umbrians: for *Penda* being a Heathen, and the British King,
though in name a Christian, yet in deeds more bloody then
20 the Pagan, nothing was omitted of barbarous cruelty in the
slaughter of Sex or Age; *Kedwalla* threatning to root out
the whole Nation, though then newly Christian. For the
Britans, and, as *Beda* saith, eev'n to his dayes, accounted
Saxon Christianity no better then Paganism, and with them
25 held as little Communion. From these calamities no refuge
being left but flight, *Paulinus* taking with him *Ethilburga*
the Queen and her Children, aided by *Bassus,* one of *Edwins*
Captains, made escape by Sea to *Eadbald* King of *Kent:* who

receaving his Sister with all kindness, made *Paulinus* Bishop
of *Rochester,* where he ended his days. After *Edwin,* the
Kingdom of *Northumberland* became divided as before, each
rightfull Heir seising his part; in *Deira Osric,* the Son of
5 *Elfric, Edwins* Uncle, by profession a Christian, and baptiz'd
by *Paulinus;* in *Bernicia, Eanfrid,* the Son of *Ethelfrid;* who
all the time of *Edwin,* with his Brother *Oswald,* and many
of the young Nobility, liv'd in *Scotland* exil'd, and had bin
there taught and baptiz'd. No sooner had they gott'n each a
10 Kingdom, but both turn'd recreant, sliding back into their
old Religion; and both were the same year slain; *Osric* by a
sudden eruption of *Kedwalla,* whom he in a strong Town
had unadvisedly beseig'd; *Eanfrid* seeking peace, and incon-
sideratly with a few surrendring himself. *Kedwalla* now
15 rang'd at will through both those Provinces, useing cruelly
his Conquest; when *Oswald* the Brother of *Eanfrid* with a   634.
small but Christian Army, unexpectedly coming on, de-
feated and destroy'd both him and his huge Forces, which
he boasted to be invincible, by a little River running into
20 *Tine,* neer the antient *Roman* Wall then call'd *Denisburn,*
the place afterwards *Heav'n field,* from the Cross reported
miraculous for Cures, which *Oswald* there erected before the
Battail, in tok'n of his Faith against the great number of his
Enemies. Obtaining the Kingdom, he took care to instruct
25 again the people in Christianity. Sending therfore to the
Scotish Elders, *Beda* so terms them, among whom he had
receav'd Baptism, requested of them som faithfull Teacher,
who might again settle Religion in his Realm, which the late

troubles had impar'd; they as readily hearkning to his request, send *Aidan* a Scotch Monk and Bishop, but of singular
zeal and meekness, with others to assist him, whom at thir
own desire he feated in *Lindisfarne,* as the Episcopal Seat,
5 now *Holy Iland:* and being the Son of *Ethelfrid,* by the Sister of *Edwin,* as right Heir, others failing, easily reduc'd
both Kingdoms of *Northumberland* as before into one; nor
of *Edwins* Dominion lost any part, but enlarg'd it rather;
over all the fowr *British* Nations, *Angles, Britans, Picts* and
10 *Scots,* exerciseing regall Authority. Of his Devotion, Hu-
mility, and Almes-deeds, much is spok'n; that he disdain'd
not to be the interpreter of *Aidan,* preaching in Scotch or
bad English, to his Nobles and Houshold Servants; and had
the poor continually serv'd at his Gate, after the promiscuous
15 manner of those times: his meaning might be upright, but
the manner more antient of privat or of Church contribution, is doubtless more Evangelical. About this time, the
West-Saxons, antiently call'd *Gevissi,* by the preaching of
Berinus, a Bishop, whom Pope *Honorius* had sent, were
20 converted to the Faith with *Kinegils* thir King: him *Oswald*
receav'd out of the Font, and his Daughter in mariage. The
next year *Cuichelm* was baptiz'd in *Dorchester,* but liv'd not
to the years end. The *East-Angles* also this year were reclaim'd to the Faith of Christ, which for som years past they
25 had thrown off. But *Sigbert* the Brother of *Eorpwald* now
succeeded in that Kingdom, prais'd for a most Christian and
Learned Man: who while his Brother yet reign'd, living in
France an exile, for some displeasure conceav'd against him

635.
Sax. an.

636.

by *Redwald* his Father, lern'd there the Christian Faith; and
reigning soon after, in the same instructed his people, by the
preaching of *Felix* a *Burgundian* Bishop.

In the year 640. *Eadbald* deceasing, left to *Ercombert* his   640.
5 Son by *Emma* the French Kings Daughter, the Kingdom of
Kent; recorded the first of English Kings, who commanded
through his limits the destroying of Idols; laudably, if all
Idols without exception, and the first to have establisht *Lent*
among us, under strict penalty, not worth remembring, but
10 only to inform us, that no *Lent* was observ'd heer till his time *Mat. Wes*
by compulsion: especially being noted by some to have fraud-
ulently usurp'd upon his Elder Brother *Ermenred,* whose
right was precedent to the Crown. *Oswald* having reign'd 8   642.
years, worthy also as might seem of longer life, fell into the
15 same fate with *Edwin,* and from the same hand, in a great
Battel overcom and slain by *Penda,* at a place call'd *Maser-* *Camden.*
feild, now *Oswestre,* in *Shropshire,* miraculous, as saith *Beda,*
after his Death. His Brother *Oswi* succeeded him; reigning,
though in much trouble, 28 years; oppos'd either by *Penda,* *Bed.*
20 or his own Son *Alfred,* or his Brothers Son *Ethilwald.* Next *L. 3. c. 14*
year *Kinegils* the *West-Saxon* dying, left his Son *Kenwalk*   643.
in his stead, though as yet unconverted. About this time *Sige-* *Sax. an.*
bert, King of *East-Angles,* having lernt in *France,* ere his
coming to Reign, the manner of thir Schools, with the as-
25 sistance of some Teachers out of *Kent,* instituted a School
heer after the same Discipline, thought to be the University
of *Cambridge* then first founded: and at length weary of his
Kingly Office, betook him to a Monastical life; commend-

ing the care of Government to his Kinsman *Egric,* who had
sustain'd with him part of that burden before. It happen'd
some years after, that *Penda* made War on the *East-Angles:*
they expecting a sharp encounter, besought *Sigebert,* whom
5 they esteem'd an expert Leader, with his presence to confirm
the Souldiery: and him refuseing carried by force out of the
Monastery into the Camp; where acting the Monk rather
then the Captain, with a single wand in his hand, he was
slain with *Egric,* and his whole Army put to flight. *Anna* of
10 the Royal Stock, as next in right, succeeded; and hath the
praise of a vertuous and most Christian Prince. But *Kenwalk*   645.
the *West-Saxon* having maried the Sister of *Penda,* and di-   *Sax. an.*
vorc't her, was by him with more appearance of a just cause
vanquisht in fight, and depriv'd of his Crown: whence re-
15 tiring to *Anna* King of the *East-Angles,* after three years
abode in his Court, he there became Christian, and after-   648.
wards regain'd his Kingdom. *Oswi* in the former years of
his Reign, had sharer with him, *Oswin* Nephew of *Edwin,*
who rul'd in *Deira* 7 years, commended much for his zeal in
20 Religion, and for comliness of person, with other princely
qualities, belov'd of all. Notwithstanding which, dissentions
growing between them, it came to Armes. *Oswin* seeing
himself much exceeded in numbers, thought it more prudence, dismissing his Army, to reserve himself for some
25 better occasion. But committing his person with one faithfull attendant to the Loyalty of *Hunwald* an Earl, his imagin'd friend, he was by him treacherously discoverd, and by
command of *Oswi* slain. After whom within 12 days, and   651.
                                                              Bede.

for greif of him whose death he foretold, dy'd Bishop *Aidan,* famous for his Charity, meekness, and labour in the Gospel. The fact of *Oswi* was detestable to all; which therfore to ex- piate, a Monastery was built in the place where it was don,

5 and Prayers there daily offerd up for the Souls of both Kings, the slain and the slayer. *Kenwalk* by this time reinstall'd in his Kingdom, kept it long, but with various Fortune; for *Beda* relates him oft-times afflicted by his Enemies with great *Bed. l.* 3. losses: and in 652. by the Annals, fought a Battel (Civil War   652.

10 *Ethelwerd* calls it) at *Bradanford* by the River *Afene;* against whom, and for what cause, or who had the Victory, they write not. *Camden* names the place *Bradford* in *Wiltshire,* by the River *Avon,* and *Cuthred* his neer Kinsman, against whom he fought, but cites no Autority; certain it is, that

15 *Kenwalk* fowr years before had giv'n large possessions to his Nephew *Cuthred,* the more unlikely therefore now to have rebell'd. The next year *Peada,* whom his Father *Penda,*   653. though a Heathen, had for his Princely Vertues made Prince of *Middle-Angles,* belonging to the *Mercians,* was with that

20 people converted to the Faith. For coming to *Oswi* with re- quest to have in mariage *Alfleda* his Daughter, he was de- ni'd her but on condition, that he with all his people should receave Christianity. Heering therefore not unwillingly what was preach't to him of Resurrection and Eternal Life, much

25 persuaded also by *Alfrid* the Kings Son, who had his Sister *Kyniburg* to Wife, he easily assented, for the truths sake only as he profess'd, whether he obtain'd the Virgin or no, and was baptiz'd with all his followers. Returning, he took with

him fowr Presbyters to teach the people of his Province;
who by thir daily preaching won many. Neither did *Penda,*
though himself no Beleever, prohibit any in his Kingdome
to heer or beleeve the Gospel, but rather hated and despis'd

5 those, who professing to beleeve, atested not thir Faith by
good works; condemning them for miserable and justly to
be despis'd, who obey not that God in whom they choose to
beleeve. How well might *Penda* this Heathen rise up in judgment against many pretending Christians, both of his own

10 and these daies! yet being a man bred up to War (as no less
were others then reigning, and oft-times one against another,
though both Christians) he warr'd on *Anna,* King of the
East-Angles,* perhaps without cause, for *Anna* was esteem'd
a just man, and at length slew him. About this time the *East-*

15 *Saxons,* who as above hath bin said, had expell'd thir Bishop
Mellitus, and renounc'd the Faith, were by the means of
Oswi thus reconverted. *Sigebert* surnam'd the small, being
the Son of *Seward,* without other memory of his Reign, left
his Son King of that Province, after him *Sigebert* the Sec-

20 ond, who coming oft'n to visit *Oswi* his great friend, was by
him at several times fervently disuaded from Idolatry, and
convinc't at length to forsake it, was there baptiz'd; on his
return home taking with him *Kedda* a laborious Preacher,
afterwards made Bishop; by whose teaching with some help

25 of others, the people were again recoverd from misbeleef.
But *Sigebert* some years after, though standing fast in Religion, was by the Conspiracy of two Brethren in place neer
about him, wickedly murder'd; who being ask'd what mov'd

654.
Sax. an.

them to do a deed so hainous, gave no other then this barbarous answer; that they were angry with him for being
so gentle to his Enemies, as to forgive them thir injuries
whenever they besought him. Yet his Death seems to have
5 happ'nd not without some cause by him giv'n of Divine
displeasure. For one of those Earls who slew him, living in
unlawfull wedlock, and therfore excommunicated so severely
by the Bishop, that no man might presume to enter into his
House, much less to sit at meat with him, the King not re-
10 garding this Church censure, went to feast with him at his
invitation. Whom the Bishop meeting in his return, though
penitent for what he had don, and faln at his feet, touch'd
with the rod in his hand, and angerly thus foretold: because
thou hast neglected to abstain from the House of that Ex-
15 communicate, in that House thou shalt die; and so it fell out,
perhaps from that prediction, God bearing witness to his
Minister in the power of Church Discipline, spiritually executed, not juridically on the contemner thereof. This year   655.
655. prov'd fortunate to *Oswi,* and fatal to *Penda,* for *Oswi*
20 by the continual inrodes of *Penda,* having long endur'd much
devastation, to the endangering once by assault and fire *Beb-*   *Bed.l.3.*
banburg, his strongest City, now *Bamborrow* Castle, unable   *Camd.*
to resist him, with many rich presents offerd to buy his
Peace. Which not accepted by the Pagan, who intended
25 nothing but destruction to that King, though more then
once in affinity with him, turning guifts into vows, he implores Divine Assistance, devoting, if he were deliverd from
his Enemy, a Child of one year old, his Daughter to be a

Nun, and 12 portions of land whereon to build Monasteries.
His vows, as may be thought, found better success then his
profferd guifts; for heerupon with his Son *Alfrid,* gathering
a small power, he encounterd and discomfited the *Mercians,*   *Camden.*
5 30 times exceeding his in number, and led on by expert Captains: at a place call'd *Loydes,* now *Leeds* in *Yorkeshire.* Besides this *Ethelwald,* the Son of *Oswald,* who rul'd in *Deira,*
took part with the *Mercians,* but in the fight withdrew his
Forces, and in a safe place expected the event: with which
10 unseasonable retreat, the *Mercians* perhaps terrifi'd and misdoubting more danger, fled; thir Commanders, with *Penda*
himself, most being slain, among whom *Edilhere* the Brother of *Anna,* who rul'd after him the *East-Angles,* and was
the Author of this War; many more flying were drown'd in
15 the River, which *Beda* calls *winved,* then swoln above his
Banks. The Death of *Penda,* who had bin the Death of so   *Mat West.*
many good Kings, made generall rejoicing, as the Song witness'd. At the River *Winwed, Anna* was aveng'd. To *Edel-*
here succeeded *Ethelwald* his Brother, in the *East-Angles;* to
20 *Sigebert* in the *East-Saxons, Suidhelm* the Son of *Sexbald,*
saith *Bede,* the Brother of *Sigebert,* saith *Malmsbury;* he was   *Bed. l. 3. c. 22.*
baptiz'd by *Kedda,* then residing in the *East-Angles,* and by
Ethelwald the King, receav'd out of the Font. But *Oswi* in
the strength of his late Victory, within three years after sub-   658.
25 du'd all *Mercia,* and of the Pictish Nation greatest part, at   *Sax. an.*
which time he gave to *Peada* his Son in Law the Kingdome
of *South-Mercia,* divided from the Northern by *Trent.* But   659.
Peada the Spring following, as was said, by the Treason of   *Sax. an.*

his Wife the Daughter of *Oswi,* married by him for a special Christian, on the Feast of *Easter,* not protected by the holy time, was slain. The *Mercian* Nobles, *Immin, Eaba,* and *Eadbert,* throwing off the Government of *Oswi,* set up *Wul-*
5 *fer* the other Son of *Penda* to be thir King, whom till then they had kept hid, and with him adherd to the Christian Faith. *Kenwalk* the *West-Saxon,* now settl'd at home, and desirous to enlarge his Dominion, prepares against the *Britans,* joins Battel with them at *Pen* in *Somersetshire,* and over
10 coming persues them to *Pedridan.* Another fight he had with them before, at a place call'd *Witgeornesbrug,* barely mention'd by the Monk of *Malmsbury.* Nor was it long ere he fell at variance with *Wulfer* the Son of *Penda,* his old Enemy, scarce yet warm in his Throne, fought with him at
15 *Possentesburg,* on the *Easter* Holy-days, and as *Ethelwerd* saith, took his Prisner; but the *Saxon* Annals, quite otherwise, that *Wulfer* winning the field, wasted the *West-Saxon* Country as far as *Eskesdun;* nor staying there, took and wasted the Ile of *Wight,* but causing the Inhabitants to be
20 baptiz'd, till then unbeleevers, gave the Iland to *Ethelwald* King of *South-Saxons,* whom he had receav'd out of the Font. The year 664. a Synod of Scotish and English Bishops, in the presence of *Oswi* and *Alfred* his Son, was held at a Monastery in those parts, to debate on what Day *Easter*
25 should be kept; a controversie which long before had disturb'd the Greek and Latin Churches: wherin the Scots not agreeing with the way of *Rome,* nor yeilding to the disputants on that side, to whom the King most enclin'd, such as

661.
Sax. an.

664.
Bed.

were Bishops heer, resign'd, and return'd home with thir
Disciples. Another clerical question was there also much con-
troverted, not so superstitious in my opinion as ridiculous,
about the right shaving of crowns. The same year was seen
5 an Eclips of the Sun in *May,* followed by a sore pestilence
beginning in the South, but spreading to the North, and over
all *Ireland* with great mortality. In which time the *East-* *Malms.*
Saxons after *Swithelms* Decease, being govern'd by *Siger*
the Son of *Sigebert* the small, and *Sebbi* of *Seward,* though
10 both subject to the *Mercians.* *Siger* and his people unstedie
of Faith, supposing that this Plague was come upon them
for renouncing thir old Religion, fell off the second time to
Infidelity. Which the *Mercian* King *Wulfer* understanding,
sent *Jarumannus* a Faithfull Bishop, who with other his fel-
15 low Labourers, by sound Doctrin and gentle dealing, soon
recur'd them of thir second relaps. In *Kent, Ercombert* expiring, was succeeded by his Son *Ecbert.* In whose fowrth   668.
year, by means of *Theodore,* a learned Greekish Monk of   *Sax. ann.*
Tarsus, whom Pope *Vitalian* had ordain'd Archbishop of
20 *Canterbury,* the Greek and Latin Tongue, with other liberal
Arts, Arithmetic, Music, Astronomie, and the like; began
first to flourish among the *Saxons;* as did also the whole
Land, under potent and religious Kings, more then ever before, as *Bede* affirms, till his own days. Two years after, in   670.
25 *Northumberland* dy'd *Oswi,* much addicted to Romish   *Sax. an.*
Rites, and resolv'd, had his Disease releas'd him, to have
ended his days at *Rome: Ecfrid* the eldest of his Sons begot   673.
in Wedlock, succeeded him. After other three years, *Ecbert*   *Sax. an.*

in *Kent* deceasing, left nothing memorable behind him, but the general suspition to have slain or conniv'd at the slaughter of his Uncles two Sons, *Elbert,* and *Egelbright.* In recompence whereof, he gave to the Mother of them part of *Tanet,* wherein to build an Abbey; the Kingdom fell to his Brother *Lothair.* And much about this time, by best account it should be, however plac'd in *Beda,* that *Ecfrid* of *Northumberland,* having War with the *Mercian Wulfer,* won from him *Lindsey,* and the Country thereabout. *Sebbi* having reign'd over the *East-Saxons* 30 years, not long before his Death, though long before desireing, took on him the Habit of a Monk; and drew his Wife at length, though unwilling, to the same Devotion. *Kenwalk* also dying, left the Government to *Sexburga* his Wife, who out-liv'd him in it but one year, driv'n out, saith *Mat. West.* by the Nobles, disdaining Female Government. After whom several petty Kings, as *Beda* calls them, for ten years space divided the *West-Saxons;* others name two, *Escwin* the Nephew of *Kinigils,* and *Kentwin* the Son, not petty by thir deeds: for *Escwin* fought a Battell with *Wulfer,* at *Bedanhafde,* and about year after both deceas'd; but *Wulfer* not without a stain left behind him, of selling the Bishoprick of *London,* to *Wini* the first Simonist we read of in this story; *Kenwalk* had before expell'd him from his Chair at *Winchester; Ethelred* the Brother of *Wulfer* obtaining next the Kingdom of *Mercia,* not only recoverd *Lindsey,* and what besides in those parts *Wulfer* had lost to *Ecfrid* some years before, but found himself strong enough to extend his Armes another way, as far as *Kent,* wasting that Country without respect to

Malms.

Bed. l. 4.

674.
Bed. l. 4.
Sax. an.
Malms.
676.

Church or Monastery, much also endamaging the City of
Rochester: Notwithstanding what resistance *Lothair* could *Bed. l.* 4. *c.* 12.
make against him. In *August* 678. was seen a Morning Comet 678.
for 3 Months following, in manner of a fiery Pillar. And the
5 *South-Saxons* about this time were converted to the Christian
Faith, upon this occasion. *Wilfrid* Bishop of the *Northum-*
brians entring into contention with *Ecfrid* the King, was by
him depriv'd of his Bishoprick, and long wandring up and 679.
down as far as *Rome,* return'd at length into *England,* but not
10 dareing to approach the North, whence he was banish'd, be-
thought him where he might to best purpose elsewhere exercise his Ministery. The South of all other *Saxons* remain'd yet
Heathen; but *Edilwalk* thir King not long before had bin
baptiz'd in *Mercia,* persuaded by *Wulfer,* and by him, as hath
15 bin said, receav'd out of the Font. For which relations sake *Bed. l.* 4. *c.* 13.
he had the Ile of *Wight,* and a Province of the *Meannari* ad- *Camd.*
joining, giv'n him on the Continent about *Meanesborow* in
Hantshir, which *Wulfer* had a little before gott'n from *Ken-*
walk. Thether *Wilfrid* takes his journey, and with the help of
20 other Spiritual Labourers about him, in short time planted
there the Gospel. It had not rain'd, as is said, of three years
before in that Country, whence many of the people daily perish'd by Famin; till on the first day of thir public Baptism,
soft and plentifull showers descending, restor'd all abundance
25 to the Summer following. Two years after this, *Kentwin* the 681.
other *West-Saxon* King above-nam'd, chac'd the *Welch-Brit-* *Sax. an.*
ans, as is Chronicl'd without circumstance, to the very Sea
shoar. But in the year, by *Beda's* reck'ning, 683, *Kedwalla* a 683.
Sax. an.

West-Saxon of the Royal Line (whom the *Welch* will have to
be *Cadwallader,* last King of the *Britans*) thrown out by faction, return'd from banishment, and invaded both *Kentwin,*
if then living, or whoever else had divided the succession of
5 *Kenwalk,* slaying in fight *Edelwalk* the *South-Saxon,* who   *Bed. l. 4. c*
oppos'd him in their aid; but soon after was repuls'd by two of
his Captains, *Bertune,* and *Andune,* who for a while held the
province in thir power. But *Kedwalla* gathering new force,   *Malms.*
with the slaughter of *Bertune,* and also of *Edric* the successor   684.
10 of *Edelwalk,* won the Kingdom. But reduc'd the people to
heavy thraldome. Then addressing to Conquer the Ile of   *Bed. l. 4.*
Wight, till that time *Pagan,* saith *Beda* (others otherwise, as
above hath bin related) made a vow, though himself yet unbaptiz'd, to devote the fowrth part of that Iland, and the spoils
15 therof, to holy uses. Conquest obtain'd, paying his vow as
then was the beleef, he gave his fowrth to Bishop *Wilfrid,* by
chance there present; and he to *Bertwin* a Priest, his Sisters
Son, with commission to baptise all the vanquisht, who meant
to save thir lives. But the two young Sons of *Arwald,* King of
20 that Iland, met with much more hostility; for they at the Enemies approach flying out of the Ile, and betray'd where they
were hid not far from thence, were led to *Kedwalla,* who lay
then under Cure of some wounds receav'd, and by his appointment, after instruction and Baptism first giv'n them, harshly
25 put to death, which the youths are said above thir Age to have
Christianly sufferd. In *Kent, Lothair* dy'd this year of his
wounds receav'd in fight against the *South-Saxons,* led on by
Edric, who descending from *Ermenred,* it seems challeng'd

the Crown; and wore it, though not commendably, one year   685.
Malms.
and a half: but coming to a violent Death, left the land expos'd
a prey either to home-bred usurpers, or neighbouring invaders.
Among whom *Kedwalla,* taking advantage from thir civil
5 distempers, and marching easily through the *South-Saxons,*
whom he had subdu'd, sorely harrass'd the Country, untouch'd of a long time by any hostile incursion. But the *Kent-*
ish men, all parties uniteing against a common Enemy, with
joint powr so oppos'd him, that he was constrain'd to retire
10 back; his Brother *Mollo* in the flight with 12 men of his   *Sax. an.*
Malms.
Company, seeking shelter in a House, was beset and therin
burnt by the persuers: *Kedwalla* much troubl'd at so great a
loss, recalling and soon rallying his disorderd Forces, return'd
fiercely upon the chaseing Enemy; nor could be got out of the   686.
15 Province, till both by fire and Sword, he had aveng'd the
Death of his Brother. At length *Victred* the Son of *Ecbert,*   687.
attaining the Kingdome, both settl'd at home all things in
peace, and secur'd his Borders from all outward Hostility.
While thus *Kedwalla* disquieted both *West* and *East,* after   *Bed.*
20 his winning the Crown, *Ecfrid* the *Northumbrian,* and *Eth-*
elred the *Mercian,* fought a sore Battel by the River *Trent;*
wherin *Elfwin* Brother to *Ecfrid,* a youth of 18 years, much
belov'd, was slain; and the accident likely to occasion much
more sheding of blood, peace was happily made by the grave
25 exhortation of Archbishop *Theodore,* a pecuniary fine only
paid to *Ecfrid,* as some satisfaction for the loss of his Brothers
life. Another adversity befell *Ecfrid* in his Family, by means
of *Ethildrith* his Wife, King *Anna's* Daughter, who having

tak'n him for hir Husband, and professing to love him above
all other men, persisted twelve years in the obstinat refusal of
his bed, therby thinking to live the purer life. So perversly
then was chastity instructed against the Apostles rule. At
5 length obtaining of him with much importunity her departure, she veild her self a Nun, then made Abbess of *Ely,*
dy'd 7 years after the pestilence; and might with better war-
rant have kept faithfully her undertak'n Wedlock, though
now canoniz'd St. *Audrey* of *Ely.* In the mean while *Ecfrid*
10 had sent *Bertus* with a power to subdue *Ireland,* a harmless
Nation, saith *Beda,* and ever friendly to the English; in both
which they seem to have left a posterity much unlike them at
this day: miserably wasted, without regard had to places hallow'd or profane, they betook them partly to thir Weapons,
15 partly to implore divine aid; and, as was thought, obtain'd it
in thir full avengement upon *Ecfrid.* For he the next year,
against the mind and persuasion of his sagest friends, and especially of *Cudbert* a famous Bishop of that Age, marching
unadvisedly against the *Picts,* who long before had bin subject
20 to *Northumberland,* was by them feigning flight, drawn
unawares into narrow streights overtopt with Hills, and cut
off with most of his Army. From which time, saith *Bede,*
military valour began among the *Saxons* to decay, nor only
the *Picts* till then peaceable, but some part of the *Britans* also
25 recover'd by Armes thir liberty for many years after. Yet *Aldfrid* elder, but base Brother to *Ecfrid,* a man said to be learned
in the Scriptures, recall'd from *Ireland,* to which place in his
Brothers Reign he had retir'd, and now succeeding, upheld

with much honour, though in narrower bounds, the residue
of his Kingdome. *Kedwalla* having now with great disturbance of his Neighbours reign'd over the *West-Saxons* two
years, besides what time he spent in gaining it, wearied per-
5 haps with his own turbulence, went to *Rome,* desirous there to
receave Baptism, which till then his worldly affairs had deferr'd, and accordingly, on *Easter* Day, 689. he was baptiz'd
by *Sergius* the Pope, and his name chang'd to *Peter.* All which
notwithstanding, surpris'd with a Disease, he outliv'd not the
10 Ceremony so far sought, much above the space of 5 weeks, in
the Thirtieth year of his Age, and in the Church of St. *Peter*
was there buried, with a large Epitaph upon his Tomb. Him
succeeded *Ina* of the Royal Family, and from the time of his
coming in, for many years oppress'd the Land with like greev-
15 ances, as *Kedwalla* had done before him, insomuch that in
those times there was no Bishop among them. His first expedition was into *Kent,* to demand satisfaction for the burning
of *Mollo: Victred* loth to hazard all for the rash act of a few,
deliver'd up 30 of those that could be found accessory, or as
20 others say, pacifi'd *Ina* with a great sum of money. Mean
while, at the incitement of *Ecbert,* a devout Monk, *Wilbrod*
a Priest eminent for learning, past over Sea, having 12 others
in Company, with intent to preach the Gospel in *Germany.*
And coming to *Pepin* Cheif Regent of the *Franks,* who a little
25 before had conquer'd the hither *Frisia,* by his countnance and
protection, promise also of many benefits to them who should
beleeve, they found the work of conversion much the easier,
and *Wilbrod* the first Bishoprick in that Nation. But two

689.

Malms.
Sax. an.
Ethelwerd.
694.

Priests, each of them *Hewald* by name, and for distinction surnam'd from the colour of thir Hair, the black and the white, by his example, piously affected to the Souls of thir Country-men the old *Saxons,* at thir coming thether to con-
5 vert them met with much worse entertainment. For in the House of a Farmer who had promis'd to convey them, as they desir'd, to the Governour of that Country, discoverd by thir daily Ceremonies to be Christian Priests, and the cause of thir coming suspected, they were by him and his Heathen Neigh-
10 bours cruelly butcherd; yet not unaveng'd, for the Governour enrag'd at such violence offerd to his Strangers, sending Armed Men, slew all those Inhabitants, and burnt thir Village. After three years in *Mercia, Ostrid* the Queen, Wife to   697.
Ethelred, was kill'd by her own Nobles, as *Beda*'s Epitome
15 records; *Florence* calls them *Southimbrians,* negligently omit-   698.
ting the cause of so strange a fact. And the year following,
Bertred a *Northumbrian* General was slain by the *Picts. Eth-*
elred 7 years after the violent Death of his Queen, put on the   704.
Monk, and resign'd his Kingdome to *Kenred* the Son of
20 *Wulfer* his Brother. The next year, *Aldfrid* in *Northumber-*   705.
land dy'd, leaving *Osred* a Child of 8 years to succeed him.
Fowr years after which, *Kenred* having a while with praise   709.
govern'd the *Mercian* Kingdome, went to *Rome* in the time
of Pope *Constantine,* and shorn a Monk spent there the resi-
25 due of his daies. *Kelred* succeeded him, the Son of *Ethelred,*
who had reign'd the next before. With *Kenred* went *Offa* the
Son of *Siger,* King of *East-Saxons,* and betook him to the same
habit, leaving his Wife and Native Country; a comely Person

in the prime of his youth, much desir'd of the people; and such his vertue by report, as might have otherwise bin worthy to have reign'd. *Ina* the *West-Saxon* one year after fought a Battell, at first doubtfull, at last successfull, against *Gerent* King

5 of *Wales.* The next year *Bertfrid,* another *Northumbrian* Captain, fought with the *Picts,* and slaughterd them, saith *Huntingdon,* to the full avengment of *Ecfrids* Death. The fowrth year after, *Ina* had another doubtfull and cruell Battel at *Wodnesburg* in *Wiltshire,* with *Kelred* the *Mercian,* who

10 dy'd the year following a lamentable Death: for as he sat one day feasting with his Nobles, suddenly possess'd with an evill Spirit, he expir'd in despair, as *Boniface* Archbishop of *Ments,* an English man, who taxes him for a defiler of Nuns, writes by way of caution to *Ethelbald,* his next of Kin, who suc-

15 ceeded him. *Osred* also the young *Northumbrian* King, slain by his Kindred in the 11. of his Reign, for his vitious life and incest committed with Nuns; was by *Kenred* succeeded and aveng'd, he reigning two years left *Osric* in his room. In whose *7th* year, if *Beda* calculate right, *Victred* King of *Kent*

20 deceas'd, having reign'd 34 years, and some part of them with *Suebhard,* as *Beda* testifies. He left behind him three Sons, *Ethelbert, Eadbert,* and *Alric* his Heirs. Three years after which, appear'd two Comets about the Sun, terrible to behold, the one before him in the Morning, the other after him in the

25 Evening, for the space of two weeks in *January,* bending thir blaze toward the North, at which time the Saracens furiously invaded *France,* but were expell'd soon after with great overthrow. The same year in *Northumberland, Osric* dying or

710.
Sax. an.
Huntingd.
711.
Bed. Epit.

715.

Sax. an.
Sax. an.
Huntingd.
716.

718.

L. 5. c. 9.
725.
728.

Bed. l. 5. c. 24.

slain, adopted *Kelwulf* the Brother of *Kenred* his Successor, to whom *Beda* dedicates his story; but writes this only of him, that the beginning, and the process of his Reign met with many adverse commotions, wherof the event was then doubt-

5 fully expected. Mean while *Ina* 7 years before, having slain *Kenwulf,* to whom *Florent* gives the addition of *Clito,* giv'n usually to none but of the blood Royal, and the 4*th.* year after overthrown and slain *Albright* another *Clito,* driv'n from *Taunton* to the *South-Saxons* for aid, vanquish't also the *East-*

10 *Angles* in more then one Battel, as *Malmsbury* writes, but not the year, whether to expiate so much blood, or infected with the contagious humour of those times, *Malmsbury* saith, at the persuasion of *Ethelburga* his Wife, went to *Rome,* and there ended his dayes; yet this praise left behind him, to have made

15 good Laws, the first of *Saxon* that remain extant to this day, and to his Kinsman *Edelard,* bequeath'd the Crown; No less then the whole Monarchy of *England* and *Wales.* For *Ina,* if we beleeve a digression in the Laws of *Edward* Confessor, was the first King Crown'd of English and British, since the *Sax-*

20 *ons* entrance; of the British by means of his second Wife, some way related to *Cadwallader* last King of *Wales,* which I had not noted being unlikely, but for the place where I found it. After *Ina,* by a surer Author, *Ethelbald* King of *Mercia* Bede. commanded all the Provinces on this side *Humber,* with thir   731.

25 Kings: the *Picts* were in league with the English, the *Scots* peaceable within thir bounds, and the *Britans* part were in thir own Goverment, part subject to the English. In which peacefull state of the land, many in *Northumberland,* both

Nobles and Commons, laying aside the exercise of Armes, betook them to the Cloister: and not content so to do at home,
many in the days of *Ina,* Clerks and Laics, Men and Woemen,
hasting to *Rome* in Herds, thought themselves no where sure
5 of Eternal Life, till they were Cloisterd there. Thus representing the state of things in this Iland, *Beda* surceas'd to write.
Out of whom cheifly hath bin gatherd, since the *Saxons* arrival, such as hath bin deliverd, a scatterd story pickt out heer
and there, with some trouble and tedious work from among
10 his many Legends of Visions and Miracles; towards the latter
end so bare of civill matters, as what can be thence collected
may seem a Calendar rather than a History, tak'n up for the
most part with succession of Kings, and computation of years,
yet those hard to be reconcil'd with the *Saxon Annals.* Thir
15 actions we read of, were most commonly Wars, but for what
cause wag'd, or by what Councells carried on, no care was
had to let us know: wherby thir strength and violence we understand, of thir wisedom, reason, or justice, little or nothing,
the rest superstition and monastical affectation; Kings one
20 after another leaving thir Kingly Charge, to run thir heads
fondly into a Monks Cowle: which leaves us uncertain, whether
Beda was wanting to his matter, or his matter to him. Yet
from hence to the *Danish* Invasion it will be worse with us,
destitute of *Beda.* Left only to obscure and blockish Chron-
25 icles; whom *Malmsbury,* and *Huntingdon,* (for neither they
then we had better Authors of those times) ambitious to
adorn the History, make no scruple oft-times, I doubt to inter-
line with conjectures and surmises of thir own: them rather

then imitate, I shall choose to represent the truth naked, though as lean as a plain Journal. Yet *William* of *Malmsbury* must be acknowledg'd, both for stile and judgment, to be by far the best Writer of them all: but what labour is to be en-

5 dur'd, turning over Volumes of Rubbish in the rest, *Florence* of *Worster, Huntingdon, Simeon* of *Durham, Hoveden, Mathew* of *Westminster,* and many others of obscurer note, with all thir monachisms, is a penance to think. Yet these are our only Registers, transcribers one after another for the most

10 part, and somtimes worthy enough for the things they regis- ter. This travail rather then not know at once what may be known of our antient story, sifted from Fables and imperti- nences, I voluntarily undergo; and to save others, if they please the like unpleasing labour; except those who take pleas-

15 ure to be all thir life time, rakeing in the Foundations of old Abbies and Cathedrals; but to my task now as it befalls. In the year 733. on the 18*th.* Kalends of *September,* was an Eclipse of the Sun about the third howr of day, obscureing almost his whole Orb as with a black sheild. *Ethelbald* of

20 *Mercia,* beseig'd and took the Castle or Town of *Somerton:* and two years after, *Beda* our Historian dy'd, some say the year before. *Kelwulf* in *Northumberland* three years after became Monk in *Lindisfarne,* yet none of the severest, for he brought those Monks from milk and water, to Wine and Ale;

25 in which doctrin no doubt but they were soon docil, and well might, for *Kelwulf* brought with him good provision, great treasure and revenues of land, recited by *Simeon,* yet all under pretense of following (I use the Authors words) poor *Christ,*

733.
Sax. an.
Ethelwer

735.
738.
Malms.

by voluntary poverty: no marvel then if such applause were
giv'n by Monkish Writers to Kings turning Monks, and much
cunning perhaps us'd to allure them. To *Eadbert* his Unkle's
Son, he left the Kingdom, whose brother *Ecbert,* Archbishop
5 of *York* built a Library there. But two years after, while *Eadbert* was busied in War against the *Picts, Ethelbald* the *Mercian,* by foul fraud, assaulted part of *Northumberland* in his
absence, as the supplement of *Beda's* Epitomy records. In the
West-Saxons, Edelard who succeeded *Ina,* having bin much
10 molested in the beginning of his Reign, with the Rebellion of
Oswald his Kinsman, who contended with him for the right
of succession, overcoming at last those troubles, dy'd in Peace
741, leaving *Cuthred* one of the same linage to succeed him:
who at first had much War with *Ethelbald* the *Mercian,* and
15 various success, but joyning with him in League two years
after, made War on the Welch: *Huntingdon* doubts not to
give them a great Victory. And *Simeon* reports another Battel fought between *Britans* and *Picts* the year ensueing. Now
was the Kingdome of *East-Saxons* drawing to a Period, for
20 *Sigeard* and *Senfred* the Sons of *Sebbi* having reign'd a while,
and after them young *Offa,* who soon quitted his Kingdome
to go to *Rome* with *Kenred,* as hath been said, the Goverment was conferr'd on *Selred* Son of *Sigebert* the good, who
having rul'd 38 years, came to a violent death; how or where-
25 fore, is not set down. After whom *Swithred* was the last King,
driv'n out by *Ecbert* the *West-Saxon:* but *London,* with the
Countries adjacent, obey'd the *Mercians* till they also were
dissolv'd. *Cuthred* had now reign'd about nine years, when

740.

741.
Malms.
Sax. an.
743.
Sim. Dun.

744.
Hoved.
Malms.

Sax. an.

746.

Kinric his Son a valiant young Prince, was in a military tu-   748.
mult slain by his own Souldiers. The same year *Eadbert* dying   *Sax. an.*
in *Kent,* his Brother *Edilbert* reign'd in his stead. But after two   *Huntin*
years, the other *Eadbert* in *Northumberland,* whose War with   750.
5 the *Picts* hath bin above-mention'd, made now such Progress
there, as to subdue *Kyle,* so saith the Auctarie of *Bede,* and
other Countries thereabout, to his dominion; While *Cuthred*
the *West-Saxon* had a fight with *Ethelhun,* one of his Nobles,
a stout Warrier, envi'd by him in some matter of the Com-
10 mon-wealth, as far as by the Latin of *Ethelwerd* can be under-   *Huntin*
stood (others interpret it Sedition) and with much ado over-   752.
coming, took *Ethelhun* for his valour into favour, by whom   *Camde*
faithfully serv'd in the twelf or thirteenth of his Reign, he
encounter'd in a set Battell with *Ethelbald* the Mercian at
15 *Beorford,* now *Burford* in *Oxfordshire;* one year after against   753.
the Welch, which was the last but one of his life. *Hunting-*
don, as his manner is to comment upon the annal Text,
makes a terrible description of that fight between *Cuthred*
and *Ethelbald,* and the Prowess of *Ethelhun,* at *Beorford,* but
20 so affectedly, and therfore suspiciously, that I hold it not
worth rehersal; and both in that and the latter conflict, gives
Victory to *Cuthred;* after whom *Sigebert,* uncertain by what   *Sax. an.*
right, his Kinsman, saith *Florent,* step'd into the Throne,   754.
whom hated for his cruelty and other evil doings, *Kimwulf*   *Malms.*
25 joining with most of the Nobility, dispossess'd of all but
Hamshir, that Province he lost also within a year, together   755.
with the love of all those who till then remain'd his adherents,
by slaying *Cumbran,* one of his Cheif Captains, who for a long

time had faithfully serv'd, and now disuaded him from in-   *Huntingd.*
Huntingd.
censing the people by such Tyrannical practices. Thence flying for safety into *Andreds* Wood, forsak'n of all, he was at
length slain by the Swineheard of *Cumbran* in revenge of his
5 Maister, and *Kinwulf* who had undoubted right to the Crown,
joyfully saluted King. The next year *Eadbert* the *Northum-*   756.
Camden.
brian joining forces with *Unust* King of the *Picts,* as *Simeon*
writes, beseig'd and took by surrender the City *Alcluith,* now
Dunbritton in *Lennox,* from the *Britans* of *Cumberland;* and
10 ten days after, the whole Army perishd about *Niwanbirig,* but
to tell us how, he forgetts. In *Mercia, Ethelbald* was slain, at   Camd.
757.
Sax. an.
Epit. Bed.
Sim. Dun.
a place call'd *Secandune,* now *Seckinton* in *Warwickshire,*
the year following, in a bloody fight against *Cuthred,* as
Huntingdon surmises, but *Cuthred* was dead two or three
15 years before; others write him murder'd in the night by his
own Guard, and the Treason, as some say, of *Beornred,* who
succeeded him; but ere many Months, was defeated and slain
by *Offa.* Yet *Ethelbald* seems not without cause, after a long
and prosperous Reign, to have fall'n by a violent Death; not
20 shameing on the vain confidence of his many Alms, to commit uncleanness with consecrated Nuns, besides Laic Adulteries, as the Arch-Bishop of *Ments* in a letter taxes him and
his Predecessor, and that by his example most of his Peers did
the like; which adulterous doings he foretold him were likely
25 to produce a slothfull off-spring, good for nothing but to be   758.
the ruin of that Kingdome, as it fell out not long after. The
next year *Osmund,* according to *Florence,* ruleing the *South-*
Saxons, and *Swithred* the *East, Eadbert* in *Northumberland,*

following the steps of his Predecessor, got him into a Monks *Sim. Du*
Hood; the more to be wonder'd, that having reign'd worth- *Eccles. L*
ily 21 years, with the love and high estimation of all, both at
home and abroad, able still to govern, and much entreated by
5 the Kings his Neighbours, not to lay down his charge; with
offer on that condition to yeild up to him part of thir own
Dominion, he could not be mov'd from his resolution, but relinquish'd his Regal Office to *Oswulf* his Son; who at the years   759.
end, though without just cause, was slain by his own Servants.
10 And the year after dy'd *Ethelbert,* Son of *Victred,* the second
of that name in *Kent.* After *Oswulf, Ethelwald,* otherwise   762.
call'd *Mollo,* was set up *King;* who in his third year had a   *Sim. Du*
great Battel at *Eldune,* by *Melros,* slew *Oswin* a great Lord, *Mat Wc*
rebelling, and gain'd the Victory. But the third year after,   765.
15 fell by the treachery of *Alcred,* who assum'd his place. The   *Sim. Du*
fowrth year after which, *Cataracta* an antient and fair City in   769.
Yorkeshire, was burnt by *Arnred* a certain Tyrant, who the
same year came to like end. And after five years more, *Alcred*   774.
the King depos'd and forsak'n of all his people, fled with a   *Sim. Du*
20 few, first to *Bebba,* a strong City of those parts, thence to
Kinot King of the *Picts. Ethelred* the Son of *Mollo,* was
crown'd in his stead. Mean while *Offa* the *Mercian,* growing
powerfull, had subdu'd a Neighbouring people by *Simeon,*
call'd *Hestings;* and fought successfully this year with *Alric*
25 King of *Kent,* at a place call'd *Ottanford:* the Annals also
speak of wondrous Serpents then seen in *Sussex.* Nor had
Kinwulf the *West-Saxon* giv'n small proof of his valour in
several Battels against the Welch heretofore; but this year

775. meeting with *Offa*, at a place call'd *Besington*, was put
to the worse, and *Offa* won the Town for which they contended. In *Northumberland*, *Ethelred* having caus'd three
of his Nobles, *Aldwulf*, *Kinwulf*, and *Ecca*, treacherously to
5 be slain by two other Peers, was himself the next year driv'n
into banishment, *Elfwald* the Son of *Oswulf* succeeding in
his place, yet not without civil broils; for in his second year
Osbald and *Ethelheard*, two Noblemen, raising Forces against
him, routed *Bearne* his General, and persueing, burnt him at
10 a place call'd *Seletune*. I am sensible how wearisom it may
likely be to read of so many bare and reasonless Actions, so
many names of Kings one after another, acting little more
then mute persons in a Scene: what would it be to have in-
serted the long Bead-roll of Archbishops, Bishops, Abbots,
15 Abbesses, and thir doeings, neither to Religion profitable, nor
to morality, swelling my Authors each to a voluminous
body, by me studiously omitted; and left as their propriety,
who have a mind to write the Ecclesiastical matters of those
Ages; neither do I care to wrincle the smoothness of History
20 with rugged names of places unknown, better harp'd at in
Camden, and other Chorographers. Six years therfore pass'd
over in silence, as wholely of such Argument, bring us to
relate next the unfortunate end of *Kinwulf* the *West-Saxon;*
who having laudably reign'd about 31 years, yet suspecting
25 that *Kineard* Brother of *Sigebert* the former King, intended
to usurp the Crown after his Decease, or revenge his Brothers
expulsion, had commanded him into banishment; but he
lurking heer and there on the borders with a small Company,

775.
Sax. an.
778.
Sim. Dun.

780.
Sim. Dun.

786.
Ethelwerd.
Malms.

Sax. ann.

having had intelligence that *Kenwulf* was in the Country *Camd.*
thereabout, at *Merantun,* or *Merton* in *Surrey,* at the House
of a Woeman whom he lov'd, went by night and beset the
place. *Kenwulf* over-confident either of his Royal presence,
5 or personal valour, issuing forth with the few about him, runs
feirsly at *Kineard,* and wounds him sore, but by his followers hem'd in, is kill'd among them. The report of so great
an accident soon running to a place not far off, where many
more attendants awaited the Kings return, *Osric* and *Wivert,*
10 two Earles hasted with a great number to the House, where
Kineard and his fellows yet remain'd. He seeing himself
surrounded, with fair words and promise of great guifts, attempted to appease them; but those rejected with disdain,
fights it out to the last, and is slain with all but one or two of
15 his retinue, which were nigh a hunderd. *Kinwulf* was succeeded by *Birthric,* being both descended of *Kerdic* the
Founder of that Kingdome. Not better was the end of *Elf-*   *788.*
wald in *Northumberland,* two years after slain miserably by   *Sim. Du*
the conspiracy of *Siggan,* one of his Nobles, others say of the   *Malms.*
20 whole people at *Scilcester* by the Roman Wall; yet undeserv-
edly, as his Sepulchre at *Hagustald,* now *Hexham* upon *Tine,*   *Camd.*
and some miracles there said to be done, are alleg'd to witness;
and *Siggan* 5 years after laid violent hands on himself. *Osred*   *Malms.*
Son of *Alcred* advanc't into the room of *Elfwald,* and within
25 one year driv'n out, left his seat vacant to *Ethelred* Son of
Mollo, who after ten years of banishment (impris'nment,
saith *Alcuin*) had the Scepter put again into his hand. The   *Sim. Du*
third year of *Birthric* King of *West-Saxons,* gave beginning   *789.*

from abroad to a new and fatal revolution of calamity on this
Land. For three Danish Ships, the first that had bin seen heer
of that Nation arriving in the West, to visit these, as was suppos'd, Foren Merchants, the Kings gatherer of Customes tak-
5 ing Horse from *Dorchester,* found them Spies and Enemies.
For being commanded to come and give account of thir lade-
ing at the Kings Custome House, they slew him and all who
came with him; as an earnest of the many slaughters, rapines,
and hostilities, which they return'd not long after to commit *Pontan. L. 3.*
10 over all the Iland. Of this Danish first arrival, and on a sudden worse then hostile Aggression, the Danish History far
otherwise relates, as if thir landing had bin at the mouth of
Humber, and thir spoilfull march far into the Country;
though soon repelld by the Inhabitants, they hasted back as fast
15 to thir Ships: But from what cause, what reason of state, what
Authority or publick counsell the invasion proceeded, makes
not mention, and our wonder yet the more, by telling us that
Sigefrid then King in *Denmarke,* and long after, was a man
studious more of peace and quiet then of warlike matters.
20 These therefore seem rather to have bin some wanderers at *Pontan. L. 4.*
Sea, who with publick Commission, or without, through love
of spoil, or hatred of Christianity, seeking booties on any land
of Christians, came by chance or weather on this shore. The 790.
next year *Osred* in *Northumberland,* who driv'n out by his *Sim. Dun.*
25 Nobles had giv'n place to *Ethelred,* was tak'n and forcibly
shav'n a Monk at *Yorke.* And the year after, *Oelf,* the *Oelf-* 791.
win, Sons of *Elfwald,* formerly King, were drawn by fair *Sim. Dun.*
promises from the principal Church of *Yorke,* and after by

command of *Ethelred,* cruelly put to Death at *Wonwaldre-mere,* a Village by the great Pool in *Lancashire,* now call'd *Winandermere.* Nor was the third year less bloody; for *Osred,* who not likeing a shav'n Crown, had desir'd banish-
5 ment and obtain'd it, returning from the Ile of *Man* with small Forces, at the secret but deceitfull call of certain Nobles, who by Oath had promis'd to assist him, was also tak'n, and by *Ethelred* dealt with in the same manner; who the better to avouch his Cruelties, therupon married *Elfled* the Daughter
10 of *Offa:* for in *Offa* was found as little Faith or mercy. He the same year having drawn to his Palace *Ethelbrite* King of *East-Angles,* with fair invitations to marry his Daughter, caus'd him to be there inhospitably beheaded, and his King-dome wrongfully seis'd, by the wicked counsel of his Wife,
15 saith *Mat. West.* annexing thereto a long unlikely Tale. For which violence and bloodshed to make attonement, with Fry-ers at lest, he bestows the reliques of St. *Alban,* in a shrine of Pearl and Gold. Far worse it far'd the next year with the reliques in *Lindisfarne;* where the *Danes* landing, pillag'd
20 that Monastery, and of Fryers kill'd some, carried away oth-ers Captive, sparing neither Preist nor Lay: which many strange thunders and fiery Dragons, with other impressions in the air seen frequently before, were judg'd to foresignifie. This year *Alric* third Son of *Victred* ended in *Kent* his long
25 Reign of 34 years: with him ended the race of *Hengist:* thenceforth whomsoever wealth or faction advanc'd, took on him the name and state of a King. The *Saxon Annals* of 784. name *Ealmund* then reigning in *Kent;* but that consists not

Camden.
792.
Sim. Dun
Sim. Dun
Eccles. L.

793.
Sim. Dun

with the time of *Alric,* and I find him no where else men-
tiond. The year following was remarkable for the Death of 794.
Malms.
Offa the *Mercian,* a strenuous and suttle King; he had much
intercourse with *Charles* the Great, at first enmity, to the in-
5 terdicting of commerce on either side, at length much amity
and firm League, as appears by the Letter of *Charles* himself
yet extant, procur'd by *Alcuin* a learned and prudent man,
though a Monk, whom the Kings of *England* in those days
had sent Orator into *France,* to maintain good correspondence
10 between them and *Charles* the Great. He granted, saith
Huntingdon, a perpetual tribute to the Pope out of every
House in his Kingdome; for yeilding perhaps to translate the *Asser. Men.*
Sim. Dun.
Primacy of *Canterbury* to *Lichfeild* in his own Dominion.
He drew a trench of wondrous length between *Mercia* and
15 the *British* Confines, from Sea to Sea. *Ecferth* the Son of *Offa,*
a Prince of great hope, who also had bin Crown'd 9 years before his Fathers Decease, restoring to the Church what his
Father had seis'd on: yet within fowr Months by a sickness
ended his Reign. And to *Kenulf* next in right of the same
20 Progeny bequeath'd his Kingdome. Mean while the *Danish*
Pirats who still wasted *Northumberland,* ventring on shoar
to spoil another Monastery at the mouth of the River *Don,*
were assail'd by the English, thir Cheif Captain slain on the
place; then returning to Sea, were most of them Ship-wrack'd;
25 others driv'n again on shoar, were put all to the Sword. *Simeon* attributes this thir punishment to the power of St. *Cudbert,* offended with them for the rifling of his Covent. Two 796.
Sim. Dun.
years after this, dy'd *Ethelred* twice King, but not exempted

at last from the fate of many his predecessors, miserably slain
by his people, some say deservedly, as not inconscious with
them who train'd *Osred* to his ruin. *Osbald* a Nobleman exalted to the Throne, and in less then a month, deserted and
5 expell'd, was forc'd to fly at last from *Lindisfarne* by Sea to
the *Pictish* King, and dy'd an Abbot. *Eardulf* whom *Ethelred*
six years before had commanded to be put to Death at *Ripun,*
before the Abbey-Gate, dead as was suppos'd, and with solemn
Dirge carried into the Church, after midnight found there
10 alive, I read not how, then banish'd, now recall'd, was in
Yorke created King. In *Kent, Ethelbert* or *Pren,* whom the
Annals call *Eadbright* (so different they often are one from
another, both in timeing and in nameing) by some means
having usurp'd regal power, after two years Reign contending
15 with *Kenulf* the *Mercian,* was by him tak'n Pris'ner, and soon
after, out of pious commiseration let go: but not receav'd of
his own, what became of him, *Malmsbury* leaves in doubt.
Simeon writes, that *Kenulf* commanded to put out his Eyes,
and lop off his hands; but whether the sentence were executed
20 or not, is left as much in doubt by his want of expression. The
second year after this, they in *Northumberland* who had con-   798.
spir'd against *Ethelred,* now also raising War against *Eardulf,*   *Sim. D*
under *Wada* thir Cheif Captain, after much havock on either
side at *Langho,* by *Whaley* in *Lancashire,* the Conspirators
25 at last flying, *Eardulf* return'd with Victory. The same year
London, with a great multitude of her Inhabitants, by a sudden fire was consum'd. The year 800. made way for great   800.
alteration in *England,* uniting her seaven Kingdoms into

one, by *Ecbert* the famous *West-Saxon;* him *Birthric* dying
Childless left next to reign, the only surviver of that linage,
descended from *Inegild* the Brother of King *Ina.* And accord- *Malms.*
ing to his Birth liberally bred, he began early from his youth to
5 give signal hopes of more then ordinary worth growing up
in him; which *Birthric* fearing, and with all his juster title to
the Crown, secretly sought his life, and *Ecbert* perceaving,
fled to *Offa* the *Mercian;* but he having married *Eadburg* his
Daughter to *Birthric,* easily gave ear to his Embassadors com- *Sax. an.*
10 ing to require *Ecbert;* he again put to his shifts, escap'd thence
into *France;* but after three years banishment there, which
perhaps contributed much to his education, *Charles* the Great
then reigning, he was call'd over by the publick voice (for
Birthric was newly dead) and with general applause created
15 King of *West-Saxons.* The same day *Ethelmund* at *Kinneres-*
ford, passing over with the *Worcestershire* men, was met by
Weolstan another Nobleman with those of *Wiltshire,* between whom happ'nd a great fray, wherin the *Wiltshire* men
overcame, but both Dukes were slain, no reason of thir quar-
20 rel writ'n; such bickerings to recount, met oft'n in these our
Writers, what more worth is it then to Chronicle the Wars of
Kites, or Crows, flocking and fighting in the Air? The year   801.
following, *Eardulf* the *Northumbrian,* leading forth an Army *Sim. Dun.*
against *Kenulf* the *Mercian,* for harboring certain of his Ene-
25 mies, by the diligent mediation of other Princes and Prelats,
Armes were laid aside, and amity soon sworn between them.
But *Eadburga* the Wife of *Birthric,* a woeman every way   *Malms. L. 2.*
wicked, in malice especially cruel, could not or car'd not to   *Asser.*
                                                               802.
                                                               Sim. Dun.

appease the general hatred justly conceiv'd against her; accustom'd in her Husbands days to accuse any whom she spighted; and not prevailing to his ruin, her practice was by poison secretly to contrive his Death. It fortun'd that the King
5 her Husband, lighting on a Cup which she had temperd, not for him, but for one of his great Favourites, whom she could not harm by accuseing, sip'd therof only, and in a while after still pineing away, ended his days; the favourite drinking deeper found speedier the operation. She fearing to be ques-
10 tiond for these facts, with what treasure she had, pass'd oversea to *Charles* the Great, whom with rich guifts coming to his presence, the Emperour courtly receav'd with this pleasant proposal: Choose *Eadburga,* which of us two thou wilt, me or my Son (for his Son stood by him) to be thy Husband. She
15 no dissembler of what she lik'd best, made easie answer. Were it in my choise, I should choose of the two your Son rather, as the younger man. To whom the Emperour between jest and earnest, hadst thou chosen me, I had bestow'd on thee my Son; but since thou hast chos'n him, thou shalt have
20 neither him nor me. Nevertheless he assign'd her a rich Monastery to dwell in as Abbess; for that life it may seem, she chose next to profess; but being a while after detected of unchastity, with one of her followers, she was commanded to depart thence; from that time wandring poorly up and down
25 with one Servant, in *Pavia* a City of *Italy,* she finish'd at last in beggery her shamefull life. In the year 805. *Cuthred,*   805.
whom *Kenulf* the *Mercian* had, instead of *Pren,* made King   *Malms.*
in *Kent,* having obscurely reign'd 8 years, decea'd. In *North-*   *Sax. ann.*

umberland, *Eardulf* the year following was driv'n out of his
Realm by *Alfwold*, who Reign'd two years in his room; after
whom *Eandred* Son of *Eardulf* 33 years; but I see not how this
can stand with the sequel of story out of better Authors: Much

5 less that which *Buchanan* relates, the year following, of *Acaius*
King of *Scots*, who having reign'd 32 years, and dying in 809,
had formerly aided (but in what year of his Reign tells not)
Hungus King of *Picts* with 10000 *Scots*, against *Athelstan* a
Saxon or English-man, then wasting the *Pictish* Borders; that

10 *Hungus* by the aid of those *Scots* and the help of St. *Andrew*
thir Patron, in a Vision by night, and the appearance of his
cross by day, routed the astonisht English, and slew *Athel-*
stan in fight. Who this *Athelstan* was, I believe no man knows;
Buchanan supposes him to have been some *Danish* Com-

15 mander, on whom King *Alured*, or *Alfred*, had bestow'd
Northumberland; but of this I find no footstep in our antient
Writers; and if any such thing were done in the time of *Al-*
fred, it must be little less then 100 years after; this *Athelstan*
therefore, and this great overthrow, seems rather to have bin

20 the fancy of some Legend then any warrantable Record. Mean
while *Ecbert,* having with much Prudence, Justice, and Clemency, a work of more then one year, establisht his Kingdome
and himself in the affections of his people, turns his first enterprise against the *Britans,* both them of *Cornwal* and those

25 beyond *Seavern,* subdueing both. In *Mercia, Kenulf* the 6th.
year after, having reign'd with great praise of his religious
mind and vertues both in Peace and War, deceas'd. His Son
Kenelm, a Child of seaven years, was committed to the care of

806.
Huntingd.
Sim. Dun.
808.
Mat. West.

809.

Sim. Dun.
813.
Sax. an.

819.
Sax. an.
Malms.

his Elder Sister *Quendrid;* who with a female ambition aspiring to the Crown, hir'd one who had the charge of his nurture, to murder him, led into a woody place upon pretence of hunting. The murder, as is reported, was miraculously reveal'd; but to tell how, by a Dove droping a writt'n note on the Altar at *Rome,* is a long story, told, though out of order, by *Malmsbury;* and under the year 821. by *Mat. West.* where I leave it to be sought by such as are more credulous then I wish my Readers. Only the note was to this purpose.

> *Low in a mead of Kine under a Thorn,*
> *Of head bereft li'th poor* Kenelm *King-born.*

Keolwulf the Brother of *Kenulf,* after one years Reign was driv'n out by one *Bernulf* an Usurper: who in his third year, uncertain whether invading or invaded, was by *Ecbert,* though with great loss on both sides, overthrown and put to flight at *Ellandune* or *Wilton:* yet *Malmsbury* accounts this Battel fought in 806, a wide difference, but frequently found in thir computations. *Bernulf* thence retireing to the *East-Angles,* as part of his Dominion by the late seisure of *Offa,* was by them met in the field and slain: but they doubting what the *Mercians* might do in revenge hereof, forthwith yielded themselves both King and people to the Sovrantie of *Ecbert.* As for the Kings of *East-Angles,* our Annals mention them not since *Ethelwald;* him succeeded his Brothers Sons, as we find in *Malmsbury, Aldulf* (a good King, well acquainted with *Bede*) and *Elwold* who left the Kingdome to *Beorn,* he to *Ethelred* the Father of *Ethelbrite,* whom *Offa*

820.
Ingulf.
823.
Sax. an.

Florent.
Genealog
Bed.
L. 2. c. 15

perfidiously put to Death. *Simeon* and *Hoveden,* in the year
749. write that *Elfwald* King of *East-Angles* dying, *Hum-
beanna* and *Albert* shar'd the Kingdom between them; but
where to insert this among the former successions is not easie,
5 nor much material: after *Ethelbrite,* none is nam'd of that
Kingdom till thir submitting now to *Ecbert:* he from this
Victory against *Bernulf* sent part of his Army under *Ethelwulf* his Son, with *Alstan* Bishop of *Shirburn,* and *Wulferd*
a Chief Commander, into *Kent.* Who finding *Baldred* there
10 reigning in his 18*th.* year, overcame and drove him over the
Thames; whereupon all *Kent, Surrey, Sussex,* and lastly *Essex,* with her King *Swithred,* became subject to the Dominion
of *Ecbert.* Neither were these all his exploits of this year, the
first in order set down in *Saxon Annals,* being his fight against
15 the *Devonshire Welch,* at a place call'd *Gafulford,* now
Camelford in *Cornwal. Ludiken* the *Mercian,* after two years   Camd.
preparing to avenge *Bernulf* his Kinsman on the *East-Angles,*   825.
Ingulf.
was by them with his five Consuls, as the Annals call them,
surpris'd and put to the Sword: and *Withlaf* his successor first
20 vanquisht, then upon submission with all *Mercia,* made tributary to *Ecbert.* Mean while the *Northumbrian* Kingdom of it
self was fall'n to shivers; thir Kings one after another so oft'n
slain by the people, no man dareing, though never so ambitious, to take up the Scepter which many had found so hot,
25 (the only effectual cure of ambition that I have read) for the
space of 33 years, after the Death of *Ethelred* Son of *Mollo,*
as *Malmsbury* writes, there was no King: many Noblemen
and Prelats were fled the Country. Which mis-rule among

them, the *Danes* having understood, oft-times from thir Ships
entring far into the land, infested those parts with wide de-
population, wasting Towns, Churches, and Monasteries, for
they were yet Heathen: The *Lent* before whose coming, on
5 the North-side of St. *Peters* Church in *Yorke,* was seen from
the roof to rain blood. The causes of these calamities, and the
ruin of that Kingdom, *Alcuin,* a learned Monk living in those
days, attributes in several Epistles, and well may, to the general ignorance and decay of lerning, which crept in among
10 them after the Death of *Beda,* and of *Ecbert* the Archbishop;
thir neglect of breeding up youth in the Scriptures, the spruce
and gay apparel of thir Preists and Nuns, discovering thir vain
and wanton minds, examples are also read, eev'n in *Beda*'s
days, of thir wanton deeds: thence Altars defil'd with per-
15 juries, Cloisters violated with Adulteries, the Land polluted
with blood of thir Princes, civil dissentions among the people,
and finally all the same vices which *Gildas* alleg'd of old to
have ruin'd the *Britans.* In this estate *Ecbert,* who had now
conquerd all the South, finding them in the year 827. (for he   827.
20 was march'd thether with an Army to compleat his Conquest
of the whole Iland) no wonder if they submitted themselves
to the yoke without resistance, *Eandred* thir King becoming
Tributary. Thence turning his forces the year following, he   828.
subdu'd more throughly what remain'd of *North-Wales.*   *Mat. Wes*

The End of the Fourth Book.

THE HISTORY OF BRITAIN.

THE FIFTH BOOK

THE summe of things in this Iland, or the best part
therof, reduc't now under the power of one man;
and him one of the worthiest, which, as far as can be
found in good Authors, was by none attain'd at any time heer
5 before unless in Fables; men might with some reason have
expected from such Union, peace and plenty, greatness, and
the flourishing of all Estates and Degrees: but far the contrary
fell out soon after, Invasion, Spoil, Desolation, slaughter of
many, slavery of the rest, by the forcible landing of a fierce
10 Nation; *Danes* commonly call'd, and somtimes *Dacians,* by
others, the same with *Normans;* as barbarous as the *Saxons*
themselves were at first reputed, and much more; for the
Saxons first invited came hither to dwell; these unsent for, un-   *Calvisius.*
provok'd, came only to destroy. But if the *Saxons,* as is above
15 related, came most of them from *Jutland* and *Anglen,* a part
of *Denmarke,* as *Danish* Writers affirm, and that *Danes* and
Normans are the same; then in this invasion, *Danes* drove out
Danes, thir own posterity. And *Normans* afterwards, none   *Pontan.*
but antienter *Normans.* Which invasion perhaps, had the   *hist. Dan.*
20 Heptarchie stood divided as it was, had either not bin attempted, or not uneasily resisted; while each Prince and
people, excited by thir neerest concernments, had more indus-
triously defended thir own bounds, then depending on the
neglect of a deputed Governour, sent oft-times from the re-

mote residence of a secure Monarch. Though as it fell out in those troubles, the lesser Kingdoms revolting from the *West-Saxon* yoke, and not aiding each other, too much concern'd with thir own safety, it came to no better pass; while severally they sought to repell the danger nigh at hand, rather then jointly to prevent it farre off. But when God hath decreed servitude on a sinful Nation, fitted by thir own vices for no condition but servile, all Estates of Government are alike unable to avoid it. God had purpos'd to punish our instrumental punishers, though now Christians, by other Heathen, according to his Divine retaliation; invasion for invasion, spoil for spoil, destruction for destruction. The *Saxons* were now full as wicked as the *Britans* were at their arrival, brok'n with luxurie and sloth, either secular or superstitious; for laying aside the exercise of Arms, and the study of all vertuous knowledge, some betook them to over-worldly or vitious practice, others to religious Idleness and Solitude, which brought forth nothing but vain and delusive visions; easily perceav'd such, by thir commanding of things, either not belonging to the Gospel, or utterly forbidden, Ceremonies, Reliques, Monasteries, Masses, Idols, add to these ostentation of Alms, got ofttimes by rapine and oppression, or intermixt with violent and lustfull deeds, sometimes prodigally bestow'd as the expiation of cruelty and bloodshed. What longer suffering could there be, when Religion it self grew so void of sincerity, and the greatest shews of purity were impur'd?

Ecbert.

ECBERT in full highth of glory, having now enjoy'd his Conquest seaven peacefull years, his victorious Army long since disbanded, and the exercise of Armes perhaps laid aside, the more was found unprovided against a sudden storm of *Danes* from the Sea, who landing in the 32. of his Reign, wasted *Shepey* in *Kent. Ecbert* the next year, gathering an Army, for he had heard of thir arrival in 35 Ships, gave them Battail by the River *Carr* in *Dorsetshire;* the event wherof was, that the *Danes* kept thir ground, and encampt where the field was fought; two *Saxon* Leaders, *Dudda* and *Osmund,* and two Bishops, as some say, were there slain. This was the only check of Fortune we read of, that *Ecbert* in all his time re-ceav'd. For the *Danes* returning two years after with a great Navy, and joining Forces with the *Cornish,* who had enterd League with them, were overthrown and put to flight. Of these invasions against *Ecbert,* the *Danish* History is not silent; whether out of thir own Records or ours, may be justly doubted; for of these times at home, I find them in much uncertainty, and beholding rather to Out-landish Chronicles then any Records of thir own. The Victor *Ecbert,* as one who had done enough, seasonably now, after prosperous success, the next year with glory ended his days, and was buried at *Winchester.*

832.
Sax. an.
833.
Sax. an.

835.
Sax. an.
Pontan. hist.
Dan. L. 4.

836.
Sax. an.

Ethelwolf.

ETHELWOLF the Son of *Ecbert* succeeded, by *Malms-bury* describ'd a man of mild nature, not inclin'd to War, or delighted with much Dominion; that therfore con-

tented with the antient *West-Saxon* bounds, he gave to *Ethel-*   *Mat. W*
stan his Brother, or Son, as some write, the Kingdome of
Kent and *Essex.* But the *Saxon* Annalist, whose Autority is
Elder, saith plainly, that both these Countries and *Sussex,*
5 were bequeath'd to *Ethelstan* by *Ecbert* his Father. The un-
warlike disposition of *Ethelwolf,* gave encouragement no
doubt, and easier entrance to the *Danes,* who came again the
next year with 33 Ships; but *Wulfheard,* one of the Kings   837.
Sax. an
Chief Captains, drove them back at *Southamton* with great
10 slaughter; himself dying the same year, of Age, as I suppose,
for he seems to have bin one of *Ecberts* old Commanders,
who was sent with *Ethelwolf* to subdue *Kent. Ethelhelm*
another of the Kings Captains with the *Dorsetshire* men, had
at first like success against the *Danes* at *Portsmouth;* but they
15 reinforcing stood thir ground, and put the English to rout.
Worse was the success of Earl *Herebert* at a place call'd *Meres-*
war, slain with the most part of his Army. The year following
in *Lindsey* also, *East-Angles,* and *Kent,* much mischief was   838.
Sax. an
839.
don by thir landing; where the next year, embold'nd by suc-   *Sax. an*
20 cess, they came on as far as *Canterbury, Rochester,* and *Lon-*
don it self, with no less cruel hostility: and giving no respit to
the peaceable mind of *Ethelwolf,* they yet return'd with the
next year in 35 Ships, fought with him, as before with his   840.
Sax. an
Father, at the River *Carr,* and made good thir ground. In   *Sim. D*
25 *Northumberland, Eandred* the Tributary King deceasing, left   *Mat. W*
844.
the same tenure to his Son *Ethelred* driv'n out in his fowrth
year, and succeeded by *Readwulf,* who soon after his Coronation hasting forth to Battel against the *Danes* at *Alvetheli,*

fell with the most part of his Army; and *Ethelred* like in fortune to the former *Ethelred,* was re-exalted to his Seat. And
to be yet further like him in Fate, was slain the fowrth year
after. *Osbert* succeeded in his room. But more southerly, the
5 *Danes* next year after met with some stop in the full course of
thir outragious insolences. For *Earnulf* with the men of *Somerset, Alstan* the Bishop, and *Osric* with those of *Dorsetshire,*
setting upon them at the Rivers mouth of *Pedridan,* slaughterd them in great numbers, and obtain'd a just Victory. This
10 repulse queld them, for ought we hear, the space of six years;
Then also renewing thir invasion with little better success.
For *Keorle* an Earl, aided with the Forces of *Devonshire,*
assaulted and over-threw them at *Wigganbeorch* with great
destruction; as prosperously were they fought with the same
15 year at *Sandwich,* by King *Ethelstan,* and *Ealker* his General,
thir great Army defeated, and nine of thir Ships tak'n, the rest
driv'n off, however to ride out the Winter on that shoar, *Asser*
saith, they then first winter'd in *Shepey Ile.* Hard it is, through
the bad expression of these Writers, to define this fight,
20 whether by Sea or Land; *Hoveden* terms it a Sea fight. Nevertheless with 50 Ships (*Asser* and others add 300) they enterd
the mouth of *Thames,* and made excursions as far as *Canterbury* and *London,* and as *Ethelwerd* writes, destroy'd both;
of *London, Asser* signifies only that they pillag'd it. *Bertulf*
25 also the *Mercian,* successor of *Withlaf,* with all his Army they
forc'd to fly, and him beyond the Sea. Then passing over
Thames with thir powers into *Surrey,* and the *West-Saxons,*
and meeting there with King *Ethelwolf* and *Ethelbald* his

845.
Sax. an.

851.
Sax. an.
Asser.

Huntingd.
Mat West.

Son, at a place call'd *Ak-Lea,* or *Oak-Lea,* they receav'd a total
defeat with memorable slaughter. This was counted a lucky
year to *England,* and brought to *Ethelwolf* great reputation.
Burhed therfore, who after *Bertulf* held of him the *Mercian*
5 Kingdom, two years after this, imploring his aid against the
North-Welch, as then troublesome to his Confines, obtain'd
it of him in person, and therby reduc'd them to obedience.
This done, *Ethelwolf* sent his Son *Alfrid* a Child of five years,
well accompanied to *Rome,* whom *Leo* the Pope both conse-
10 crated to be King afterward, and adopted to be his Son; at
home *Ealker* with the Forces of *Kent,* and *Huda* with those
of *Surrey,* fell on the *Danes* at thir landing in *Tanet,* and at
first put them back; but the slain and drown'd were at length
so many on either side, as left the loss equal on both: which
15 yet hinderd not the solemnity of a marriage at the feast of
Easter, between *Burhed* the *Mercian,* and *Ethelswida* King
Ethelwolf's Daughter. Howbeit the *Danes* next year winterd
again in *Shepey.* Whom *Ethelwolf* not finding human health
sufficient to resist, growing daily upon him, in hope of divine
20 aid, registerd in a Book, and dedicated to God the tenth part
of his own lands, and of his whole Kingdome, eas'd of all
impositions, but converted to the maintenance of Masses and
Psalms weekly to be sung for the prospering of *Ethelwolf* and
his Captains, as appears at large by the Patent it self, in *Wil-*
25 liam of *Malmsbury. Asser* saith, he did it for the redemtion
of his Soul and the Soul of his Ancestors. After which, as
having done some great matter to shew himself at *Rome,* and
be applauded of the Pope; he takes a long and cumbersome

853.
*Sax. an.
Asser.*

Malms.
854.
Sax. an.

journey thether with young *Alfrid* again, and there staies a   855.
year, when his place requir'd him rather heer in the field   *Asser.*
against Pagan Enemies left wintring in his land. Yet so much
manhood he had, as to return thence no Monk; and in his way
5 home took to Wife *Judith* Daughter of *Charles* the bald, King
of *France*. But ere his return, *Ethelbald* his eldest Son, *Alstan*   *Asser.*
his trusty Bishop, and *Enulf* Earl of *Somerset* conspir'd
against him; thir complaints were, that he had tak'n with
him *Alfrid* his youngest Son to be there inaugurated King,
10 and brought home with him an out-landish Wife; for which
they endeavourd to deprive him of his Kingdom. The disturbance was expected to bring forth nothing less then War:
but the King abhorring civil discord, after many conferences
tending to peace, condescended to divide the Kingdom with
15 his Son; division was made, but the matter so carried, that the
Eastern and worst part was malignly afforded to the Father:
The Western and best giv'n to the Son, at which many of the
Nobles had great indignation, offring to the King thir utmost
assistance for the recovery of all; whom he peacefully dissuad-
20 ing, sat down contented with his portion assign'd. In the
East-Angles, Edmund lineal from the antient stock of those
Kings, a youth of 14 years only, but of great hopes, was with
consent of all but his own Crown'd at *Burie*. About this time,   857.
as *Buchanan* relates, the *Picts,* who not long before had by
25 the *Scots* bin driv'n out of thir Countrey, part of them coming to *Osbert* and *Ella,* then Kings of *Northumberland,* obtain'd aid against *Donaldus* the *Scotish* King, to recover thir
antient possession. *Osbert* who in person undertook the expe-

dition, marching into *Scotland,* was at first put to a retreat;
but returning soon after on the *Scots,* over-secure of thir suppos'd Victory, put them to flight with great slaughter, took
Pris'ner thir King, and persu'd his Victory beyond *Sterlin-*
5 *bridge.* The *Scots* unable to resist longer, and by Embassadors
entreating peace, had it granted them on these conditions:
the *Scots* were to quit all they had possess'd within the Wall
of *Severus:* the limits of *Scotland* were beneath *Sterlinbridge*
to be the River *Forth,* and on the other side, *Dunbritton*
10 *Frith;* from that time so call'd of the *Brittish* then seated in
Cumberland, who had joind with *Osbert* in this Action, and
so far extended on that side the *Brittish* limits. If this be true,
as the *Scotch* Writers themselv's witness (and who would think
them Fabulous to the disparagement of thir own Country?)
15 how much wanting have bin our Historians to thir Countries
Honour, in leting pass unmention'd an exploit so memorable,
by them rememberd and attested, who are wont ofter to ex-
tenuate then to amplifie aught done in *Scotland* by the English? *Donaldus* on these conditions releas't, soon after dyes;
20 according to *Buchanan,* in 858. *Ethelwolf* Chief King in
England, had the year before ended his life, and was buried as
his Father at *Winchester.* He was from his youth much ad-   *Mat. W*
dicted to devotion; so that in his Fathers time he was ordain'd
Bishop of *Winchester;* and unwillingly, for want of other
25 Legitimate Issue, succeeded him in the Throne; mannaging
therfore his greatest affairs by the activity of two Bishops,
Alstan of *Sherburne,* and *Swithine* of *Winchester.* But *Alstan*   *Malms.*
is noted of Covetousness and Oppression, by *William* of

Malmsbury; the more vehemently no doubt for doing some
notable damage to that Monastery. The same Author writes,   *Sigon. de*
that *Ethelwolf* at *Rome,* paid a Tribute to the Pope, continu'd   *regn. Ital.*
to his dayes. However he were facil to his Son, and seditious   *L. 5.*
5 Nobles, in yeilding up part of his Kingdome, yet his Queen
he treated not the less honourably, for whomsoever it displeas'd. The *West-Saxons* had decreed ever since the time of   *Asser.*
Eadburga, the infamous Wife of *Birthric,* that no Queen
should sit in State with the King, or be dignifi'd with the
10 Title of Queen. But *Ethelwolf* permitted not that *Judith* his
Queen should loose any point of Regal State by that Law.
At his Death, he divided the Kingdom between his two Sons,
Ethelbald, and *Ethelbert;* to the younger *Kent, Essex, Surrey,*
Sussex, to the Elder all the rest; to *Peter* and *Paul* certain
15 revenues yearly, for what uses let others relate, who write also
his Pedigree, from Son to Father, up to *Adam.*

Ethelbald, and *Ethelbert.*

E THELBALD, unnatural and disloyal to his Father, fell   *Asser.*
  justly into another, though contrary sin, of too much   *Malms.*
                                                          Sim. Dun.
20 love to his Fathers Wife; and whom at first he oppos'd coming into the Land, her now unlawfully marrying, he takes
into his Bed; but not long enjoying, dy'd at three years end,
without doing aught more worthy to be rememberd; having   860.
reign'd two years with his Father, impiously usurping, and   *Sax. an.*
25 three after him, as unworthily inheriting. And his hap was all
that while to be unmolested by the *Danes;* not of Divine favour doubtless, but to his greater condemnation, living the

more securely his incestuous life. *Huntingdon* on the other
side much praises *Ethelbald,* and writes him buried at *Sherburn,* with great sorrow of the people, who miss'd him long
after. *Mat. West.* saith, that he repented of his incest with
5 *Judith,* and dismiss'd her: but *Asser* an Eye witness of those
times, mentions no such thing.

Ethelbert alone.

ETHELBALD by Death remov'd, the whole Kingdom
came rightfully to *Ethelbert* his next Brother. Who
10 though a Prince of great Vertue and no blame, had as short a
Reign allotted him as his faulty Brother, nor that so peacefull;
once or twice invaded by the *Danes.* But they having landed
in the West with a great Army, and sackt *Winchester,* were
met by *Osric* Earl of *Southampton,* and *Ethelwolf* of *Bark-
15 shire,* beat'n to thir Ships, and forc't to leave thir booty. Five
years after, about the time of his Death, they sat foot again in
Tanet; the Kentish men wearied out with so frequent Alarms,
came to agreement with them for a certain sum of money; but
ere the peace could be ratifi'd, and the money gatherd, the
20 *Danes* impatient of delay by a sudden eruption in the night,
soon wasted all the *East* of *Kent.* Mean while or something
before, *Ethelbert* deceasing was buried as his Brother at
Sherburne.

*855.
Sax. an.*

Ethelred.

25 ETHELRED the third, Son of *Ethelwolf,* at his first
coming to the Crown was entertain'd with a fresh invasion of *Danes,* led by *Hinguar* and *Hubba,* two Brothers, who

*866.
Sax. an.
Hunting*

now had got footing among the *East-Angles;* there they winterd, and coming to terms of peace with the Inhabitants, furnish'd themselves of Horses, forming by that means many Troops with Riders of thir own: These Pagans, *Asser* saith,

5 came from the River *Danubius.* Fitted thus for a long expe- 867.
dition, they ventur'd the next year to make thir way over land *Sax. an.*
and over *Humber,* as far as *Yorke,* them they found to thir hands imbroil'd in civil dissentions; thir King *Osbert* they had thrown out, and *Ella* Leader of another faction chosen in

10 his room; who both, though late, admonish'd by thir com-
mon danger, towards the years end with united powers made head against the *Danes* and prevail'd; but persueing them over-eagerly into *Yorke,* then but slenderly wall'd, the *North-* *Asser.*
umbrians were every where slaughter'd, both within and

15 without; thir Kings also both slain, thir City burnt, saith
Malmsbury, the rest as they could, made thir peace, over-run and vanquisht as far as the River *Tine,* and *Egbert* of English race appointed King over them. *Bromton* no antient Author (for he wrote since *Mat. West.*) nor of much credit, writes a

20 particular cause of the *Danes* coming to *Yorke:* that *Bruern* a
Nobleman, whose Wife King *Osbert* had ravisht, call'd in *Hinguar* and *Hubba* to revenge him. The example is remark-able if the truth were as evident. Thence victorious, the *Danes* 868.
next year enterd into *Mercia* towards *Nottingham,* where they

25 spent the Winter. *Burhed* then King of that Country, unable
to resist, implores the aid of *Ethelred* and young *Alfred* his Brother, they assembling thir Forces and joining with the *Mercians* about *Nottingham,* offer Battel: the *Danes* not dar- *Asser.*

ing to come forth, kept themselves within that Town and
Castle, so that no great fight was hazarded there; at length
the *Mercians* weary of long suspence, enterd into conditions
of peace with thir Enemies. After which the *Danes* returning
5 back to *Yorke,* made thir abode there the space of one year,
committing, some say, many cruelties. Thence imbarking to
Lindsey, and all the Summer destroying that Country, about
September they came with like fury into *Kesteven,* another
part of *Lincolnshire,* where *Algar* the Earl of *Howland* now
10 *Holland,* with his Forces, and two hunderd stout Souldiers
belonging to the Abbey of *Croiland,* three hunderd from
about *Boston, Morcard* Lord of *Brunne,* with his numerous
Family, well train'd and arm'd: *Osgot* Governour of *Lincoln*
with 500. of that City, all joyning together, gave Battel to the
15 *Danes,* slew of them a great multitude, with three of thir
Kings, and persu'd the rest to thir Tents; but the night following, *Gothrun, Baseg, Osketil, Halfden,* and *Hamond,*
five Kings, and as many Earls, *Frena, Hinguar, Hubba,*
Sidroc the Elder and Younger, coming in from several parts
20 with great forces and spoils, great part of the English began
to slink home. Nevertheless *Algar* with such as forsook him
not, all next day in order of Battel facing the *Danes,* and sus-
taining unmov'd the brunt of thir assaults, could not with-
hold his men at last from persueing thir counterfitted fight;
25 wherby op'nd and disorder'd, they fell into the snare of thir
Enemies, rushing back upon them. *Algar* and those Captains
fore-nam'd with him, all resolute men, retreating to a hill
side, and slaying of such as follow'd them, manifold thir own

869.
Sim. Dun

870.
Ingulf.

number, dy'd at length upon heaps of dead which they had
made round about them. The *Danes* thence passing on into
the Country of *East-Angles,* rifl'd and burnt the Monastery
of *Elie,* overthrew Earl *Wulketul* with his whole Army, and
5 lodg'd out the Winter at *Thetford;* where King *Edmund*
assailing them, was with his whole Army put to flight, himself tak'n, bound to a stake, and shot to Death with Arrows,
his whole Country subdu'd. The next year with great supplies, 871.
Sax. an.
saith *Huntingdon,* bending thir march toward the *West-*
10 *Saxons,* the only people now left, in whom might seem yet to
remain strength or courage likely to oppose them, they came
to *Reading,* fortifi'd there between the two Rivers of *Thames,*
and *Kenet,* and about three dayes after, sent out wings of Horse
under two Earls to forage the Country; but *Ethelwulf* Earl of *Asser.*
15 *Barkshire,* at *Englefeild* a Village nigh, encounterd them,
slew one of thir Earls, and obtain'd a great Victory. Four
dayes after came the King himself and his Brother *Alfred*
with the main Battail; and the *Danes* issuing forth, a bloody
fight began, on either side great slaughter, in which Earl
20 *Ethelwulf* lost his life; but the *Danes* loosing no ground, kept
thir place of standing to the end. Neither did the English for
this make less hast to another conflict at *Escesdunc,* or *Ash-*
down, four dayes after, where both Armies with thir whole
force on either side met. The *Danes* were imbattail'd in two
25 great Bodies, the one led by *Bascai* and *Halfden,* thir two
Kings, the other by such Earls as were appointed; in like
manner the English divided thir powers, *Ethelred* the King
stood against their Kings; and though on the lower ground,

and coming later into the Battail from his orisons, gave a fierce onset, wherin *Bascai* (the *Danish* History names him *Ivarus* the Son of *Regnerus*) was slain. *Alfred* was plac'd against the Earls, and beginning the Battail ere his Brother came into the

5 field, with such resolution charg'd them, that in the shock most of them were slain; they are nam'd *Sidroc* Elder and Younger, *Osbern, Frean, Harald;* at length in both Divisions, the *Danes* turn thir backs; many thousands of them cut off, the rest persu'd till night. So much the more it may be won-

10 derd to hear next in the Annals, that the *Danes* 14 days after such an overthrow, fighting again with *Ethelred* and his Brother *Alfred* at *Basing,* under conduct, saith the *Danish* History, of *Agnerus* and *Hubbo,* Brothers of the slain *Ivarus,* should obtain the Victory; especially since the new supply of

15 *Danes* mention'd by *Asser,* arriv'd after this action. But after *Pontan.* two Months, the King and his Brother fought with them again *Dan. L.* at *Mertun,* in two Squadrons as before, in which fight hard it is to understand who had the better; so darkly do the *Saxon Annals* deliver thir meaning with more then wonted infancy.

20 Yet these I take (for *Asser* is heer silent) to be the Chief Foun- tain of our story, the ground and basis upon which the Monks later in time gloss and comment at thir pleasure. Nevertheless it appears, that on the *Saxon* part, not *Heamund* the Bishop only, but many valiant men lost thir lives. This fight was

25 follow'd by a heavy Summer Plague; wherof, as is thought, King *Ethelred* dy'd in the fifth of his Reign, and was buried *Camd.* at *Winburne,* where his Epitaph inscribes that he had his Deaths wound by the *Danes,* according to the *Danish* History

872. Of all these terrible landings and devastations by the *Danes,* from the days of *Ethelwolf* till thir two last Battels with *Ethelred,* or of thir Leaders, whether Kings, Dukes, or Earls, the *Danish* History of best credit saith nothing; So

5 little Wit or Conscience it seems they had to leave any memory of thir brutish, rather then manly actions; unless we shall suppose them to have come, as above was cited out of *Asser,* from *Danubius,* rather then from Denmarke, more probably some barbarous Nations of *Prussia,* or *Livonia,* not long before

10 seated more Northward on the *Baltic* Sea.

Alfred.

ALFRED the fourth Son of *Ethelwolf,* had scarce perform'd his Brothers obsequies, and the solemnity of his own Crowning, when at the months end in hast with a

15 small power he encounterd the whole Army of *Danes* at *Wilton,* and most part of the day foyl'd them; but unwarily following the Chase, gave others of them the advantage to rally; who returning upon him now weary, remain'd Masters of the field. This year, as is affirm'd in the Annals, nine Bat-

20 tels had bin fought against the *Danes* on the South-side of *Thames,* besides innumerable excursions made by *Alfred* and other Leaders; one King, nine Earls were fall'n in fight, so that weary on both sides at the years end, League or Truce was concluded. Yet next year the *Danes* took thir march to *Lon-*

25 *don,* now expos'd thir prey, there they winterd, and thether came the *Mercians* to renue peace with them. The year following they rov'd back to the parts beyond *Humber,* but

872.
Sax. an.

winter'd at *Torksey* in *Lincolnshire,* where the *Mercians* now
the third time made peace with them. Notwithstanding
which, removing their Camp to *Rependune* in *Mercia,* now
Repton upon *Trent* in *Darbishire,* and there wintring, they
5 constrein'd *Burhed* the King to fly into Forein parts, makeing
seisure of his Kingdome, he running the direct way to *Rome;*
with better reason then his Ancestors, dy'd there, and was
buried in a Church by the English School. His Kingdom the
Danes farm'd out to *Kelwulf,* one of his Houshold Servants
10 or Officers, with condition to be resign'd them when they
commanded. From *Rependune* they dislodg'd, *Hafden* thir
King leading part of his Army Northward, winterd by the
River *Tine,* and subjecting all those quarters, wasted also the
Picts and *British* beyond: but *Cuthrun, Oskitell,* and *An-*
15 *wynd,* other three of thir Kings moving from *Rependune,*
came with a great Army to *Grantbrig,* and remain'd there a
whole year. *Alfred* that Summer purposing to try his Fortune
with a Fleet at Sea (for he had found that the want of Shipping and neglect of Navigation, had expos'd the Land to these
20 Piracies) met with 7 *Danish* Rovers, took one, the rest escaping; an acceptable success from so small a beginning: for the
English at that time were but little experienc't in Sea affairs.
The next years first motion of the *Danes* was towards *War-*
ham Castle: where *Alfred* meeting them, either by policy, or
25 their doubt of his power; *Ethelwerd* saith, by money brought
them to such terms of peace, as that they swore to him upon a
hallow'd Bracelet, others say upon certain Reliques (a Solemn
Oath it seems which they never voutsaf'd before to any other

873.
Sax. an.
Camden
874.
Sax. an.

875.
Sax. an.

876.
Sax. an.

Florent.

Nation) forthwith to depart the land: but falsifying that
Oath, by night with all the Horse they had (*Asser* saith, *Florent.*
slaying all the Horseman he had) stole to *Exeter,* and there
winterd. In *Northumberland, Hafden* thir King began to
5 settle, to divide the land, to till, and to inhabit. Mean while
they in the West who were march'd to *Exeter,* enterd the City,
coursing now and then to *Warham;* but thir Fleet the next 877.
year sailing or rowing about the West, met with such a tem- *Sax. an.*
pest neer to *Swanswich,* or *Gnavewic,* as wrack'd 120 of
10 thir Ships, and left the rest easie to be maisterd by those
Gallies which *Alfred* had set there to guard the Seas, and
streit'n *Exeter* of provision. He the while beleagering them *Asser.*
in the City; now humbl'd with the loss of thir Navy (two
Navies, saith *Asser,* the one at *Gnavewic,* the other at *Swan-*
15 *wine*) distress'd them so, as that they gave him as many
hostages as he requir'd, and as many Oaths, to keep thir covnanted peace, and kept it. For the Summer coming on, they
departed into *Mercia,* wherof part they divided amongst
themselves, part left to *Kelwulf* thir substituted King. The 878.
20 twelftide following, all Oaths forgott'n, they came to *Chip-* *Sax. ann.*
penham in *Wiltshire,* dispeopleing the Countries round, dis-
possessing some, driving others beyond the Sea; *Alfred* himself with a small Company was forc'd to keep within Woods
and Fenny places, and for some time all alone, as *Florent*
25 saith, sojourn'd with *Dunwulf* a Swine-heard, made afterwards for his devotion, and aptness to learning, Bishop of
Winchester. *Hafden* and the Brother of *Hinguar,* coming *Sim. Dun.*
with 23 Ships from *North-wales,* where they had made great

spoil, landed in *Devonshire,* nigh to a strong Castle nam'd
Kinwith; whereby the Garrison issuing forth unexpectedly,
they were slain with 12 hunderd of thir men. Mean while   *Asser.*
the King about *Easter,* not despairing of his affairs, built a
5 Fortress at a place call'd *Athelney* in *Somersetshire,* therin
valiantly defending himself and his followers, frequently sallying forth. The *7th.* week after, he rode out to a place call'd
Ecbryt-stone in the East part of *Selwood:* thether resorted to
him with much gratulation the *Somerset* and *Wiltshire* men,
10 with many out of *Hamshire,* some of whom a little before had
fled thir Country; with these marching to *Ethandune* now   *Camd.*
Edindon in *Wiltshire,* he gave Battel to the whole *Danish*
power, and put them to flight. Then beseiging thir Castle,
within fourteen days took it. *Malmsbury* writes, that in this
15 time of his recess, to go a spy into the *Danish* Camp, he took
upon him with one Servant the habit of a Fidler; by this
means gaining access to the Kings Table, and somtimes to his
Bed-Chamber, got knowledge of thir secrets, thir careless encamping, and thereby this opportunity of assailing them on a
20 sudden. The *Danes* by this misfortune brok'n, gave him more
hostages, and renu'd thir Oaths to depart out of his Kingdom.
Thir King *Gytro,* or *Gothrun,* offer'd willingly to receave
Baptism, and accordingly came with 30 of his friends, to a
place call'd *Aldra,* or *Aulre,* neer to *Athelney,* and were   *Camd.*
25 baptiz'd at *Wedmore;* where *Alfred* receav'd him out of the
Font, and nam'd him *Athelstan.* After which, they abode
with him 12 daies, and were dismiss't with rich presents.   879.
Whereupon the *Danes* remov'd next year to *Cirencester,*   *Sax. an.*

thence peaceably to the *East-Angles;* which *Alfred,* as some
write, had bestow'd on *Gothrun* to hold of him; the bounds
wherof may be read among the Laws of *Alfred.* Others of
them went to *Fulham* on the *Thames,* and joining there with
5 a great Fleet newly come into the River, thence pass'd over
into *France* and *Flanders,* both which they enterd so far conquering or wasting, as witness'd sufficiently, that the *French*
and *Flemish* were no more able then the *English,* by Policy
or prowess to keep off that *Danish* inundation from thir land.
10 *Alfred* thus rid of them, and intending for the future to prevent thir landing; three years after (quiet the mean while)   882.
with more Ships and better provided, puts to Sea, and at first   *Sax. an.*
met with four of theirs, wherof two he took, throwing the
men over-board, then with two others, wherin were two of
15 thir Princes, and took them also, but not without some loss of
his own. After three years another Fleet of them appear'd on   885.
these Seas, so huge that one part thought themselves sufficient *Sax. an.*
to enter upon *East-France,* the other came to *Rochester,* and
beleaguerd it, they within stoutly defending themselves, till
20 *Alfred* with great Forces, coming down upon the *Danes,*
drove them to thir Ships, leaving for hast all thir Horses behind them. The same year *Alfred* sent a Fleet toward the
East-Angles, then inhabited by the *Danes,* which at the mouth *Sim. Dun.*
of *Stour,* meeting with 16 *Danish* Ships, after some flight took
25 them all, and slew the Souldiers aboard; but in thir way home
lying careless, were overtak'n by another part of that Fleet,
and came off with loss, whereupon perhaps those *Danes* who
were settl'd among the *East-Angles,* erected with new hopes,

violated the peace which they had sworn to *Alfred,* who spent   886.
Sax. an.
the next year in repairing *London,* (beseiging, saith *Hunting-*
don) much ruind and unpeopl'd by the *Danes;* the *Lon-*
doners, all but those who had bin led away Captive, soon re-
5 turn'd to thir dwellings, and *Ethred* Duke of *Mercia,* was by   *Sim. Du*
893.
Sax. an.
the King appointed thir Governour. But after 13 years respite
of peace, another *Danish* Fleet of 250 Sail, from the *East* part
of *France* arriv'd at the mouth of a River in *East Kent,* call'd
Limen, nigh to the great Wood *Andred,* famous for length
10 and bredth; into that Wood they drew up this Ships four mile
from the Rivers mouth, and built a Fortress. After whom
Haesten with another *Danish* Fleet of 80 Ships, entring the
mouth of *Thames,* built a Fort at *Middleton,* the former Army
remaining at a place call'd *Apeltre.* *Alfred* perceaving this,
15 took of those *Danes* who dwelt in *Northumberland,* a new
Oath of Fidelity, and of those in *Essex,* hostages, lest they
should joyn, as they were wont, with thir Countrymen newly
arriv'd. And by the next year, having got together his Forces,   894.
Sax. an.
between either Army of the *Danes* encamp'd so, as to be ready
20 for either of them, who first should happ'n to stir forth;
Troops of Horse also he sent continually abroad, assisted by
such as could be spar'd from strong places, wherever the
Countries wanted them, to encounter forageing parties of the
Enemy. The King also divided sometimes his whole Army,
25 marching out with one part by turns, the other keeping in-
trencht. In conclusion rowling up and down, both sides met
at *Farnham* in *Surrey;* where the *Danes* by *Alfreds* Horse
Troops were put to flight, and crossing the *Thames* to a cer-

tain Iland neer *Coln* in *Essex,* or as *Camden* thinks, by *Cole-
brooke,* were beseig'd there by *Alfred* till provision fail'd the
beseigers, another part staid behind with thir King wounded.
Mean while *Alfred* preparing to reinforce the seige in *Colney,*
5 the *Danes* of *Northumberland* breaking Faith, came by Sea
to the *East-Angles,* and with a hundred Ships Coasting Southward, landed in *Devonshire,* and beseig'd *Exeter;* thether
Alfred hasted with his powers, except a Squadron of *Welch*
that came to *London:* with whom the Citizens marching
10 forth to *Beamflet,* where *Haesten* the *Dane* had built a strong
Fort, and left a Garrison, while he himself with the main of
his Army was enterd far into the Country, luckily surprise the
Fort, maister the Garrison, make prey of all they find there;
thir Ships also they burnt or brought away with good booty,
15 and many Prisners, among whom, the Wife and two Sons of
Heasten were sent to the King, who forthwith set them at
liberty. Whereupon *Heasten* gave Oath of Amitie and Hostages to the King; he in requital, whether freely, or by agreement, a summe of money. Nevertheless without regard of
20 Faith giv'n, while *Alfred* was busied about *Exeter,* joining
with the other *Danish* Army, he built another Castle in *Essex*
at *Shobcrie,* thence marching Westward by the *Thames,*
aided with *Northumbrian* and *East-Anglish Danes,* they
came at length to *Severn,* pillaging all in thir way. But, *Eth-*
25 *red, Ethelm,* and *Ethelnoth,* the Kings Captains, with united
Forces pitch'd nigh to them at *Buttingtun,* on the *Severn* Camden.
Bank in *Montgomery-shire,* the River running between, and
there many weeks attended; the King mean while blocking

up the *Danes* who beseig'd *Exeter,* having eat'n part of thir
Horses, the rest urg'd with hunger broke forth to thir fellows,
who lay encamp't on the East-side of the River, and were all
there discomfitted, with some loss of valiant men on the Kings
5 party; the rest fled back to *Essex* and thir Fortress there. Then
Laf, one of their Leaders, gatherd before Winter a great Army
of *Northumbrian* and *East-Anglish Danes,* who leaving thir
money, Ships, and Wives with the *East-Angles,* and marching
day and night, sat down before a City in the West call'd
10 *Wirheal* neer to *Chester,* and took it ere they could be overtak'n. The English after two daies seige hopeless to dislodge
them, wasted the Country round to cut off from them all
provision, and departed. Soon after which, next year the
Danes no longer able to hold *Wirheal,* destitute of Vittles,
15 enterd *North-Wales;* thence lad'n with spoils, part return'd
into *Northumberland,* others to the *East-Angles* as far as
Essex, where they seis'd on a small Iland call'd *Meresig.* And
heer again the Annals record them to beseige *Exeter,* but without coherence of sence or story. Others relate to this purpose,
20 that returning by Sea from the Seige of *Exeter,* and in thir
way landing on the Coast of *Sussex,* they of *Cichester* sallied
out and slew of them many hunderds, taking also some of thir
Ships. The same year they who possess'd *Meresig,* intending
to winter thereabout, drew up thir Ships, some into the
25 *Thames,* others into the River *Lee,* and on the Bank therof
built a Castle twenty miles from *London;* to assault which the
Londoners aided with other Forces march'd out the Summer
following, but were soon put to flight, loosing fowr of the

895.
Sax. an.

Sim. Du
Florent.

896.
Sax. an.

Kings Captains. *Huntingdon* writes quite the contrary, that these fowr were *Danish* Captains, and the overthrow theirs: but little credit is to be plac'd in *Huntingdon* single. For the King therupon with his Forces, lay encamp't neerer the City,

5 that the *Danes* might not infest them in time of Harvest; In the mean time, suttlely devising to turn *Lee* stream several waies; wherby the *Danish* Bottoms were left on dry ground: which they soon perceaving, march'd over Land to *Quatbrig* on the *Severn,* built a Fortress and winterd there; while thir

10 Ships left in *Lee,* were either brok'n or brought away by the *Londoners;* but thir Wives and Children they had left in safety with the *East-Angles.* The next year was pestilent, and besides the common sort took away many great Earls, *Kel-mond* in *Kent, Brithulf* in *Essex, Wulfred* in *Hampshire,*

897.
Sax. an.

15 with many others; and to this evill, the *Danes* of *Northum-berland* and *East-Angles* ceas'd not to endamage the *West-Saxons,* especially by stealth, robbing on the South-shoar in certain long Gallies. But the King causing to be built others twice as long as usually were built, and some of 60 or 70 Oars

20 higher, swifter and steddier then such as were in use before either with *Danes* or *Frisons,* his own invention, some of these he sent out against six *Danish* Pirats, who had done much harm in the Ile of *Wight* and parts adjoining. The bickering was doubtfull and intricate, part on the water, part on

25 the Sands; not without loss of some eminent men on the English side. The Pirats at length were either slain or tak'n, two of them stranded; the men brought to *Winchester,* where the King then was, were executed by his command; one of

them escap'd to the *East-Angles,* her men much wounded: the same year not fewer then twenty of thir Ships perish'd on the South Coast with all thir men. And *Rollo* the *Dane* or *Norman* landing heer, as *Mat. West.* writes, though not in
5 what part of the Iland, after an unsuccessful fight against those Forces which first oppos'd him, sail'd into *France* and conquerd the Country, since that time called *Normandy.* This is the summe of what pass'd in three years against the *Danes,* returning out of *France,* set down so perplexly by the
10 *Saxon* Annalist, ill-guifted with utterance, as with much ado can be understood sometimes what is spok'n, whether meant of the *Danes,* or of the *Saxons.* After which troublesome time, *Alfred* enjoying three years of peace, by him spent, as his manner was, not idely or voluptuously, but in all vertuous
15 emploiments both of mind and body, becoming a Prince of his Renown, ended his daies in the year 900. the 51. of his Age, the 30*th* of his Reign, and was buried regally at *Winchester;* he was born at a place call'd *Wanading* in *Barkshire,* his Mother *Osburga* the Daughter of *Oslac* the Kings Cup-
20 bearer, a *Goth* by Nation, and of noble descent. He was of person comlier then all his Brethren, of pleasing Tongue and gracefull behaviour, ready wit and memory; yet through the fondness of his Parents towards him, had not bin taught to read till the twelfth year of his Age; but the great desire of
25 learning which was in him, soon appear'd, by his conning of *Saxon* Poems day and night, which with great attention he heard by others repeated. He was besides, excellent at Hunting, and the new Art then of Hawking, but more exemplary

900.
Asser.

in devotion, having collected into a Book certain Prayers and
Psalms, which he carried ever with him in his Bosome to use
on all occasions. He thirsted after all liberal knowledge, and
oft complain'd that in his youth he had no Teachers, in his
5 middle Age so little vacancy from Wars and the cares of his
Kingdome, yet leasure he found sometimes, not only to learn
much himself, but to communicate therof what he could to his
people, by translating Books out of Latin into English,
Orosius, Boethius, Beda's History and others, permitted none
10 unlern'd to bear Office, either in Court or Common-wealth;
at twenty years of age not yet reigning, he took to Wife *Egels-
witha* the Daughter of *Ethelred* a *Mercian* Earl. The extremi-
ties which befell him in the sixt of his Reign, *Neothan* Abbot
told him, were justly come upon him for neglecting in his
15 younger days the complaints of such as injur'd and oppress'd
repair'd to him, as then second person in the Kingdome for
redress; which neglect were it such indeed, were yet excusable in a youth, through jollity of mind unwilling perhaps to
be detain'd long with sad and sorrowfull Narrations; but from
20 the time of his undertaking regal charge, no man more patient in hearing causes, more inquisitive in examining, more
exact in doing justice, and providing good Laws, which are
yet extant; more severe in punishing unjust judges or obsti-
nate offenders. Theeves especially and Robbers, to the terrour
25 of whom in cross waies were hung upon a high Post certain
Chains of Gold, as it were dareing any one to take them
thence; so that justice seem'd in his daies not to flourish only,
but to tryumph: no man then hee more frugal of two pretious

things in mans life, his time and his revenue; no man wiser in
the disposal of both. His time, the day, and night, he distributed by the burning of certain Tapours into three equall
portions: the one was for devotion, the other for publick or
5 private affairs; the third for bodily refreshment: how each
hour past, he was put in minde by one who had that Office.
His whole annual revenue, which his first care was should be
justly his own, he divided into two equall parts; the first he
imploi'd to secular uses, and subdivided those into three, the
10 first to pay his Souldiers, Household-Servants and Guard, of
which divided into three Bands, one attended monthly by
turn; the second was to pay his Architects and workmen,
whom he had got together of several Nations; for he was also
an Elegant Builder; above the Custome and conceit of English-
15 men in those days: the third he had in readiness to releive or
honour Strangers according to thir worth, who came from all
parts to see him and to live under him. The other equal part of
his yearly wealth the dedicated to religious uses, those of fowr
sorts; the first to releive the poor, the second to the building
20 and maintenance of two Monasteries, the third of a School,
where he had perswaded the Sons of many Noblemen to study
sacred knowledge and liberal Arts, some say at *Oxford;* the
fourth was for the releif of Foreign Churches, as far as *India*   *Malms.*
to the shrine of St. *Thomas,* sending thether *Sigelm* Bishop of
25 *Sherburn,* who both return'd safe, and brought with him
many rich Gems and Spices; guifts also and a letter he receav'd from the Patriarch of *Jerusalem,* sent many to *Rome,*
and for them receav'd reliques. Thus far, and much more

might be said of his noble mind, which renderd him the miror
of Princes; his body was diseas'd in his youth with a great
soreness in the Seige, and that ceasing of it self, with another
inward pain of unknown cause, which held him by frequent
5 fits to his dying day; yet not disinabl'd to sustain those many
glorious labours of his life both in peace and war.

Edward the Elder.

EDWARD the Son of *Alfred* succeeded, in learning not *Malms.*
equal, in power and extent of Dominion, surpassing
10 his Father. The beginning of his Reign had much disturbance *Huntingd.*
by *Ethelwald* an ambitious young man, Son of the Kings
Uncle, or Cosin German, or Brother, for his Genealogy is
variously deliverd. He vainly avouching to have equal right $_s\begin{matrix}901.\\ Sax.\,an.\end{matrix}$
with *Edward* of succession to the Crown, posses'd himself of
15 *Winburne* in *Dorset,* and another Town diversly nam'd, giving out that there he would live or dye; but encompass'd with
the Kings Forces at *Badburie* a place nigh, his heart failing
him, he stole out by night, and fled to the *Danish* Army beyond *Humber.* The King sent after him, but not overtaking,
20 found his Wife in the Town, whom he had married out of a
Nunnery, and commanded her to be sent back thether. About   902.
this time the *Kentish* men, against a multitude of *Danish*
Pirats, fought prosperously at a place call'd *Holme,* as *Hoveden* records. *Ethelwald* aided by the *Northumbrians* with
25 Shipping, three years after, sailing to the *East-Angles,* per- $\begin{matrix}905.\\ Sax.\,ann.\end{matrix}$
swaded the *Danes* there to fall into the Kings Territory, who
marching with him as far as *Crecklad,* and passing the

Thames there, wasted as far beyond as they durst venture, and
lad'n with spoils return'd home. The King with his powers
makeing speed after them, between the *Dike* and *Ouse,* suppos'd to be *Suffolk* and *Cambridge-shire,* as far as the Fenns
5 Northward, laid wast all before him. Thence intending to
return, he commanded that all his Army should follow him
close without delay; but the *Kentish* men, though oft'n call'd
upon, lagging behind, the *Danish* Army prevented them, and
join'd Battel with the King: where Duke *Sigulf* and Earl
10 *Sigelm,* with many other of the Nobles were slain; on the
Danes part, *Eoric* thir King, and *Ethelwald* the Author of this
War, with others of high note, and of them greater number,
but with great ruin on both sides; yet the *Danes* kept in thir
power the burying of thir slain. What ever follow'd upon this
15 conflict, which we read not, the King two years after with the
Danes, both of *East-Angles,* and *Northumberland* concluded
peace, which continu'd three years, by whomsoever brok'n:
for at the end thereof King *Edward* raising great Forces out
of *West-Sex* and *Mercia,* sent them against the *Danes* beyond
20 *Humber;* where staying five weeks, they made great spoil and
slaughter. The King offer'd them terms of peace, but they re-
jecting all, enterd with the next year into *Mercia,* rendring no
less hostility then they had suffer'd; but at *Tetnal* in *Stafford-
shire,* saith *Florent,* were by the English in a set Battel over-
25 thrown. King *Edward* then in *Kent,* had got together of
Ships about a hunderd Sail, others gon Southward, came back
and met him. The *Danes* now supposing that his main Forces
were upon the Sea, took liberty to rove and plunder up and

907.
Sax. an.

910.
Sax. an.

911.
Sax. an.

down, as hope of prey led them, beyond *Severn*. The King *Ethelwerd.*
guessing what might imbold'n them, sent before him the
lightest of his Army to entertain them; Then following with
the rest, set upon them in thir return over *Cantbrig* in *Gloster-*
5 *shire,* and slew many thousands, among whom *Ecwils,*
Hafden, and *Hinguar* thir Kings, and many other harsh
names in *Huntingdon;* the place also of this fight is variously
writt'n by *Ethelwerd* and *Florent,* call'd *Wodensfeild.* The
year following *Ethred* Duke of *Mercia,* to whom *Alfred* had   912.
10 giv'n *London,* with his daughter in marriage; now dying,   *Sax. an.*
King *Edward* resum'd that City, and *Oxford,* with the Countries adjoining, into his own hands, and the year after, built,   913.
or much repair'd by his Souldiers, the Town of *Hertford* on   *Sax. an.*
either side *Lee,* and leaving a sufficient number at the work,
15 march'd about middle Summer, with the other part of his
Forces into *Essex,* and encamp'd at *Maldon,* while his Souldiers built *Witham;* where a good part of the Country, subject
formerly to the *Danes,* yeilded themselves to his protection.
Fowr years after (*Florent* allows but one year) the *Danes*   917.
20 from *Leister* and *Northampton,* falling into *Oxfordshire,*   *Sax. ann.*
committed much rapine, and in some Towns therof great
slaughter; while another party wasting *Hertfordshire,* met
with other Fortune; for the Countrypeople inur'd now to such
kind of incursions, joining stoutly together, fell upon the
25 spoilers, recover'd thir own goods, with some booty from thir
Enemies. About the same time *Elfled* the Kings Sister sent
her Army of *Mercians* into *Wales,* who routed the *Welch,*   *Huntingd.*
took the Castle of *Bricnam-mere* by *Brecknock,* and brought   *Camd.*

away the Kings Wife of that Country with other Prisners. Not
long after she took *Derby* from the *Danes,* and the Castle by a
sharp assault. But the year ensueing brought a new Fleet of   918.
Sax. an.
Danes to *Lidwic* in *Devonshire,* under two Leaders, *Otter* and
5 *Roald;* who sailing thence Westward about the lands end,
came up to the mouth of *Severn;* there landing wasted the
Welch Coast, and *Irchenfeild* part of *Herefordshire;* where
they took *Kuneleac* a *British* Bishop, for whose ransome King
Edward gave forty pound, but the men of *Hereford* and
10 *Glostershire* assembling, put them to flight; slaying *Roald*
and the Brother of *Otter,* with many more, persu'd them to a
Wood, and there beset, compel'd them to give hostages of
present departure. The King with his Army sat not far off,
securing from the South of *Severn* to *Avon;* so that op'nly
15 they durst not, by night they twice ventur'd to land; but
found such welcome, that few of them came back; the rest
anchord by a small Iland where many of them famish'd;
then sailing to a place call'd *Deomed,* they cross'd into *Ireland.* The King with his Army went to *Buckingham,* staid
20 there a moneth, and built two Castles or Forts on either Bank
of *Ouse* ere his departing, and *Turkitel* a *Danish* Leader, with
those of *Bedford* and *Northampton,* yeilded him subjection.
Wherupon the next year he came with his Army to the Town   919.
Sax. an.
of *Bedford,* took possession therof, staid there a month, and
25 gave order to build another part of the Town, on the South-
side of *Ouse.* Thence the year following went again to *Maldon,*   920.
Sax. an.
repair'd and fortifi'd the Town. *Turkitel* the *Dane* having
small hope to thrive heer, where things with such prudence

were mannag'd against his interess, got leave of the King, with as many voluntaries as would follow him, to pass into *France*. Early the next year King *Edward* re-edifi'd *Tove-chester,* now *Torchester;* and another City in the Annals 921. *Sax. an.*

5 call'd *Wigingmere.* Mean while the *Danes* of *Leister* and *Northampton-shire;* not likeing perhaps to be neighbour'd with Strong Towns, laid Seige to *Torchester;* [but they within repelling the assault one whole day till supplies came] quitted the Seige by night; and persu'd close by the beseig'd, between

10 *Birnwud* and *Ailsbury* were surpris'd, many of them made Prisners, and much of thir bagage lost. Other of the *Danes* at *Huntingdon,* aided from the *East-Angles,* finding that Castle not commodious, left it, and built another at *Temsford,* judging that place more opportune from whence to make thir

15 excursions; and soon after went forth with design to assail *Bedford:* but the Garrison issuing out, slew a great part of them, the rest fled. After this a greater Army of them gatherd out of *Mercia* and the *East-Angles,* came and beseig'd the City call'd *Wigingmere* a whole Day; but finding it defended

20 stoutly by them within, thence also departed, driving away much of thir Cattel: wherupon the English from Towns and Citties round about joining Forces, laid Seige to the Town and Castle of *Temsford,* and by assault took both; slew thir King with *Toglea* a Duke, and *Mannan* his Son an Earl, with

25 all the rest there found; who chose to die rather then yeild. Encourag'd by this, the men of *Kent, Surrey,* and part of *Essex,* enterprise the Seige of *Colchester,* nor gave over till they won it, sacking the Town and putting to Sword all the

Danes therein, except some who escap'd over the Wall. To the
succour of these, a great number of *Danes* inhabiting Ports
and other Towns in the *East-Angles,* united thir Force; but
coming too late, as in revenge beleaguerd *Maldon;* but that
5 Town also timely reliev'd, they departed, not only frustrate
of thir design, but so hotly persu'd, that many thousands of
them lost thir lives in the flight. Forthwith King *Edward* with
his *West-Saxons* went to *Passham* upon *Ouse,* there to guard
the passage, while others were building a stone Wall about
10 *Torchester;* to him there Earl *Thurfert,* and other Lord
Danes, with thir Army thereabout as far as *Weolud,* came and
submitted. Wherat the Kings Souldiers joyfully cry'd out to
be dismiss't home: therfore with another part of them he
enterd *Huntingdon,* and repair'd it, where breaches had bin
15 made; all the people thereabout returning to obedience. The
like was done at *Colnchester* by the next remove of his Army,
after which both *East* and *West-Angles,* and the *Danish*
Forces among them, yeilded to the King, swearing Allegiance
to him both by Sea and Land: the Army also of *Danes* at
20 *Grantbrig,* surrendring themselves took the same Oath. The
Summer following he came with his Army to *Stamford,*   922.
built a Castle there on the South-side of the River, where all *Sax. an*
the people of those quarters acknowledg'd him supream.
Dureing his abode there, *Elfled* his Sister a martial Woman,
25 who after her Husbands Death would no more marry, but
gave her self to public affairs, repairing and fortifying many
Towns, warring sometimes, dy'd at *Tamworth* the Cheif
Seat of *Mercia,* wherof by guift of *Alfred* her Father, she was

Lady or Queen; wherby that whole Nation became obedient
to King *Edward,* as did also *North-Wales* with *Howel, Cle-
daucus,* and *Jeothwell* thir Kings. Thence passing to *Nottingham,* he enterd and repair'd the Town, plac'd there part
5 English, part *Danes,* and receav'd fealty from all in *Mercia*
of either Nation. The next Autumn, coming with his Army   923.
Sax. an.
into *Cheshire,* he built and fortifi'd *Thelwel;* and while he
staid there, call'd another Army out of *Mercia,* which he sent
to repair and fortifie *Manchester.* About Midsummer follow-   924.
Sax. an.
10 ing he march'd again to *Nottingham,* built a Town over
against it on the South-side of that River, and with a Bridg
joyn'd them both; thence journied to a place call'd *Bedecan-
willan* in *Pictland;* there also built and fenc'd a City on the
Borders, where the King of *Scots* did him honour as to his
15 Sovran, together with the whole *Scotish* Nation; the like did
Reginald and the Son of *Eadulf, Danish* Princes, with all the
Northumbrians, both English, and *Danes.* The King also of
a people thereabout call'd *Streatgledwalli* (the *North Welch,*
as *Camden* thinks, of *Strat-Cluid* in *Denbigh-shire,* perhaps
20 rather the *British* of *Cumberland*) did him homage, and not
undeserv'd. For *Buchanan* himself confesses, that this King
Edward with a small number of men compar'd to his Ene-   *Buch. L. 6.*
mies, overthrew in a great Battel, the whole united power both
of *Scots* and *Danes,* slew most of the *Scotish* Nobility, and
25 forc'd *Malcolmb,* whom *Constantine* the *Scotch* King had
made General, and design'd Heir of his Crown, to save himself by flight for wounded. Of the English, he makes *Athelstan* the Son of *Edward* Chief Leader; and so far seems to

confound times and actions, as to make this Battel the same
with that fought by *Athelstan,* about 24 years after at *Bruneford,* against *Anlaf* and *Constantine,* wherof hereafter. But
here *Buchanan* takes occasion to inveigh against the English
5 Writers, upbraiding them with ignorance, who affirm *Athel-*   *Buch. L*
stan to have bin supream King of *Britain, Constantine* the
Scotish King with others to have held of him: and denies that
in the Annals of *Marianus Scotus,* any mention is to be found
therof; which I shall not stand much to contradict, for in
10 *Marianus,* whether by Surname or by Nation *Scotus,* will be
found as little mention of any other *Scotish* affairs, till the time
of King *Dunchad* slain by *Machetad,* or *Mackbeth,* in the
year 1040. which gives cause of suspition, that the affairs
of *Scotland* before that time were so obscure as to be unknown
15 to thir own Countryman, who liv'd and wrote his Chronicle
not long after. But King *Edward* thus nobly doing, and thus   925.
honour'd, the year following dy'd at *Farendon;* a builder and   *Sax. an.*
restorer eev'n in War, not a destroyer of his Land. He had   *Huntin*
by several Wives many Childern; his eldest Daughter *Ed-*   *Mat We*
20 *gith* he gave in marriage to *Charles* King of *France,* Grand-
Child of *Charles* the *Bald* above-mention'd; of the rest in
place convenient. His Laws are yet to be seen. He was buried
at *Winchester,* in the Monastery by *Alfred* his Father. And a
few days after him dy'd *Ethelwerd* his Eldest Son, the Heir of
25 his Crown. He had the whole Iland in subjection, yet so as
petty Kings reign'd under him. In *Northumberland,* after
Ecbert whom the *Danes* had set up, and the *Northumbrians*   *Sim. Du*
yet unruly under thir yoke, at the end of 6 years had expell'd,

one *Ricsig* was set up King, and bore the name 3 years; then another *Ecbert,* and *Guthred;* the latter, if we beleeve Legends, of a Servant made King by command of St. *Cudbert,* in a Vision; and enjoyn'd by another Vision of the same Saint,

5 to pay well for his Royalty many Lands and privileges to his Church and Monastery. But now to the story.

Athelstan.

ATHELSTAN next in Age to *Ethelward* his Brother, who deceas'd untimely few days before, though born

10 of a Concubine, yet for the great appearance of many vertues in him, and his Brethren being yet under Age, was exalted to   926.
the Throne, at *Kingstone* upon *Thames,* and by his Fathers last Will, saith *Malmsbury,* yet not without some opposition of one *Alfred* and his Accomplices; who not likeing he should

15 reign, had conspir'd to seise on him after his Fathers Death, and to put out his Eyes. But the Conspiratours discovered, and *Alfred* denying the Plot, was sent to *Rome,* to assert his inno-   *Malms.*
cence before the Pope; where taking his Oath on the Altar, he fell down immediatly, and carried out by his Servants,

20 three daies after dy'd. Mean while beyond *Humber,* the *Danes,* though much aw'd were not idle. *Inguald* one of thir   *Sim. Dun.*
Kings took possession of *Yorke, Sitric* who some years before had slain *Niel* his Brother, by force took *Davenport* in *Cheshire;* and however he defended these doing; grew so consid-

25 erable, that *Athelstan* with great solemnity gave him his   *Malms.*
Sister *Edgith* to Wife: but he enjoy'd her not long, dying ere   *Mat. West.*
the years end, nor his Sons *Anlaf* and *Guthfert* the Kingdome,

driv'n out the next year by *Athelstan;* not unjustly saith *Hunt-* 927.
Sax. an.
ingdon, as being first raisers of the War. *Simeon* calls him
Gudfrid a *British* King, whom *Athelstan* this year drove out
of his Kingdome; and perhaps they were both one, the name
5 and time not much differing, the place only mistak'n. *Malms-*
bury differs in the name also, calling him *Aldulf* a certain
Rebel. Them also I wish as much mistak'n, who write that
Athelstan, jealous of his younger Brother *Edwin's* towardly
vertues, least added to the right of Birth, they might some 933.
Sim. Du
10 time or other call in question his illegitimate precedence,
caus'd him to be drown'd in the Sea; expos'd, some say, with
one Servant in a rott'n Bark, without Sail or Oar; where the
youth far off land, in rough weather despairing, threw himself over-board; the Servant more patient, got to land and
15 reported the success. But this *Malmsbury* confesses to be
sung in old Songs, not read in warrantable Authors: and
Huntingdon speaks as of a sad accident to *Athelstan,* that he
lost his Brother *Edwin* by Sea; far the more credible, in that
Athelstan, as is writ'n by all, tenderly lov'd and bred up the
20 rest of his Brethren, of whom he had no less cause to be jeal-
ous. And the year following he prosperd better then from so 934.
Sax. an.
Sim. Du
foul a fact, passing into *Scotland* with great Puissance, both
by Sea and Land, and chaceing his Enemies before him, by
Land as far as *Dunfeoder,* and *Wertermore,* by Sea as far as
25 *Cathness.* The cause of this expedition, saith *Malmsbury,* was
to demand *Gudfert* the Son of *Sitric,* thether fled, though not
deny'd at length by *Constantine,* who with *Eugenius* King of
Cumberland, at a place call'd *Dacor* or *Dacre* in that Shire,

surrenderd himself and each his Kingdome to *Athelstan,* who
brought back with him for hostage the Son of *Constantine.*
But *Gudfert* escaping in the mean while out of *Scotland,* and
Constantine exasperated by this invasion, perswaded *Anlaf*
5 the other Son of *Sitric* then fled into *Ireland,* others write
Anlaf King of *Ireland* and the *Iles,* his Son in law, with 615
Ships, and the King of *Cumberland* with other forces, to his
aid. This within fowr years effected, they enterd *England* by
Humber, and fought with *Athelstan* at a place call'd *Wen-*
10 *dune,* others term it *Brunanburg,* others *Bruneford,* which
Ingulf places beyond *Humber, Camden* in *Glendale* of *North-*
umberland on the *Scotch* Borders; the bloodiest fight, say
Authors, that ever this Iland saw, to describe which, the
Saxon Annalist wont to be sober and succinct, whether the
15 same or another writer, now labouring under the weight of
his Argument, and over-charg'd, runs on a sudden into such
extravagant fansies and metaphors, as bare him quite beside
the scope of being understood. *Huntingdon,* though himself
peccant enough in this kind, transcribes him word for word
20 as a pastime to his Readers. I shall only summe up what of
him I can attain, in usuall language. The Battel was fought
eagerly from morning till night; some fell of King *Edwards*
old Army, try'd in many a Battel before; but on the other
side great multitudes, the rest fled to thir Ships. Five Kings,
25 and 7 of *Anlafs* Chief Captains were slain on the place, with
Froda a *Norman* Leader; *Constantine* escap'd home, but lost
his Son in the fight, if I understand my Author; *Anlaf* by Sea
to *Dublin,* with a small remainder of his great hoast. *Malms-*

bury relates this War, adding many circumstances after this manner. That *Anlaf* joining with *Constantine* and the whole power of *Scotland,* besides those which he brought with him out of *Ireland,* came on far Southwards, till *Athelstan* who
5 had retir'd on set purpose to be the surer of his Enimies, en- clos'd from all succour and retreat, met him at *Bruneford.* *Anlaf* perceaving the valour and resolution of *Athelstan,* and mistrusting his own Forces though numerous, resolv'd first to spie in what posture his Enemies lay: and imitating per-
10 haps what he heard attempted by King *Alfred* the Age before, in the habit of a Musitian, got access by his lute and voice to the Kings tent, there playing both the minstrel and the spie: then towards Evening dismis't, he was observ'd by one who had bin his Souldier and well knew him, veiwing earnestly
15 the Kings Tent, and what approaches lay about it, then in the twilight to depart. The Souldier forthwith acquaints the King, and by him blam'd for letting go his Enemy, answerd, that he had giv'n first his military Oath to *Anslaf,* whom if he had betrai'd, the King might suspect him of like treasonous minde
20 towards himself; which to disprove, he advis'd him to remove his Tent a good distance off; and so don, it happ'nd that a Bishop with his retinue coming that night to the Army, pich'd his Tent in the same place, from whence the King had remov'd. *Anlaf* coming by night as he had design'd, to assault
25 the Camp and especially the Kings Tent, finding there the Bishop in stead, slew him with all his followers. *Athelstan* took the Allarm, and as it seems, was not found so unpro- vided, but that the day now appearing, he put his men in

order, and maintain'd the fight till Evening; wherin *Constantine* himself was slain with five other Kings, and twelve Earls, the Annals were content with seav'n, in the rest not disagreeing. *Ingulf* Abbot of *Croyland* from the autority of *Turketul*
5 a principal Leader in this Battel, relates it more at large to this effect: that *Athelstan* above a mile distant from the place where execution was done upon the Bishop and his supplies, allarm'd at the noise, came down by break of day, upon *Anlaf* and his Army, overwatch't and wearied now with the slaugh-
10 ter they had made, and something out of order, yet in two main Battels. The King therfor in like manner dividing, led the one part consisting most of *West Saxons*, against *Anlaf* with his *Danes* and *Irish*, committing the other to his Chancellor *Turketul*, with the *Mercians* and *Londoners* against
15 *Constantine* and his *Scots*. The showr of Arrows and Darts over-pass't, both Battells attack'd each other with a close and terrible ingagement, for a long space neither side giving ground. Till the Chancellor *Turketul*, a man of great stature and strength, taking with him a few *Londoners*, of select
20 valour, and *Singin* who led the *Worstershire* men, a Captain of undaunted courage, broke into the thickest, making his way first through the *Picts* and *Orkeners*, then through the *Cumbrians* and *Scots*, and came at length where *Constantine* himself fought, unhors'd him, and us'd all means to take him
25 alive; but the *Scots* valiantly defending thir King, and laying load upon *Turketul*, which the goodness of his Armour well endur'd, he had yet bin beat'n down, had not *Singin* his faithfull second at the same time slain *Constantine;* which once

known, *Anlaf* and the whole Army betook them to flight,
wherof a huge multitude fell by the Sword. This *Turketul* not
long after leaving worldly affairs, became Abbot of *Croyland,*
which at his own cost he had repair'd, from *Danish* ruins, and
5 left there this memorial of his former actions. *Athelstan*
with his Brother *Edmund* victorious, thence turning into
Wales, with much more ease vanquish'd *Ludwal* the King,
and possest his land. But *Malmsbury* writes, that commiserat-
ing human chance, as he displac'd, so he restor'd both him and
10 *Constantine* to thir Regal State; for the surrender of *King
Constantine* hath bin above spok'n of. However the *Welch*
did him homage at the City of *Hereford,* and covnanted
yearly payment of Gold 20 pound, of Silver 300, of *Oxen* 25
thousand, besides Hunting Dogs and Hawks. He also took
15 *Exeter* from the *Cornish Britans,* who till that time had equal
right there with the English, and bounded them with the
River *Tamar,* as the other *Brittish* with *Wey.* Thus dreaded
of his Enemies, and renown'd far and neer, three years after
he dy'd at *Gloster,* and was buried with many Trophies at
20 *Malmsbury,* where he had caus'd to be laid his two Cosin
Germans, *Edwin* and *Ethelstan,* both slain in the Battel
against *Anlaf.* He was 30 years old at his coming to the
Crown, mature in wisdom from his Childhood, comly of
person and behaviour; so that *Alfred* his Grandfather in
25 blessing him was wont to pray he might live to have the Kingdome, and put him yet a Child into Souldiers habit. He had
his breeding in the Court of *Elfled* his Aunt, of whose vertues
more then female we have related, sufficient to evince that his

941.
Sax. an.
Malms.
Ingulf.

mother, though said to be no wedded Wife, was yet such of parentage and worth, as the Royal line disdain'd not, though the Song went in *Malmsburies* daies (for it seems he refus'd not the autority of Ballats for want of better) that his mother
5 was a Farmers Daughter, but of excellent feature; who dreamt one night she brought forth a Moon that should enlight'n the whole land: which the Kings Nurse hearing of, took her home and bred up Courtly; that the King coming one day to visit his Nurse, saw there this Damsel, lik'd her, and by earnest
10 suit prevailing, had by her this famous *Athelstan,* a bounteous, just and affable King, as *Malmsbury* sets him forth; nor less honour'd abroad by Foren Kings, who sought his Friendship by great guifts or affinity; that *Harold* King of *Noricum* sent him a Ship, whose Prow was of gold, sails purple, and
15 other golden things, the more to be wonderd at, sent from *Noricum,* whether meant *Norway* or *Bavaria,* the one place so far from such superfluity of wealth, the other from all Sea: the Embassadors were *Helgrim* and *Offrid,* who found the King at *Yorke.* His Sisters he gave in marriage to greatest
20 Princes, *Elgif* to *Otho* Son of *Henry* the Emperour, *Egdith* to a certain Duke about the *Alpes, Edgiv* to *Ludwic* King of *Aquitain,* sprung of *Charles* the Great, *Ethilda* to *Hugo* King of *France,* who sent *Aldulf* Son of *Baldwin,* Earl of *Flanders,* to obtain her. From all these great suitors, especially from the
25 Emperour and King of *France,* came rich presents, Horses of excellent Breed, gorgeous Trappings and Armour, Reliques, Jewels, Odors, Vessels of *Onyx,* and other pretious things, which I leave poetically describ'd in *Malmsbury,* tak'n, as he

confesses, out of an old versifier, some of whose verses he
recites. The only blemish left upon him, was the exposing of
his Brother *Edwin,* who disavow'd by Oath the treason
wherof he was accus'd, and implor'd an equall hearing. But
5 these were Songs, as before hath bin said, which add also that
Athelstan, his anger over, soon repented of the fact, and put
to Death his Cup-bearer, who had induc't him to suspect and
expose his Brother, put in mind by a word falling from the
Cup-bearers own mouth, who slipping one day as he bore the
10 Kings Cup, and recovring himself on the other leg, said
aloud, fatally as to him it prov'd, one Brother helps the other.
Which words the King laying to heart, and pondring how ill
he had done to make away his Brother, aveng'd himself first
on the adviser of that fact, took on him seav'n years penance,
15 and as *Mat. West.* saith, built two Monasteries for the Soul of
his Brother. His Laws are extant among the Laws of other
Saxon Kings to this day.

Edmund.

EDMUND not above 18 years old succeeded his Brother   942.
20 Athelstan, in courage not inferiour. For in the second   *Sax. an.*
of his Reign he free'd *Mercia* of the *Danes* that remain'd there,
and took from them the Citties of *Lincoln, Nottingham,*
Stamford, Darby, and *Leister,* where they were plac'd by
King *Edward,* but it seems gave not good proof of thir fidelity.
25 *Simeon* writes that *Anlaf* setting forth from *Yorke,* and having wasted Southward as far as *Northampton,* was met by
Edmund at *Leister;* but that ere the Battails join'd, peace was
made between them by *Odo* and *Wulstan* the two Archbish-

ops, with conversion of *Anlaf;* for the same year *Edmund* receav'd at the Font-stone this or another *Anlaf,* as saith *Huntingdon,* not him spok'n of before, who dy'd this year (so uncertain they are in the story of these times also) and held
5 *Reginald* another King of the *Northumbers,* while the Bishop confirm'd him: thir limits were divided North and South by *Watling-street.* But spirituall kindred little avail'd to keep peace between them, whoever gave the cause; for we read him two years after driving *Anlaf* (whom the Annals now first
10 call the Son of *Sitric*) and *Suthfrid* Son of *Reginald* out of *Northumberland,* takeing the whole Country into subjection. *Edmund* the next year harras'd *Cumberland,* then gave it to *Malcolm* King of *Scots,* thereby bound to assist him in his Wars, both by Sea and Land; *Mat. West.* adds that in this
15 action *Edmund* had the aid of *Leolin* Prince of *Northwales,* against *Dummail* the *Cumbrian* King, him depriving of his Kingdome, and his two Sons of thir sight. But the year after he himself by strange accident came to an untimely Death, feasting with his Nobles on St. *Austins* Day at *Puclekerke* in
20 *Glostershire,* to celebrat the memory of his first converting the *Saxons.* He spi'd *Leof* a noted Theef, whom he had banish'd, sitting among his Guests; wherat transported with too much vehemence of Spirit, though in a just cause, riseing from the Table he ran upon the Theef, and catching his hair,
25 pull'd him to the ground. The Theef who doubted from such handling no less then his Death intended, thought to die not unreveng'd; and with a short Dagger strook the King, who still laid at him, and little expected such assassination, mor-

944.
Sax. an.

945.
Sax. an.

946.
Sax. an.
Camden.

tally into the brest. The matter was done in a moment, ere
men set at Table could turn them, or imagin at first what the
stir meant, till perceaving the King deadly wounded, they
flew upon the murderer and hew'd him to peeces; who like a
5 wild Beast at abbay, seeing himself surrounded, desperatly
laid about him, wounding some in his fall. The King was
buried at *Glaston,* wherof *Dunstan* was then Abbot, his Laws
yet remain to be seen among the Laws of other *Saxon* Kings.

Edred.

10 **E**DRED the third Brother of *Athelstan,* the Sons of
Edmund being yet but Children, next reign'd, not
degenerating from his worthy predecessors, and Crown'd at
Kingston. Northumberland he throughly subdu'd, the *Scots*
without refusal swore him Allegiance; yet the *Northumbri-*
15 *ans,* ever of doubtfull Faith, soon after chose to themselves
one *Eric* a *Dane. Huntingdon* still haunts us with this *Anlaf*
(of whom we gladly would have bin ridd) and will have him
before *Eric* recall'd once more and reign fowr years, then
again put to his shifts. But *Edred* entring into *Northumber-*
20 *land,* and with spoils returning, *Eric* the King fell upon his
rear. *Edred* turning about, both shook off the Enemy, and
prepar'd to make a second inroad: which the *Northumbrians*
dreading rejected *Eric,* slew *Amaneus* the Son of *Anlaf,* and
with many presents appeasing *Edred,* submitted again to his
25 Goverment; not from that time had Kings, but were govern'd
by Earls, of whom *Osulf* was the first. About this time *Wul-*
stan Archbishop of *York,* accus'd to have slain certain men

950.
Sim. Du

Hoved.

953.
Sim. Du

of *Thetford* in revenge of thir Abbot whom the Townsmen had slain, was committed by the King to close Custody; but soon after enlarg'd, was restor'd to his place. *Malmsbury* writes that his crime was to have conniv'd at the revolt of his
5 Countrymen: but King *Edred* two years after sick'ning in the flowr of his youth, dy'd much lamented, and was buried at *Winchester*.

955.
Sim. Dun.

Edwi.

E*DWI* the Son of *Edmund* now come to Age, after his
10 Uncle *Edred*'s Death took on him the Goverment, and was Crown'd at *Kingston*. His lovely person sirnam'd him the Fair, his actions are diversly reported, by *Huntingdon* not thought illaudable. But *Malmsbury* and such as follow him write far otherwise, that he married or kept as Concubine,
15 his neer Kinswoman, some say both her and her Daughter; so inordinatly giv'n to his pleasure, that on the very day of his Coronation, he abruptly withdrew himself from the Company of his Peers, whether in Banquet or Consultation, to sit wantoning in the Chamber with this *Algiva,* so was her
20 name, who had such power over him. Wherat his Barons offended, sent Bishop *Dunstan,* the boldest among them, to request his return: he going to the Chamber, not only interrupted his dalliance and rebuk'd the Lady, but takeing him by the hand, between force and persuasion, brought him back to
25 his Nobles. The King highly displeas'd, and instigated perhaps by her who was so prevalent with him, not long after sent *Dunstan* into banishment, caus'd his Monastery to be rifl'd, and became an Enemy of all Monks. Wherupon *Odo*

Ethelwerd.

Mat. West.

956.

Archbishop of *Canterbury* pronounc't a separation or divorce
of the King from *Algiva*. But that which most incited *William* of *Malmsbury* against him, he gave that Monastery to be
dwelt in by secular Preists, or, to use his own phrase, made it
5 a stable of Clerks; at length these affronts done to the Church
were so resented by the people, that the *Mercians* and *Northumbrians* revolted from him, and set up *Edgar* his Brother,   *Hoved.*
leaving to *Edwi* the *West-Saxons* only, bounded by the River   957.
Thames; with greif wherof, as is thought, he soon after ended   *Sax. an.*
10 his daies, and was buried at *Winchester*. Mean while *Elfsin*   958.
Bishop of that place after the Death of *Odo,* ascending by   *Mat. West*
Simony to the Chair of *Canterbury,* and going to *Rome* the
same year for his Pall, was froz'n to Death in the *Alps*.

Edgar.

15 **E**DGAR by his Brothers Death now King of all *England*   959.
    at 16 years of Age, call'd home *Dunstan* out of *Flan-*   *Malms.*
ders, where he liv'd in exile. This King had no War all his
Reign; yet allways well prepar'd for War, govern'd the Kingdom in great Peace, Honour, and Prosperity, gaining thence
20 the Sirname of Peaceable, much extoll'd for Justice, Clemency, and all Kingly Vertues, the more, ye may be sure, by
Monks, for his building so many Monasteries; as some write,   *Mat. Wes.*
every year one: for he much favour'd the Monks against secular Preists, who in the time of *Edwi* had got possession in most
25 of thir Convents. His care and wisdome was great in guard-
ing the Coast round with stout ships, to the number of 3600,
Mat. West. reck'ns them 4800, divided into fowr Squadrons,

to sail to and fro about the fowr quarters of the land, meeting each other; the first 1200 sail from East to West, the second of as many from West to East, the third and fowrth between North and South, himself in the Summer time with his Fleet.

5 Thus he kept out wisely the force of Strangers, and prevented Forein War; but by thir too frequent resort hither in time of peace, and his too much favouring them, he let in thir vices unaware. Thence the people, saith *Malmsbury,* learnt of the out-landish *Saxons* rudeness, of the *Flemish* daintiness and

10 softness; of the *Danes* Drunk'ness; though I doubt these vices are as naturally homebred heer as in any of those Countries. Yet in the Winter and Spring time he usually rode the Circuit as a Judge Itinerant through all his Provinces, to see justice well administerd, and the poor not oppress'd. Theeves and

15 Robbers he rooted almost out of the Land, and wild Beasts of prey altogether; enjoining *Ludwal* King of *Wales* to pay the yearly tribute of 300 Wolves, which he did for two years together, till the third year no more were to be found, nor ever after; but his Laws may be read yet extant. Whatever was the

20 cause he was not Crown'd till the 30. of his Age, but then with great splendor and magnificence at the City of *Bath,* in the Feast of *Pentecost.* This year dy'd *Swarling* a Monk of *Croyland,* the 142. year of his Age, and another soon after him in the 115*th.* in that Fenny and watrish air, the more remark-

25 able. King *Edgar* the next year went to *Chester,* and summoning to his Court there all the Kings that held of him, took homage of them: thir names are *Kened* King of *Scots, Malcolm* of *Cumberland, Maccuse* of the Iles, five of *Wales,*

*973.
Sax. an.
Ingulf.*

*974.
Sax. an.*

Dufwal, Huwal, Grifith, Jacob, Judethil, these he had in such
aw, that going one day into a Gally, he caus'd them to take
each man his Oar, and row him down the River *Dee,* while
he himself sat at the Stern: which might be done in meriment
5 and easily obei'd; if with a serious brow, discoverd rather
vain glory and insulting haughtiness, then moderation of
mind. And that he did it seriously tryumphing, appears by
his words then utterd, that his successors might then glory to
be Kings of *England,* when they had such honour done them.
10 And perhaps the Divine power was displeas'd with him for
taking too much honour to himself; since we read that the
year following he was tak'n out of this life by sickness in the   975.
highth of his glory and the prime of his Age, buried at *Glaston*
Abby. The same year, as *Mat. West.* relates, he gave to *Kened*
15 the *Scottish* King, many rich presents, and the whole Country
of *Laudian,* or *Lothien,* to hold of him on condition that he
and his successors should repair to the English Court at high
Festivals when the King sat Crown'd, gave him also many
lodging places by the way, which till the days of *Henry* the
20 second were still held by the Kings of *Scotland.* He was of
Stature not tall, of body slender, yet so well made, that
in strength he chose to contend with such as were thought
strongest, and dislik'd nothing more then that they should
spare him for respect or fear to hurt him. *Kened* King of
25 *Scots* then in the Court of *Edgar,* sitting one day at Table
was heard to say jestingly among his Servants, he wonderd
how so many Provinces could be held in subjection by such a
little dapper man: his words were brought to the Kings Ear;

HISTORY OF BRITAIN 245

he sends for *Kened* as about some private business, and in talk
drawing him forth to a secret place, takes from under his garment two Swords which he had brought with him, gave one
of them to *Kened;* and now saith he, it shall be try'd which
5 ought to be the subject; for it is shamefull for a King to boast
at Table, and shrink in fight. *Kened* much abash'd fell presently at his Feet, and besought him to pardon what he had
simply spok'n, no way intended to his dishonour or disparagement: wherewith the King was satisfi'd. *Camden* in his
10 description of *Ireland,* cites a Charter of King *Edgar,* wherin
it appears, he had in subjection all the Kingdomes of the Iles
as far as *Norway,* and had subdu'd the greatest part of *Ireland*
with the City of *Dublin:* but of this other Writers make no
mention. In his youth having heard of *Elfrida,* Daughter to
15 *Ordgar* Duke of *Devonshire,* much commended for her
Beauty, he sent Earl *Athelwold,* whose loyalty he trusted
most, to see her; intending, if she were found such as answerd
report, to demand her in marriage. He at the first view tak'n
with her presence, disloyally, as it oft happ'ns in such emploi-
20 ments, began to sue for himself; and with consent of her
Parents obtain'd her. Returning therfore with scarce an ordinary commendation of her Feature, he easily took off the
Kings mind, soon diverted another way. But the matter coming to light how *Athelwold* had forestall'd the King, and
25 *Elfrida*'s Beauty more and more spok'n of, the King now
heated not only with a relapse of Love, but with a deep sence
of the abuse, yet dissembling his disturbance, pleasantly told
the Earl, what day he meant to come and visit him and his fair

Wife. The Earl seemingly assur'd his welcome, but in the
mean while acquainting his Wife, earnestly advis'd her to
deform her self, what she might, either in dress or otherwise,
lest the King, whose amorous inclination was not unknown,
should chance to be attracted. She who by this time was not
ignorant, how *Athelwold* had stepd between her and the
King, against his coming arraies her self richly, useing whatever art she could devise might render her the more amiable;
and it took effect. For the King inflam'd with her love the
more for that he had bin so long defrauded and rob'd of her,
resolv'd not only to recover his intercepted right, but to punish the interloper of his destind spouse, and appointing with
him as was usual, a day of hunting, drawn aside in a Forest,
now call'd *Harewood,* smote him through with a Dart. Some
censure this act as cruel and tyrannical, but considerd well,
it may be judg'd more favourably, and that no man of sensible
Spirit but in his place, without extraordinary perfection,
would have done the like: for next to life what worse treason
could have bin committed against him? it chanc'd that the
Earls base Son coming by upon the fact, the King sternly
ask'd him how he lik'd this Game; he submisly answering,
that whatsoever pleas'd the King, must not displease him; the
King return'd to his wonted temper, took an affection to the
youth, and ever after highly favour'd him, making amends
in the Son for what he had done to the Father. *Elfrida* forthwith he took to Wife, who to expiate her former Husbands
Death, though therin she had no hand, coverd the place of his
bloodshed with a Monastery of Nuns to sing over him. An-

other fault is laid to his charge, no way excusable, that he took a Virgin *Wilfrida* by force out of the Nunnery, where she was plac'd by her friends to avoid his persuit, and kept her as his Concubine; but liv'd not obstinatly in the offence; for sharply

5 reprov'd by *Dunstan* he submitted to 7 years penance, and for that time to want his Coronation: But why he had it not before, is left unwritt'n. Another story there goes of *Edgar,* fitter for a Novel then a History; but as I find it in *Malmsbury,* so I relate it. While he was yet unmarried, in his youth he

10 abstain'd not from Women, and coming on a day to *Andover,* caus'd a Dukes Daughter there dwelling, reported rare of Beauty, to be brought to him. The mother not dareing flatly to deny, yet abhorring that her Daughter should be so deflour'd, at fit time of night sent in her attire, one of her waiting Maids;

15 a Maid it seems not unhansom nor unwitty; who suppli'd the place of her young Lady. Night pass'd, the Maid going to rise, but day-light scarse yet appearing, was by the King askt why she made such hast, she answer'd, to do the work which her Lady had set her; at which the King wondring, and with

20 much ado staying her to unfold the riddle, for he took her to be the Dukes Daughter, she falling at his Feet besought him, that since at the command of her Lady she came to his Bed, and was enjoy'd by him, he would be pleas'd in recompence to set her free from the hard service of her Mistress. The King

25 a while standing in a study whether he had best be angry or not, at length turning all to a jest, took the Maid away with him, advanc'd her above her Lady, lov'd her and accompanied with her only, till he married *Elfrida.* These only are

his faults upon record, rather to be wonderd how they were so few, and so soon left, he coming at 16 to the Licence of a Scepter; and that his vertues were so many and so mature, he dying before the Age wherin wisdome can in others attain to
5 any ripeness: however with him dy'd all the *Saxon* glory. From henceforth nothing is to be heard of but thir decline and ruin under a double Conquest, and the causes foregoing; which, not to blur or taint the praises of thir former actions and liberty well defended, shall stand severally related, and
10 will be more then long enough for another Book.

The End of the Fifth Book.

THE HISTORY OF
BRITAIN.

THE SIXTH BOOK

EDWARD the eldest Son of *Edgar* by *Egelfleda* his first
Wife, the Daughter of Duke *Ordmer,* was according
to right and his Fathers Will, plac'd in the Throne;
Elfrida his second Wife, and her faction only repineing, who
5 labour'd to have had her Son *Ethelred* a Child of 7 years, preferr'd before him; that she under that pretence might have
rul'd all. Mean while Comets were seen in Heav'n, portend-
ing not Famin only, which follow'd the next year, but the
troubl'd State of the whole Realm not long after to ensue. The
10 troubles begun in *Edwi*'s daies, between Monks and secular
Priests, now reviv'd and drew on either side many of the
Nobles into parties. For *Elfere* Duke of the *Mercians,* with
many other Peers, corrupted as is said with guifts, drove the *Florent.*
Monks out of those Monasteries where *Edgar* had plac'd *Sim. Dun.*
15 them, and in thir stead put secular Priests with thir Wives.
But *Ethelwin* Duke of *East-Angles,* with his Brother *Elfwold,*
and Earl *Britnoth* oppos'd them, and gathering an Army
defended the Abbies of *East-Angles* from such intruders. To
appease these tumults, a Synod was call'd at *Winchester,* and
20 nothing there concluded, a general Councel both of Nobles
and Prelates, was held at *Caln* in *Wiltshire,* where while the
dispute was hot, but chiefly against *Dunstan,* the room
wherin they sat fell upon thir heads, killing some, maiming

others, *Dunstan* only escaping upon a beam that fell not, and the King absent by reason of his tender Age. This accident quieted the controversie, and brought both parts to hold with *Dunstan* and the Monks. Mean while the King addicted to a
5 Religious life, and of a mild Spirit, simply permitted all things to the ambitious will of his Step-mother and her Son *Ethelred:* to whom she displeas'd that the name only of King was wanting, practis'd thenceforth to remove King *Edward* out of the way; which in this manner she brought about. *Edward* on a
10 day wearied with hunting, thirsty and alone, while his attendance follow'd the Dogs, hearing that *Ethelred* and his mother lodg'd at *Corvesgate* (*Corfe* Castle, saith *Camden,* in the Ile of *Purbeck*) innocently went thether. She with all shew of kindness welcoming him, commanded drink to be
15 brought forth, for it seems he lighted not from his Horse; and while he was drinking, caus'd one of her Servants, privately before instructed, to stab him with a poignard. The poor youth who little expected such unkindness there, turning speedily the Reins, fled bleeding; till through loss of blood falling
20 from his Horse, and expiring, yet held with one foot in the Stirrop, he was dragg'd along the way, trac'd by his blood, and buried without honour at *Werham,* having reign'd about 3 years: but the place of his burial not long after grew famous for miracles. After which by Duke *Elfer* (who, as *Malmsbury*
25 saith, had a hand in his Death) he was Royally enterr'd at *Skepton* or *Shaftsbury*. The murdress *Elfrida* at length repenting spent the residue of her daies in sorrow and great penance.

978.
Malms.

Ethelred.

ETHELRED second Son of *Edgar* by *Elfrida* (for *Ed-mund* dy'd a Child) his Brother *Edward* wickedly re-mov'd, was now next in right to succeed, and accordingly
5 Crown'd at *Kingston:* reported by some, fair of visage, comly of person, elegant of behaviour; but the event will shew that with many sluggish and ignoble vices he quickly sham'd his outside; born and prolong'd a fatal mischeif of the people, and the ruin of his Country; whereof he gave early signes
10 from his first infancy, bewraying the Font and Water while the Bishop was baptizing him. Whereat *Dunstan* much troubl'd, for he stood by and saw it, to them next him broke into these words, By God and Gods Mother this Boy will prove a Sluggard. Another thing is writt'n of him in his Childhood;
15 which argu'd no bad nature, that hearing of his Brother *Ed-wards* cruel Death, he made loud lamentation; but his furious mother offended therwith, and having no rod at hand, beat him so with great Wax Candles, that he hated the sight of them ever after. *Dunstan* though unwilling set the Crown
20 upon his head; but at the same time foretold op'nly, as is reported, the great evils that were to come upon him and the Land, in avengment of his Brothers innocent blood. And about the same time, one midnight, a Cloud some-times bloody, sometimes fiery, was seen over all *England;*
25 and within three years the *Danish* Tempest, which had long surceast, revolv'd again upon this Iland. To the more ample relating whereof, the *Danish* History, at least thir latest

979.
Malms.

Florent.
Sim. Dun.

Sim. Dun.

982.
Malms.

and diligentest Historian, as neither from the first landing of
Danes, in the Reign of *West-Saxon Brithric,* so now again
from first to last, contributes nothing; busied more then
anough to make out the bare names and successions of thir
5 uncertain Kings, and thir small actions at home: unless out of
him I should transcribe what hee takes, and I better may,
from our own Annals; the surer, and the sadder witnesses of
thir doings here, not glorious, as they vainly boast, but most
inhumanly Barbarous. For the *Danes* well understanding, *Eadmer.*
10 that *England* had now a slothfull King to thir wish, first *Florent.*
landing at *Southhampton* from 7 great Ships, took the Town,
spoil'd the Country, and carried away with them great pillage; nor was *Devonshire* and *Cornwall* uninfested on the *Hoved.*
shore; Pirats of *Norway* also harried the Coast of *West-*
15 *Chester:* and to add a worse calamity, the City of *London* was *Sim. Dun*
burnt, casually or not, is not writt'n. It chanc'd fowr years *Hoved.*
after, that *Ethelred* beseig'd *Rochester,* some way or other *Malms.*
offended by the Bishop therof. *Dunstan* not approving the *Ingulf.*
cause, sent to warn him that he provoke not St. *Andrew*
20 the Patron of that City, nor wast his Lands; an old craft of
the Clergy to secure thir Church Lands, by entailing them on
some Saint; the King not hark'ning, *Dunstan* on this condition that the seige might be rais'd, sent him a hunderd pound,
the money was accepted and the seige dissolv'd. *Dunstan* rep-
25 rehending his avarice, sent him again this word, because thou
hast respected money more then Religion, the evils which I
foretold shall the sooner come upon thee; but not in my days, *987.*
for so God hath spok'n. The next year was calamitous, bring- *Malms.*

ing strange fluxes upon men, and murren upon Cattel. *Dun-*
stan the year following dy'd, a strenuous Bishop, zealous
without dread of person, and for ought appeers, the best of
many Ages, if he busied not himself too much in secular af-
5 fairs. He was Chaplain at first to King *Athelstan,* and *Ed-*
mund who succeeded, much imploi'd in Court affairs, till
envi'd by some who laid many things to his charge, he was by
Edmund forbidd'n the Court, but by the earnest mediation,
saith *Ingulf,* of *Turkitul* the Chancellour, receav'd at length
10 to favour, and made Abbot of *Glaston,* lastly by *Edgar* and the
generall Vote, Archbishop of *Canterbury.* Not long after his
Death, the *Danes* arriving in *Devonshire* were met by *Goda*
Lieutenant of that Country, and *Strenwold* a valiant Leader,
who put back the *Danes,* but with loss of thir own lives. The
15 third year following, under the conduct of *Justin* and *Guth-*
mund the Son of *Steytan,* they landed and spoil'd *Ipswich,*
fought with *Britnoth* Duke of the *East-Angles* about *Maldon,*
where they slew him; the slaughter else had bin equal on both
sides. These and the like depredations on every side the Eng-
20 lish not able to resist, by counsel of *Siric* then Archbishop of
Canterbury, and two Dukes, *Ethelward* and *Alfric;* it was
thought best for the present to buy that with Silver which they
could not gain with thir Iron; and Ten Thousand pound was
paid to the *Danes* for peace. Which for a while contented; but
25 taught them the ready way how easiest to come by more. The
next year but one they took by storm and rifl'd *Bebbanburg*
an antient City nigh *Durham:* sailing thence into the mouth
of *Humber,* they wasted both sides therof, *Yorkeshire* and

988.
Malms.

991.
Sim. Dun.

993.
Sim. Dun.

Lindsey, burning and destroying all before them. Against these went out three Noblemen, *Frana, Frithegist,* and *Godwin,* but being all *Danes* by the Fathers side, willingly began flight, and forsook thir own Forces betray'd to the Enemy.

5 No less treachery was at Sea; for *Alfric* the Son of *Elfer* Duke of *Mercia,* whom the King for some offence had banish'd but now recall'd, sent from *London* with a Fleet to surprise the *Danes,* in some place of disadvantage, gave them over night intelligence therof, then fled to them himself; which his

10 Fleet, said *Florent,* perceaveing, persu'd, took the Ship, but miss'd of his person; the *Londoners* by chance grapling with the *East-Angles* made them fewer, saith my Authour, by many thousands. Others say, that by this notice of *Alfric,* the *Danes* not only escap'd, but with a greater Fleet set upon the

15 English, took many of thir Ships, and in tryumph brought them up the *Thames,* intending to beseige *London:* for *Anlaf* King of *Norway,* and *Swane* of *Denmarke,* at the head of these, came with 94 Gallies. The King for this treason of *Alfric,* put out his Sons Eyes; but the *Londoners* both by land

20 and water, so valiantly resisted thir beseigers, that they were forc't in one day with great loss to give over. But what they could not on the City, they wreck'd themselves on the Countries round about, wasting with Sword and fire all *Essex, Kent,* and *Sussex.* Thence horsing thir Foot, diffus'd far

25 wider thir outragious incursions, without mercy either to Sex or Age. The slothfull King instead of Warlike opposition in the Field, sends Embassadors to treat about another payment; the sum promisd was now 16 thousand pound; till which

Florent.
Hunting

994.
Sim. Dur

Malms.

paid, the *Danes* winterd at *Southampton; Ethelred* inviteing
Anlaf to come and visit him at *Andover:* where he was *Malms.*
royally entertain'd, some say baptiz'd, or confirm'd, adopted
Son by the King, and dismis't with great presents, promising
5 by Oath to depart and molest the Kingdome no more; which *Huntingd.*
he perform'd, but the calamity ended not so, for after some
intermission of thir rage for three years, the other Navy of   997.
Danes sailing about to the West, enterd *Severn,* and wasted   *Sim. Dun.*
one while *South Wales,* then *Cornwall* and *Devonshire,* till at
10 length they winterd about *Tavistoc.* For it were an endless
work to relate how they wallow'd up and down to every particular place, and to repeat as oft what devastations they
wrought, what desolations left behinde them, easie to be
imagin'd. In summ, the next year they afflicted *Dorsetshire,*   998.
15 *Hamshire,* and the Ile of *Wight;* by the English many reso-   *Sim. Dun.*
lutions were tak'n, many Armies rais'd, but either betray'd by
the falshood, or discourag'd by the weakness of thir Leaders,
they were put to rout, or disbanded themselves. For Souldiers
most commonly are as thir Commanders, without much odds
20 of valour in one Nation or other, only as they are more or less
wisely disciplin'd and conducted. The following year brought   999.
them back upon *Kent,* where they enterd *Medway,* and be-   *Sim. Dun.*
seig'd *Rochester;* but the *Kentish* men assembling, gave them
a sharp encounter, yet that suffic'd not to hinder them from
25 doing as they had done in other places. Against these depopu-
lations, the King levied an Army; but the unskillfull Leaders
not knowing what to do with it when they had it, did but
drive out time, burd'ning and impoverishing the people,

consuming the publick treasure, and more imboldning the
Enemy, then if they had sat quiet at home. What cause mov'd
the *Danes* next year to pass into *Normandy,* is not recorded;
but that they return'd thence more outragious then before.
5 Mean while the King, to make some diversion, undertak's an
expedition both by Land and Sea into *Cumberland,* where the
Danes were most planted; there and in the Ile of *Man,* or as
Camden saith, *Anglesey,* imitating his Enemies in spoiling
and unpeopleing; the *Danes* from *Normandy* arriving in the
10 River *Ex,* laid seige to *Exeter;* but the Cittizens, as those of
London, valorously defending themselves, they wreck'd thir
anger, as before, on the Villages round about. The Country
people of *Somerset* and *Devonshire* assembling themselves at
Penho, shew'd thir readiness, but wanted a head; and besides,
15 being then but few in number, were easily put to flight; the
Enemy plundring all at will, with loaded spoils pass'd into
the Ile of *Wight;* from whence all *Dorsetshire,* and *Hamshire,*
felt again thir fury. The *Saxon* Annals write, that before thir
coming to *Exeter,* the *Hamshire* men had a bickering with
20 them, wherin *Ethelward* the Kings General was slain, adding
other things hardly to be understood, and in one antient Copy;
so end. *Ethelred,* whom no adversity could awake from his
soft and sluggish life, still coming by the worse at fighting, by
the advice of his Peers not unlike himself, sends one of his gay
25 Courtiers, though looking loftily, to stoop basely and propose
a third tribute to the *Danes:* they willingly hark'n, but the
summ is enhaunc't now to 24 thousand pound, and paid; the
Danes therupon abstaining from hostility. But the King to

1000.
Sim. Dun

1001.
Sim. Dun

1002.
Sim. Dun

strengthen his House by some potent affinity, marries *Em-*
ma, whom the *Saxons* call *Elgiva,* Daughter of *Richard* Duke
of *Normandy.* With him *Ethelred* formerly had War or no   *Malms.*
good correspondence, as appears by a Letter of Pope *John* the   *Calvis.*
5 *15th.* who made peace between them about eleaven years before; puft up now with his suppos'd access of strength by this
affinity, he caus'd the *Danes* all over *England,* though now   *Florent.*
living peaceably, in one day perfidiously to be massacherd,   *Huntingd.*
both Men, Women, and Childern; sending privat Letters to
10 every Town and Citty, wherby they might be ready all at the
same hower; which till the appointed time (being the 9*th* of   *Calvisius.*
July) was conceal'd with great silence, and perform'd with
much unanimity; so generally hated were the *Danes. Mat.*
West. writes, that this execution upon the *Danes* was ten years
15 after; that *Huna* one of *Ethelreds* Chief Captains, complaining of the *Danish* insolencies in time of peace, thir pride, thir
ravishing of Matrons and Virgins, incited the King to this
massacher, which in the madness of rage made no difference
of innocent or nocent. Among these, *Gunhildis* the Sister of
20 *Swane* was not spar'd, though much deserving not pitty only,
but all protection: she with her Husband Earl *Palingus,* coming to live in *England,* and receaving Christianity, had her
Husband and young Son slain before her face, her self then
beheaded, foretelling and denouncing that her blood would   *Mat. West.*
25 cost *England* dear. Some say this was done by the Traitor
Edric, to whose custody she was committed; but the massacher was some years before *Edric's* advancement; and if it
were done by him afterward, it seems to contradict the privat

correspondence which he was thought to hold with the *Danes.*
For *Swane* breathing revenge, hasted the next year into *Eng-*
land, and by the treason or negligence of Count *Hugh,* whom
Emma had recommended to the Government of *Devonshire,*
5　sack'd the City of *Exeter,* her Wall from East to West-gate
brok'n down: after this wasting *Wiltshire,* the people of that
County, and of *Hamshire,* came together in great numbers
with resolution stoutly to oppose him, but *Alfric* thir General,
whose Sons Eyes the King had lately put out, madly thinking
10　to revenge himself on the King, by ruining his own Country,
when he should have orderd his Battel, the Enemy being at
hand, fain'd himself tak'n with a vomiting; wherby his Army
in great discontent, destitute of a Commander, turn'd from
the Enemy; who streight took *Wilton* and *Salsbury,* carrying
15　the pillage therof to his Ships. Thence the next year landing
on the Coast of *Norfolk,* he wasted the Country, and set *Nor-*
wich on fire; *Ulfketel* Duke of the *East-Angles,* a man of great
valour, not having space to gather his Forces, after consultation had, thought it best to make peace with the *Dane,* which
20　he breaking within three weeks, issu'd silently out of his Ships,
came to *Thetford,* staid there a night, and in the Morning left
it flameing. *Ulketel* hearing this, commanded some to go and
break, or burn his Ships; but they not dareing or neglecting,
he in the mean while with what secresie and speed was pos-
25　sible, drawing together his Forces, went out against the
Enemy, and gave them a feirce onset retreating to thir Ships;
but much inferiour in number, many of the Cheif *East-*
Angles, there lost thir lives. Nor did the *Danes* come off with-

1003.
Sim. Dun.

1004.
Sim. Dun

out great slaughter of thir own; confessing that they never
met in *England* with so rough a charge. The next year, whom 1005.
Sim. Dun.
War could not, a great Famin drove *Swane* out of the Land.
But the Summer following, another great Fleet of *Danes*
5 enterd the Port of *Sandwich,* thence powrd out over all *Kent* 1006.
Sim. Dun.
and *Sussex,* made prey of what they found. The King levying
an Army out of *Mercia,* and the *West-Saxons,* took on him for
once the Manhood to go out and face them; But they who held
it safer to live by rapine, then to hazard a Battel, shifting
10 lightly from place to place, frustrated the slow motions of a
heavy Camp, following thir wonted course of robbery, then
running to thir Ships. Thus all *Autumn* they wearied out the
Kings Army, which gone home to winter, they carried all thir
pillage to the Ile of *Wight,* and there staid till *Christmas;* at
15 which time the King being in *Shropshire,* and but ill imploi'd
(for by the procurement of *Edric,* he caus'd, as is thought, *Florent.*
Alfhelm a noble Duke, treacherously to be slain, and the
Eyes of his two Sons to be put out) they came forth again,
over-running *Hamshire,* and *Barkeshire,* as far as *Reading*
20 and *Wallingford:* thence to *Ashdune,* and other places thereabout, neither known nor of tolerable pronuntiation; and
returning by another way, found many of the people in
Armes by the River *Kenet;* but making thir way through,
they got safe with vast booty to thir Ships. The King and his 1007.
Sim. Dun.
25 Courtiers wearied out with thir last Summers jaunt after the
nimble *Danes* to no purpose, which by proof they found too
toilsome for thir soft Bones, more us'd to Beds and Couches,
had recourse to thir last and only remedy, thir Cofers; and

send now the fourth time to buy a dishonorable peace, every
time still dearer, not to be had now under 36 thousand pound
(for the *Danes* knew how to milk such easie Kine) in name
of Tribute and expences: which out of the people over all
5 *England,* already half beggerd, was extorted and paid. About
the same time *Ethelred* advanc'd *Edric,* surnam'd *Streon,*
from obscure condition to be Duke of *Mercia,* and marry
Edgitha the Kings Daughter. The cause of his advancement,
Florent of *Worster,* and *Mat. West.* attribute to his great
10 wealth, gott'n by fine policies and a plausible tongue: he
prov'd a main accessory to the ruin of *England,* as his actions
will soon declare. *Ethelred* the next year somewhat rowsing
himself, ordain'd that every 310 Hides (a Hide is so much
land as one Plow can sufficiently till) should set out a Ship or
15 Gally, and every nine Hides find a Corslet and Head-peice:
new Ships in every Port were builded, vittl'd, fraught with
stout Mariners and Souldiers, and appointed to meet all at
Sandwich. A man might now think that all would go well;
when suddenly a new mischief sprung up, dissention among
20 the great ones; which brought all this diligence to as little
success as at other times before. *Bithric* the Brother of *Edric,*
falsly accus'd *Wulnoth* a great Officer set over the *South-
Saxons,* who fearing the potency of his Enemies, with 20
Ships got to Sea, and practis'd piracy on the Coast. Against
25 whom, reported to be in a place where he might be easily surpris'd, *Bithric* sets forth with 80 Ships; all which driv'n back
by a Tempest and wrackt upon the shoar, were burnt soon
after by *Wulnoth.* Disheart'nd with this misfortune, the King

1008.
Sim. Dun

returns to *London;* the rest of his Navy after him; and all this
great preparation to nothing. Wherupon *Turkill,* a *Danish*
Earl, came with a Navy to the Ile of *Tanet,* and in *August* a
far greater, led by *Heming* and *Ilaf* joyn'd with him. Thence
5 coasting to *Sandwich,* and landed, they went onward and
began to assault *Canterbury,* but the Citizens and East Kentish
men, coming to composition with them for three thousand
pound, they departed thence to the Ile of *Wight,* robbing and
burning by the way. Against these the King levies an Army
10 through all the land, and in several quarters places them nigh
the Sea, but so unskillfully or unsuccessfully, that the *Danes*
were not therby hinderd from exerciseing thir wonted Robberies. It happ'nd that the *Danes* one day were gone up into
the Country, far from thir Ships, the King having notice
15 therof, thought to intercept them in thir return; his men
were resolute to overcome or die, time and place advantagious;
but where courage and fortune was not wanting, there wanted
Loyalty among them. *Edric* with suttle arguments that had
a shew of deep policy, disputed and perswaded the simplicity
20 of his Fellow Counsellers, that it would be best consulted at
that time to let the *Danes* pass without ambush or intercep-
tion. The *Danes* where they expected danger, finding none,
pass'd on with great joy and booty to thir Ships. After this,
sailing about *Kent,* they lay that Winter in the *Thames,*
25 forcing *Kent* and *Essex* to contribution, oft-times attempting
the City of *London,* but repuls't as oft to thir great loss. Spring
begun, leaving thir Ships, they pass'd through *Chiltern* Wood
into *Oxfordshire,* burnt the City, and thence returning with

1009.
Sim. Dun.

1010.
Sim. Dun.
Florent.

divided forces wasted on both sides the *Thames;* but hearing, that an Army from *London* was marcht out against them, they on the North-side, passing the River at *Stanes,* join'd with them on the South into one body, and enrich't with great
5 spoils, came back through *Surrey* to thir Ships; which all the Lent-time they repair'd. After *Easter,* sailing to the *East-Angles* they arriv'd at *Ipswich,* and came to a place call'd *Ringmere,* where they heard that *Ulfketell* with his Forces lay, who with a sharp encounter soon entertain'd them; but
10 his men at length giving back, through the suttlety of a *Danish* Servant among them who began the flight, lost the field; though the men of *Cambridgeshire* stood to it valiantly. In this Battel *Ethelstan* the Kings Son in Law, with many other Noblemen, was slain; wherby the *Danes* without more re-
15 sistance, three months together had the spoiling of those Countries and all the Fenns, burnt *Thetford* and *Grantbrig,* or *Cambridge;* thence to a hilly place not far off, call'd by *Huntingdon Balesham,* by *Camden Gogmagog* Hills, and the Villages therabout they turn'd thir fury, slaying all they met
20 save one man, who getting up into a Steeple, is said to have defended himself against the whole *Danish* Army. They therefore so leaving him, thir Foot by Sea, thir Horse by land through *Essex,* return'd back lad'n to thir Ships left in the *Thames.* But many daies pass'd not between, when salying
25 again out of thir Ships as out of Savage Denns, they plunderd over again all *Oxfordshire,* and added to thir prey *Bucking-* Huntin, *ham, Bedford,* and *Hertfordshire;* then like wild Beasts glutted, returning to thir Caves. A third excursion they made

into *Northamptonshire,* burnt *Northampton,* ransacking the
Country round; then as to fresh pasture betook them to the
West-Saxons, and in like sort harrasing all *Wiltshire,* return'd, as I said before, like wild Beasts or rather Sea-Monsters
5 to thir Water-stables, accomplishing by *Christmas* the Circuit
of thir whole years good Deeds; an unjust and inhuman
Nation, who receaving or not receaving tribute where none
was owing them, made such destruction of mankind, and
rapine of their lively-hood, as is a misery to read. Yet here
10 they ceas'd not, for the next year repeating the same cruel- 1011.
ties on both sides the *Thames,* one way as far as *Hunt-* *Sim. Dun.*
ingdon, the other as far as *Wiltshire* and *Southhampton,*
sollicited again by the King for peace, and receaving thir
demands both of tribute and contribution, they slighted
15 thir faith; and in the beginning of *September* laid seige
to *Canterbury.* On the twentieth day, by the treachery of
Almere the Archdeacon, they took part of it and burnt it,
committing all sorts of massacher as a sport; some they threw
over the Wall, others into the fire, hung some by the privy
20 members, infants pull'd from thir mothers breasts, were
either tost on spears, or Carts drawn over them; Matrons and
Virgins by the hair dragd and ravish't. *Alfage* the grave
Archbishop, above others hated of the *Danes,* as in all Coun- *Eadmer.*
sells and actions to his might thir known opposer, tak'n, *Malms.*
Eadmer.
25 wounded, imprison'd in a noisom Ship; the multitude are 1012.
tith'd, and every tenth only spar'd. Early the next year before *Sim. Dun.*
Easter, while *Ethelred* and his Peers were assembl'd at *Lon-*
don, to raise now the fifth Tribute amounting to 48 thousand

pound, the *Danes* at *Canterbury* propose to the Archbishop, who had bin now seav'n months thir Prisoner, life and lib- *Eadmer* erty, if he pay them three thousand pound; which he refuseing as not able of himself, and not willing to extort it from

5 his Tennants, is permitted till the next *Sunday* to consider; then hal'd before thir Counsel, of whom *Turkill* was Cheif, and still refuseing, they rise most of them being drunk, and beat him with the blunt side of thir Axes, then thrust forth deliver him to be pelted with stones; till one *Thrum* a converted

10 *Dane,* pittying him half dead, to put him out of pain; with a pious impiety, at one stroak of his Ax on the head dispatch'd him. His body was carried to *London,* and there buried, thence afterward remov'd to *Canterbury.* By this time the tribute paid, and peace so oft'n violated sworn again by the

15 *Danes,* they dispers'd thir Fleet; forty five of them, and *Turkill* thir Cheif staid at *London* with the King, swore him Allegeance to defend his Land against all strangers, on condition only to be fed and cloth'd by him. But this voluntary friendship of *Turkill* was thought to be deceitfull, that stay-

20 ing under this pretence he gave intelligence to *Swane,* when most it would be seasonable to come. In *July* therfore of the $\begin{smallmatrix}1013\\ Sim. D\end{smallmatrix}$ next year, King *Swane* arriving at *Sandwich,* made no stay there, but sailing first to *Humber,* thence into *Trent,* landed and encamp'd at *Gainsburrow:* whither without delay re-

25 pair'd to him the *Northumbrians,* with *Uthred* thir Earl; those of *Lindsey* also, then those of *Fisburg,* and lastly all on the North of *Watling-street* (which is a high way from East to West Sea) gave Oath and Hostages to obey him. From

whom he commanded Horses and provision for his Army, taking with him besides Bands and Companies of thir choicest men; and committing to his Son *Canute* the care of his Fleet and hostages; he marches towards the *South Mercians,* com-

5 manding his Souldiers to exercise all Acts of hostility; with the terror wherof fully executed, he took in few daies the City of *Oxford,* then *Winchester;* thence tending to *London,* in his hasty passage over the *Thames,* without seeking Bridge or Ford, lost many of his men. Nor was his expedition against

10 *London* prosperous; for assaying all means by force or wile to take the City, wherin the King then was, & *Turkill* with his *Danes,* he was stoutly beat'n off as at other times. Thence back to *Wallingford* and *Bath* directing his course, after usual havock made, he sate a while and refresh'd his Army. There

15 *Ethelm* an Earl of *Devonshire,* and other great Officers in the West yeilded him subjection. These things flowing to his wish, he betook him to his Navy, from that time stil'd and accounted King of *England,* if a Tyrant, saith *Simeon,* may be call'd a King. The *Londoners* also sent him hostages and

20 made thir peace, for they fear'd his fury. *Ethelred* thus reduc't to narrow compass, sent *Emma* his Queen, with his two Sons had by her, and all his treasure to *Richard* the 2*d.* her Brother, Duke of *Normandy;* himself with his *Danish* Fleet abode some while at *Greenwich,* then sailing to the Ile of

25 *Wight,* pass'd after *Christmas* into *Normandy;* where he was honourably receav'd at *Roan* by the Duke, though known to have born himself churlishly and proudly towards *Emma* his *Malms.* Sister, besides his dissolute Company with other women.

Mean while *Swane* ceas'd not to exact almost insupportable
tribute of the people, spoiling them when he listed; besides,
the like did *Turkill* at *Greenwich*. The next year beginning, 1014.
Sim. Dun
Swane sickens and dyes; some say terrifi'd and smitt'n by an *Mat. Wes*
5 appearing shape of St. *Edmund* arm'd, whose Church at *Bury*
he had threat'nd to demolish; but the authority hereof relies
only upon the Legend of St. *Edmund.* After his Death the
Danish Army and Fleet made his Son *Canute* thir King; but
the Nobility and States of *England* sent Messengers to *Ethel-*
10 *red,* declareing that they preferr'd none before thir Native
Sovran, if he would promise to govern them better then he
had done, and with more Clemency. Wherat the King rejoicing, sends over his Son *Edward* with Embassadors to
court both high and low, and win thir love, promising largly
15 to be thir mild and devoted Lord, to consent in all things to
thir will, follow thir counsel, and whatever had been done or
spok'n by any man against him, freely to pardon; if they
would loyally restore him to be thir King. To this the people
cheerfully answer'd, and amity was both promisd and con-
20 firm'd on both sides. An Embassey of Lords is sent to bring
back the King honourably; he returns in *Lent* and is joyfully
receav'd of the people, marches with a strong Army against
Canute; who having got Horses and joyn'd with the men of
Lindsey, was preparing to make spoil in the Countries adjoin-
25 ing; but by *Ethelred* unexpectedly coming upon him, was
soon driv'n to his Ships, and his Confederats of *Lindsey* left
to the anger of thir Country-men, executed without mercy
both by fire and Sword. *Canute* in all hast sailing back to

Sandwich, took the hostages giv'n to his Father from all parts
of *England,* and with slit Noses, Ears cropt, and hands chop't
off, setting them ashore, departed into *Denmarke.* Yet the
people were not disburd'nd, for the King rais'd out of them
5   30 thousand pound to pay his Fleet of *Danes* at *Greenwich.*
To these evills the Sea in *October* pass'd his bounds, over-
whelming many Towns in *England,* and of thir inhabitants
many thousands. The year following an Assembly being at
Oxford, Edric of *Streon,* having invited two Noblemen, *Sige-*
10 *ferth,* and *Morcar,* the Sons of *Earngrun* of *Seav'nburg* to his
Lodging, secretly murderd them: the King, for what cause is
unknown, seis'd thir Estates, and caus'd *Algith* the Wife of
Sigeferth to be kept at *Maidulfsburg,* now *Malmsbury;* whom
Edmund the Prince there married against his Fathers minde,
15 then went and possesd thir lands, making the people there
subject to him. *Mat. West.* saith, that these two were of the
Danes who had seated themselves in *Northumberland,* slain
by *Edric* under colour of Treason laid to thir charge. They
who attended them without, tumulting at the Death of thir
20 Maisters, were beat'n back; and driv'n into a Church, and
defending themselves were burnt there in the Steeple. Mean
while *Canute* returning from *Denmarke* with a great Navy,
200 Ships richly gilded and adorn'd, well fraught with Arms
and all provision; and, which *Encomium Emmæ* mentions
25 not, two other Kings, *Lachman* of *Sweden, Olav* of *Norway,*
arriv'd at *Sandwich;* And, as the same Authour then living
writes, sent out spies to discover what resistance on land was
to be expected; who return'd with certain report, that a great

1015.
Sim. Dun.

Malms.

Leges. Ed.
Conf. Tit.
deduct.
Norman.

Army of English was in readiness to oppose them. *Turkill,*
who upon the arrival of these *Danish* Powers, kept faith no
longer with the English, but joining now with *Canute,* as it
were to reingratiate himself after his revolt, whether real or *Encom. E*
5 complotted, councell'd him (being yet young) not to land,
but leave to him the management of this first Battel; the King
assented, and he with the Forces which he had brought, and
part of those which arriv'd with *Canute,* landing to thir wish
encounterd the English, though double in number, at a place
10 call'd *Scorastan,* and was at first beaten back with much loss.
But at length animating his men with rage only and despair,
obtain'd a clear Victory, which won him great reward and
possessions from *Canute.* But of this action no other writer
makes mention: from *Sandwich* therefore sailing about to
15 the River *Frome,* and there landing, over all *Dorset, Sommer-*
set, and *Wiltshire,* he spread wastfull hostility. The King lay *Camd.*
then sick at *Cosham* in this County; though it may seem
strange how he could lie sick there in the midst of his Enemies. Howbeit *Edmund* in one part, and *Edric* of *Streon* in
20 another, rais'd Forces by themselves; but so soon as both
Armies were united, the Traytor *Edric* being found to practice against the life of *Edmund,* he remov'd with his Army
from him; whereof the Enemy took great advantage. *Edric*
easily enticeing the 40 Ships of *Danes* to side with him, re-
25 volted to *Canute,* the *West-Saxons* also gave pledges and fur-
nished him with Horses. By which means the year ensueing, *1016.*
he with *Edric* the Traytor, passing the *Thames* at *Creclad,* *Sim. Dun*
about twelftide, enterd into *Mercia,* and especially *Warwick-*

shire, depopulating all places in thir way. Against these, Prince *Edmund,* for his hardiness call'd *Ironside,* gather'd an Army; but the *Mercians* refus'd to fight unless *Ethelred* with the *Londoners* came to aid them; and so every man return'd
5 home. After the Festival, *Edmund* gathering another Army besought his Father to come with the *Londoners,* and what force besides he was able; they came with great strength gott'n together, but being come, and in a hopefull way of good success, it was told the King, that unless he took the
10 better heed, some of his own Forces would fall off and betray him. The King daunted with this perhaps cunning whisper of the Enemy, disbanding his Army, returns to *London.* *Edmund* betook him into *Northumberland,* as some thought to raise fresh Forces; but he with Earl *Uthred* on the one side,
15 and *Canute* with *Edric* on the other, did little else but wast the Provinces; *Canute* to Conquer them, *Edmund* to punish them, who stood neuter; for which cause *Stafford, Shropshire,* and *Lestershire,* felt heavily his hand; while *Canute,* who was ruining the more Southern Shires, at length march'd into
20 *Northumberland;* which *Edmund* hearing dismiss'd his Forces and came to *London.* *Uthred* the Earl hasted back to *Northumberland,* and finding no other remedy, submitted himself with all the *Northumbrians,* giving hostages to *Canute.* Nevertheless by his command or connivence, and the
25 hand of one *Turebrand,* a *Danish* Lord; *Uthred* was slain, and *Iric* another *Dane* made Earl in his stead. This *Uthred* Son of *Walteof,* as *Simeon* writes, in his treatise of the Seige of *Durham,* in his youth obtain'd a great Victory against

Malcolm Son of *Kened* King of *Scots,* who with the whole
power of his Kingdome was fall'n into *Northumberland,* and
laid seige to *Durham.* *Walteof* the old Earl unable to resist,
had secur'd himself in *Bebbanburg,* a strong Town, but
5 *Uthred* gathering an Army rais'd the Seige, slew most of the
Scots, thir King narrowly escaping, and with the heads of thir
slain fixt upon Poles beset round the Walls of *Durham.* The
year of this exploit *Simeon* cleers not, for in 969. and in the
Reign of *Ethelred* as he affirms, it could not bee. *Canute* by
10 another way returning Southward, joyfull of his success, before *Easter* came back with all the Army to his Fleet. About
the end of *April* ensueing, *Ethelred* after a long, troublesome
and ill govern'd Reign, ended his daies at *London,* and was
buried in the Church of St. *Paul.*

15 ## *Edmund Ironside.*

AFTER the decease of *Ethelred,* they of the Nobility *Florent.*
who were then at *London* together with the Citizens, *Aelred in*
chose *Edmund* his Son (not by *Emma,* but a former Wife the *the life of*
Daughter of Earl *Thored*) in his Fathers room; but the Arch- *Ed. Conf*
20 bishops, Abbots, and many of the Nobles assembling together
elected *Canute;* and coming to *Southamton* where he then
remain'd, renounc'd before him all the race of *Ethelred,* and
swore him fidelity: he also swore to them, in matters both
religious and secular, to be thir faithfull Lord. But *Edmund* *Florent.*
25 with all speed going to the *West-Saxons,* was joyfully receav'd *Sim. Dun*
of them as thir King, and of many other Provinces by their
example. Mean while *Canute* about mid *May* came with his

whole Fleet up the River to *London;* then causing a great
Dike to be made on *Surrey* side, turn'd the stream and drew
his Ships thether West of the Bridge; then begirting the City
with a broad and deep trench, assail'd it on every side; but
5 repulst as before by the valorous Defendants, and in despair
of success at that time, leaving part of his Army for the defence of his Ships, with the rest sped him to the *West-Saxons,*
ere *Edmund* could have time to assemble all his powers: who
yet with such as were at hand invoking divine aid, encounterd
10 the *Danes* at *Pen* by *Gillingham* in *Dorsetshire,* and put him
to flight. After mid-summer, encreast with new Forces, he met
with him again at a place call'd *Sherastan,* now *Sharstan;* but
Edric, Almar, and *Algar,* with the *Hamshire* and *Wiltshire*
men, then sideing with the *Danes,* he only maintain'd the
15 fight, obstinatly fought on both sides, till night and weariness
parted them. Day light returning renu'd the conflict; wherein
the *Danes* appearing inferiour, *Edric* to dishart'n the English
cuts off the Head of one *Osmer,* in countnance and hair somewhat resembling the King, and holding it up, cries aloud to
20 the English, that *Edmund* being slain and this his head, it
was time for them to flie; which falacy *Edmund* perceaving,
and op'nly shewing himself to his Souldiers, by a spear thrown   *Malms.*
at *Edric,* that missing him yet slew one next him, and through
him another behinde, they recoverd heart, and lay sore upon
25 the *Danes* till night parted them as before: for ere the third
morn, *Canute* sensible of his loss, march'd away by stealth to
his Ships at *London,* renuing there his leagre. Some would
have this Battell at *Sherastan* the same with that at *Scorastan*

before mention'd, but the circumstance of time permits not that, having bin before the landing of *Canute*, this a good while after, as by the Process of things appears: from *Sherastan* or *Sharstan*, *Edmund* return'd to the *West-Saxons*, whose

5 valour *Edric* fearing, least it might prevail against the *Danes*, sought pardon of his revolt, and obtaining it swore loyalty to the King, who now the third time coming with an Army from the *West-Saxons* to *London*, rais'd the Seige, chaseing *Canute* and his *Danes* to thir Ships. Then after two daies passing the

10 *Thames* at *Branford*, and so coming on thir backs, kept them so turn'd, and obtain'd the Victory: then returns again to his *West Saxons*, and *Canute* to his Seige, but still in vain; riseing therfore thence, he enterd with his Ships a River then call'd *Arenne;* and from the Banks therof wafted *Mercia;* thence

15 thir Horse by land, thir Foot by Ship came to *Medway*. *Edmund* in the mean while with multipli'd Forces out of many Shires, crossing again at *Branford*, came into *Kent*, seeking *Canute;* encounterd him at *Otford*, and so defeated, that of his Horse, they who escap'd fled to the Ile of *Sheppey*, and a

20 full Victory he had gain'd, had not *Edric* still the Traytor by some wile or other detain'd his persuit: and *Edmund* who never wanted courage, heer wanted prudence to be so misled, ever after forsak'n of his wonted Fortune. *Canute* crossing with his Army into *Essex*, thence wasted *Mercia* worse then

25 before, and with heavy prey return'd to his Ships: them *Edmund* with a collected Army persueing, overtook at a place call'd *Assandune*, or *Asseshill*, now *Ashdown* in *Essex;* the *Camden.* Battel on either side was fought with great vehemence; but

perfidious *Edric* perceaving the Victory to incline towards *Edmund,* with that part of the Army which was under him, fled, as he had promis'd *Canute,* and left the King over-match't with numbers: by which desertion the English were over-
5 thrown, Duke *Alfric,* Duke *Godwin,* and *Ulfketel* the valiant Duke of *East-Angles,* with a great part of the Nobility slain, so as the English of a long time had not receav'd a greater blow. Yet after a while *Edmund* not absurdly call'd *Ironside,* preparing to try again his Fortune in another feild, was hin-
10 derd by *Edric* and others of his faction, adviseing him to make peace and divide the Kingdome with *Canute.* To which *Ed-* *Camd.* mund over-rul'd, a treaty appointed, and pledges mutually giv'n, both Kings met together at a place call'd *Deorhirst* in *Glostershire; Edmund* on the West side of *Severn, Canute* on
15 the East with thir Armies, then both in person wafted into an Iland, at that time call'd *Olanege,* now *Alney* in the midst of *Camd.* the River; swearing amity and brotherhood, they parted the Kingdome between them. Then interchanging Armes and the habit they wore, assessing also what pay should be allotted to
20 the Navy; they departed each his way. Concerning this interveiw and the cause therof, others write otherwise; *Malmsbury,* that *Edmund* greiving at the loss of so much blood spilt for the ambition only of two men striveing who should reign, of his own accord sent to *Canute,* offering him single Com-
25 bate, to prevent in thir own cause the effusion of more blood then thir own; that *Canute* though of courage anough, yet not unwisely doubting to adventure his body of small Timber, against a man of Iron sides, refus'd the Combate, offring to

divide the Kingdome; this offer pleasing both Armies, *Edmund* was not difficult to consent; and the decision was, that he as his hereditary Kingdome should rule the *West-Saxons,* and all the *South, Canute* the *Mercians,* and the *North. Huntingdon* follow'd by *Mat. West.* relates, that the Peers on every side wearied out with continuall warfare, and not refraining to affirm op'nly, that they two who expected to reign singly, had most reason to fight singly, the Kings were content; the Iland was thir lists, the Combate Knightly; till *Knute* finding himself too weak, began to parle, which ended as is said before. After which the *Londoners* bought thir peace of the *Danes,* and permitted them to winter in the City. But King *Edmund* about the Feast of St. *Andrew,* unexpectedly deceas'd at *London,* and was buried neer to *Edgar* his Grandfather at *Glaston.* The cause of his so sudden death is uncertain; common fame, saith *Malmsbury,* laies the guilt therof upon *Edric,* who to please *Canute,* allur'd with promise of reward two of the Kings Privy Chamber, though at first abhorring the fact, to assassinate him at the stool, by thrusting a sharp Iron into his hinder parts. *Huntingdon,* and *Mat. West.* relate it done at *Oxford* by the Son of *Edric,* and something vary in the manner, not worth recital. *Edmund* dead, *Canute* meaning to reign sole King of *England,* calls to him all the Dukes, Barons, and Bishops of the Land, cunningly demanding of them who were witnesses what agreement was made between him and *Edmund* dividing the Kingdome, whether the Sons and Brothers of *Edmund* were to govern the *West-Saxons* after him, *Canute* living? they who understood his

meaning, and fear'd to undergo his anger, timorously answerd, that *Edmund* they knew had left no part therof to his Sons or Brethren, living or dying; but that he intended *Canute* should be thir Guardian, till they came to age of reigning. *Simeon*
5 affirms, that for fear or hope of reward they attested what was not true: notwithstanding which he put many of them to death not long after.

Canute, or *Knute.*

CANUTE having thus sounded the Nobility, and by them understood, receav'd thir Oath of fealty, they
10 the pledge of his bare hand, and Oath from the *Danish* Nobles; wherupon the House of *Edmund* was renounc't, and *Canute* Crown'd. Then they enacted, that *Edwi* Brother of *Edmund,* a Prince of great hope, should be banish't the
15 Realm. But *Canute* not thinking himself secure while *Edwi* liv'd, consulted with *Edric* how to make him away; who told him of one *Ethelward* a decay'd Nobleman, likeliest to do the work. *Ethelward* sent for, and tempted by the King in privat, with largest rewards, but abhorring in his mind the deed,
20 promisd to do it when he saw his opportunity; and so still deferr'd it. But *Edwi* afterwards receav'd into favour as a snare, was by him or some other of his false freinds, *Canute* contriving it, the same year slain. *Edric* also counsel'd him to dispatch *Edward* and *Edmund,* the Sons of *Ironside;* but the
25 King doubting that the fact would seem too foul done in *England,* sent them to the King of *Sweden,* with like intent; but he disdaining the Office, sent them for better safety to *Solomon* King of *Hungary;* where *Edmund* at length dy'd,

1017.
Sim. Dun.
Sax. an.

but *Edward* married *Agatha* Daughter to *Henry* the *German* Emperour. A digression in the Laws of *Edward* Confessor under the Title of *Lex Noricorum* saith, that this *Edward* for fear of *Canute,* fled of his own accord to *Malesclot* King of
5 the *Rugians,* who receav'd him honourably, and of that Country gave him a Wife. *Canute* settl'd in his Throne, divided the Government of his Kingdom into fowr parts; the *West-Saxons* to himself, the *East-Angles* to Earl *Turkill,* the *Mercians* to *Edric,* the *Northumbrians* to *Eric;* then made peace
10 with all Princes round about him, and his former Wife being dead, in *July* married *Emma* the Widow of King *Ethelred.* The *Christmas* following was an ill Feast to *Edric,* of whose Treason, the King having now made use as much as serv'd his turn, and fearing himself to be the next betray'd, caus'd
15 him to be slain at *London* in the Palace, thrown over the City Wall, and there to lie unburied; the head of *Edric* fixt on a pole, he commanded to be set on the highest Tower of *London,* as in a double sence he had promis'd him, for the murder of King *Edmund* to exalt him above all the Peers of *England.*
20 *Huntingdon, Malmsbury,* and *Mat. West.* write, that suspecting the Kings intention to degrade him from his *Mercian* Dukedome, and upbraiding him with his merits, the King enrag'd, caus'd him to be strangl'd in the room, and out at a Window thrown into the *Thames.* Another writes, that *Eric*
25 at the Kings command struck off his head. Other great men though without fault, as Duke *Norman* the Son of *Leofwin,* *Ethelward* Son of Duke *Agelmar,* he put to death at the same time, jealous of thir power or familiarity with *Edric:* and

Encom. *Ingulf.*

notwithstanding peace, kept still his Army; to maintain
which, the next year he squees'd out of the English, though
now his subjects, not his Enemies, 72, some say, 82 thousand
pound, besides 15 thousand out of *London*. Mean while great
5 War arose at *Carr,* between *Uthred* Son of *Waldef,* Earl of
Northumberland, and *Malcolm* Son of *Kened* King of *Scots,*
with whom held *Eugenius* King of *Lothian*. But heer *Simeon*
the relater seems to have committed some mistake, having
slain *Uthred* by *Canute* two years before, and set *Eric* in his
10 place: *Eric* therfore it must needs be, not *Uthred,* who man-
ag'd this War against the *Scots*. About which time in a Convention of *Danes* at *Oxford,* it was agreed on both parties to
keep the Laws of *Edgar; Mat. West.* saith, of *Edward* the
Elder. The next year *Canute* sail'd into *Denmarke,* and there
15 abode all Winter. *Huntingdon* and *Mat. West.* say, he went
thether to repress the *Swedes,* and that the night before a
Battel to be fought with them, *Godwin* stealing out of the
Camp with his English, assaulted the *Swedes,* and had got the
victory ere *Canute* in the morning knew of any fight. For
20 which bold enterprise, though against Discipline, he had the
English in more esteem ever after. In the Spring at his return
into *England,* he held in the time of *Easter* a great assembly
at *Chirchester,* and the same year was with *Turkill* the *Dane*
at the dedication of a Church by them built at *Assendune,* in
25 the place of that great Victory which won him the Crown.
But suspecting his greatness, the year following banish'd him
the Realm, and found occasion to do the like by *Eric* the
Northumbrian Earl upon the same jealousie. Nor yet content

1018.
Sim. Dun.
Huntingd.
Mat. West.

1019.
Sim. Dun.

1020.
Sim. Dun.

1021.
Sim. Dun.
Malms.
1028.
Sim. Dun.

with his Conquest of *England,* though now above ten years
enjoy'd, he pass'd with 50 Ships into *Norway,* dispossess'd
Olave thir King, and subdu'd the land, first with great
summes of money sent the year before to gain him a party,
5 then coming with an Army to compell the rest. Thence returning King of *England, Denmarke,* and *Norway,* yet not
secure in his mind, under colour of an Embassey he sent into
banishment *Hacun* a powerfull *Dane,* who had married the
Daughter of his Sister *Gunildis,* having conceav'd some sus-
10 pition of his practices against him: but such course was tak'n,
that he never came back; either perishing at Sea, or slain by
contrivance the next year in *Orkney. Canute* therefore having thus establish't himself by bloodshed and oppression, to
wash away, as he thought, the guilt therof, sailing again into
15 *Denmark,* went thence to *Rome,* and offerd there to St. *Peter*
great guifts of Gold and Silver, and other pretious things; besides the usuall tribute of *Romscot,* giving great Alms by the
way, both thether and back again, freeing many places of
Custom and Toll with great expence, where strangers were
20 wont to pay, having vow'd great amendment of life at the
Sepulchre of *Peter* and *Paul,* and to his whole people in a large
letter writt'n from *Rome* yet extant. At his return therfore he
built and dedicated a Church to St. *Edmund* at *Bury,* whom
his Ancestors had slain, threw out the secular Preists who had
25 intruded there, and plac'd Monks in thir stead; then going
into *Scotland,* subdu'd and receav'd homage of *Malcolm,* and
two other Kings there, *Melbeath,* and *Jermare.* Three years
after having made *Swane* his suppos'd Son by *Algiva* of

1029.
Sim. Dut

1030.
Sim. Dut
1031.
Sim. Dut

Hunting

1032.
Sim. Dut

Hunting
1035.
Sim. Dut

Northamton, Duke *Alfhelms* Daughter (for others say the
Son of a Preist whom *Algiva* barren had got ready at the time
of her feign'd labour) King of *Norway,* and *Hardecnute* his   *Florent.*
Son by *Emma* King of *Denmark,* and design'd *Harold* his
5 Son by *Algiva* of *Northamton* King of *England,* dy'd at
Shaftsbury, and was buried at *Winchester* in the old Monas-   *Florent.*
tery. This King, as appears, ended better then he began, for
though he seems to have had no hand in the Death of *Ironside,*
but detested the fact, and bringing the murderers, who came
10 to him in hope of great reward, forth among his Courtiers, as
it were to receave thanks, after they had op'nly related the
manner of thir killing him, deliver'd them to deserved punishment, yet he spar'd *Edric* whom he knew to be the prime
Authour of that detestable fact; till willing to be rid of him,
15 grown importune upon the confidence of his merits, and upbraided by him that he had first relinquisht, then extinguisht
Edmund for his sake; angry to be so upbraided, therfore said
he with a chang'd countnance, Traytor to God and to me,
thou shalt die; thine own mouth accuses thee to have slain thy
20 Master my confederate Brother, and the Lords Anointed.
Whereupon although present and privat Execution was in   *Malms.*
rage done upon *Edric,* yet he himself in cool blood scrupl'd
not to make away the Brother and Childern of *Edmund,* who
had better right to be the Lords Anointed heer then himself.
25 When he had obtain'd in *England* what he desir'd, no wonder
if he sought the love of his conquerd Subjects for the love of
his own quiet, the maintainers of his wealth and state, for his
own profit. For the like reason he is thought to have married

Emma, and that *Richard* Duke of *Normandy* her Brother might the less care what became of *Elfred* and *Edward,* her Sons by King *Ethelred.* He commanded to be observ'd the antient *Saxon* Laws, call'd afterwards the Laws of *Edward*
5 the Confessor, not that hee made them, but strictly observ'd them. His Letter from *Rome* professes, if he had done aught amiss in his youth, through negligence or want of due temper, full resolution with the help of God to make amends, by governing justly and piously for the future; charges and adjures
10 all his Officers and Vicounts, that neither for fear of him, or favour of any person, or to enrich the King, they suffer injustice to be done in the land; commands his treasurers to pay all his Debts ere his return home, which was by *Denmarke,* to compose matters there; and what his Letter profess'd, he
15 perform'd all his life after. But it is a fond conceit in many great ones, and pernicious in the end, to cease from no violence till they have attain'd the utmost of thir ambitions and desires; then to think God appeas'd by thir seeking to bribe him with a share however large of thir ill-gott'n spoils, and then
20 lastly to grow zealous of doing right, when they have no longer need to do wrong. Howbeit *Canute* was famous through *Europe,* and much honour'd of *Conrade* the Emperour, then at *Rome,* with rich guifts and many grants of what he there demanded for the freeing of passages from Toll and
25 Custome. I must not omit one remarkable action done by him, as *Huntingdon* reports it, with great Scene of circumstance, and emphatical expression, to shew the small power of Kings in respect of God; which, unless to Court-Parasites, needed no

such laborious demonstration. He caus'd his Royal Seat to be
set on the shoar, while the Tide was coming in; and with all
the state that Royalty could put into his countnance, said thus
to the Sea: Thou Sea belongst to me, and the Land wheron I
5 sit is mine; nor hath any one unpunish't resisted my commands: I charge thee come no furder upon my Land, neither
presume to wet the Feet of thy Sovran Lord. But the Sea, as
before, came rowling on, and without reverence both wet and
dash'd him. Wherat the King quickly riseing, wish'd all
10 about him to behold and consider the weak and frivolous
power of a King, and that none indeed deserv'd the name of a
King, but he whose Eternal Laws both Heav'n, Earth, and
Sea obey. A truth so evident of it self, as I said before, that
unless to shame his Court Flatterers who would not else be
15 convinc't, *Canute* needed not to have gone wet-shod home:
The best is, from that time forth he never would wear a
Crown, esteeming Earthly Royalty contemptible and vain.

Harold.

HAROLD for his swiftness surnam'd *Harefoot,* the   *Florent.*
20 Son of *Canute* by *Algiva* of *Northampton* (though   *Bromton.*
                                                             Huntingd.
some speak doubtfully as if she bore him not, but had him of   *Mat. West.*
a Shoo-makers Wife, as *Swane* before of a Preist; others of a   *Mat. West.*
Maid-Servant, to conceal her barrenness) in a great Assembly
at *Oxford,* was by Duke *Leofric* and the *Mercians,* with the
25 *Londoners,* according to his Fathers Testament, elected King;
but without the Regal Habiliments, which *Ælnot* the Arch-   *Encom. Em.*
bishop having in his Custody, refus'd to deliver up, but to the

Sons of *Emma,* for which Harold ever after hated the Clergy;
and (as the Clergy are wont thence to inferr) all Religion.
Godwin Earl of *Kent,* and the West-Saxons with him, stood
for *Hardecnute. Malmsbury* saith, that the contest was be-
5 tween Dane and English; that the Danes and Londoners
grown now in a manner Danish, were all for *Hardecnute;* but
he being then in *Denmarke, Harold* prevail'd, yet so as that the
Kingdom should be divided between them; the West and
Southpart reserv'd by *Emma* for *Hardecnute,* till his return.
10 But *Harold* once advanc't into the Throne, banish'd *Emma*
his Mother-in-law, seis'd on his Fathers Treasure at *Win-*
chester, and there remain'd. *Emma* not holding it safe to
abide in *Normandy* while Duke *William* the Bastard was
yet under Age, retir'd to *Baldwin* Earl of *Flanders.* In the
15 mean while *Alfred* and *Edward* Sons of *Ethelred,* accompanied with a small number of Norman Souldiers in a few
Ships, coming to visit thir mother *Emma* not yet departed the
land, and perhaps to see how the people were inclin'd to restore them thir right; *Elfred* was sent for by the King then at
20 *London;* but in his way met at *Guilford* by Earl *Godwin,* who
with all seeming freindship entertain'd him, was in the night
surpris'd and made Prisner, most of his Company put to
various sorts of cruel Death, decimated twice over, then
brought to *London,* was by the King sent bound to *Eely,* had
25 his Eyes put out by the way, and deliverd to the Monks there,
dy'd soon after in thir Custody. *Malmsbury* gives little credit
to this story of *Elfred,* as not Chronicl'd in his time, but rumour'd only. Which *Emma* however nearing, sent away her

1036.
Sim. Dun

Son *Edward,* who by good hap accompanied not his Brother, with all speed into *Normandy.* But the Authour of *Encomium Emmæ,* who seems plainly (though nameless) to have been some Monk, yet liv'd, and perhaps wrote within the same
5 year when these things were done; by his relation differing from all others, much aggravates the cruelty of *Harold,* that he not content to have practis'd in secret (for op'nly he durst not) against the life of *Emma,* sought many treacherous ways to get her Son within his power; and resolv'd at length to forge
10 a Letter in the name of thir mother, inviting them into *England,* the Copy of which Letter he produces writt'n to this purpose.

E MMA *in name only Queen, to her Sons* Edward *and* Alfrid *imparts motherly salutation. While we severally*
15 *bewail the Death of our Lord the King, most Dear Sons, and while daily yee are depriv'd more and more of the Kingdom your Inheritance; I admire what Counsel yee take, knowing that your intermitted delay, is a daily strengthning to the Reign of your Usurper, who incessantly goes about from*
20 *Town to City, gaining the Chief Nobles to his party, either by gifts, prayers, or threats. But they had much rather one of you should reign over them, then to be held under the power of him who now over-rules them. I entreat therefore that one of you come to me speedily, and privatly; to receive from me*
25 *wholsom Counsel, and to know how the business which I intend shall be accomplisht. By this Messenger present, send back what you determine. Farewell, as dear both as my own Heart.*

These Letters were sent to the Princes then in *Normandy,*
by express Messengers, with presents also as from thir mother;
which they joyfully receiving, return word by the same Messengers, that one of them will be with her shortly; naming
5 both the time and place. *Alfrid* therefore the younger (for
so it was thought best) at the appointed time, with a few Ships
and small numbers about him appearing on the Coast, no
sooner came ashore but fell into the snare of Earl *Godwin,*
sent on purpose to betray him; as above was related. *Emma*
10 greatly sorrowing for the loss of her Son, thus cruelly made
away, fled immediatly with some of the Nobles her faith-
fullest adherents into *Flanders,* had her dwelling assign'd at
Bruges by the Earl; where having remain'd about two years,   1039.
she was visited out of *Denmarke* by *Hardecnute* her Son; and   *Sim. Dun*
15 he not long had remain'd with her there, when *Harold* in
England, having done nothing the while worth memory,   *Huntingd*
save the taxing of every Port at 8 marks of Silver to 16   1040.
Ships, dy'd at *London,* some say at *Oxford,* and was buried   *Sim. Dun*
at *Winchester.* After which, most of the Nobility, both   *Malms.*
20 Danes and English now agreeing, send Embassadors to *Har-*
decnute still at *Bruges* with his mother, entreating him to
come and receave as his right the Scepter, who before Mid-
somer came with 60 Ships, and many Souldiers out of *Den-*
marke.
25   *Hardecnute.*

HARDECNUTE receav'd with acclamation, and seated
in the Throne, first call'd to mind the injuries done
to him or his Mother *Emma* in the time of *Harold;* sent

Alfric Archbishop of *Yorke*, *Godwin* and others, with *Troud* his Executioner to *London*, commanding them to dig up the body of King *Harold*, and throw it into a Ditch; but by a second order, into the *Thames*. Whence tak'n up by a Fisher-
5 man, and convei'd to a Church-yard in *London*, belonging to the Danes, it was enterr'd again with honour. This done he levied a sore Tax, that 8 marks to every Rower, and twelve to every Officer in his Fleet should be paid throughout *England;* by which time they who were so forward to call him over, had
10 anough of him; for he, as they thought, had too much of theirs. After this he call'd to account *Godwin* Earl of *Kent,* and *Leving* Bishop of *Worster,* about the Death of *Elfred* his half Brother, which *Alfric* the Archbishop laid to thir charge; the King depriv'd *Leving* of his Bishoprick, and gave it to his
15 accuser: but the year following, pacifi'd with a round summe restor'd it to *Leving*. *Godwin* made his peace by a sumptuous *Malms.* present, a Gally with a guilded stem bravely rigg'd, and 80 Souldiers in her, every one with Bracelets of gold on each Arm, weighing 16 ounces, Helmet, Corslet, and Hilts of his
20 Sword guilded; a Danish Curtax listed with gold or silver, hung on his left shoulder, a Sheild with boss and nailes guilded in his left hand, in his right a Launce: besides this, he took his Oath before the King, that neither of his own councel or will, but by the command of *Harold* he had done what he did, to
25 the putting out of *Elfreds* Eyes. The like Oath took most of the Nobility for themselves, or in his behalf. The next year,   1041.
Sim. Dun.
Hardecnute sending his Housecarles, so they call'd his Officers, to gather the Tribute impos'd; two of them rigorous in

thir Office, were slain at *Worster* by the people; wherat the King enrag'd, sent *Leofric* Duke of *Mercia,* and *Seward* of *Northumberland,* with great Forces and Commission to slay the Citizens, rifle and burn the City, wast the whole Province.

5 Affrighted with such news, all the people fled; the Countrymen whither they could, the Cittizens to a small Iland in *Severn,* call'd *Beverege,* which they fortifi'd and defended stoutly, till peace was granted them, and freely to return home. But thir City they found sack't and burnt; wherwith the King

10 was appeas'd. This was commendable in him, however cruel to others, that toward his half brethren, though Rivals of his Crown, he shew'd himself always tenderly affectiond; as now towards *Edward,* who without fear came to him out of *Normandy,* and with unfeigned kindness receav'd, remain'd

15 safely and honorably in his Court. But *Hardecnute* the year following, at a Feast wherin *Osgod* a great Danish Lord gave his Daughter in marriage at *Lambeth,* to *Prudon* another potent Dane; in the midst of his mirth, sound and healthfull to sight, while he was drinking fell down speechless, and so

20 dying, was buried at *Winchester* beside his Father. He was it seems a great lover of good chere; sitting at Table fowr times a day, with great variety of Dishes and superfluity to all Commers. Wheras, saith *Huntingdon,* in our time Princes in thir houses made but one meal a day. He gave his Sister *Gunildis,*

25 a Virgin of rare Beauty, in marriage to *Henry* the *Alman* Emperour; and to send her forth pompously, all the Nobility contributed thir Jewels and richest Ornaments. But it may seem a wonder that our Historians, if they deserve that name,

1042.
Sim. Du

should in a matter so remarkable, and so neer thir own time, so much differ. *Huntingdon* relates against the credit of all other records, that *Hardecnute* thus dead, the English rejoycing at this unexpected riddance of the Danish yoke, sent over to

5 *Elfred* the Elder Son of *Emma* by King *Ethelred,* of whom we heard but now, that he dy'd Prisner at *Eely,* sent thether by *Harold* six year before; that he came now out of *Normandy,* with a great number of men to receave the Crown; that Earl *Godwin* aiming to have his Daughter Queen of *England*

10 by marrying her to *Edward* a simple youth, for he thought *Elfred* of a higher Spirit then to accept her, persuaded the Nobles that *Elfred* had brought over too many Normans, had promis'd them lands heer, that it was not safe to suffer a Warlike and suttle Nation to take root in the Land, that these were to

15 be so handl'd as none of them might dare for the future to flock hither, upon pretence of relation to the King; therupon by common consent of the Nobles, both *Elfred* and his Company were dealt with as was above related; that they then sent for *Edward* out of *Normandy,* with hostages to be left there

20 of thir faithfull intentions to make him King, and thir desires not to bring over with him many Normans; that *Edward* at thir call came then first out of *Normandy;* wheras all others agree that he came voluntarily over to visit *Hardecnute,* as is before said, and was remaining in the Court at the time of his

25 Death. For *Hardecnute* dead, saith *Malmsbury, Edward* doubting greatly his own safety, determin'd to rely wholly on the advice and favour of Earl *Godwin,* desiring therfore by messengers to have privat speech with him, the Earl a while

deliberated: at last assenting, Prince *Edward* came, and would have fall'n at his feet; but that not permitted, told him the danger wherin he thought himself at present, and in great perplexity besought his help to convey him some whether out of
5 the Land. *Godwin* soon apprehending the fair occasion that now as it were prompted him how to advance himself and his Family, cherfully exhorted him to remember himself the Son of *Ethelred,* the Grandchild of *Edgar,* right Heir to the Crown, at full Age; not to think of flying but of reigning, which might
10 easily be brought about if he would follow his Counsel; then setting forth the power and authority which he had in *England,* promisd it should be all his to set him on the Throne, if he on his part would promise and swear to be for ever his friend, to preserve the honour of his House, and to marry his Daughter.
15 *Edward,* as his necessity then was, consented easily, and swore to whatever *Godwin* requir'd. An Assembly of States therupon met at *Gillingham,* where *Edward* pleaded his right; and by the powerfull influence of *Godwin* was accepted. Others, as *Bromton,* with no probability write, that *Godwin* at this time
20 was fled into *Denmarke,* for what he had done to *Elfred,* return'd and submitted himself to *Edward* then King, was by him charg'd op'nly with the Death of *Elfred,* and not without much ado, by the intercession of *Leofric* and other Peers, receav'd at length into favour.

25   *Edward* the Confessor.

GLAD were the English deliverd so unexpectedly from thir Danish Maisters, and little thought how neer another Conquest was hanging over them. *Edward,* the

Easter following, Crown'd at *Winchester,* the same year accompanied with Earl *Godwin, Leofric,* and *Siward,* came
again thether on a sudden, and by thir Counsel seis'd on the
treasure of his Mother *Emma.* The cause alleg'd is, that she
5 was hard to him in the time of his banishment; and indeed
she is said not much to have lov'd *Ethelred* her former Husband, and thereafter the Childern by him; she was moreover
noted to be very covetous, hard to the poor, and profuse to
Monasteries. About this time also King *Edward,* according to
10 promise, took to Wife *Edith* or *Egith* Earl *Godwins* Daughter, commended much for beauty, modesty, and, beyond what
is requisite in a woman, learning. *Ingulf* then a youth lodging
in the Court with his Father, saw her oft, and coming from the
School, was sometimes met by her and pos'd, not in Grammar
15 only, but in Logic. *Edward* the next year but one, made ready
a strong Navy at *Sandwich* against *Magnus* King of *Norway,*
who threat'nd an invasion; had not *Swane* King of *Denmarke*
diverted him by a War at home to defend his own land, not
out of good will to *Edward,* as may be suppos'd, who at the
20 same time express'd none to the Danes, banishing *Gunildis*
the Neece of *Canute* with her two Sons, and *Osgod* by sirname
Clapa, out of the Realm. *Swane* over-powred by *Magnus,*
sent the next year to entreat aid of King *Edward; Godwin*
gave counsel to send him 50 Ships fraught with Souldiers;
25 but *Leofric* and the general voice gain-saying, none were sent.
The next year *Harold Harvager* King of *Norway* sending
Embassadors, made peace with King *Edward;* but an Earth-
quake at *Worster* and *Darby,* Pestilence and Famin in many
places, much lesse'nd the enjoyment therof. The next year

Henry the Emperour displeas'd with *Baldwin* Earl of *Flan-* 1049.
Sim. Dun.
ders, had streit'nd him with a great Army by land; and send-
ing to King *Edward,* desir'd him with his Ships to hinder
what he might, his escape by sea. The King therfore with a
5 great Navy coming to *Sandwich,* there staid till the Emperour
came to an agreement with Earl *Baldwin.* Mean while *Swane*
Son of Earl *Godwin,* who not permitted to marry *Edgiva* the
Abbess of *Chester* by him deflour'd, had left the land, came
out of *Denmarke* with 8 Ships, feigning a desire to return into
10 the Kings favour; and *Beorn* his Cousin German, who commanded part of the Kings Navy, promis'd to intercede that
his Earldome might be restor'd him. *Godwin* therfore and
Beorn with a few Ships, the rest of the Fleet gone home, coming to *Pevensey* (but *Godwin* soon departing thence in persuit
15 of 29 Danish Ships who had got much booty on the Coast of
Essex, and perish'd by tempest in thir return) *Swane* with his
Ships comes to *Beorn* at *Pevensey,* guilefully requests him to
sail with him to *Sandwich,* and reconcile him to the King, as
he had promis'd. *Beorn* mistrusting no evill where he in-
20 tended good, went with him in his Ship attended by three
only of his Servants: but *Swane* set upon barbarous cruelty,
not reconciliation with the King, took *Beorn* now in his power
and bound him; then coming to *Dertmouth,* slew and buried
him in a deep Ditch. After which, the men of *Hastings* took
25 six of his Ships and brought them to the King at *Sandwich;*
with the other two he escap'd into *Flanders,* there remaining
till *Aldred* Bishop of *Worster* by earnest mediation wrought
his peace with the King. About this time King *Edward* sent *Mat. Wes*

to Pope *Leo,* desiring absolution from a vow, which he had
made in his younger years, to take a journey to *Rome,* if God
voutsaf'd him to reign in *England;* the Pope dispenc'd with
his vow, but not without the expence of his journey giv'n to
5 the poor, and a Monastery built or re-edifi'd to St. *Peter:* who
in a Vision to a Monk, as is said, chose *Westminster,* which
King *Edward* thereupon rebuilding endow'd with large privileges and revennues. The same year, saith *Florent* of *Worster,*
certain Irish Pirats with 36 Ships enterd the mouth of *Severn,*
10 and with the aid of *Griffin* Prince of *South-Wales,* did some
hurt in those parts: then passing the River *Wey,* burnt *Duned-*
ham, and slew all the Inhabitants they found. Against whom
Aldred Bishop of *Worster,* with a few out of *Gloster* and
Herefordshire, went out in hast: but *Griffin* to whom the
15 Welch and Irish had privily sent Messengers, came down upon
the English with his whole power by night, and early in the
morning suddenly assaulting them, slew many, and put the
rest to flight. The next year but one, King *Edward* remitted
the Danish Tax, which had continu'd 38 years heavy upon the
20 land since *Ethelred* first paid it to the *Danes,* and what remain'd therof in his treasury he sent back to the owners: but
through imprudence laid the foundation of a far worse mischeif to the English; while studying gratitude to those Normans, who to him in exile had bin helpfull; he call'd them
25 over to public Offices heer, whom better he might have repaid
out of his privat purse; by this means exasperating either Nation one against the other, and making way by degrees to the
Norman Conquest. *Robert* a Monk of that Country, who had

1051.
Sim. Dun.

Ingulf.

bin serviceable to him there in time of need, he made Bishop,
first of *London,* then of *Canterbury; William* his Chaplain
Bishop of *Dorchester.* Then began the English to lay aside thir *Ingulf.*
own antient Customes, and in many things to imitate French
5 manners, the great Peers to speak French in thir Houses,
in French to write thir Bills and Letters, as a great peece of
Gentility, asham'd of thir own: a presage of thir subjection
shortly to that people, whose fashions and language they affected so slavishly: But that which gave begining to many
10 troubles ensueing, happ'nd this year, and upon this occasion.
Eustace Earl of *Boloign,* Father of the famous *Godfrey* who *Malms.*
won *Jerusalem* from the Saracens, and Husband to *Goda*
the Kings Sister, having bin to visit King *Edward,* and returning by *Canterbury* to take Ship at *Dover,* one of his Har-
15 bingers insolently seeking to lodge by force in a House there,
provok'd so the Master therof, as by chance or heat of anger
to kill him. The Count with his whole train going to the
House where his Servant had bin kill'd, slew both the slayer
and 18 more who defended him. But the Townsmen running
20 to Arms, requited him with the slaughter of 21 more of his
Servants, wounded most of the rest; hee himself with one or
two hardly escapeing; ran back with clamour to the King;
whom seconded by other Norman Courtiers, he stirr'd up to
great anger against the Cittizens of *Canterbury.* Earl *Godwin*
25 in hast is sent for, the cause related and much aggravated by
the King against that City, the Earl commanded to raise
Forces, and use the Cittizens therof as Enemies. *Godwin,* sorry
to see strangers more favour'd of the King then his native

people, answerd, that it were better to summon first the Cheif
men of the Town into the Kings Court, to charge them with
Sedition, where both parties might be heard, that not found
in fault they might be acquitted, if otherwise, by fine or loss
5 of life might satisfie the King whose peace they had brok'n,
and the Count whom they had injur'd; till this were done refuseing to prosecute with hostile punishment them of his own
County unheard, whom his Office was rather to defend. The
King displeas'd with his refusal, and not knowing how to
10 compell him, appointed an Assembly of all the Peers to be
held at *Gloster,* where the matter might be fully try'd; the Assembly was full and frequent according to summons; but
Godwin mistrusting his own cause, or the violence of his ad-
versaries; with his two Sons, *Swane* and *Harold,* and a great
15 power gatherd out of his own and his Sons Earldomes, which
contein'd most of the South-East and West parts of *England,*
came no furder then *Beverstan,* giving out that thir Forces
were to go against the Welch, who intended an irruption into
Herefordshire; and *Swane* under that pretence lay with part
20 of his Army thereabout. The Welch understanding this device, and with all diligence clearing themselves before the
King, left *Godwin* detected of false accusation in great hatred
to all the Assembly. *Leofric* therfore and *Siward* Dukes of
great power, the former in *Mercia,* the other in all parts be-
25 yond *Humber,* both ever faithfull to the King, send privily
with speed to raise the Forces of thir Provinces. Which *Godwin* not knowing, sent boldly to King *Edward,* demanding
Count *Eustace* and his followers together with those *Boloigni-*

ans, who as *Simeon* writes, held a Castle in the jurisdiction of
Canterbury. The King as then having but little force at hand,
entertain'd him a while with treaties and delays, till his sum-
mond Army drew nigh, then rejected his demands. *Godwin*
5 thus match'd, commanded his Sons not to begin fight against
the King; begun with, not to give ground. The Kings Forces
were the flower of those Counties whence they came, and   *Sim. Du*
eager to fall on: But *Leofric* and the wiser sort detesting civil
War, brought the matter to this accord, that Hostages giv'n on
10 either side, the whole cause should be again debated at *London.* Thether the King and Lords coming with thir Army,
sent to *Godwin* and his Sons (who with thir powers were
come as far as *Southwarke*) commanding thir appearance
unarm'd with only 12 attendants, and that the rest of thir
15 Souldiers they should deliver over to the King. They to appear
without pledges before an adverse faction deny'd; but to
dismiss thir Souldiers refus'd not, nor in ought else to obey the
King as far as might stand with honour and the just regard of
thir safety. This answer not pleasing the King, an edict was
20 presently issu'd forth, that *Godwin* and his Sons within five
days depart the Land. He who perceav'd now his numbers to
diminish, readily obey'd, and with his Wife and three Sons,
Tosti, Swane, and *Cyrtha,* with as much treasure as thir Ship
could carry, embarking at *Thorney,* sail'd into *Flanders* to
25 Earl *Baldwin,* whose Daughter *Judith Tosti* had married:
for *Wulnod* his fourth Son was then hostage to the King in
Normandy; his other two, *Harold* and *Leofwin,* taking Ship
at *Bristow,* in a Vessel that lay ready there belonging to

Swane, pass'd into *Ireland.* King *Edward* persueing his displeasure, divorc'd his Wife *Edith* Earl *Godwins* Daughter,
sending her despoil'd of all her Ornaments to *Warewel* with
one waiting Maid, to be kept in custody by his Sister the
5 Abbess there. His reason of so doing was as harsh as his act,   *Malms.*
that she only, while her neerest relations were in banishment,
might not, though innocent, enjoy ease at home. After this,
William Duke of *Normandy* with a great number of followers
coming into *England,* was by King *Edward* honorably enter-
10 tain'd and led about the Cities, and Castles, as it were to shew
him what ere long was to be his own (though at that time, saith
Ingulf, no mention thereof pass'd between them) then after
some time of his abode heer, presented richly and dismiss'd,
he return'd home. The next year Queen *Emma* dy'd, and   1052.
15 was buried at *Winchester.* The Chronicle attributed to *John*   *Sim. Dun.*
Bromton a *Yorkshire* Abbot, but rather of some nameless
Author living under *Edward* the 3*d.* or later, reports that the
year before, by *Robert* the Archbishop she was accus'd both of
consenting to the Death of her Son *Alfred,* and of prepareing
20 poyson for *Edward* also; lastly of too much familiarity with
Alwin Bishop of *Winchester;* that to approve her innocence,
praying over-night to St. *Swithun,* she offerd to pass blindfold
between certain Plow-shares red hot, according to the Ordalian
Law, which without harm she perform'd; that the King ther-
25 upon receav'd her to honour, and from her and the Bishop,
penance for his credulity; that the Archbishop asham'd of his
accusation fled out of *England:* which besides the silence of
antienter Authors (for the Bishop fled not till a year after)

brings the whole story into suspition, in this more probable,
if it can be proov'd, that in memory of this deliverance from
the nine burning Plow-shares, Queen *Emma* gave to the Abbey
of St. *Swithune* nine Mannors, and Bishop *Alwin* other nine.

5 About this time *Griffin* Prince of *South-Wales* wasted *Here-*
fordshire; to oppose whom the people of that Country with
many Normans, garrisond in the Castle of *Hereford,* went out
in Armes, but were put to the worse, many slain, and much
booty driv'n away by the Welch. Soon after which, *Harold*

10 and *Leofwin,* Sons of *Godwin,* coming into *Severn* with many
Ships, in the Confines of *Somerset* and *Dorset-shire,* spoil'd
many Villages, and resisted by those of *Somerset* and *Devon-*
shire, slew in fight more then 30 of thir principal men, many
of the common sort, and return'd with much booty to thir

15 Fleet. King *Edward* on the other side made ready above 60 *Malms.*
Ships at *Sandwich* well stor'd with men and provision, under
the conduct of *Odo* and *Radulf* two of his Norman Kindred,
enjoyning them to find out *Godwin,* whom he heard to be at
Sea. To quick'n them, he himself lay on ship-board, oft-times

20 watch'd and sail'd up and down in search of those Pirats. But
Godwin, whether in a mist, or by other accident, passing by
them, arriv'd in another part of *Kent,* and dispersing secret
messengers abroad, by fair words allur'd the cheif men of
Kent, Sussex, Surrey, and *Essex* to his party; which news

25 coming to the Kings fleet at *Sandwich,* they hasted to find
him out; but missing of him again, came up without effect to
London. Godwin advertisd of this, forthwith sail'd to the Ile
of *Wight;* where at length his two sons *Harold* and *Leofwin*

finding him, with thir united Navy lay on the coast, forbear-
ing other hostility then to furnish themselves with fresh
victual from Land as they needed. Thence as one fleet they set
forward to *Sandwich,* using all fair means by the way to
5 encrease thir numbers both of Mariners and Souldiers. The
King then at *London,* startl'd at these tydings, gave speedy
order to raise Forces in all parts which had not revolted from
him; but now too late, for *Godwin* within a few days after
with his Ships or Gallies came up the River *Thames* to *South-*
10 *wark,* and till the tide return'd had conference with the *Lon-*
doners; whom by fair speeches, for he was held a good Speaker
in those times, he brought to his bent. The tide returning, and
none upon the Bridge hindring, he row'd up in his Gallies
along the South bank; where his Land-army now come to
15 him, in array of battel stood on the shore, then turning toward
the North side of the River, where the Kings Gallies lay in
some readiness, and Land-forces also not far off, he made shew
as offring to fight; but they understood one another, and the
souldiers on either side soon declar'd thir resolution not to fight
20 *English* against *English.* Thence coming to treaty, the King
and the Earl reconcil'd, both armies were dissolv'd, *Godwin*
and his sons restor'd to their former dignities, except *Swane,*
who touch't in conscience for the slaughter of *Beorn* his kinsman, was gone bare-foot to *Jerusalem,* and returning home,
25 dy'd by sickness or *Saracens* in *Lycia;* his wife *Edith, Godwins*
daughter, King *Edward* took to him again, dignify'd as before. Then were the *Normans,* who had done many unjust
things under the Kings authority, and giv'n him ill counsel

against his people, banish't the Realm, some of them not blameable permitted to stay. *Robert* Archbishop of *Canterbury, William* of *London, Ulf* of *Lincoln,* all *Normans,* hardly escaping with thir followers, got to Sea. The Arch-

5　bishop went with his complaint to *Rome;* but returning, dy'd in *Normandy* at the same Monastery from whence he came. *Osbern* and *Hugh* surrender'd thir Castles, and by permission of *Leofric* pass'd through his Counties with thir *Normans* to *Macbeth* King of *Scotland.* The year following *Rhese* brother

10　to *Griffin,* Prince of South *Wales,* who by inrodes had done much damage to the *English* tak'n at *Bulendun,* was put to death by the Kings appointment, and his head brought to him at *Gloster.* The same year at *Winchester* on the second holy-day of *Easter,* Earl *Godwin* sitting with the King at table,

15　sunk down suddenly in his seat as dead: his three sons *Harold, Tosti,* and *Gyrtha,* forthwith carried him into the Kings Chamber, hoping he might revive: but the malady had so seis'd him, that the fifth day after he expir'd. The *Normans* who hated *Godwin* give out, saith *Malmsbury,* that mention

20　happ'ning to be made of *Elfred,* and the King thereat looking sowerly upon *Godwin,* he to vindicate himself, utter'd these words, Thou, O King, at every mention made of thy brother *Elfred,* look'st frowningly upon me: but let God not suffer me to swallow this morsel, if I be guilty of ought done against

25　his life or thy advantage; that after these words, choak't with the morsel tak'n, he sunk down and recover'd not. His first wife was the sister of *Canute,* a woman of much infamy for the trade she drove of buying up *English* Youths and Maids

1053.
Sim. Du

to sell in *Denmarke,* whereof she made great gain; but ere
long was struck with thunder, and dy'd. The year ensuing, 1054.
Sim. Dun.
Siward Earl of *Northumberland,* with a great number of
horse and foot, attended also by a strong fleet at the Kings
5 appointment, made an expedition into *Scotland,* vanquish't
the Tyrant *Macbeth,* slaying many thousands of *Scots* with
those *Normans* that went thether, and plac'd *Malcolm* Son of
the *Cumbrian* King in his stead; yet not without loss of his
own Son, and many other both English and Danes. Told of *Huntingd.*
10 his Sons Death, he ask'd whether he receav'd his Deaths
wound before or behind? when it was answerd before, I am
glad, saith hee; and should not else have thought him, though
my Son, worthy of Burial. In the mean while King *Edward*
being without Issue to succeed him, sent *Aldred* Bishop of
15 *Winchester* with great presents to the Emperour, entreating
him to prevail with the King of *Hungary,* that *Edward* the
remaining Son of his Brother *Edmund Ironside,* might be
sent into *England. Siward* but one year surviving his great 1055.
Sim. Dun.
Victory, dy'd at *Yorke;* reported by *Huntingdon* a man of
20 Giant-like stature, & by his own demeanour at point of Death
manifested, of a rough and meer souldierly mind. For much
disdaining to die in bed by a disease, not in the field fighting
with his enemies, he caus'd himself compleatly arm'd, and
weapon'd with battel-ax and shield to be set in a chair, whether
25 to fight with death, if he could be so vain, or to meet him
(when far other weapons and preparations were needful) in
a Martial bravery; but true fortitude glories not in the seats of
War, as they are such, but as they serve to end War soonest by

a victorious Peace. His Earldom the King bestow'd on *Tosti*
the Son of Earl *Godwin:* and soon after in a Convention held
at *London,* banish't without visible cause, *Huntingdon* saith
for treason, *Algar* the Son of *Leofric;* who passing into *Ire-*
5 *land,* soon return'd with eighteen ships to *Griffin* Prince of
South *Wales,* requesting his aid against King *Edward.* He
assembling his Powers, enter'd with him into *Hereford-shire;*
whom *Radulf* a timorous Captain, Son to the Kings Sister,
not by *Eustace,* but a former husband, met two miles distant
10 from *Hereford;* and having hors'd the *English* who knew
better to fight on foot, without stroke he with his *French* and
Normans beginning to flie, taught the *English* by his example. *Griffin* and *Algar* following the chase, slew many,
wounded more, enter'd *Hereford,* slew seven Canons de-
15 fending the Minster, burnt the Monasterie and Reliques, then
the City; killing some, leading captive others of the Citizens,
return'd with great spoils; whereof King *Edward* having
notice, gather'd a great Army at *Gloster* under the conduct of
Harold now Earl of *Kent;* who strenuously pursuing *Griffin,*
20 enter'd *Wales,* and encamp'd beyond *Straddale.* But the
enemy flying before him farther into the Country, leaving
there the greater part of his Army with such as had charge to
fight, if occasion were offer'd, with the rest he return'd, and
fortifi'd *Hereford* with a wall and gates. Mean while *Griffin*
25 and *Algar* dreading the diligence of *Harold,* after many
messages to and fro, concluded a Peace with him. *Algar* discharging his fleet with pay at West *Chester,* came to the King,
and was restor'd to his Earldom. But *Griffin* with breach of

faith, the next year set upon *Leofgar* the Bishop of *Hereford* 1056.
Sim. Dun.
and his Clerks then at a place call'd *Glastbrig* with *Agelnoth*
Vicount of the shire, and slew them; but *Leofric, Harold,*
and King *Edward* by force, as is likeliest, though it be not
5 said how, reduc'd him to Peace. The next year *Edward* Son 1057.
Sim. Dun.
of *Edmund Ironside,* for whom his Uncle King *Edward* had
sent to the Emperour, came out of *Hungary,* design'd Successor to the Crown; but within a few days after his coming
dy'd at *London,* leaving behind him *Edgar Atheling* his Son,
10 *Margaret* and *Christina* his Daughters. About the same time
also dy'd Earl *Leofric* in a good old age, a man of no less vertue
then power in his time, religious, prudent, and faithful to his
Country, happily wedded to *Godiva* a woman of great praise.
His Son *Algar* found less favour with King *Edward,* again 1058.
Sim. Dun.
15 banish't the year after his Fathers death; but he again by the
aid of *Griffin* and a fleet from *Norway,* maugre the King,
soon recover'd his Earldom. The next year *Malcolm* King of 1059.
Sim. Dun.
Scots coming to visit King *Edward,* was brought on his way
by *Tosti* the *Northumbrian* Earl, to whom he swore brother-
20 hood: yet the next year but one, while *Tosti* was gone to *Rome* 1061.
Sim. Dun.
with *Aldred* Archbishop of *York* for his Pall, this sworn
brother taking advantage of his absence, roughly harrass'd
Northumberland. The year passing to an end without other
matter of moment, save the frequent inrodes and robberies of
25 *Griffin,* whom no bonds of faith could restrain, King *Edward*
sent against him after *Christmas Harold* now Duke of West- 1062.
Sim. Dun.
Saxons with no great body of Horse from *Gloster,* where he
then kept his Court, whose coming heard of, *Griffin* not dar-

ing to abide, nor in any part of his Land holding himself
secure, escap't hardly by Sea, ere *Harold* coming to *Rudeland,*
burnt his Palace and Ships there, returning to *Gloster* the same
day: But by the middle of *May* setting out with a fleet from
5 *Bristow,* he sail'd about the most part of *Wales,* and met by
his brother *Tosti* with many Troops of Horse, as the King had
appointed, began to waste the Country; but the *Welch* giving
pledges, yeilded themselves, promis'd to become tributary,
and banish *Griffin* thir Prince; who lurking somewhere, was
10 the next year tak'n and slain by *Griffin* Prince of North *Wales;*
his head with the head and tackle of his Ship sent to *Harold,*
by him to the King, who of his gentleness made *Blechgent*
and *Rithwallon* or *Rivallon* his two Brothers Princes in his
stead; they to *Harold* in behalf of the King swore fealty and
15 tribute. Yet the next year *Harold* having built a fair house at
a place call'd *Portascith* in *Monmouth-shire,* and stor'd it with
provision, that the King might lodge there in time of hunting,
Caradoc the Son of *Griffin* slain the year before, came with a
number of men, slew all he found there, and took away the
20 provision. Soon after which the *Northumbrians* in a tumult
at *York,* beset the Palace of *Tosti* their Earl, slew more then
200 of his Souldiers and Servants, pillag'd his Treasure, and
put him to flie for his life. The cause of this insurrection they
alledg'd to be, for that the Queen *Edith* had commanded in
25 her Brother *Tosti*'s behalf, *Gospatric* a noble man of that
Country to be treacherously slain in the Kings Court; and that
Tosti himself the year before with like treachery had caus'd to
be slain in his Chamber *Gamel* and *Ulf* two other of thir

1063.
Sim. Dun

1064.
Sim. Dun

1065.
Sim. Dun
Camden.

noble men, besides his intolerable exactions and oppressions.
Then in a manner the whole Country coming up to complain
of their grievances, met with *Harold* at *Northampton,* whom
the King at *Tosti's* request had sent to pacifie the *Northum-*
5   *brians;* but they laying op'n the cruelty of his Government,
and thir own birth-right of freedom not to endure the tyranny
of any Governour whatsoever, with absolute refusal to admit
him again, and *Harold* hearing reason, all the complices of
Tosti were expell'd the Earldom. He himself banish't the
10 Realm, went in *Flanders; Morcar* the Son of *Algar* made Earl
in his stead. *Huntingdon* tells another cause of *Tosti's* banishment, that one day at *Windsor,* while *Harold* reach'd the
Cup to King *Edward, Tosti* envying to see his younger Brother in greater favour then himself, could not forbear to run furi-
15 ously upon him, and catching hold of his Hair, the scuffle was
soon parted by other attendants rushing between, and *Tosti*
forbidd'n the Court. He with continu'd fury rideing to *Here-*
ford, where *Harold* had many Servants, preparing an entertainment for the King, came to the House and set upon them
20 with his followers; then lopping off Hands, Armes, Legs of
some, Heads of others, threw them into Butts of Wine, Meath,
or Ale, which were laid in for the Kings drinking: and at his
going away charg'd them to send him this word, that of other
fresh meats he might bring with him to his Farm what he
25 pleas'd, but of Sowce he should find plenty provided ready for
him: that for this barbarous Act the King pronounc't him
banish'd; that the Northumbrians taking advantage at the
Kings displeasure and sentence against him, rose also to be re-

veng'd of his cruelties done to themselves; but this no way
agrees, for why then should *Harold* or the King so much labour with the Northumbrians to re-admit him, if he were a
banish'd man for his Crimes done before? About this time it   *Malms.*
5 happ'nd that *Harold* putting to Sea one day for his pleasure, in
a Fisher Boat, from his Mannor at *Boseham* in *Sussex,* caught
with a Tempest too far off land, was carried into *Normandy;*
and by the Earl of *Pontiew,* on whose Coast he was driv'n, at
his own request brought to Duke *William,* who entertaining
10 him with great courtesie, so far won him, as to promise the
Duke by Oath of his own accord, not only the Castle of *Dover*
then in his tenure, but the Kingdome also after King *Edwards*
Death to his utmost endeavour, therupon betrothing the Dukes
Daughter then too young for marriage, and departing richly
15 presented. Others say, that King *Edward* himself after the
Death of *Edward* his Nephew, sent *Harold* thether, on purpose to acquaint Duke *William* with his intention to bequeath
him his Kingdom: but *Malmsbury* accounts the former story
to be the truer. *Ingulf* writes, that King *Edward* now grown   *Leges Ed.*
20 old, and perceaving *Edward* his Nephew both in body and   *Conf. Tit.*
mind unfit to govern, especially against the pride and inso-   *Lex Noric*
lence of *Godwins* Sons, who would never obey him; Duke
William on the other side of high merit, and his Kinsman by
the Mother, had sent *Robert* Archbishop of *Canterbury,* to
25 acquaint the Duke with his purpose, not long before *Harold*
came thether. The former part may be true, that King *Edward*
upon such considerations had sent one or other; but Archbishop *Robert* was fled the land, and dead many years before.

Eadmer and *Simeon* write, that *Harold* went of his own accord into *Normandy,* by the Kings permission or connivence,
to get free his Brother *Wulnod* and Nephew *Hacun* the Son
of *Swane,* whom the King had tak'n hostages of *Godwin* and
5 sent into *Normandy;* that King *Edward* foretold *Harold,* his
journey thether would be to the detriment of all *England* and
his own reproach; that Duke *William* then acquainted *Harold,* how *Edward* ere his coming to the Crown had promisd,
if ever he attain'd it, to leave Duke *William* Successor after
10 him. Last of these *Mathew Paris* writes, that *Harold* to get
free of Duke *William,* affirm'd his coming thether not to
have been by accident or force of Tempest, but on set purpose,
in that privat manner to enter with him into secret confed-
eracie; so variously are these things reported. After this King
15 *Edward* grew sickly, yet as he was able kept his *Christmas* at
London, and was at the Dedication of St. *Peters* Church in
Westminster, which he had rebuilt; but on the Eve of *Epiph-
anie,* or *Twelftide,* deceas'd much lamented, and in the
Church was Entoomb'd. That he was harmless and simple, is
20 conjecturd by his words in anger to a Peasant who had cross'd
his Game (for with Hunting and Hawking he was much delighted) by God and Gods Mother, said hee, I shall do you as
shrew'd a turn if I can; observing that Law-Maxim, the best
of all his Successors, that the King of *England* can do no
25 wrong. The softness of his Nature gave growth to factions of
those about him, Normans especially and English; these complaining that *Robert* the Archbishop was a sower of dissention
between the King and his people, a traducer of the English;

1066.
Sim. Dun.

the other side, that *Godwin* and his Sons bore themselves arrogantly and proudly towards the King, usurping to themselves
equall share in the Government; ofttimes making sport with   *Hunting*
his simplicity, that through thir power in the land, they made
5 no scruple to kill men of whose inheritance they took a likeing, and so to take possession. The truth is, that *Godwin* and
his Sons did many things boistrously and violently, much
against the Kings minde; which not able to resist, he had, as
some say, his Wife *Edith Godwins* Daughter in such aversa-
10 tion, as in bed never to have touch'd her; whether for this cause
or mistak'n Chastitie, not commendable; to enquire further is
not material. His Laws held good and just, and long after
desir'd by the English of thir Norman Kings, are yet extant.
He is said to be at Table not excessive, at Festivals nothing
15 puft up with the costly Robes he wore, which his Queen with
curious Art had woven for him in Gold. He was full of Alms-
deeds, and exhorted the Monks to like Charitie. He is said
to be the first of English Kings that cur'd the Disease call'd
thence the Kings Evil; yet *Malmsbury* blames them who at-
20 tribute that Cure to his Royaltie, not to his Sanctitie; said
also to have cur'd certain blinde men with the water wherin
he had wash'd his hands. A little before his Death, lying
speechless two days, the third day after a deep sleep, he was
heard to pray, that if it were a true Vision, not an Illusion
25 which he had seen, God would give him strength to utter it,
otherwise not. Then he related how he had seen two devout
Monks, whom he knew in *Normandy,* to have liv'd and dy'd
well, who appearing told him they were sent Messengers

from God to foretell, that because the great ones of *England,*
Dukes, Lords, Bishops, and Abbots, were not Ministers of
God but of the Devil, God had deliverd the Land to thir
Enemies; and when he desir'd that he might reveal this
5 Vision, to the end they might repent, it was answerd; they
neither will repent, neither will God pardon them; at this
relation others trembling, *Stigand* the Simonious Archbishop,
whom *Edward* much to blame had sufferd many years to sit
Primate in the Church, is said to have laugh't, as at the fea-
10 vourish Dream of a doteing old man; but the event prov'd
it true.

Harold Son of Earl *Godwin.*

HAROLD, whether by King *Edward* a little before his   *Hoved.*
Death ordain'd Successor to the Crown, as *Simeon* of   *Florent.*
15 *Durham,* and others affirm; or by the prevalence of his faction,
excluding *Edgar* the right Heir, Grandchild to *Edmund*
Ironside, as *Malmsbury* and *Huntingdon* agree, no sooner
was the Funeral of King *Edward* ended, but on the same day
was elected and Crown'd King: and no sooner plac't in the
20 Throne, but began to frame himself by all manner of com-
pliances to gain affection, endeavour'd to make good Laws,
repeal'd bad, became a great Patron to Church and Church-
men, courteous and affable to all reputed good, a hater of evill
doers, charg'd all his Officers to punish Theeves, Robbers, and
25 all disturbers of the peace, while he himself by Sea and Land
labourd in the defence of his Country: so good an actor is
ambition. In the mean while a blazing Star, 7 Mornings
together, about the end of *April,* was seen to stream terribly,

not only over *England,* but other parts of the World; foretelling heer, as was thought, the great changes approaching: plainliest prognosticated by *Elmer* a Monk of *Malmsbury,* who could not foresee, when time was, the breaking of his
5 own Legs for soaring too high. He in his youth strangely aspiring, had made and fitted Wings to his Hands and Feet; with these on the top of a Tower, spread out to gather air, he flew more then a Furlong; but the wind being too high, came fluttering down, to the maiming of all his Limbs; yet so con-
10 ceited of his Art, that he attributed the cause of his fall to the want of a Tail, as Birds have, which he forgot to make to his hinder parts. This story, though seeming otherwise too light in the midst of a sad narration, yet for the strangness therof, I thought worthy anough the placeing as I found it plac't in my
15 Authour. But to digress no farder, *Tosti* the Kings Brother coming from *Flanders,* full of envy at his younger Brothers advancement to the Crown, resolv'd what he might to trouble his Reign; forcing therfor them of *Wight Ile* to contribution, he sail'd thence to *Sandwich,* committing Piracies on the
20 Coast between. *Harold* then residing at *London,* with a great number of Ships drawn together, and of Horse Troops by Land, prepares in person for *Sandwich:* wherof *Tosti* having   *Malms.* notice, directs his course with 60 Ships towards *Lindsey,* taking with him all the Sea-men he found, willing or unwill-
25 ing: where he burnt many Villages, and slew many of the Inhabitants; but *Edwin* the *Mercian* Duke, and *Morcar* his Brother, the *Northumbrian* Earl, with thir Forces on either side, soon drove him out of the Country. Who thence betook

him to *Malcolm* the Scottish King, and with him abode the
whole Summer. About the same time Duke *William* sending
Embassadors to admonish *Harold* of his promise and Oath,
to assist him in his Plea to the Kingdom, he made answer,

5 that by the death of his Daughter betroth'd to him on that
condition, he was absolv'd of his Oath, or not Dead, he could   *Eadmer.*
not take her now an out-landish woman, without consent of
the Realm; that it was presumptuously done and not to be
persisted in, if without consent or knowledge of the States,

10 he had sworn away the right of the Kingdome; that what
he swore was to gain his liberty, being in a manner then his
Prisner; that it was unreasonable in the Duke to require or
expect of him the foregoing of a Kingdome, conferr'd upon
him with universal favour and acclamation of the people: to

15 this flat deniall he added contempt, sending the Messengers
back, saith *Mathew Paris,* on maim'd Horses. The Duke thus
contemptuously put off, addresses himself to the Pope, setting
forth the Justice of his cause, which *Harold,* whether through
haughtiness of mind, or distrust, or that the ways to *Rome*

20 were stop'd, sought not to do. Duke *William,* besides the
promise and Oath of *Harold,* alleg'd that King *Edward* by
the advice of *Seward, Godwin* himself, and *Stigand* the Archbishop, had giv'n him the right of succession, and had sent
him the Son and Nephew of *Godwin,* pledges of the guift; the

25 Pope sent to Duke *William,* after this demonstration of his
right, a consecrated Banner. Wherupon he having with great
care and choice got an Army of tall and stout Souldiers, under
Captains of great skill and mature Age, came in *August* to the

Port of St. *Valerie*. Mean while *Harold* from *London* comes
to *Sandwich,* there expecting his Navy; which also coming,
he sails to the Ile of *Wight;* and having heard of Duke *William*'s preparations and readiness to invade him, kept good
5 watch on the Coast, and Foot Forces every where in fit places
to guard the shoar. But ere the middle of *September,* provision failing when it was most needed, both Fleet and Army
return home. When on a sudden, *Harold Harvager* King of *Malms.*
Norway, with a Navy of more then 500 great Ships, (others *Mathew*
Paris.
10 less'n them by two hunderd, others augment them to a thousand) appears at the mouth of *Tine;* to whom Earl *Tosti* with
his Ships came as was agreed between them; whence both
uniting, set sail with all speed and enterd the River *Humber.*
Thence turning into *Ouse,* as far as *Rical,* landed; and won
15 *Yorke* by assault. At these tideings *Harold* with all his power
hasts thetherward; but ere his coming, *Edwin* and *Morcar* at
Fulford by *Yorke,* on the North side of *Ouse,* about the Feast
of St. *Mathew* had giv'n them Battel; successfully at first, but
over-born at length with numbers; and forc't to turn thir
20 backs, more of them perish'd in the River, then in the Fight.
The Norwegians taking with them 500 Hostages out of
Yorke, and leaving there 150 of thir own, retir'd to thir Ships.
But the fift day after, King *Harold* with a great and well appointed Army, coming to *York,* and at *Stamford*-Bridge, or *Camd.*
25 *Battell*-Bridge on *Darwent,* assailing the Norwegians, after
much bloodshed on both sides, cut off the greatest part of
them with *Harfager* thir King, and *Tosti* his own Brother.
But *Olave* the Kings Son, and *Paul* Earl of *Orkney,* left with

many Souldiers to guard the Ships, surrendring themselves with Hostages and Oath giv'n never to return as Enemies, he sufferd freely to depart with 20 Ships and the small remnant of thir Army. One man of the Norwegians is not to be for- *Malms.*
5 gott'n, who with incredible valour keeping the Bridge a long hour against the whole English Army, with his single resistance delai'd thir Victorie; and scorning offerd life, till in the end no man dareing to graple with him, either dreaded as too strong, or contemn'd as one desperate, he was at length shot
10 dead with an Arrow; and by his fall op'nd the passage of persuit to a compleat Victorie. Wherwith *Harold* lifted up in minde, and forgetting now his former shews of popularitie, defrauded his Souldiers thir due and well deserved share of the spoils. While these things thus past in *Northumberland,*
15 Duke *William* lay still at St. *Valerie;* his Ships were readie, but the wind serv'd not for many days; which put the Souldierie into much discouragement and murmur, taking this for an unlucky sign of thir success; at last the wind came favourable, the Duke first under sail awaited the rest at Anchor,
20 till all coming forth, the whole Fleet of 900 Ships with a prosperous gale arriv'd at *Hastings.* At his going out of the *Sim. Dun.* Boat by a slip falling on his hands, to correct the Omen, a Souldier standing by said aloud, that thir Duke had tak'n possession of *England.* Landed, he restrein'd his Army from
25 wast and spoil, saying, that they ought to spare what was thir own. But these are things related of *Alexander* and *Cæsar,* and I doubt thence borrow'd by the Monks to inlay thir story. The Duke for 15 days after landing kept his men quiet within

the Camp, having tak'n the Castle of *Hastings,* or built a Fortress there. *Harold* secure the while and proud of his new
Victorie, thought all his Enemies now under foot: but sitting
jollily at dinner, news is brought him, that Duke *William* of
5 *Normandy* with a great multitude of Horse and Foot, Slingers
and Archers, besides other choice Auxiliaries which he had
hir'd in *France,* was arriv'd at *Pevensey. Harold* who had
expected him all the Summer, but not so late in the year as
now it was, for it was *October;* with his Forces much dimin-
10 ish't after two sore conflicts and the departing of many others
from him discontented, in great hast marches to *London.*
Thence not tarrying for supplies which were on thir way
towards him, hurries into *Sussex* (for he was always in hast
since the day of his Coronation) and ere the third part of his
15 Army could be well put in order, findes the Duke about 9
mile from *Hastings,* and now drawing nigh, sent spies before
him to survey the strength and number of his Enemies: them,
discoverd such, the Duke causing to be led about, and after
well fill'd with meat and drink sent back. They not over-wise,
20 brought word that the Dukes Army were most of them
Priests; for they saw thir faces all over shav'n; the English
then useing to let grow on thir upper-lip large Mustachio's, as
did antiently the *Britans.* The King laughing answerd, that
they were not Priests, but valiant and hardy Souldiers. There-
25 fore said *Girtha* his Brother, a youth of noble courage and
understanding above his Age, Forbear thou thy self to fight,
who art obnoxious to Duke *William* by Oath, let us unsworn
undergo the hazard of Battel, who may justly fight in the

defence of our Country; thou reserv'd to fitter time, maist either reunite us flying, or revenge us dead. The King not hark'ning to this, least it might seem to argue fear in him or a bad cause, with like resolution rejected the offers of Duke

5 *William* sent to him by a Monk before the Battel, with this only answer hastily deliverd, let God judge between us. The offers were these, that *Harold* would either lay down the Scepter, or hold it of him, or try his title with him by single Combate in the sight of both Armies, or referr it to the Pope.

10 These rejected, both sides prepar'd to fight the next morning, the English from singing and drinking all night, the Normans from confession of thir sins and communion of the host. The English were in a streit disadvantagious place, so that many discourag'd with thir ill ordering, scarse having room

15 where to stand, slip'd away before the onset, the rest in close order with thir Battel-Axes and Shields, made an impenetrable Squadron: the King himself with his Brothers on foot stood by the Royal Standard, wherin the figure of a man fighting was inwov'n with gold and pretious Stones. The Norman

20 Foot, most Bowmen, made the formost Front, on either side Wings of Horse somewhat behind. The Duke Arming, and his Corslet giv'n him on the wrong side, said pleasantly, *the strength of my Dukedom will be turn'd now into a Kingdom.* Then the whole Army singing the Song of *Rowland,* the re-

25 membrance of whose exploits might hart'n them, imploring lastly Divine help, the Battel began; and was fought sorely on either side; but the main body of English Foot by no means would be brok'n, till the Duke causing his men to feign flight,

drew them out with desire of pursuit into op'n disorder, then
turn'd suddenly upon them so routed by themselves, which
wrought thir overthrow; yet so they dy'd not unmanfully,
but turning oft upon thir Enemies, by the advantage of an
5 upper ground, beat them down by heaps, and fill'd up a great
Ditch with thir Carcasses. Thus hung the Victory wavering
on either side, from the third hour of day to Evening; when
Harold having maintain'd the fight with unspeakable courage and personal valour, shot into the head with an Arrow,
10 fell at length, and left his Souldiers without heart longer to
withstand the unwearied Enemy. With *Harold* fell also his
two Brothers, *Leofwin,* and *Girtha,* with them greatest part of
the English Nobility. His Body lying dead a Knight or Souldier wounding on the thigh, was by the Duke presently turn'd
15 out of military service. Of Normans and French were slain
no small number; the Duke himself also that day not a little
hazarded his person, having had three choice Horses kill'd
under him. Victory obtain'd, and his dead carefully buried,
the English also by permission, he sent the body of *Harold*
20 to his mother without ransom, though she offered very much
to redeem it, which having receav'd, she buried at *Waltham,* in
a Church built there by *Harold.* In the mean while, *Edwin*
and *Morcar,* who had withdrawn themselves from *Harold,*
hearing of his Death, came to *London;* sending *Aldgith* the
25 Queen thir Sister with all speed to *West-Chester. Aldred*
Archbishop of *York,* and many of the Nobles, with the
Londoners would have set up *Edgar* the right Heir, and prepar'd themselves to fight for him; but *Morcar* and *Edwin* not

likeing the choice, who each of them expected to have been
chos'n before him, withdrew thir Forces and return'd home.
Duke *William* contrary to his former resolution, if *Florent* of   *Sim. Dun.*
Worster, and they who follow him say true, wasting, burning,
5 and slaying all in his way, or rather, as saith *Malmsbury,* not
in hostile but in regal manner came up to *London,* met at
Barcham by *Edgar,* with the Nobles, Bishops, Citizens, and
at length *Edwin* and *Morcar,* who all submitted to him, gave
hostages, and swore fidelity, he to them promis'd peace and
10 defence; yet permitted his men the while to burn and make
prey. Coming to *London* with all his Army, he was on *Christmass* day sollemly Crown'd in the great Church at *Westminster,* by *Aldred* Archbishop of *York,* having first giv'n
his Oath at the Altar in presence of all the people, to defend
15 the Church, well govern the people, maintain right Law;
prohibit rapine and unjust judgment. Thus the English, while
they agreed not about the choice of thir native King, were
constrein'd to take the Yoke of an out-landish Conquerer.
With what minds and by what course of life they had fitted
20 themselves for this servitude, *William* of *Malmsbury* spares
not to lay op'n. Not a few years before the Normans came,
the Clergy, though in *Edward* the Confessors daies, had lost
all good literature and Religion, scarse able to read and understand thir Latin Service: he was a miracle to others who knew
25 his Grammar. The Monks went clad in fine stuffs, and made
no difference what they eat; which though in it self no fault,
yet to their Consciences was irreligious. The great men giv'n
to gluttony and dissolute life, made a prey of the common

people, abuseing thir Daughters whom they had in service, then turning them off to the Stews, the meaner sort tipling together night and day, spent all they had in Drunk'ness, attended with other Vices which effeminate mens minds.
5 Whence it came to pass, that carried on with fury and rashness more then any true fortitude or skill of War, they gave to *William* thir Conquerour so easie a Conquest. Not but that some few of all sorts were much better among them; but such was the generality. *And as the long suffering of God permits*
10 *bad men to enjoy prosperous daies with the good, so his severity oft times exempts not good men from thir share in evil times with the bad.*

If these were the Causes of such misery and thraldom to those our Ancestors, with what better close can be concluded,
15 then here in fit season to remember this Age in the midst of her security, to fear from like Vices without amendment the Revolution of like Calamities.

FINIS.

THE DIGRESSION

The Digression in Miltons History of England.
To come in Lib. 3. page 114. after these words.
[from one misery to another.]

BUT because the gaining or loosing of libertie is the greatest change to better or to worse that may befall a
nation under civil government, and so discovers, as
nothing more, what degree of understanding, or capacitie,
what disposition to justice and civilitie there is among them, I
suppose it will bee many wayes profitable to resume a while
the whole discourse of what happn'd in this Iland soone after
the Romans goeing out: and to consider what might bee the
reason, why, seeing other nations both antient and modern
with extreame hazard & danger have strove for libertie as a
thing invaluable, & by the purchase thereof have soo enobl'd
thir spirits, as from obscure and small to grow eminent and
glorious commonwealths, why the Britans having such a
smooth occasion giv'n them to free themselves as ages have
not afforded, such a manumission as never subjects had a
fairer, should let it pass through them as a cordial medcin
through a dying man without the least effect of sence or
natural vigor. And no less to purpose if not more usefully to
us it may withal bee enquir'd, since god after 12 ages and
more had drawne so neare a parallel betweene their state and
ours in the late [p. 2] commotions, why they who had the

chiefe mannagement ther-in having attain'd, though not so easilie, to a condition which had set before them civil goverment in all her formes, and giv'n them to bee masters of thir own choise, were not found able after so many years doeing
5 and undoeing to hitt so much as into any good and laudable way that might show us hopes of a just and well amended common-wealth to come. For those our ancestors it is alledg'd, that thir youth and chiefe strength was carried over sea to serve the Empire, that the Scots and Picts and Saxons lay
10 sore upon them without respit. And yet wee heare the Romans telling them that thir enimies were not stronger then they: when as one legion drove them twice out of the Ile at first encounter. Nor could the Brittans be so ignorant of warr whome the Romans had then newly instructed; or if they
15 were to seeke, alike were thir enimies, rude and naked barbarians. But that they were so timorous and without heart, as Gildas reportes them, is no way credible; for the same hee reportes of those whom the Romans testifie to have found valiant. Wherof those alsoe gave not the least prooff, when a
20 few of them, and these in thir greatest weakness takeing courage, not defended themselves onely against the Scots and Picts, but repuls'd them well beaten home. [p. 3]. Of these who sway'd most in the late troubles, few words as to this point may suffice. They had armies, leaders and successes to
25 thir wish; but to make use of so great advantages was not thir skill. To other causes therefore and not to want of force, or warlike manhood in the Brittans, both those and these lately, wee must impute the ill husbanding of those faire oppor-

tunities, which might seeme to have put libertie, so long desir'd, like a bird into thir hands. Of which other causes
equally belonging both to ruler, priest, and people above hath
bin related: which as they brought those antient natives to
5 miserie and ruin by libertie which rightly us'd might have
made them happie, so brought they these of late after many
labours, much blood-shed, & vast expence, to ridiculous frus-
tration, in whom the like deffects, the like miscarriages noto-
riouslie appear'd, with vices not less hatefull or inexcusable;
10 nor less inforcing, whosoever shall write thir storie, to revive
those antient complaints of Gildas as deservedly on these lately
as on those his times. For a parlament being call'd, and as was
thought many things to redress, the people with great courage
& expectation to be now eas'd of what discontented them
15 chose to thir behoof in parlament such as they thought best
affected to the public good, & some indeed men of wisdome
and integritie. [p. 4]. The rest, and to be sure the greatest
part, whom wealth and ample possessions or bold and active
ambition rather then merit had commended to the same
20 place, when once the superficial zeale and popular fumes
that acted thir new magistracie were cool'd and spent in
them, straite every one betooke himself, setting the common-
wealth behinde and his private ends before, to doe as his owne
profit or ambition led him. Then was justice delai'd & soone
25 after deny'd, spite and favour determin'd all: hence faction,
then treacherie both at home & in the field, ev'ry where
wrong & oppression, foule and dishonest things commited
daylie, or maintain'd in secret or in op'n. Some who had bin

call'd from shops & warehouses without other merit to sit in
supreme councels & committies, as thir breeding was, fell to
hucster the common-wealth; others did thereafter as men
could sooth and humour them best: so that hee onely who
5 could give most, or under covert of hypocritical zeal insinuate
basest enjoy'd unworthylie the rewards of learning & fidel-
itie, or escap'd the punishment of his crimes and misdeeds.
Thir votes and ordinances which men look'd should have
contain'd the repealing of bad laws & the immediate consti-
10 tution of better, resounded with nothing els but new impositions, taxes, excises, yearlie, monthlie, weeklie, not to reck'n
the offices, gifts, and preferments bestow'd and shar'd among
themselves. They in the meane while who were ever faith-
fullest to thir cause, and [p. 5] freely aided them in person,
15 or with thir substance when they durst not compel either,
slighted soone after and quite bereav'd of thir just debts by
greedy sequestration, were toss'd up and downe after miserable attendance from one committie to another with peti-
tions in thir hands, yet either miss'd the obtaining of thir suit,
20 or if it were at length granted by thir orders, meere shame &
reason oft times extorting from them at least a show of justice, yet by thir sequestrators & subcommitties abroad, men
for the most part of insatiable hands, & noted disloyaltie,
those orders were commonlie disobey'd; which for certaine
25 durst not have bin, without secret complyance if not compact
with some superiours able to beare them out. Thus were thir
friends confiscate in thir enimies, while they forfeted thir
debtors to the state as they call'd it, but indeed to the ravening

seisure of innumerable theeves in office, yet were withall no
less burden'd in all extraordinarie assessments and oppressions then whom they tooke to be disaffected. Nor were wee
happier creditours to the state then to them who were seques-
5 ter'd as the states enimies; for that faith which ought to bee
kept as sacred and inviolable as any thing holy, the public
faith, after infinite summs receiv'd & all the wealth of the
church, not better imploy'd, but swallow'd up into a private gulfe, was not ere long asham'd to confess bankrupt.
10 And now besides [p. 6] the sweetness of briberie and other
gaine with the love of rule, thir owne guiltiness and the
dreaded name of just account, which the people had long
call'd for, discover'd plainelie that there were of thir owne
number who secretly contriv'd and fomented those troubles
15 and combustions in the land which openly they sate to remedy, & would continually finde such worke, as should keepe
them from ever being brought to the terrible stand of laying
downe thir authoritie for lack of new buisness, or not drawing it out to any length of time though upon the nesessarie
20 ruin of a whole nation. And if the state were in this plight,
religion was not in much better: to reforme which a certaine
number of divines were call'd, neither chosen by any rule or
custome ecclesiastical, nor eminent for either piety or knowledge above others left out; onelie as each member of parla-
25 ment in his private fancie thought fit, so elected one by one.
The most of them were such as had preach'd and cry'd downe
with great show of zeal the avarice & pluralities of bishops and
prelates; that one cure of soules was a full imployment for one

spiritual pastor how able so ever, if not a charge rather above
humane strength. [p. 7]. Yet these conscientious men, ere
any part of the worke for which they came together, and that
on the public salarie, wanted not impudence to the ignominie
5 and scandal of thir pastor-like proffession & especially of thir
boasted reformation, to seise into thir hands or not unwill-
inglie to accept (besides one sometimes two or more of the
best Livings) collegiat master-ships in the universitie, rich
lectures in the cittie, setting saile to all windes that might
10 blow gaine into thir covetous bosomes. By which meanes
those great rebukers of nonresidence among so many distant
cures were not asham'd to be seen so quicklie pluralists and
nonresidents themselves, to a feareful condemnation doubtless
by thir owne mouthes. And yet the main doctrin for which
15 they tooke such pay, and insisted upon with more vehemence
then gospel, was but to tell us in effect that thir doctrin was
worth nothing and the spiritual power of thir ministrie less
availeable then bodilie compulsion; perswading the magistrate
to use it as a stronger means to subdue & bring in conscience
20 then evangellic perswasion. But while they taught compulsion without convincement (which not long before they so
much complain'd of as executed unchristianlie [p. 8] against
themselves) thir intents were cleere to be no other then to have
set up a spiritual tyrannie by a secular power to the advancing
25 of thir owne authoritie above the magistrate; And well did
thir disciples manifest themselves to be no better principl'd
then thir teachers, trusted with committiships and other
gainfull offices, upon their commendations for zealous &, as

they stick'd not to term them, godlie men, but executing thir
places more like childern of the devil, unfaithfully, unjustly,
unmercifully, and where not corruptly, stupidly. So that between them the teachers and these the disciples, there hath
5 not bin a more ignominious and mortal wound to faith, to
pietie, nor more cause of blaspheming giv'n to the enimies of
god and of truth since the first preaching of reformation;
which needed most to have begun in the forwardest reformers
themselves. The people therefore looking one while on the
10 statists, whom they beheld without constancie or firmness
labouring doubtfully beneath the weight of thir own too high
undertakings, busiest in pettie things, triffling in the maine,
deluded & quite alienated, express'd divers wayes thir dis-
affection; some despising whom before they honour'd; some
15 deserting, some inveighing, some conspireing against them.
Then looking on the [p. 9] Church-men, most of whom they
saw now to have preach't thir own bellies, rather then the
gospel, many illiterate, persecutors more then lovers of the
truth, covetous, worldlie, to whom not godliness with con-
20 tentment seem'd great gaine, but godliness with gaine seem'd
great contentment, like in many things whereof they had
accus'd thir predecessors. Looking on all these the people,
who had bin kept warme a while by the affected zele of thir
pulpits, after a false heat became more cold & obdurate then
25 before; som turning to leudness, som to flat atheisme, put
beside thir old religion, & scandalis'd in what they expected
should be new. Thus they who but of late were extoll'd as
great deliverers, and had a people wholy at thir devotion, by

so discharging thir trust as wee see, did not onely weak'n and
unfitt themselves to be dispencers of what libertie they pretended,* but unfitted also the people, now growne worse &
more disordinate, to receave or to digest any libertie at all.

5 For stories teach us that libertie sought out of season in a corrupt and degenerate age brought Rome it self into further
slaverie. For libertie hath [p. 10] a sharp and double edge
fitt onelie to be handl'd by just and vertuous men, to bad and
dissolute it becomes a mischief unwieldie in thir own hands.

10 Neither is it compleatlie giv'n, but by them who have the
happie skill to know what is greivance and unjust to a people;
and how to remove it wiselie; that good men may enjoy the
freedom which they merit and the bad the curb which they
need. But to doe this and to know these exquisit proportions,

15 the heroic wisdom which is requir'd surmounted far the prin-
ciples of narrow politicians: what wonder then if they sunke
as those unfortunate Britans before them, entangl'd and oppress'd with things too hard and generous above thir straine
and temper. For Britain (to speake a truth not oft spok'n)

20 as it is a land fruitful enough of men stout and couragious in
warr, so is it naturallie not over fertil of men able to govern
justlie & prudently in peace; trusting onelie on thir Mother-
witt, as most doo, & consider not that civilitie, prudence, love
of the public more then of money or vaine honour are to this

25 soile in a manner out-landish; grow not here but in minds
well implanted with solid & elaborate breeding; too impolitic
els and too crude, if not [p. 11] headstrong and intractable to

* MS pretented

the industrie and vertue either of executing or understanding
true civil goverment. Valiant indeed and prosperous to winn
a field but to know the end and reason of winning, unjudi-
cious and unwise, in good or bad success alike unteachable.
5 For the sunn, which wee want, ripens witts as well as fruits;
and as wine and oyle are imported to us from abroad, so must
ripe understanding and many civil vertues bee imported into
our minds from forren writings & examples of best ages: wee
shall else miscarry still and com short in the attempt of any
10 great enterprise. Hence did thir victories prove as fruitless as
thir losses dangerous, and left them still conquering under the
same grievances that men suffer conquer'd, which was indeed
unlikely to goe otherwise, unless men more then vulgar, bred
up, as few of them were, in the knowledge of Antient and
15 illustrious deeds, invincible against money, and vaine titles,
impartial to friendships and relations had conducted thir affaires. But then from the chapman to the retaler many, whose
ignorance was more audacious then the rest, were admitted
with all thir sordid rudiments to beare no mean sway among
20 them both in church [p. 12] and state. From the confluence
of all these errors, mischiefs, & misdemeanors, what in the
eyes of man could be expected but what befel those antient
inhabitants whom they so much resembl'd, confusion in the
end. But on these things and this parallel having anough in-
25 sisted, I returne back to the storie which gave matter to this
digression.

A BRIEF HISTORY OF
MOSCOVIA

The Authour's

PREFACE.

THE study of Geography is both profitable and de-
lightfull; but the Writers thereof, though some of
them exact enough in setting down Longitudes and
Latitudes, yet in those other relations of Manners, Religion,
5 Government and such like, accounted Geographical, have
for the most part miss'd their proportions. Some too brief
and deficient satisfy not; others too voluminous and impertinent cloy and weary out the Reader; while they tell long
Stories of absurd Superstitions, Ceremonies, quaint Habits,
10 and other petty Circumstances little to the purpose. Whereby
that which is usefull, and onely worth observation, in such a
wood of words, is either overslip't, or soon forgotten: which
perhaps brought into the mind of some men, more learned
and judicious, who had not the leisure or purpose to write
15 an entire Geography, yet at least to assay something in the
description of one or two Countreys, which might be as a
Pattern or Example, to render others more cautious hereafter,
who intended the whole work. And this perhaps induc'd
Paulus Jovius to describe onely Muscovy and Britain.
20 Some such thoughts, many years since; led me at a vacant
time to attempt the like argument; and I began with Muscovy, as being the most northern Region of Europe reputed
civil; and the more northern Parts thereof, first discovered

by English *Voiages. Wherein I saw I had by much the advantage of* Jovius. *What was scatter'd in many Volumes, and observ'd at several times by Eye-witnesses, with no cursory pains I laid together, to save the Reader a far longer*
5 *travaile of wandring through so many desert Authours; who yet with some delight drew me after them, from the eastern Bounds of* Russia, *to the Walls of* Cathay, *in several late Journeys made thither overland by* Russians, *who describe the Countreys in their way far otherwise than our*
10 *common Geographers. From proceeding further other occasions diverted me. This Essay, such as it is, was thought by some, who knew of it, not amiss to be published; that so many things remarkable, dispers'd before, now brought under one view, might not hazard to be otherwise lost, nor*
15 *the labour lost of collecting them.*

J. M.

ADVERTISEMENT.

This Book was writ by the Authour's own hand, before he lost his sight. And sometime before his death dispos'd of it to be printed. But it being small, the Bookseller hop'd to have procured some other suitable Piece of the same Authour's to have joyn'd with it, or else it had been publish'd 'ere now.

MOSCOVIA:

Or, Relations of Moscovia,

As far as hath been discover'd by English Voyages;

Gather'd from the Writings of several Eye-witnesses: And of other less-known Countries lying Eastward of *Russia* as far as *Cathay,* lately discovered at several times by *Russians.*

CHAP. I.

A brief Description.

THE Empire of *Moscovia,* or as others call it, *Russia,* is bounded on the North with *Lapland* and the Ocean; Southward by the *Crim Tartar;* on the West
5 by *Lituania, Livonia* and *Poland;* on the East by the River *Ob,* or *Oby,* and the *Nagayan Tartars* on the *Volga,* as far as *Astracan.*

The north parts of this Country are so barren, that the In- The North habitants fetch their Corn a 1000 miles, and so cold in Winter *Hack.* 251. and East,
10 that the very Sap of their Wood-fewel burning on the fire, freezes at the Brands end where it drops. The Mariners which were left a shipboard in the first English Voyage thither, in *Hack.* vol. 1. going up onely from their Cabins to the Hatches, had their 248. breath so congeal'd by the cold, that they fell down as it were
15 stifl'd. The Bay of Saint *Nicholas,* where they first put in, Saint lyeth in 64 degrees; call'd so from the Abby there built of *Hack.* 376. *Nicholas,*

Wood; wherein are 20 Monks; unlearned, as then they found
them, and great Drunkards: their Church is fair, full of Im-
ages, and Tapers. There are besides but 6 Houses, whereof one
built by the English. In the Bay over against the Abby is *Rose*   *Rose Isla*
5 *Island,* full of damask and red Roses, Violets, and wild Rose-   *Hack.* 36
mary; the Isle is in circuit 7 or 8 miles: about the midst of *May*
the snow there is clear'd, having two months been melting;
then the ground in 14 daies is dry, and Grass knee-deep within
a month: after *September* Frost returns, and Snow a yard
10 high: it hath a House built by the English near to a fresh fair
Spring. North-east of the Abby on the other side of *Dvina* is
the Castle of *Archangel;* where the English have another   *Archang*
House. The River *Dvina* beginning about 700 miles within   *Dvina.*
the Country, having first receiv'd *Pinega* falls here into the   *Pinega.*
15 Sea, very large and swift, but shallow. It runneth pleasantly
between Hills on either side; beset like a Wilderness with high
Firre, and other Trees: their Boats of Timber without any
Iron in them, are either to sail, or to be drawn up with Ropes
against the stream.
20   North-east beyond *Archangel* standeth *Lampas,* where twice   *Lampas,*
a year is kept a great Fair of *Russes, Tartars* and *Samoeds:* and   284.
to the Land-ward *Mezen,* and *Slobotca* two Towns of traffick
between the River *Pechora,* or *Petzora,* and *Dvina;* To Sea-   *Candinos*
ward lies the Cape of *Candinos,* and the Island of *Colgoieve*   *Colgoieve*
                                                         Pur. par.
25 about 30 leagues from the Bar of *Pechora* in 69 degrees.   533.
    The River *Pechora* or *Petzora* holding his course through
Siberia, how far, the *Russians* thereabouts know not, runneth
into the Sea at 72. mouths, full of Ice: abounding with Swans,

Ducks, Geese and Partridge, which they take in *July,* sell the
Feathers, and salt the Bodies for Winter Provision. On this
River spreading to a Lake stands the Town of *Pustozera* in 68
degrees, having some 80, or 100 Houses, where certain Mer-
5 chants of *Hull* winter'd in the year 1611. The Town *Pechora*
small and poor hath 3 Churches. They traded there up the
River 4 daies journey to *Oustzilma* a small Town of 60
Houses. The *Russians* that have travail'd, say that this River
springs out of the Mountains of *Jougoria* and runs through
10 *Permia.* Not far from the Mouth thereof are the Straits of
Vaigats, of which hereafter: more eastward is the Point of
Naramzy, and next to that, the River *Ob.* Beyond which, the
Muscovites have extended lately their dominion. Touching
the *Riphœan* Mountains whence *Tanais* was anciently thought
15 to spring, our men could hear nothing; but rather that the
whole Country is Champain, and in the northmost part huge
and desert Woods of Firre, abounding with Black Wolves,
Bears, Buffs, and another Beast call'd Rossomakka, whose
Female bringeth forth by passing through some narrow place,
20 as between two Stakes; and so presseth her Womb to a dis-
burthening. Travailing southward they found the Country
more pleasant, fair and better inhabited, Corn, Pasture, Mead-
ows and huge Woods. *Arkania* (if it be not the same with
Archangel) is a place of English trade, from whence a days
25 journey distant, but from Saint *Nicholas* a 100 versts, *Col-*
mogro stands on the *Dvina:* a great Town not wall'd, but
scatter'd. The English have here Lands of their own, given
them by the Emperour, and fair Houses; not far beyond,

Pustozera,
ibid. *Purc.*

Purc. 549.

545, 551.

Riphœan
Mountains.

From Saint
Nicholas
to *Mosco.*
Arkania,
546, 542.

Colmogro,
Hack. 376.

Pinega running between Rocks of Alabaster and great Woods, meets with *Dvina.* From *Colmogro* to *Ustiug* are 500 versts *Ustiug.* or little miles, an ancient City upon the Confluence of *Juga,* and *Sucana* into *Dvina* which there first receives his name. *Hack.* 31

5 Thence continuing by water to *Wologda;* a great City so *Wologd* nam'd of the River which passes through the midst; it hath a Castle wall'd about with Brick and Stone, and many wooden Churches, two for every Parish, the one in Winter to be heated, the other us'd in Summer; this is a Town of much Traffick a

10 1000 miles from Saint *Nicholas.* All this way by water no lodging is to be had but under open Sky by the River side, and other provision onely what they bring with them. From *Wo-logda* by *Sled* they go to *Yeraslave* on the *Volga,* whose *Yeraslav* breadth is there at least a mile over; and thence runs 2700 versts

15 to the *Caspian* Sea, having his head Spring out of *Bealozera,* *Hack.* 37 which is a Lake, amidst whereof is built a strong Tower 248. wherein the Kings of *Moscovy* reserve their Treasure in time of War. From this Town to *Rostove,* then to *Pereslave* a great Town situate on a fair Lake; thence to *Mosco.*

20 Between *Yeraslave* and *Mosco* which is 200 miles, the Country is so fertile, so populous and full of Villages, that in a forenoon 7 or 800 *Sleds* are usually seen coming with Salt 251. Fish, or laden back with Corn. 335.
Mosco.

Mosco the chief City, lying in 55 degrees, distant from

25 Saint *Nicholas* 1500 miles, is reputed to be greater than *Lon-don* with the Suburbs, but rudely built, their Houses and 313. Churches most of Timber, few of Stone, their Streets un-pav'd; it hath a fair Castle four-square, upon a Hill, two miles

about, with Brick Walls very high, and some say 18 foot
thick, 16 Gates, and as many Bulwarks; in the Castle are kept
the chief Markets, and in Winter on the River being then firm
Ice. This River *Moscua* on the south-west side encloses the
5 Castle, wherein are nine fair Churches with round gilded
Towers, and the Emperour's Palace; which neither within,
nor without is equal for state to the King's Houses in *England*
but rather like our Buildings of old fashion with small Windows, some of Glass, some with Latices, or Iron Bars.

10   They who travail from *Mosco* to the *Caspian,* go by Water   South-east.
down the *Moscua* to the River *Occa;* then by certain Castles   *Hack.* 325.
to *Rezan,* a famous City now ruinate; the 10*th* day to *Nysnov-*
ogrod where *Occa* falls into *Volga,* which the *Tartars* call
Edel. From thence the 11*th* day to *Cazan* a *Tartan* City of
15 great wealth heretofore, now under the *Russian;* wall'd at
first with Timber and Earth, but since by the Emperour *Va-*
siliwich with free Stone. From *Cazan* to the River *Cama*
falling into *Volga* from the Province of *Permia,* the People
dwelling on the left side are *Gentiles,* and live in Woods with-
20 out Houses: beyond them to *Astracan, Tartars* of *Mangat,*   334.
and *Nagay;* on the right side those of *Crimme.* From *Mosco*
to *Astracan* is about 600 leagues. The Town is situate in an
Island on a Hill-side wall'd with Earth, but the Castle with
Earth and Timber; the Houses except that of the Governour's,
25 and some few others, poor and simple; the Ground utterly
barren, and without Wood: they live there on Fish, and Stur-
geon especially; which hanging up to dry in the Streets and
Houses brings whole swarms of Flies, and infection to the

Aire, and oft great Pestilence. This Island in length 12 leagues, 3 in breadth is the *Russian* limit toward the Caspian, which he keeps with a strong Garrison; being 20 leagues from that Sea into which *Volga* falls at 70 mouths. From Saint
5 *Nicholas,* or from *Mosco* to the *Caspian* they pass in 46 daies and nights, most part by Water.

West-ward from Saint *Nicholas* 1200 miles, is the City *Novogrod* 58 degrees, the greatest Mart-town of all this Dominion, and in bigness not inferior to *Mosco*. The way thither
10 is through the western bottom of Saint *Nicholas* Bay, and so along the Shoar full of dangerous Rocks to the Monastery *Solofky,* wherein are at least 200 Monks; the People thereabout in a manner Savages, yet Tenants to those Monks. Thence to the dangerous River *Owiga,* wherein are Water-
15 falls as steep as from a Mountain, and by the violence of their descent kept from freezing; so that the Boats are to be carried there a mile over land: which the Tenants of that Abby did by command, and were guides to the Merchants without taking any reward. Thence to the Town *Povensa* standing within a
20 mile of the famous Lake *Onega* 320 miles long; and in some places 70, at narrowest 25 broad, and of great depth. Thence by some Monasteries to the River *Swire;* then into the Lake *Ladiscay* much longer then *Onega:* after which into the River *Volhusky* which through the midst of *Novogrod* runs into
25 this Lake, and this Lake into the *Baltick* sound by *Narv* and *Revel.* Their other Cities toward the western bound are *Plesco, Smolensko* or *Vobsco.*

The Emperour exerciseth absolute power: if any man die

West.
Novogro&
365.

Governm
Hac. 240.

without male Issue, his Land returns to the Emperour. Any rich man who through age, or other impotence is unable to serve the Publick, being inform'd of, is turn'd out of his Estate, and forc'd with his Family to live on a small Pension,

5 while some other more deserving, is by the Duke's authority put into possession. The manner of informing the Duke is thus. Your Grace, saith one, hath such a Subject, abounding with Riches, but for service of the State unmeet, and you have others poor and in want, but well able to doe their Country

10 good service. Immediately the Duke sends forth to enquire, and calling the Rich man before him, Friend, saith he, you have too much Iiving, and are unserviceable to your Prince; less will serve you, and the rest maintain others who deserve more. The man thus call'd to impart his Wealth, repines not,

15 but humbly answers, that all he hath is God's, and the Duke's: as if he made restitution of what more justly was anothers, than parted with his own. Every Gentleman hath rule and justice over his own Tenants: if the Tenants of two Gentlemen agree not, they seek to compose it, if they cannot, each

20 brings his Tenant before the high Judge of that Country. They have no Lawyers, but every man pleads his own Cause, or else by Bill or Answer in writing delivers it with his own hands to the Duke: yet Justice by corruption of inferiour Officers is much perverted. Where other proof is wanting, they

25 may try the matter by personal combat, or by champion. If a Debtor be poor, he becomes bondman to the Duke, who lets out his labour till it pay the dept; till then he remains in bond- *Hac.* 309. age: another tryal they have by lots.

The Revenues of the Emperour are what he list, and what Revenues
his Subjects are able; and he omits not the coursest means to
raise them: for in every good Town there is a drunken Tav-
ern, call'd a *Cursemay,* which the Emperour either lets out to *Hac.* 314
5 farm, or bestowes on some Duke, or Gentleman in reward of
his Service; who for that time is Lord of the whole Town,
robbing and spoiling at his pleasure; till being well enricht, he
is sent at his own charge to the Wars, and there squeez'd of
his ill-got wealth; by which means the waging of war is to the
10 Emperour little or nothing chargeable.

The *Russian* armeth not less in time of war than 300 thou- Forces.
sand men; half of whom he takes with him into the Field, the *Hac.* 239 250.
rest bestows in Garrisons on the Borders. He presseth no
Husband or Merchant, but the Youth of the Realm. He useth
15 no Foot, but such as are Pioners, or Gunners, of both which
sort 30 thousand. The rest being Horsemen, are all Archers,
and ride with a short Stirrup after the *Turkish.* Their Armour is a Coat of Plate, and a Skull on their Heads. Some of
their Coats are cover'd with Velvet, or cloth of Gold; for they
20 desire to be gorgeous in Arms, but the Duke himself above
measure: his Pavilion cover'd with cloth of Gold, or Silver,
set with pretious Stones. They use little Drums at the Saddle
bow instead of Spurs; for at sound thereof the Horses run
more swiftly.

25 They fight without order; nor willingly give battail but by *Hac.* 314 250.
stealth or ambush; of cold and hard Diet marvelously patient;
for when the Ground is cover'd with Snow froz'n a yard thick,
the common Souldier will lie in the Field two months to-

gether without Tent, or covering over head; onely hangs up
his Mantle against that part from whence the Weather drives,
and kindling a little fire, lies him down before it, with his
Back under the Wind: his Drink, the cold Stream mingl'd
5 with Oat-meal, and the same all his Food: his Horse fed with
Green Wood and Bark, stands all this while in the open Field,
yet does his service. The Emperour gives no pay at all, but to
Strangers; yet repaies good deserts in war with certain Lands
during life; and they who oftenest are sent to the wars, think
10 themselves most favour'd, though serving without Wages. *Hac.* 316.
On the 1 2*th* of *December* yearly the Emperour rides into the
Field which is without the City, with all his Nobility on Jen-
nets and Turky Horses in great state: before him 5000 Har-
quebusiers, who shoot at a bank of Ice till they beat it down,
15 the Ordnance, which they have very fair of all sorts, they plant
against two wooden Houses fill'd with earth at least 30 foot
thick, and beginning with the smallest, shoot them all off
thrice over, having beat those two Houses flat. Above the rest
6 great Cannon they have, whose Bullet is a yard high, so that
20 a man may see it flying; then out of Morter-pieces they shoot
wild-fire into the Aire. Thus the Emperour having seen what
his Gunners can doe, returns home in the same order.

They follow the *Greek* Church, but with excess of Super- Religion.
stitions; their Service is in the *Russian* Tongue. They hold the *Hac.* 253.
25 Ten Commandments not to concern them, saying that God
gave them under the Law, which *Christ* by his death on the
Cross hath abrogated: the Eucharist they receive in both
kinds; they observe 4 Lents, have Service in their Churches

daily, from two hours before dawn to Evening; yet for Whor- 242, 321.
dom, Drunkenness and Extortion none worse than the Clergy.

They have many great and rich Monasteries, where they 320.
keep great hospitality. That of *Trojetes* hath in it 700 Friers,
5 and is wall'd about with Brick very strongly, having many
Pieces of Brass Ordnance on the Walls; most of the Lands,
Towns and Villages within 40 miles belong to those Monks,
who are also as great Merchants as any in the Land. During
Easter Holy-daies when two Friends meet they take each
10 other by the hand; one of them saying, the Lord is risen; the
other answering, it is so of a truth; and then they kiss, whether 318.
Men or Women. The Emperour esteemeth the Metropolitan
next to God, after our Lady, and Saint *Nicholas,* as being his
spiritual Officer, himself but his temporal. But the *Musco-*
15 *vites* that border on *Tartaria* are yet *Pagans.* 320, 254.

When there is love between two, the Man among other Marriage
trifling Gifts, sends to the Woman a Whip, to signify, if she of- *Hac.* 322
fend, what she must expect; and it is a Rule among them, that
if the Wife be not beaten once a week, she thinks her self not
20 belov'd, and is the worse; yet are they very obedient, and stir
not forth, but at some Seasons. Upon utter dislike, the Husbands divorces; which Liberty no doubt they receiv'd first with 314.
their Religion from the *Greek* Church, and the Imperial Laws.

Their Dead they bury with new Shooes on their Feet, as to Burial.
25 a long Journey; and put Letters testimonial in their Hands to 242, 254,
Saint *Nicholas,* or Saint *Peter,* that this was a *Russe* of *Russes* 323.
and dy'd in the true Faith; which, as they believe, Saint *Peter*
having read, forthwith admits him into Heaven.

They have no Learning, nor will suffer to be among them; Manners. 241, 314. their greatest friendship is in drinking; they are great Talkers, Lyars, Flatterers and Dissemblers. They delight in gross Meats and noysom Fish; their Drink is better, being sundry

5 sorts of Meath; the best made with Juice of a sweet and crimson Berry call'd *Maliena,* growing also in *France;* other sorts 323. with Black-cherry, or divers other Berries: another Drink they use in the Spring drawn from the Birch-tree Root, whose Sap after *June* dries up. But there is no People that live so miser-

10 ably as the Poor of *Russia;* if they have Straw and Water they make shift to live; for Straw dry'd and stampt in Winter time is their Bread; in Summer Grass and Roots; at all times Bark of Trees is good Meat with them; yet many of them die in the Street for hunger, none relieving, or regarding them.

15 When they are sent into Foreign Countries, or that Stran- Habit. 239. gers come thither, they are very sumptuous in apparel, else the Duke himself goes but meanly.

In Winter they travail onely upon Sleds, the Wayes being Travailing. 314. hard, and smooth with Snow, the Rivers all froz'n: one Horse

20 with a Sled will draw a man 400 miles in 3 daies; in Summer the way is deep, and travailing ill. The *Russe* of better sort goes not out in Winter, but on his Sled; in Summer on his Horse: in his Sled he sits on a Carpet, or a white Bears Skin; the Sled drawn with a Horse well deckt, with many Fox or

25 Wolve Tayles about his Neck, guided by a Boy on his Back, other Servants riding on the tayle of the Sled.

The *Russian* Sea breeds a certain Beast which they call a Beasts. 252. Morse; who seeks his Food on the Rocks, climing up with help of his Teeth; whereof they make as great account, as we of the Elephant's Tooth.

CHAP. II.

Of Samoedia, Siberia, *and other Countries north-east subject to the* Muscovites.

5 NORTH-EAST of *Russia* lieth *Samoedia* by the River *Ob.* This Country was first discover'd by *Oneke* a *Russian;* who first trading privately among them in rich Furrs got great Wealth, and the knowledge of their Country; then reveal'd his discovery to *Boris*
10 Protectour to *Pheodor,* shewing how beneficial that Country gain'd, would be to the Empire. Who sending Ambassadours among them gallantly attir'd, by fair means won their subjection to the Empire; every Head paying yearly two Skins of richest Sables. Those Messengers travailing also 200 leagues
15 beyond *Ob* east-ward, made report of pleasant Countries, abounding with Woods and Fountains, and People riding on Elks and Loshes, others drawn on Sleds by Rain-deer, others by Dogs as swift as Deer. The *Samoeds* that came along with those Messengers returning to *Mosco* admir'd the stateliness
20 of that City, and were as much admir'd for excellent Shooters, hitting every time the breadth of a penny, as far distant as hardly could be discern'd.

The River *Ob* is reported by the *Russes* to be in breadth the sayling of a Summer's day: but full of Islands and Shoals, hav-
25 ing neither Woods, nor, till of late, Inhabitants. Out of *Ob* they turn into the River *Tawze.* The *Russians* have here, since

Purch. part. 3. 543, 540. Molgom

the *Samoeds* yielded them subjection, two Governours with
3 or 400 Gunners; have built Villages and some small Castles;
all which Place they call *Mongozey,* or *Molgomzay.* Further
up-land they have also built other Cities of Wood, consisting   524.
5 chiefly of *Poles, Tartars* and *Russes,* fugitive or condemned
men; as *Vergateria, Siber,* whence the whole Country is
nam'd, *Tinna,* thence *Tobolsca* on this side *Ob,* on the Rivers   526.
Irtis, and *Tobol,* chief Seat of the *Russian* Governour; above
that, *Zergolta* in an Island of *Ob,* where they have a Custom-
10 house, beyond that on the other side *Ob, Narim,* and *Tooina*
now a great City. Certain Churches also are erected in those   526, 527.
Parts; but no man forc'd to Religion; beyond *Narim* east-
ward on the River *Telta* is built the Castle of *Comgoscoi,* and
all this Plantation began since the year 1590. with many other
15 Towns like these. And these are the Countries from whence
come all the Sables and rich Furrs.

    The *Samoeds* have no Towns, or certain place of abode, but   Manners
up and down where they find Moss for their Deer; they live   of the *Samoeds.*
in companies peaceably, and are govern'd by some of the An-   522, 555.
20 cientest amongst them, but are Idolaters. They shoot wondrous cunningly; their Arrow heads are sharpned Stones, or
Fish-bones, which latter serve them also for Needles, their
Thread being the Sinews of certain small Beasts, wherewith
they sowe the Furrs which cloath them; the furry side in Sum-
25 mer outward, in Winter inward. They have many Wives, and
their Daughters they sell to him who bids most; which, if they
be not lik't, are turn'd back to their Friends, the Husband
allowing onely to the Father what the marriage Feast stood

him in. Wives are brought to bed there by their Husbands,
and the next day go about as before. They till not the Ground;
but live on the Flesh of those Wild Beasts which they hunt.
They are the onely Guides to such as travaile *Jougoria, Sibe-*   548.
5   *ria,* or any of those north-east parts in Winter; being drawn
on Sleds with Bucks, riding post day and night, if it be Moon-
light; and lodge on the Snow under Tents of Deer Skins in
whatever place they find enough of white Moss to feed their
Sled Staggs, turning them loose to dig it up themselves out of
10   the deep Snow: another *Samoede* stepping to the next Wood,
brings in store of Firing; round about which they lodge within
their Tents, leaving the top open to vent Smoak; in which
manner they are as warm as the Stoves in *Russia.* They carry
Provision of Meat with them, and partake besides of what
15   Fowle or Venison the *Samoede* kills with shooting by the
way; their Drink is melted Snow. Two Deer being yoak'd to
a Sled riding post will draw 200 miles in 24 hours without
resting, and laden with their Stuff will draw it 30 miles in 12.

CHAP. III.

Of Tingoesia, *and the Countries adjoyning eastward, as far*
20   *as* Cathay.

BEYOND *Narim* and *Comgoscoi* the Souldiers of those   *Pur.* par.
Garrisons travailing by appointment of the *Russian*   527.
Governour in the year 1605. found many goodly
Countries not inhabited; many vast Deserts, and Rivers, till at
25   the end of ten weeks they spy'd certain Cottages, and Herds,

or companies of People, which came to them with reverent behaviour, and signify'd to the *Samoeds* and *Tartars,* which
were Guides to the *Russian* Souldiers, that they were call'd
Tingoesi; that their dwelling was on the great River *Jenissey.*   *Jenissey.*
5 This River is said to be far bigger than *Ob;* distant from the   527.
Mouth thereof 4 daies and nights sayling; and likewise falls   551.
into the Sea of *Naramzie;* it hath high Mountains on the East,   546.
some of which cast out Fire, to the West a plain and fertil
Country, which in the Spring time it overflowes about 70   527.
10 leagues; all that time the Inhabitants keep them in the Mountains, and then return with their Cattel to the Plain. The *Tin-*   Manners.
goesi are a very gentle Nation, they have great swoln Throats
like those in *Italy* that live under the *Alpes;* at perswasion of   *Ibid.*
the *Samoeds* they forthwith submitted to the *Russian* Gov-
15 ernment; and at their request travailing the next year to discover still east-ward, they came at length to a River, which the
Savages of that place call'd *Pisida,* somewhat less than *Jenis-*   528.
sey; beyond which hearing ofttimes the towling of Brazen
Bells, and sometimes the noise of Men and Horses, they durst
20 not pass over; they saw there certain Sayles afar off, square,
and therefore suppos'd to be like *Indian* or *China* Sayles, and
the rather for that they report that great Guns have been heard
shot off from those Vessels. In *April,* and *May* they were
much delighted with the fair prospect of that Country, re-
25 plenish't with many rare Trees, Plants and Flowers, Beasts
and Fowle. Some think here to be the Borders of *Tangut* in   543.
the north of *Cathay.* Some of those *Samoeds* about the Year
1610. travail'd so far till they came in view of a White City;   546.

and heard a great din of Bells, and report there came to them Men all arm'd in Iron from head to foot. And in the Year 1611. divers out of *Cathay,* and others from *Alteen Czar* who stiles himself the golden King, came and traded at *Zergolta,* 5 or *Surgoot* on the River *Ob,* bringing with them Plates of Silver. Whereupon *Michael Pheodorowick* the *Russian* Emperour in the Year 1619. sent certain of his People from *Tooma* to *Alteen,* and *Cathay,* who return'd with Ambassadours from those Princes. These relate, that from *Tooma* in 797. 10 ten daies and a half, three daies whereof over a Lake, where Rubies and Saphirs grow, they came to the *Alteen* King, or King of *Alty;* through his Land in five weeks they pass'd into the Country of *Sheromugaly* or *Mugalla,* where reigned a Queen call'd *Manchika;* whence in four daies they came to 15 the Borders of *Cathay,* fenc't with a stone Wall, 15 fathom high; along the side of which, having on the other hand many pretty Towns belonging to Queen *Manchika,* they travail'd ten daies without seeing any on the Wall till they came to the Gate. Where they saw very great Ordnance lying, 20 and 3000 men in watch. They traffick with other Nations at the Gate, and very few at once are suffered to enter. They were travailing from *Tooma* to this Gate 12 weeks; and from thence to the great City of *Cathay* ten daies. Where being conducted to the House of Ambassadours, within a few daies 25 there came a Secretary from King *Tambur* with 200 Men well apparell'd, and riding on Asses, to feast them with divers sorts of Wine, and to demand their Message; but having brought no Presents with them, they could not be admitted

to his sight; onely with his Letter to the Emperour they return'd as is aforesaid, to *Tobolsca*. They report that the Land
of *Mugalla* reaches from *Boghar* to the north Sea, and hath
many Castles built of Stone four-square, with Towers at the
5 Corners cover'd with glazed Tiles; and on the Gates Alarum-
Bells or Watch-Bells twenty pound weight of Metal; their
Houses built also of Stone, the Seelings cunningly painted
with Flowers of all Colours. The People are Idolaters; the
Country exceeding fruitfull. They have Asses and Mules, but
10 no Horses. The People of *Cathay* say that this great Wall
stretches from *Boghar* to the north Sea four months journey
with continual Towers a flight-shot distant from each other,
and Beacons on every Tower; and that this Wall is the bound
between *Mugalla* and *Cathay*. In which are but five Gates;
15 those narrow, and so low, that a Horse-man sitting upright
cannot ride in. Next to the Wall is the City *Shirokalga;* it
hath a Castle well furnish't with short Ordnance, and small
Shot, which they who keep watch on the Gates, Towers and
Walls, duly at Sun-set and rising discharge thrice over. The
20 City abounds with rich Merchandize, Velvets, Damasks,
Cloth of Gold and Tissue, with many sorts of Sugars. Like to
this is the City *Yara,* their Markets smell odoriferously with
Spices, and *Tayth* more rich than that. *Shirooan* yet more
magnificent, half a day's journey through, and exceeding
25 populous. From hence to *Cathaia* the imperial City is two
daies journey, built of White-stone four-square, in circuit four
daies going, corner'd with four White Towers, very high and
great, and others very fair along the Wall, white intermingl'd

799.

with blew, and Loop-holes furnisht with Ordnance. In midst
of this White City stands a Castle built of Magnet, where the
King dwels, in a sumptuous Palace, the top whereof is over-
laid with Gold. The City stands on even ground encompass'd
5 with the River *Youga,* 7 daies journey from the Sea. The
People are very fair, but not warlike, delighting most in rich
Traffick. These Relations are referr'd hither, because we have
them from *Russians;* who report also, that there is a Sea beyond *Ob* so warm that all kind of Sea-Fowl live thereabout as   806.
10 well in Winter as in Summer. Thus much briefly of the Sea
and Lands between *Russia,* and *Cathay.*

CHAP. IV.

The Succession of Moscovia *Dukes and Emperours taken out
of their Chronicles by a* Polack *with some later Additions.*

THE great Dukes of *Muscovy* derive their Pedegree,
15 though without ground, from *Augustus Cæsar:*
whom they fable to have sent certain of his Kindred
to be Governours over many remote Provinces; and among
them, *Prussus* over *Prussia;* him to have had his Seat on the
eastern *Baltick* Shoar by the River *Wixel;* of whom *Rurek,*
20 *Sinaus,* and *Truuor* descended by the Fourth Generation,
were by the *Russians* living then without Civil Government
sent for in the Year 573. to bear rule over them; at the per-   573.
swasion of *Gostomislius* chief Citizen of *Novogrod.* They
therefore taking with them *Olechus* their Kinsman divided
25 those Countries among themselves, and each in his Province
taught them Civil Government.

Ivorson of *Rurek,* the rest dying without Issue, became
Successour to them all; being left in nonage under the protection of *Olechus.* He took to wife *Olha* Daughter to a Citizen
of *Plesco;* of whom he begat *Stoslaus;* but after that, being
5 slain by his Enemies, *Olha* his Wife went to *Constantinople,*
and was there baptiz'd *Helena.*

Stoslaus fought many Battails with his Enemies; but was
at length by them slain, who made a Cup of his Scull engrav'n
with this Sentence in Gold; Seeking after other Mens he lost
10 his own. His Sons were *Teropolchus, Olega* and *Volodimir.*

Volodimir having slain the other two, made himself sole
Lord of *Russia;* yet after that fact enclining to Christian Religion, had to wife *Anna* Sister of *Basilius* and *Constantine*
Greek Emperours; and with all his People in the Year 988. 988.
15 was baptiz'd, and call'd *Basilius.* Howbeit *Zonaras* reporteth
that before that time *Basilius* the *Greek* Emperour sent a
Bishop to them; at whose preaching they not being mov'd,
but requiring a Miracle, he, after devout Prayers, taking the
Book of Gospel into his hands, threw it before them all into
20 the Fire: which remaining there unconsum'd, they were converted.

Volodimir had eleven Sons among whom he divided his
Kingdom; *Boristus* and *Glebus* for their holy Life register'd
Saints; and their Feast kept every year in *November* with
25 great solemnity. The rest through contention to have the sole
Government, ruin'd each other; leaving onely *Jaroslaus* in-
heritour of all.

Volodimir Son of *Jaroslaus* kept his Residence in the an-

cient City *Kiow* upon the River *Boristenes*. And after many
conflicts with the Sons of his Uncles; and having subdu'd all
was call'd *Monomachus*. He made war with *Constantine* the
Greek Emperour, wasted *Thracia,* and returning home with
5 great spoils to prepare new war, was appeas'd by *Constantine,*
who sent *Neophytus* Bishop of *Ephesus,* and *Eustathius* Abbot
of *Jerusalem,* to present him with part of our Saviour's Cross,
and other rich Gifts, and to salute him by the name of *Czar,*
or *Cæsar:* with whom he thenceforth enter'd into league and
10 amity.

    After him in order of descent *Vuszevolodus, George, De-
metrius.*

    Then *George,* his Son, who in the Year 1237. was slain in   1237.
battail by the *Tartar* Prince *Bathy,* who subdu'd *Muscovia*
15 and made it tributary. From that time the *Tartarians* made
such Dukes of *Russia,* as they thought would be most pliable
to their ends; of whom they requir'd, as oft as Ambassadours
came to him out of *Tartary,* to go out and meet them; and in
his own Court to stand bare-headed, while they sate and de-
20 liver'd their Message. At which time the *Tartars* wasted also
Polonia, Silesia, and *Hungaria,* till Pope *Innocent* the Fourth
obtain'd peace of them for 5 years. This *Bathy,* say the *Russians,* was the Father of *Tamerlan,* whom they call *Temirkutla.*

    Then succeeded *Jaroslaus* the Brother of *George,* then
25 *Alexander* his Son.

    Daniel the Son of *Alexander* was he who first made the
City of *Mosco* his Royal Seat, builded the Castle, and took on
him the Title of great Duke.

John the Son of *Daniel* was sirnamed *Kaleta,* that word signifying a Scrip, out of which, continually carried about with him, he was wont to deal his Almes.

His Son *Simeon* dying without Issue left the Kingdom to
5 *John* his next Brother; and he to his Son *Demetrius,* who left two Sons, *Basilius* and *George.*

Basilius reigning had a Son of his own name, but doubting lest not of his own Body, through the suspicion he had of his Wife's Chastity, him he disinherits, and gives the Dukedom
10 to his Brother *George.*

George putting his Nephew *Basilius* in prison, reigns; yet at his death, either through remorse, or other cause surrenders him the Dukedom.

Basilius unexpectedly thus attaining his supposed right, en-
15 joy'd it not long in quiet; for *Andrew* and *Demetrius* the two Sons of *George* counting it injury not to succeed their Father, made war upon him, and surprizing him on a suddain, put out his Eyes. Notwithstanding which, the *Boiarens,* or Nobles kept their allegiance to the Duke though blind, whom there-
20 fore they call'd *Cziemnox.*

John Vasiliwich his Son was the first who brought the *Russian* Name out of obscurity into renown. To secure his own Estate he put to death as many of his Kindred as were likely to pretend; and stil'd himself great Duke of *Wolodi-*
25 *miria, Muscovia, Novogardia, Czar* of all *Russia.* He won *Plesco* the onely walled City in all *Muscovy,* and *Novogrod* the richest, from the *Lituanians,* to whom they had been sub-ject 50 years before; and from the latter carried home 300

Waggons laden with Treasure. He had war with *Alexander* King of *Poland,* and with the *Livonians;* with him, on pretence of withdrawing his Daughter *Helena,* whom he had to wife, from the *Greek* Church to the *Romish;* with the *Livo-* 5 *nians* for no other cause, but to enlarge his Bounds: though he were often foyl'd by *Plettebergius* great Master of the *Prussian* Knights. His Wife was Daughter to the Duke of *Tyversky;* of her he begat *John;* and to him resigned his Dukedom; giving him to wife the Daughter of *Steven,* Palatine of 10 *Moldavia;* by whom he had Issue *Demetrius,* and deceas'd soon after. *Vasiliwich* therefore reassuming the Dukedom married a second Wife *Sophia* Daughter to *Thomas Palæologus:* who is said to have receiv'd her Dowry out of the Pope's Treasury, upon promise of the Duke to become *Romish.*

15   This Princess of a haughty mind, often complaining that she was married to the *Tartars* Vassal, at length by continual perswasions, and by a wile found means to ease her Husband, and his Country of that Yoke. For whereas till then the *Tartar* had his Procurators, who dwelt in the very Castle of *Mosco,* 20 to oversee State-affairs, she fain'd that from Heaven she had been warn'd, to build a Temple to Saint *Nicholas* on the same place where the *Tartar* Agents had their House. Being therefore delivered of a Son, she made it her request to the Prince of *Tartary,* whom she had invited to the baptizing, that he 25 would give her that House; which obtaining she raz'd to the ground; and remov'd those Overseers out of the Castle: and so by degrees dispossess'd them of all, which they held in *Russia.* She prevail'd also with her Husband to transfer the

Dukedom from *Demetrius* the Son of *John* deceas'd, to *Ga-*
briel his eldest by her.

    Gabriel no sooner Duke, but chang'd his name to *Basilius,*
and set his mind to doe nobly; he recover'd great part of *Mus-*
5 *covy* from *Vitoldus* Duke of *Lituania;* and on the *Boristhenes*   1514.
won *Smolensko* and many other Cities in the Year 1514. He
divorc'd his first Wife, and of *Helena* Daughter to Duke
Glinsky begat *Juan Vasiliwich.*

    Juan Vasiliwich being left a Child was committed to
10 *George* his Unkle and Protector; at 25 years of age he vanquish'd the *Tartars* of *Cazan* and *Astracan,* bringing home
with him their Princes captive; made cruel war in *Livonia*
pretending right of inheritance. He seem'd exceedingly devout, and whereas the *Russians* in their Churches use out of
15 zeal and reverence to knock their Heads against the ground,
his Forehead was seldom free of swellings and bruzes, and
very often seen to bleed. The cause of his rigour in government, he alledg'd to be the malice and treachery of his Subjects. But some of the Nobles incited by his cruelty, call'd in   *Horsey's*
  Observa-
20 the Crim *Tartar* who in the Year 1571. broke into *Russia,*   *tions.*
burnt *Mosco* to the ground: he reigned 54 years; had three   1571.
Sons, of which the eldest being strook on a time by his Father,
with grief thereof dy'd; his other Sons were *Pheodor* and
Demetrius: in the time of *Juan Vasiliwich* the *English* came
25 first by Sea into the north parts of *Russia.*

    Pheodor Juanowick being under age was left to the protec-   1584.
tion of *Boris* Brother to the young Empress, and third Son by   *Hac.* vol. 1.
  466.
adoption in the Emperòur's Will. After 40 daies of mourn-   *Horsey.*

ing, the appointed time of Coronation being come, the Emperour issuing out of his Palace, the whole Clergy before him, enter'd with his Nobility the Church of *Blaueshina* or blessedness; whence after Service to the Church of *Michael,* then to
5 our Lady Church being the Cathedral. In midst whereof a Chair of Majesty was plac'd, and most unvaluable Garments put upon him: there also was the imperial Crown set on his Head by the Metropolitan, who out of a small Book in his hand read Exhortations to the Emperour, of justice and peace-
10 able government. After this rising from his Chair he was invested with an upper Robe, so thick with Orient Pearls and Stones as weigh'd 200 pounds, the Train born up by 6 Dukes; his Staff imperial was of a Unicorn's Horn three foot and a half long, beset with rich Stones: his Globe, and six Crowns
15 carried before him by Princes of the Bloud: his Horse at the Church door stood ready with a Covering of imbroidered Pearl, Saddle and all suitable to the value of 300 thousand Marks. There was a kind of Bridge made three waies, 150 fathom long, three foot high, two fathom broad, whereon the
20 Emperour with his Train went from one Church to another above the infinite throng of People making loud Acclamations; At the Emperour's returning from those Churches they were spread under-foot, with Cloth of Gold, the Porches with Red Velvet, the Bridges with Scarlet and Stammel-cloth, all
25 which, as the Emperour pass'd by, were cut and snatch't by them that stood next; besides new minted Coines of Gold and Silver cast among the People. The Empress in her Palace was plac't before a great open Window in rich and shining Robes,

among her Ladies. After this the Emperour came into Parliament, where he had a Banquet serv'd by his Nobles in princely order; two standing on either side his Chair with Battelaxes of Gold; three of the next Roomes great and large being set
5 round with Plate of Gold and Silver, from the ground up to the roof. This Triumph lasted a week, wherein many royal Pastimes were seen: after which, election was made of the Nobles to new Offices and Dignities. The conclusion of all was a Peal of 170 Brass Ordnance two miles without the City,
10 and 20000 Harquebuzes twice over: and so the Emperour with at least 50 thousand Horse return'd through the City to his Palace: where all the Nobility, Officers, and Merchants brought him rich Presents. Shortly after, the Emperour by direction of *Boris* conquer'd the large Country of *Siberia,* and
15 took Prisoner the King thereof: he remov'd also corrupt Officers and former Taxes. In sum, a great alteration in the Government follow'd, yet all quietly, and without tumult. These things reported abroad strook such awe into the neighbour Kings, that the Crim *Tartar* with his Wives also and many
20 Nobles valiant and personable men came to visit the *Russian.* There came also 12 hundred *Polish* Gentlemen, many *Circassians,* and People of other Nations to offer service; Ambassadours from the *Turk,* the *Persian, Georgian,* and other *Tartar* Princes; from *Almany, Poland, Sweden, Denmark.*
25 But this glory lasted not long through the treachery of *Boris,* who procur'd the death first of *Demetrius,* then of the Emperour himself, whereby the imperial Race after the succession of 300 years was quite extinguish't.

Boris, adopted, as before was said, third Son to *Juan Vasili-wich* without impeachment now ascended the Throne; but neither did he enjoy long, what he had so wickedly com-pass'd; Divine revenge raising up against him a Counterfeit

5 of that *Demetrius* whom he had caus'd to be murthered at *Ouglets.* This Upstart strength'd with many *Poles* and *Cossacks* appears in arms to claim his right out of the hands of *Boris,* who sent against him an Army of 200 thousand Men; many of whom revolted to this *Demetrius: Peter Basman* the

10 General returning to *Mosco* with the empty Triumph of a re-ported Victory. But the Enemy still advancing, *Boris* one day, after a plentifull Meal finding himself heavy and pain'd in his Stomach laid him down on his Bed; but 'ere his Doctours, who made great haste, came to him, was found speechless, and

15 soon after dy'd, with grief, as is suppos'd, of his ill-success against *Demetrius.* Before his death, though it were speedy, he would be shorn, and new christn'd. He had but one Son, whom he lov'd so fondly, as not to suffer him out of sight; using to say he was Lord and Father of his Son, and yet his

20 Servant, yea his Slave. To gain the Peoples love, which he had lost by his ill-getting the Empire, he us'd two Policies; first he caus'd *Mosco* to be fir'd in four places, that in the quenching thereof he might shew his great care and tenderness of the People; among whom he likewise distributed so much of his

25 Bounty, as both new-built their Houses, and repair'd their Losses. At another time the People murmuring, that the great Pestilence which had then swept away a third part of the Na-tion, was the punishment of their electing him, a Murtherer,

1604.
Pur. par
750.

to reign over them, he built Galleries around about the utmost
Wall of *Mosco;* and there appointed for one whole month 20
thousand pound to be given to the Poor; which well nigh
stopt their Mouths. After the death of *Boris, Peter Basman*
5 their onely hope and refuge, though a Young man, was sent
again to the Wars, with him many *English, Scots, French*
and *Dutch;* who all with the other General *Goleeche* fell off
to the new *Demetrius;* whose Messengers coming now to the
Suburbs of *Mosco,* were brought by the Multitude to that spa-
10 tious Field before the Castle Gate; within which the Council
were then sitting; many of whom were by the Peoples threatning call'd out and constrain'd to hear the Letters of *Deme-*
trius openly read: which, long 'ere the end, wrought so with
the Multitude, that furiously they broke into the Castle, lay-
15 ing violence on all they met; when strait appear'd coming
towards them two Messengers of *Demetrius* formerly sent,
pittifully whipt and roasted, which added to their rage. Then
was the whole City in an uproar, all the great Counselours
Houses ransack't, especially of the *Godonova's* the Kindred
20 and Family of *Boris.* Such of the Nobles that were best belov'd, by entreaty prevail'd at length to put an end to this
Tumult. The Empress flying to a safer place had her Collar of
Pearl pull'd from her Neck; and by the next Message command was given to secure her with her Son and Daughter.
25 Whereupon *Demetrius* by general consent was proclaim'd
Emperour. The Empress now seeing all lost, counsel'd the
Prince her Son to follow his Father's example; who, it seems,
had dispatch't himself by Poyson; and with a desperate cour-

age beginning the deadly Health, was pledg'd effectually by her Son; but the Daughter onely sipping, escap'd. Others ascribe this deed to the secret Command of *Demetrius,* and Self-murther imputed to them, to avoid the envy of such a
5 Command.

Demetrius Evanowich, for so he call'd himself, who suc- *Pur.* par ceeded, was credibly reported the Son of *Gregory Peupoloy* a 764. *Russe* Gentleman, and in his younger years to have been shorn a Fryar; but escaping from the Monastery, to have travail'd
10 *Germany* and other Countries, but chiefly *Poland:* where he attain'd to good sufficiency in Arms and other Experience; which rais'd in him such high thoughts, as grounding on a common belief among the *Russians,* that the young *Demetrius* was not dead, but convey'd away, and their hatred
15 against *Boris,* on this foundation with some other circumstances, to build his hopes no lower than an Empire; which on his first discovery found acceptation so generally, as planted him at length on the Royal Seat; but not so firmly as the fair beginning promis'd; for in a short while the *Russians*
20 finding themselves abus'd by an Impostor, on the sixth day after his marriage, observing when his Guard of *Poles* were most secure, rushing into the Palace before break of day, drag'd him out of his Bed, and when he had confes'd the fraud, pull'd him to pieces; with him *Peter Basman* was also
25 slain, and both their dead Bodies laid open in the Marketplace. He was of no presence, but otherwise of a princely disposition; too bountifull, which occasion'd some exactions; in other matters a great lover of justice, not unworthy the

Empire which he had gotten, and lost onely through greatness
of mind, neglecting the Conspiracy, which he knew the *Russians* were plotting. Some say their hatred grew, for that they
saw him alienated from the *Russian* Manners and Religion,
5 having made *Buchinskoy* a learned Protestant his Secretary.
Some report from *Gilbert's* relation, who was a *Scot,* and Captain of his Guard, that lying on his Bed awake, not long before the Conspiracy, he saw the appearance of an aged man
coming toward him; at which he rose, and call'd to them that
10 watch'd; but they denied to have seen any such pass by them.
He returning to his Bed, and within an hour after troubl'd
again with the same Apparition, sent for *Buchinskoy,* telling
him he had now twice the same night seen an aged man, who
at his second coming told him, that though he were a good
15 Prince of himself, yet for the injustice and oppression of his
inferiour Ministers, his Empire should be taken from him.
The Secretary counsell'd him to embrace true Religion, af-
firming that for lack thereof, his Officers were so corrupt. The
Emperour seem'd to be much mov'd, and to intend what was
20 perswaded him. But a few daies after, the other Secretary, a
Russian, came to him with a drawn Sword; of which the
Emperour made slight at first; but he after bold words assaulted him, strait seconded by other Conspiratours crying
liberty. *Gilbert* with many of the Guard oversuddenly sur-
25 pris'd retreated to *Coluga* a Town which they fortify'd; most
of the other Strangers were massacr'd, except the *English,*
whose mediation sav'd also *Buchinskoy. Shusky* who succeeded him reports in a Letter to King *James* otherwise of

him; that his right name was *Gryshca* the Son of *Boughdan;*
that to escape punishment for Villanies done, he turn'd Fryar,
and fell at last to the Black art; and fearing that the Metropolitan intended therefore to imprison him, fled into *Lettow;*
5 where by counsel of *Sigismund* the *Poland* King, he began to
call himself *Demetry* of *Ouglitts;* and by many Libels and
Spies privily sent into *Mosco,* gave out the same; that many
Letters and Messengers thereupon were sent from *Boris* into
Poland, and from the Patriarch, to acquaint them who the
10 Runnagate was; but the *Polanders* giving them no credit,
furnish't him the more with Arms and Money, notwithstanding the League; and sent the Palatine *Sandamersko* and other
Lords to accompany him into *Russia,* gaining also a Prince of
the Crim *Tartars* to his aide; that the Army of *Boris* hearing
15 of his sudden death, yielded to this *Gryshca,* who taking to
wife the Daughter of *Sandamersko,* attempted to root out the
Russian Clergy, and to bring in the *Romish* Religion, for
which purpose many Jesuits came along with him. Whereupon *Shusky* with the Nobles and Metropolitans conspiring
20 against him, in half a year gather'd all the Forces of *Moscovia,*
and surprising him found in writing under his own hand all
these his Intentions; Letters also from the Pope and Cardinals
to the same effect, not onely to set up the Religion of *Rome,*
but to force it upon all, with death to them that refus'd.

25 *Vasily Evanowich Shusky* after the slaughter of *Demetry* 1606.
or *Gryshca* was elected Emperour; having not long before
been at the Block for reporting to have seen the true *Demetrius* dead and buried; but *Gryshca* not onely recall'd him,

but advanc'd him, to be the instrument of his own ruine. He was then about the age of 50; nobly descended, never married, of great wisedom reputed, a favourer of the *English;* for he sav'd them from rifling in the former Tumults. Some say

5 he modestly refus'd the Crown, till by lot four times together it fell to him; yet after that, growing jealous of his Title, remov'd by Poyson, and other means all the Nobles that were like to stand his Rivals; and is said to have consulted with Witches of the *Samoeds, Lappians* and *Tartarians,* about the

10 same fears; and being warn'd of one *Michalowich,* to have put to death three of that name; yet a fourth was reserv'd by fate to succeed him; being then a Youth attendant in the Court, one of those that held the golden Axes, and least suspected. But before that time he also was supplanted by an-

15 other reviving *Demetrius* brought in by the *Poles;* whose counterfeited Hand, and strange relating of privatest Circumstances had almost deceiv'd *Gilbert* himself; had not their persons been utterly unlike; but *Gryshca's* Wife so far believ'd him for her Husband, as to receive him to her Bed.

20 *Shusky* besieg'd in his Castle of *Mosco,* was adventrously supply'd with some Powder and Ammunition by the *English;* and with 2000 *French, English* and *Scots,* with other Forces from *Charles* King of *Sweden.* The *English* after many miseries of cold, and hunger and assaults by the way, deserted by

25 the *French,* yielded most of them to the *Pole,* neer *Smolensko,* and serv'd him against the *Russ.* Mean while this second *Demetrius* being now rejected by the *Poles,* with those *Russians* that sided with him laid siege to *Mosco: Zolkiewsky* for *Sigis-*

Purch. part. 3. 769, *&c.*

1609.

779.

mund King of *Poland* Beleaguers on the other side with forty thousand Men; whereof 1500 *English, Scotch,* and *French.* *Shusky* despairing success betakes him to a Monastery; but with the City is yielded to the *Pole;* who turns now his force

5 against the Counterfeit *Demetrius;* he seeking to fly is by a *Tartar* slain in his Camp. *Smolensko* held out a siege of two years, then surrender'd. *Shusky* the Emperour carried away into *Poland,* there ended miserably in prison. But before his departure out of *Muscovy* the *Polanders* in his name sending

10 for the chief Nobility as to a last farewell, cause them to be entertain'd in a secret place, and there dispatch'd: by this means the easier to subdue the People. Yet the *Poles* were starv'd at length out of those Places in *Mosco* which they had fortify'd. Wherein the *Russians* who besieg'd them, found, as

15 is reported, 60 Barrels of Man's Flesh powder'd, being the Bodies of such as dy'd among them, or were slain in fight.

After which the Empire of *Russia* broke to pieces, the prey 1612. of such as could catch, every one naming himself, and striving to be accounted that *Demetrius* of *Ouglitts.* Some chose *Vlad-*

20 *islaus* King *Sigismund*'s Son, but he not accepting, they fell to a popular Government; killing all the Nobles under pretence of favouring the *Poles.* Some overtures of receiving them were made, as some say, to King *James,* and Sir *John Meric,* and Sir *William Russel* imploy'd therein. Thus *Russia*

25 remaining in this confusion, it happen'd that a mean Man, a Butcher dwelling in the North about *Dvina,* inveying against *Purch.* the baseness of their Nobility, and the corruption of Officers, part. 3. uttered words, that if they would but choose a faithfull Treas- 790.

urer to pay well the Souldiers, and a good General (naming
one *Pozarsky* a poor Gentleman, who after good service done
liv'd not far off retir'd and neglected;) that then he doubted
not to drive out the *Poles.* The People assent, and choose that
5 General: the Butcher they make their Treasurer who both so
well discharg'd their Places, that with an Army soon gather'd
they raise the siege of *Mosco,* which the *Polanders* had renew'd; and with *Boris Licin* another great Souldier of that
Countrey fall into consultation about the choise of an Emper-
10 our, and chose at last *Michalowich,* or *Michael Pheodoro-*
wich, the fatal Youth, whose name *Shusky* so fear'd.

 Michael Pheodorowich thus elected by the valour of *Po-* 1613.
zarsky and *Boris Licin,* made them both Generals of his
Forces, joyning with them another great Commander of the
15 *Cossacks* whose aid had much befriended him; the Butcher
also was made a Counselour of State. Finally a Peace was
made up between the *Russians* and the *Poles;* and that partly
by the mediation of King *James.*

CHAP. V.

The first discovery of Russia *by the North-east,* 1553 *with the*
20 English *Embassies, and Entertainments at that Court, un-*
 till the Year 1604.

T HE discovery of *Russia* by the northern Ocean, made *Hac.* vol. 1.
  first, of any Nation that we know, by *English* men, 243. 234.
  might have seem'd an enterprise almost heroick; if
25 any higher end than the excessive love of Gain and Traffick,
had animated the design. Nevertheless that in regard that

many things not unprofitable to the knowledge of Nature, and other Observations are hereby come to light, as good events ofttimes arise from evil occasions, it will not be the worst labour to relate briefly the beginning, and prosecution
5 of this adventurous Voiage; untill it became at last a familiar Passage.

When our Merchants perceiv'd the Commodities of *England* to be in small request abroad, and foreign Merchandize to grow higher in esteem and value than before, they began to
10 think with themselves how this might be remedied. And seeing how the *Spaniards* and *Portugals* had encreas'd their Wealth by discovery of new Trades and Countries, they resolv'd upon some new and strange Navigation. At the same time *Sebastian Chabota,* a man for the knowledge of Sea-
15 affairs much renown'd in those daies, happen'd to be in *London.* With him first they consult; and by his advice conclude to furnish out three Ships for the search and discovery of the northern parts. And having heard that a certain Worm is bred in that Ocean, which many times eateth through the
20 strongest Oak, they contrive to cover some part of the Keel of those Ships with thin sheets of Lead; and victual them for 18 months; allowing equally to their journey their stay, and their return. Arms also they provide and store of Munition, with sufficient Captains and Governours for so great an enterprise.
25 To which among many, and some void of experience that offer'd themselves, Sir *Hugh Willowby* a valiant Gentleman earnestly requested to have the charge. Of whom before all others both for his goodly personage, and singular skill in the

services of War, they made choise to be Admiral; and of *Rich-*
ard Chancelor, a man greatly esteem'd for his skill, to be chief
Pilot. This man was brought up by Mr. *Henry Sidney,* afterwards Deputy of *Ireland,* who coming where the Adventurers
5 were gather'd together; though then a young man, with a
grave and eloquent Speech commended *Chancelor* unto them.

After this, they omitted no enquiry after any person that
might inform them concerning those north-easterly parts to
which the Voiage tended; and two *Tartarians* then of the
10 King's Stable were sent for; but they were able to answer nothing to purpose. So after much debate it was concluded that by
the 20*th* of *May* the Ships should depart. Being come near
Greenwich where the Court then lay, presently the Courtiers
came running out, the Privy Council at the Windows, the rest
15 on the Towers and Battlements. The Mariners all apparell'd
in Watchet, or sky-coloured Cloth, discharge their Ordnance;
the noise whereof, and of the People shouting is answer'd from
the Hills and Waters with as loud an Echo. Onely the good
King *Edward* then sick beheld not this sight, but dy'd soon
20 after. From hence putting into *Harwich,* they staid long and
lost much time. At length passing by *Shetland,* they kenn'd a
far off *Ægelands,* being an innumerable sort of Islands call'd
Rost Islands in 66 degrees. Thence to *Lofoot* in 68. to *Seinam*
in 70 degrees; these Islands belong all to the Crown of *Den-*
25 *mark*. Whence departing Sir *Hugh Willowby* set out his Flag
by which he call'd together the chief men of his other Ships
to counsel; where they conclude, in case they happen'd to be
scatter'd by Tempest, that *Wardhouse* a noted Haven in *Fin-*

mark be the appointed place of their meeting. The very same day after noon so great a Tempest arose, that the Ships were some driv'n one way, some another in great peril. The General with his loudest voice call'd to *Chancelor* not to be far

5 from him; but in vain, for the admiral sayling much better than his Ship, and bearing all her Sayles was carried with great swiftness soon out of sight; but before that, the Ship-boat striking against her Ship was overwhelmed in view of the *Bonaventure* whereof *Chancelor* was Captain. The third Ship   *Hac.* 235.

10 also in the same Storm was lost. But Sir *Hugh Willowby* escaping that Storm, and wandring on those desolate Seas till the 18*th* of *September* put into a Haven where they had Weather as in the depth of Winter; and there determining to abide till Spring, sent out three men southwest to find Inhabi-

15 tants; who journy'd three daies but found none; then other three went westward four daies journey, and lastly three south-east three daies; but they all returning without news of People, or any sign of Habitation, Sir *Hugh* with the company of his two Ships abode there till *January,* as appears by

20 a Will since found in one of the Ships; but then perish'd all with cold. This River or Haven was *Arzina* in *Lapland* neer to *Kegor,* where they were found dead the year after by cer-   *Hac.* 464. tain *Russian* Fishermen. Whereof the *English* Agent at *Mosco* having notice, sent and recover'd the Ships with the dead

25 Bodies and most of the Goods, and sent them for *England;* but the Ships being unstanch, as is suppos'd, by their two years wintring in *Lapland,* sunk by the way with their Dead, and them also that brought them. But now *Chancelor* with his

Ship and Company thus left, shap'd his course to *Wardhouse,*
the place agreed on to expect the rest; where having staid 7
daies without tydings of them, he resolves at length to hold on
his Voiage; and sayl'd so far till he found no night, but con-
5 tinual day and Sun cleerly shining on that huge and vast Sea
for certain daies. At length they enter into a great Bay, nam'd,
as they knew after, from Saint *Nicholas;* and spying a Fisher-
boat, made after him to know what People they were. The
Fishermen amaz'd with the greatness of his Ship, to them a
10 strange and new sight, sought to fly; but overtak'n, in great
fear they prostrate themselves, and offer to kiss his Feet; but
he raysing them up with all signes and gestures of courtesie,
sought to win their friendship. They no sooner dismist, but
spread abroad the arrival of a strange Nation, whose human-
15 ity they spake of with great affection; whereupon the People
running together, with like return of all courteous usage receive them; offering them Victuals freely; nor refusing to
traffick, but for a loyal Custom which bound them from that,
without first the consent had of their King. After mutual de-
20 mands of each other's Nation they found themselves to be in
Russia where *Juan Vasiliwich* at that time reign'd Emperour.
To whom privily the Governour of that place sending notice
of the strange Guests that were arriv'd, held in the mean while
our Men in what suspence he could. The Emperour well
25 pleas'd with so unexpected a Message, invites them to his
Court, offring them Posthorses at his own charge, or if the
journey seem'd overlong, that they might freely traffick where
they were. But 'ere this Messenger could return, having lost

his way, the *Muscovites* themselves, loath that our men should depart which they made shew to doe, furnish't them with Guides and other Conveniences to bring them to their King's presence. *Chancelor* had now gon more than half his journey,

5 when the Sled-man sent to Court meets him on the way; delivers him the Emperour's Letters; which when the *Russes* understood, so willing they were to obey the Contents thereof, that they quarrell'd and strove who should have the preferment to put his Horses to the Sled. So after a long and trou-

10 blesome journey of 1500 miles he arriv'd at *Mosco*. After he had remain'd in the City about 12 daies, a Messenger was sent to bring them to the King's House. Being enter'd within the Court Gates, and brought into an outward Chamber, they beheld there a very honourable company to the number of a

15 hunder'd sitting all apparell'd in Cloth of gold down to their Ancles: next conducted to the Chamber of presence, there sate the Emperour on a lofty and very royal Throne; on his Head a Diadem of gold, his Robe all of Goldsmiths work, in his Hand a chrystal Sceptre garnish'd and beset with precious

20 Stones; no less was his Countenance full of majesty. Beside him stood his chief Secretary; on his other side the great Commander of silence, both in Cloth of gold; then sate his Council of 150 round about on high Seats, clad all as richly. *Chancelor* nothing abash'd made his obeysance to the Emperour

25 after the *English* manner. The Emperour having taken, and read his Letters, after some enquiry of King *Edward*'s Health, invited them to dinner, and till then dismiss'd them. But before dismission the Secretary presented their Present bare-

headed; till which time they were all cover'd; and before ad-
mittance our men had charge not to speak, but when the Emperour demanded ought. Having sat two hours in the Secretary's Chamber, they were at length call'd in to dinner; where
5 the Emperour was set at Table, now in a Robe of silver, and
another Crown on his Head. This place was call'd the golden
Palace, but without cause, for the *English* men had seen many
fairer; round about the room, but at distance, were other long
Tables; in the midst a Cupboard of huge and massy goblets,
10 and other Vessels of gold and silver; among the rest four great
Flagons nigh two yards high, wrought in the top with de-
vices of Towers and Dragons heads. The Guests ascended to
their Tables by three steps; all apparell'd in Linnen, and that
lin'd with rich Furrs. The Messes came in without order, but
15 all in Chargers of gold, both to the Emperour, and to the rest
that din'd there, which were two hundred persons; on every
Board also were set Cups of gold without number. The Ser-
vitors one hundred and forty were likewise array'd in gold,
and waited with Caps on their heads. They that are in high
20 favour sit on the same Bench with the Emperour, but far off.
Before Meat came in, according to the custom of their Kings,
he sent to every Guest a slice of Bread; whom the Officer
naming saith thus, *John Basiliwich* Emperour of *Russ,* &c.
doth reward thee with Bread, at which words all men stand
25 up. Then were Swans in several pieces serv'd in, each piece
in a several Dish, which the great Duke sends about as the
Bread, and so likewise the Drink. In dinner time he twice
chang'd his Crown, his Waiters thrice their Apparel; to whom

the Emperour in like manner gives both Bread and Drink with his own hands; which they say is done to the intent that he may perfectly know his own Household; and indeed when dinner was done, he call'd his Nobles every one before him by
5 name; and by this time Candles were brought in, for it grew dark; and the *English* departed to their Lodgings from dinner, an hour within night.

In the Year 1555. *Chancelor* made another voiage to this *Hac.* 258.
Place with Letters from Queen *Mary;* had a House in *Mosco,* 263, 465.
10 and Diet appointed him; and was soon admitted to the Emperour's presence in a large room spread with Carpets; at his entring and salutation all stood up, the Emperour onely sitting, except when the Queen's name was read, or spoken; for then he himself would rise: at dinner he sate bareheaded; his
15 Crown and rich Cap standing on a Pinacle by. *Chancelor* returning for *England, Osep Napea* Governour of *Wologda* came in his Ship Ambassadour from the *Russe;* but suffering shipwrack in *Pettislego* a Bay in *Scotland, Chancelor* who took more care to save the Ambassadour than himself was
20 drown'd, the Ship rifled, and most of her lading made booty by the People thereabout.

In the Year 1557. *Osep Napea* returned into his Countrey 310, *&c.*
with *Antony Jenkinson* who had the command of four tall Ships. He reports of a Whirlpool between the *Rost Islands*
25 and *Lofoot* call'd *Malestrand;* which from half ebb till half flood is heard to make so terrible a noise, as shakes the Doorrings of Houses in those Islands ten mile off; Whales that come within the Current thereof make a pittifull cry; Trees

carried in and cast out again have the ends and boughs of them so beaten, as they seem like the stalks of bruized Hemp. About *Zeinam* they saw many Whales very monstrous hard by their Ships; whereof some by estimation sixty foot long;
5 they roard hideously, it being then the time of their engendring. At *Wardhouse,* he saith, the Cattel are fed with Fish. Coming to *Mosco,* he found the Emperour sitting aloft in a Chair of state, richly crown'd, a Staff of gold in his hand wrought with costly stone. Distant from him sate his Brother,
10 and a Youth the Emperour's Son of *Casan* whom the *Russ* had conquer'd; there din'd with him diverse Ambassadours, Christian and Heathen, diversely apparell'd; his Brother with some of the chief Nobles sate with him at Table: the Guests were in all six hundred. In dinner time came in six Musi-
15 cians; and standing in the midst, sung three several times, but with little or no delight to our men; there din'd at the same time in other Halls two thousand *Tartars* who came to serve the Duke in his Wars. The *English* were set at a small Table by themselves direct before the Emperour; who sent them
20 diverse Bowles of Wine and Meath and many Dishes from his own hand: the Messes were but mean, but the change of Wines and several Meaths were wonderfull. As oft as they din'd with the Emperour, he sent for them in the Morning, and invited them with his own mouth. On *Christmass* day be-
25 ing invited, they had for other provision as before; but for   317. store of gold and silver Plate excessive; among which were twelve Barrels of silver, hoop'd with fine gold containing twelve gallons apiece.

1560. was the first *English* traffick to the *Narve* in *Livonia,* till then conceal'd by *Danskers* and *Lubeckers.*

1561. The same *Antony Jenkinson* made another voiage to *Mosco;* and arriv'd while the Emperour was celebrating his
5 marriage with a *Circassian* Lady; during which time the City Gates for three daies were kept shut; and all men whatsoever straitly commanded to keep within their Houses; except some of his Houshold; the cause whereof is not known.

1566. He made again the same voiage; which now men   311.
10 usually made in a month from *London* to Saint *Nicholas* with good Windes, being seven hundred and fifty leagues.

1568. *Thomas Randolf,* Esq; went Embassadour to *Mus-*   373.
covy, from Queen *Elizabeth;* and in his passage by Sea met nothing remarkable save great store of Whales, whom they
15 might see engendring together, and the Sperma-ceti swimming on the Water. At *Colmogro* he was met by a Gentleman from the Emperour, at whose charge he was conducted to *Mosco:* but met there by no man; not so much as the *English;* lodg'd in a fair House built for Ambassa-
20 dours; but there confin'd upon some suspicion which the Emperour had conceav'd; sent for at length after seventeen weeks delay, was fain to ride thither on a borrow'd Horse, his men on foot. In a Chamber before the presence were sitting about three hundred Persons, all in rich Robes
25 taken out of the Emperour's Wardrobe for that day; they sate on three ranks of Benches, rather for shew than that the Persons were of honour; being Merchants, and other mean Inhabitants. The Ambassadour saluted them, but by them

unsaluted pass'd on with his Head cover'd. At the Presence
door being receiv'd by two which had been his Guardians,
and brought into the midst, he was there will'd to stand still,
and speak his message from the Queen; at whose name the
5 Emperour stood up, and demanded her health: then giving
the Ambassadour his Hand to kiss fell to many questions. The
Present being deliver'd, which was a great silver Bowle curiously grav'n, the Emperour told him, he din'd not that day
openly because of great Affairs; but, saith he, I will send thee
10 my Dinner, and augment thy Allowance. And so dismissing
him, sent a Duke richly apparell'd soon after to his Lodging
with fifty Persons each of them carrying Meat in silver Dishes
cover'd; which himself deliver'd into the Ambassadour's own
hands tasting first of every Dish, and every sort of Drink;
15 that done, set him down with his Company, took part, and
went not thence unrewarded. The Emperour sent back with
this Ambassadour another of his own call'd *Andrew Savin.*

    1571. *Jenkinson* made a third voiage; but was staid long at
Colmogro by reason of the Plague in those Parts; at length
20 had audience where the Court then was, near to *Pereslave;* to
which place the Emperour was return'd from his *Swedish*
War with ill success; and *Mosco* the same year had been
wholly burnt by the *Crim;* in it the *English* House, and diverse *English* were smother'd in the Sellars, multitudes of
25 People in the City perish'd, all that were young led captive
with exceeding spoil.

    1583. *Juan Basiliwich* having the year before sent his Am-
bassadour *Pheodor Andrewich* about matters of Commerce, *Hac.* vol. 1.
458.

the Queen made choice of Sir *Jerom Bowes,* one of her houshold, to go into *Russia;* who being attended with more than
forty persons, and accompanied with the *Russe* returning
home, arriv'd at St. *Nicolas.* The *Dutch* by this time had in-
5 truded into the *Muscovy*-Trade; which by privilege long
before had been granted solely to the *English;* and had corrupted to their side *Shalkan* the Chancellor, with others of the
great ones; who so wrought, that a creature of their own was
sent to meet Sir *Jerom* at *Colmogro,* and to offer him occa-
10 sions of dislike: Until at *Vologda* he was receiv'd by another
from the Emperor; and at *Yeraslave* by a Duke well accompanied, who presented him with a Coach and ten Geldings.
Two miles from *Mosco* met him four Gentlemen with Two
hundred Horse, who after short salutation, told him what they
15 had to say from the Emperor, willing him to alight, which the
Ambassador soon refus'd, unless they also lighted; whereon
they stood long debating; at length agreed, great dispute
follow'd, whose foot should first touch the ground. Their
Message deliver'd, and then embracing, they conducted the
20 Ambassador to a house at *Mosco,* built for him purposely. At
his going to Court he and his followers honourably mounted
and apparell'd, the Emperour's Guard were set on either side
all the way about 6000 shot. At the Court-gate met him four
Noblemen in Cloth of Gold, and rich Furr-Caps, embroider'd
25 with Pearl and Stone; then four others of greater degree,
in which passage there stood along the Walls, and sate on
Benches seven or eight hundred men in colour'd Sattins and
Gold. At the Presence-dore met him the chief Herald, and

with him all the great Officers of Court, who brought
him where the Emperour sate: there were set by him three
Crowns of *Muscovy, Cazan* and *Astracan;* on each side
stood two young Noblemen, costly apparell'd in White;
5 each of them had a broad Axe on his shoulder; on the
Benches round sate above a hundred Noblemen. Having
giv'n the Ambassadour his hand to kiss, and enquir'd of
the Queens Health, he will'd him to go sit in the place provided for him, nigh ten paces distant; from thence to send him
10 the Queens Letters and Present. Which the Ambassadour
thinking not reasonable, step'd forward; but the Chancellor
meeting him, would have tak'n his Letters; to whom the Ambassador said, that the Queen had directed no Letters to him;
and so went on and deliver'd them to the Emperour's own
15 hands; and after a short withdrawing into the Council-Cham-
ber, where he had Conference with some of the Council, he
was call'd in to dinner: about the midst whereof, the Emperour standing up, drank a deep Carouse to the Queens Health,
and sent to the Ambassadour a great Bowl of Rhenish-Wine to
20 pledge him. But at several times being call'd for to treat about
Affairs, and not yielding ought beyond his Commission, the
Emperour not wont to be gain-say'd, one day especially broke
into passion, and with a stern countenance told him, he did
not reckon the Queen to be his fellow; for there are, quoth
25 he, her betters. The Ambassadour not holding it his part,
whatever danger might ensue, to hear any derogate from the
Majesty of his Prince, with like courage and countenance told
him, that the Queen was equal to any in Christendom who

thought himself greatest; and wanted not means to offend her
Enemies whomsoever. Yea, quoth he, what saist thou of the
French and *Spanish* Kings? I hold her, quoth the Ambassadour, equal to either. Then what to the *German* Emperour?
5 Her Father, quoth he, had the Emperour in his pay. This
answer mislik'd the Duke so far, as that he told him, were he
not an Ambassadour, he would throw him out of doors. You
may, said the Ambassadour, doe your will, for I am now fast in
your Countrey; but the Queen I doubt not will know how to
10 be reveng'd of any injury offer'd to her Ambassadour. Whereat
the Emperour in great sudden bid him get home; and he
with no more reverence than such usage requir'd, saluted the
Emperour, and went his way. Notwithstanding this, the *Mus-
covite,* soon as his mood left him, spake to them that stood by,
15 many praises of the Ambassadour, wishing he had such a
Servant, and presently after sent his chief Secretary to tell him
that whatever had pass'd in words, yet for his great respect to
the Queen, he would shortly after dispatch him with honour
and full contentment, and in the mean while he much en-
20 larg'd his entertainment. He also desir'd that the Points of
our Religion might be set down, and caus'd them to be read to
his Nobility with much approbation. And as the year before
he had sought in marriage the Lady *Mary Hastings,* which
took not effect, the Lady and her Friends excusing it, he now
25 again renu'd the motion to take to wife some one of the
Queen's Kinswomen either by sending an Embassage, or going himself with his Treasure into *England.* Now happy was
that Nobleman whom Sir *Jerom Bowes* in publick favour'd;

unhappy they who had oppos'd him: for the Emperour had beaten *Shalkan* the Chancelour very grievously for that cause, and threatn'd not to leave one of his race alive. But the Emperour dying soon after of a Surfeit, *Shalkan* to whom then
5 almost the whole Government was committed, caus'd the Ambassadour to remain close Prisoner in his House nine weeks. Being sent for at length to have his dispatch, and slightly enough conducted to the Council Chamber, he was told by *Shalkan* that this Emperour would condescend to no other
10 agreements than were between his Father and the Queen before his coming: and so disarming both him and his Company, brought them to the Emperour with many affronts in their passage, for which there was no help but patience. The Emperour saying but over what the Chancelour had said be-
15 fore, offer'd him a Letter for the Queen: which the Ambassadour, knowing it contain'd nothing to the purpose of his Embassy, refus'd, till he saw his danger grow too great; nor was he suffer'd to reply, or have his Interpreter. *Shalkan* sent him word that now the *English* Emperour was dead; and hasten'd
20 his departure, but with so many disgraces put upon him, as made him fear some mischief in his journey to the Sea; having onely one mean Gentleman sent with him to be his Convoy; he commanded the *English* Merchants in the Queen's name to accompany him, but such was his danger, that they durst
25 not. So arming himself and his Followers in the best wise he could, against any outrage, he at length recover'd the Shoar of Saint *Nicholas*. Where he now resolv'd to send them back by his Conduct some of the affronts which he had receiv'd.

Ready therefore to take Ship, he causes three or four of his
valiantest and discreetest men to take the Emperour's Letter,
and disgracefull Present, and to deliver it, or leave it at the
Lodging of his Convoy, which they safely did; though fol-
5 low'd with a great Tumult of such as would have forc'd them
to take it back.

1584. At the Coronation of *Pheodor* the Emperour, *Jerom
Horsey* being then Agent in *Russia,* and call'd for to court
with one *John de Wale* a Merchant of the *Netherlands* and a
10 Subject of *Spain,* some of the Nobles would have preferr'd the
Fleming before the *English.* But to that our Agent would in
no case agree, saying he would rather have his Leggs cut off by
the Knees, then bring his present in course after a Subject of
Spain. The Emperour and Prince *Boris* perceiving the contro-
15 versy, gave order to admit *Horsey* first: who was dismiss'd
with large Promises, and seventy Messes with three Carts of
several Meath sent after him.

1588. Dr. *Giles Fletcher* went Ambassadour from the
Queen to *Pheodor* then Emperour; whose Relations being
20 judicious and exact are best red entirely by themselves. This   508.
Emperour upon report of the great learning of *John Dee* the
Mathematician invited him to *Mosco* with offer of two thousand pound a year, and from Prince *Boris* one thousand
Marks; to have his Provision from the Emperour's Table, to
25 be honourably receiv'd, and accounted as one of the chief men
in the Land. All which *Dee* accepted not.

1604. Sir *Thomas Smith* was sent Ambassadour from King
James to *Boris* then Emperour; and staid some daies at a place

five miles from *Mosco* till he was honourably receiv'd into
the City; met on horseback by many thousands of Gentlemen and Nobles on both sides the way; where the Ambassadour alighting from his Coach and mounted on his Horse,
5 rode with his Trumpets sounding before him; till a Gentleman of the Emperour's Stable brought him a Gennet gor-
geously trapt with gold, pearl and stone, especially with a
great Chain of plated gold about his Neck, and Horses richly
adorn'd for his Followers. Then came three great Noblemen
10 with an Interpreter offring a Speech; but the Ambassadour
deeming it to be ceremony, with a brief Complement found
means to put it by. Thus alighting all, they saluted, and gave
hands mutually. Those three after a tedious preamble of the
Emperour's Title thrice repeated brought a several Comple-
15 ment of three words apiece, as namely, the first, to know how
the King did, the next, how the Ambassadour, the third, that
there was a fair House provided him. Then on they went on
either hand of the Ambassador, and about six thousand Gal-
lants behind them; still met within the City by more of greater
20 quality to the very Gate of his lodging: where fifty Gunners
were his daily Guard both at home and abroad. The Prestaves
or Gentlemen assign'd to have the care of his entertainment,
were earnest to have had the Ambassadour's Speech and Message given them in writing, that the Interpreter, as they pre-
25 tended, might the better translate it; but he admonish'd them
of their foolish demand. In the day of his audience other Gen-
nets were sent him and his Attendants to ride on, and two
white Palfreys to draw a rich Chariot, which was parcel of

the Present; the rest whereof was carried by his Followers through a lane of the Emperour's Guard; many Messengers posting up and down the while, till they came through the great Castle, to the uttermost Court gate. There met by a great

5 Duke they were brought up stairs through a Stone-gallery, where stood on each hand many in fair Coats of *Persian* Stuff, Velvet and Damask. The Ambassadour by two other Counselours being led into the presence, after his obeysance done, was to stay and hear again the long Title repeated; then the

10 particular Presents; and so deliver'd as much of his Embassage as was then requisite. After which the Emperour arising from his Throne demanded of the King's health; so did the young Prince. The Ambassadour then deliver'd his Letters into the Emperour's own hand, though the Chancelour offer'd

15 to have taken them. He bore the Majesty of a mighty Emperour; his Crown and Sceptre of pure gold, a Collar of Pearls about his Neck, his Garment of crimson Velvet embroider'd with precious stone and gold. On his right Side stood a fair Globe of beaten gold on a Pyramis with a Cross upon it; to

20 which, before he spake, turning a little he crost himself. Not much less in splendour on another Throne sate the Prince. By the Emperour stood two Noblemen in Cloth of silver, high Caps of black Furr, and Chains of gold hanging to their Feet; on their Shoulders two Poleaxes of gold; and two of silver by

25 the Prince; the ground was all cover'd with Arras or Tapistry. Dismist, and brought in again to dinner they saw the Emperour and his Son seated in state, ready to dine; each with a Skull of Pearl on their bare Heads, their Vestments chang'd. In the

midst of this Hall seem'd to stand a Pillar heap'd round to a
great height with massy Plate curiously wrought with Beasts,
Fishes and Fowl. The Emperour's Table was serv'd with two
hundred Noblemen in Coats of gold; the Princes Table with
5 young Dukes of *Casan, Astracan, Siberia, Tartaria* and *Cir-
cassia.* The Emperour sent from his Table to the Ambassadour, thirty Dishes of Meat, to each a Loaf of extraordinary
fine Bread. Then follow'd a number more of strange and rare
Dishes pil'd up by half dozens, with boyl'd, roast and bak't,
10 most part of them besawc'd with Garlick and Onions. In
midst of dinner calling the Ambassadour up to him he drank
the King's health, who receiving it from his hand, return'd to
his place, and in the same Cup being of fair Chrystal pledg'd
it with all his Company. After dinner they were call'd up to
15 drink of excellent and strong Meath from the Emperour's
hand; of which when many did but sip, he urg'd it not; saying
he was best pleas'd with what was most for their health. Yet
after that, the same day he sent a great and glorious Duke, one
of them that held the golden Poleax, with his Retinue, and
20 sundry sorts of Meath to drink merrily with the Ambassadour,
which some of the *English* did, untill the Duke and his Followers light-headed, but well rewarded with thirty yards of
Cloth of gold, and two standing Cups, departed. At second
audience the Ambassadour had like reception as before: and
25 being dismiss'd had dinner sent after him with three hundred
several Dishes of Fish, it being Lent, of such strangeness,
greatness and goodness as scarce would be credible to report.
The Ambassadour departing was brought a mile out of the

City with like honour as he was first met; where lighting from the Emperour's Sled, he took him to his Coach, made fast upon a Sled; the rest to their Sleds an easy and pleasant passage.

Names of the Authours from whence these Relations have been taken; being all either Eye-witnesses, or immediate Relaters from such as were.

THE *Journal of Sir* Hugh Willowby.
Discourse of Richard Chancelor.
Another of Clement Adams *taken from the mouth of* Chancelor.

Notes of Richard Johnson, *Servant to* Chancelor.

The Protonotaries *Register.*

Two Letters of Mr. Hen. Lane.

The several voiages of Jenkinson, Southam *and* Sparks.

The Journal of Randolf *the Embass.*

Another of Sir Jerom Bowes.

The Coronation of Pheodor *written by* Jerom Horsey.

Gourdon *of* Hull'*s Voiage to* Pechora.

The Voiage of William Pursglove, *to* Pechora.

Of Josias Logan.

Hessel Gerardus, *out of* Purchas, *part* 3. *l.* 3.

Russian *Relations in* Purch. 797. ibid. 806. ibid.

The Embassage of Sir Thomas Smith.

Papers of Mr. Hackluit.

Jansonius.

The End.

NOTES

THE HISTORY OF BRITAIN

MILTON'S *History of Britain* first appeared in print in 1670, with the following title-page: The History of Britain, *That part Especially now call'd* England. *From the first Traditional Beginning, Continu'd to the* Norman Conquest. *Collected out of the antientest and best Authours thereof by* John Milton. London, Printed by *J. M.* for *James Allestry,* at the *Rose* and *Crown* in St. *Paul's Church-Yard,* M DC LXX. As a frontispiece the volume contains an engraved portrait of Milton by Faithorne. The same text, but with the portrait omitted, and with the following title-page, was issued again in 1671: The History of Britain, That part especially now called England. From the first Traditional Beginning, Continued to the *Norman Conquest.* Collected out of the Antientest and best Authors thereof: by John Milton. London, Printed by *J. M.* for *Spencer Hickman,* at the *Rose* in St. *Paul's Church*-Yard, M DC LXXI.

The text of the present edition has been made from photostat reproductions of the copy of the edition of 1670 in the library of Harvard University. A passage which probably formed part of the third book of the *History* when it was written but which was omitted by Milton when the *History* was printed, is given separately, following the text of the *History.* This passage usually appears in modern editions of the *History,* but Masson, *Life of Milton,* Vol. VI, p. 808, questioned the propriety of giving the passage a place in the body of the text, and Firth, *Milton as an Historian,* p. 30, points out that in all probability the passage was intentionally and voluntarily omitted by Milton.

THE DIGRESSION

THIS text of the digression, or omitted passage, in Milton's *History of Britain* is printed from a manuscript of twelve pages written in a hand of the seventeenth century contained in the library of Harvard University. The manuscript version of the digression is fuller and apparently it more faithfully represents the passage as Milton wrote it than the better known printed version of 1681, published anonymously in that year under the title: *Mr. John Miltons Character of the Long Parliament and Assembly of Divines In M DC XLI*. The manuscript version also indicates a more appropriate place for the digression than the position commonly assigned to it in the later printed editions of *The History* near the beginning of the third book, after the words *in great undertakings,* p. 103, l. 20.

A BRIEF HISTORY OF MOSCOVIA

MILTON'S *Brief History of Moscovia* was not printed during his life. It was first published at London in 1682. The text of the present edition is derived from photostatic reproductions of a copy of the 1682 edition in the New York Public Library.

COLUMBIA UNIVERSITY PRESS
COLUMBIA UNIVERSITY
NEW YORK

FOREIGN AGENT
OXFORD UNIVERSITY PRESS
HUMPHREY MILFORD
AMEN HOUSE, LONDON, E.C.